DIFFERENTIAL ITEM FUNCTIONING

DIFFERENTIAL ITEM FUNCTIONING

Edited by

Paul W. Holland
Howard Wainer

Educational Testing Service

 LAWRENCE ERLBAUM ASSOCIATES, PUBLISHERS
1993   Hillsdale, New Jersey   Hove and London

Lawrence Erlbaum Associates, Inc., Publishers
365 Broadway
Hillsdale, New Jersey 07642

Library of Congress Cataloging-in-Publication Data

Differential item functioning / edited by Paul
  W. Holland, Howard Wainer (Educational Testing Service).
        p.   .cm.
  Includes bibliographical references and index.
  ISBN 0–8058–0972–4
  1. Test bias—Evaluation.   2. Test bias—Statistics.
  3. Examinations—Validity.   I. Holland, Paul W.   II. Wainer,
  Howard.   III. Educational Testing Service.
  LB3060.62.D54 1993
  371.2′6013—dc20   92–17068
                                                                            CIP

Books published by Lawrence Erlbaum Associates are printed on acid-free paper, and their
bindings are chosen for strength and durability.

Printed in the United States of America

10 9 8 7 6 5 4 3 2 1

To Linda and Roberta
who make a big DIF in our lives

Contents

Foreword:
Differential Item Functioning (DIF): A Perspective From the Air Force Human Resources Laboratory

The Manpower and Personnel Division of the Air Force Human Resources Laboratory, part of the Air Force systems Command, was pleased to have co-sponsored a conference on DIF with the Educational Testing Service. We have long been partners in psychometric progress. The purpose of the American military is to deter aggression and defend against those who would deprive us of our rights. This is done in a manner consistent with fair treatment and equality. The twin ideas of human rights and fair treatment of humans have been advanced rapidly by the American military in this century. From the World War I committee of the American Psychological Association that met in Vineland, New Jersey to the 1948 presidential order integrating the armed services three decades later, to support for advanced psychometric models of fairness, to this conference, America's military research establishment has been in the forefront of development and fair application of advanced technology.

DIF is of concern to the Air Force and to all major test developers and users. The American military is in a unique position because we develop and use our own tests. This year, more than two million young men and women will be tested for enlistment qualification and additional hundreds of thousands of tests will be administered by the service for promotion and certification purposes. These tests will materially affect the lives of these military members and the security of our country.

The issue of test and selection fairness encompasses many concepts and models. Primary to all of them is DIF. If test items operate in a differential fashion, then the scores for different groups are *per se* not comparable. This cannot lead to equitable treatment, a declared goal of the American armed forces. For the Air Force, which produces both enlisted and officer tests, certain models

of DIF detection have become an integral part of the test production and evaluation procedure. Additionally, content and construct validation of our many tests
benefit from DIF analyses. Finally, DIF models and knowledge point the way to
fuller understanding of the characteristics that cause items to differ in item
analytic difficulty and discrimination indices. In the future, DIF models will
bring fundamental change to psychometrics.

This conference and the chapters of this book provide a solid foundation for
the future development of knowledge and techniques to institutionalize fairness
in our tests and our selection and classification systems. The knowledge provided
by this conference has already been used in developing more equitable tests for
the military and civilian community. Issues discussed at this conference and
included in this volume will continue to advance research resulting in more
equitable and better tests.

Malcolm James Ree

Preface

Test fairness is a moral imperative for both the makers and the users of tests. This has been a basic tenet for more than 30 centuries. Although formal testing was well under way during the Shang Dynasty (ca. 1760–1122 B.C.), by the time of the Han Dynasty (202 B.C.–A.D.220), written examination papers were rewritten by scribes. This rewriting was to ensure the anonymity of the examinees before they were graded, thus eliminating one possible barrier to the unbiased grading of the exams. Machine scoring of multiple-choice tests is a modern equivalent, but it is a trivial component of the modern armamentarium of techniques used routinely to ensure test fairness. Three of these, of relevance to the contents of this book, are:

1. Detailed reviews of test items by subject matter experts and members of the major subgroups in society (gender, ethnic, and linguistic) that, in prospect, will be represented in the examinee population.
2. Comparisons of the predictive validity of the test done separately for each of the major subgroups of examinees.
3. Extensive statistical analyses of the relative performance of major subgroups of examinees on individual test items.

This book is concerned primarily with number 3. With the exception of chapter 19, which is concerned with formal methods for implementing number 1, the focus of this book is very tightly focused on methods for detecting test items that function differently for different groups of examinees and on using this information to improve tests.

The history of this subject is littered with unfortunate, incomplete, and misleading terminology and vocabulary, which has led to ambiguous expositions and imprecise thinking. In this account, we have tried to maintain a consistent terminology and our authors have adhered to this quite well.

To begin, we reserve the ambiguous term *item bias* to refer to an informed judgment about an item that takes into account the purpose of the test, the relevant experiences of certain subgroups of examinees taking it, and statistical information about the item. In the main, we avoid using item bias in this book and refer, more neutrally and, to our way of thinking, more appropriately, to items that function differently in different groups of examinees. For short, we call this DIFferential Item Functioning, and, for shorter, simply DIF.

DIF is a relative term. An item may perform differently for one group of examinees relative to the way it performs for another group of examinees. The examinee group of interest is the FOCAL group, and the group to which its performance on the item is being compared is the REFERENCE group. In general, there will be several FOCAL/REFERENCE pairs of groups for with DIF analyses can be made.

In DIF analyses, items play a variety of roles. When an item is examined to ascertain the degree to which it exhibits DIF for a specific FOCAL/REFERENCE pair, it is the STUDIED ITEM for that analysis.

The genesis of this book reaches back at least to the mid-1980s, when the two of us often discussed the various approaches to measuring DIF. One focus of this discussion was our differing outlooks on what some call the *observed-score* versus the *true-score* approaches to the detection of DIF. Holland, then as now, firmly believes in the practical advantages and the conceptual clarity of the observed-score approaches, whereas Wainer was and remains convinced that a model-based approach is more principled, flexible, and powerful. In the intervening years both sets of beliefs have moderated somewhat. At that time, we agreed that we were making progress in understanding this general area of applied research and that a monograph providing both theoretical justification and practical advice would be possible within a few years. In consequence, we began to seek support for the research as well as for the conference that would lead to this book. Educational Testing Service (ETS) has provided very generous support to its staff for DIF research and for the preparation of this monograph. The Air Force Human Resources Laboratory (now Armstrong Laboratory) provided support for the conference that was held at the Henry Chauncy Conference Center at ETS in October 1989. Holland was able to finish his work on this book while a Fellow at the Center for Advanced Study in the Behavioral Sciences, with support from the Spencer Foundation as well as ETS.

This volume has benefited from the good thoughts, cooperation, and diligent efforts of a large number of people and it is our pleasure to have this opportunity to acknowledge them now.

First, we thank Gregory Anrig, the president of ETS, who has been a fervent advocate of test fairness in general, and of this project in particular, since the very first days that he joined ETS. Nancy Cole participated both as an author in the book and as an interested senior manager at ETS whose background in the subject antedates our own. Our research vice president, Henry Braun, provided tireless support and has helped us in more ways than can be tersely listed here. Special thanks go to Malcolm Ree, of the Air Force's Armstrong Laboratory, whose concern with increasing the fairness and validity of testing has manifested itself in several fruitful collaborations between our two institutions.

The contributors to this volume have, and deserve, our warmest thanks. Their efforts to craft their words carefully to convey the results of extensive research has resulted, in our opinion, in a book of great value. We can only hope that they will have, by now, forgiven our occasionally impertinent requests for revisions and the seemingly endless and curious delays in the manuscript's final production.

Our good fortune to have Martha Byelich and Elizabeth Brophy as colleagues can hardly be fully recognized in a few sentences. Not only did they organize and run the conference that led to this book, but in good cheer they maintained timely control over numerous revisions of some manuscripts and, in a myriad of ways, provided the crucial help we needed to bring this book into being. We continue to wonder how they did it, but we are thankful that they did!

Paul W. Holland and Howard Wainer

INTRODUCTION AND BACKGROUND

Aristotle, in his *Metaphysics,* pointed out that "we understand those things best that we see grow from their very beginnings." We thus begin our examination of DIF with an over-the-shoulder look at the history of procedures that were developed to aid in the detection of malfunctioning items. In chapter 1, William Angoff traces the history of DIF methods from their heuristic beginnings to the more statistically rigorous methods currently available. He comments on the similarities and differences among these methods and on the language that has been developed to accurately describe exactly what it is that these methods detect. He also examines the very important set of arguments surrounding the necessity and importance of matching examinees in the two populations of interest prior to the calculation of any statistics characterizing the differential functioning of the item.

In chapter 2, Nancy Cole amplifies Angoff's concerns about the importance of a proper vocabulary to allow precision in the discussion of the technical aspects of test fairness. She then points out how an understanding of the social context in which discussions of test fairness take place are critical if one is to interpret those discussions properly.

1

Perspectives on Differential Item Functioning Methodology

William H. Angoff
Educational Testing Service

The studies of what has come to be known as *item bias* were apparently first undertaken in earnest in the 1960s. These studies were designed to develop methods for studying cultural differences and for investigating the assertion that the principal, if not the sole, reason for the great disparity in test performance between Black and Hispanic students and White students on tests of cognitive ability is that the tests contain items that are outside the realms of the minority cultures. The presumption was that these items deal with content that minority students have little occasion and less opportunity to learn. The more specific goal of these studies was, and continues to be, to identify any items that are biased against minority students and to remove them from the tests.

In parallel and contemporaneous with these studies have been the studies designed to investigate whether the tests as a whole, especially the tests used for selection, are biased against minorities, yielding lower scores for them than would be indicated by their standings on the criterion measures that these tests were intended to predict.

What set these two efforts apart, in addition to their targets of enquiry, and the different models and methods that were developed in their behalf, was that an obvious and natural external criterion existed for examining and evaluating bias in the selection test, whereas no such external criterion was thought to be readily available for evaluating bias in the items. As a consequence, investigators studying item bias resorted to the device of using the test as a whole, either directly or indirectly, as a surrogate criterion for matching the groups with respect to ability (or, to use the currently preferred term, *proficiency*). In both types of efforts it was recognized early that the study of bias would be falsely rendered if the criterion itself was inadequate in any way, most particularly if it was itself biased. Under such circumstances it is quite likely that some biased items would be found to be unbiased and other, unbiased items found to be biased.

It may be useful at this point to consider the language that we ordinarily use in connection with studies of item and test bias—in particular, the use of the word *bias* itself. Several writers (e.g., Ironson, 1982; Linn & Drasgow, 1987; Linn, Levine, Hastings, & Wardrop, 1981; and Shepard, Camilli, & Averill, 1981) have defined item bias in very much the same way, essentially: An item is biased if equally able (or proficient) individuals, from different groups, do not have equal probabilities of answering the item correctly. (The same definition, in principle, applies to bias in the test.) It is of some interest that Shepard et al. also characterized bias as "a kind of invalidity that harms one group more than another" (p. 318). The first of these definitions, it is noted, refers to the simple observation of the difference in performance; the second contains the sense of an evaluation, over and above the difference itself, and refers to its (unfair) effect on a group. The dictionary defines bias as a divergence from some expression or indication of truth. Statistically, this translates into a tendency for an estimate to deviate in one direction or another from a true value. Socially, it means something akin to prejudice, an unreasoning inclination of temperament. When the concept first acquired popular psychometric currency in the 1960s, it was used in the sense used by Shepard et al.—that a possible reason, to be investigated, for the low test performance of minorities was that the items were capitalizing unfairly on knowledge and skills that were part of the White middle-class culture, but alien to the minority cultures. In an effort to investigate the validity of this hypothesis, methods were developed by the psychometricians, and studies undertaken, to determine how aberrant items, and therefore, by one definition, biased items, could be identified. But these were only statistical findings, subject to later interpretation and judgment. Some of these aberrant items may well have been biased, in the sense of being unfairly disadvantageous, against minorities. Some others, however, were judged to be quite fair, in the sense that they called on important educational outcomes, appropriate for all students, but unequally known and understood by all students. Still other items gave no clue as to the reason for their aberrancy.

In any case, it became clear very early that there was a semantic conflict here; the word *bias* was being used simultaneously, but quite understandably, for at least two entirely different meanings, social and statistical. The consequence was that unnecessary additional confusion was being introduced into an already confused political atmosphere in which bias was alleged to be the cause of the large disparity in scores. Some suggestions were made to use a term other than *bias* for the statistical observation, quite apart from its judgmental or interpretive meaning and use, and another term to describe the judgment and evaluation of bias in the social sense. Finally, the expression *differential item functioning* (DIF) came into use, referring to the simple observation that an item displays different statistical properties in different group settings (after controlling for differences in the abilities of the groups, a topic discussed later). How the item was to be judged and used, that is, whether it was socially biased, and what disposition was to be made of it, was regarded as a quite separate matter. But semantic habits die hard. The word *bias* is particularly seductive; it is singular, brief, and concise, and lends itself comfortably to use as either noun, verb, or adjective. *Differential item functioning,* on the other hand, is long, unwieldy, and terminologically unadaptable. Nevertheless, it is the far preferable term for the objective observation, that is, without prejudgment, of a group disparity. Its freedom from evaluative overtones is worth preserving, permitting bias as a social issue to be examined quite separately.

METHODS FOR INVESTIGATING
DIFFERENTIAL ITEM FUNCTIONING

One of the first formal procedures undertaken to evaluate the extent of what was then, without the distinction just discussed, called item bias in a test was that by Cardall and Coffman (1964), in which they applied analysis of variance procedures to test the interaction of items with groups of Black and (mostly) White examinees who had taken the SAT in 1963. Essentially the same procedure was followed in connection with their studies by Cleary and Hilton (1968) and by Angoff and Sharon (1974), but the approach does not appear to have caught on very widely.

In 1972, Angoff offered a method for studying cultural differences, known variously as the *delta-plot* or *transformed item-difficulty* (TID) method. This method shortly became highly popular for reasons of its easy logic and practical simplicity, and for this reason it is described here in some detail. Although it was originally described by Thurstone (1925) in connection with his method of *absolute scaling,* the method was later applied by Tucker (1951) in a study of an academic ability scale of vocabulary items and by Gulliksen (1960) in a binational comparison of scale values of occupational prestige.

The delta-plot method calls for the calculation of item *p*-values for each of the two groups under consideration and for the conversion of each *p*-value to a normal deviate, usually expressed on a scale with a mean of 13 and standard deviation of 4. The pairs of normal deviates, one pair for each item, are then plotted on a bivariate graph with the two groups represented on the axes, each pair represented by a point on the graph. When the groups are of the same type and of the same level of proficiency, the plot of these points will ordinarily appear in the form of an ellipse extending from lower left to upper right, often representing a correlation of .98 or even higher, indicating that the rank order of difficulty of the items is essentially the same in the two groups. (See Fig. 1.1, panel a.) When the groups differ only in level of proficiency, the ellipse will be displaced vertically or horizontally, depending on which group is the more profi-

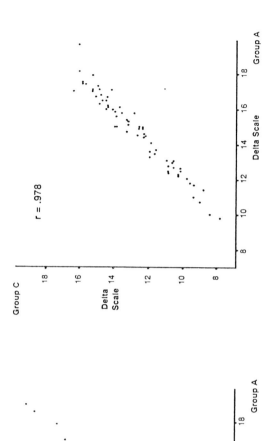

Panel A
Groups of the same type, equally proficient

Panel B
Groups of the same type, not equally proficient

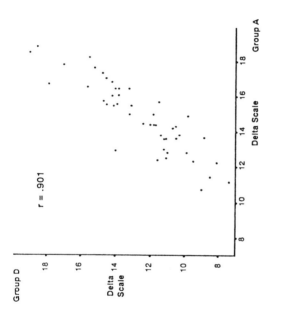

Panel C
Groups of different types, not equally proficient

FIG. 1.1.   Delta plots for different pairs of groups.

cient. (See Fig. 1.1, panel b.) However, when the groups are drawn from different types of populations, the points will be dispersed in the off-diagonal direction and the correlation represented by the points will be lower than previously indicated. The items falling at some distance from the plot of points, as measured by the distance of the item's bivariate point from the principal axis of the plot, may be regarded as contributing to the item × group interaction (Angoff & Ford, 1973). (See Fig. 1.1, panel c, in which the groups are also different in levels of proficiency.) These are the items that are especially more difficult for one group than for the other, *relative to* the other items, and are ordinarily taken to be characterized by DIF. The point is worth making here that the relative proficiencies of the two groups is of no particular significance in applying the method. What is important is the position of the points in the graph relative to one another.

A significant development, punctuating a major breakthrough in the history of test theory, was reached in the publication of F. M. Lord's dissertation (Lord, 1952) and in the Lord and Novick (1968) text, in which Lord explicated the *item response theory (IRT)* model. Within a short time thereafter it became clear that this model could be profitably applied in the study of differential item functioning. As is by now well known, the basis of the theory lay in the item response function, the S-shaped trace of the proportion of individuals at the same ability level who answer a given item correctly. Under the assumption that the ability under consideration is unidimensional and that the item measures the same ability, the trace is unique under the conditions of a particular model; except for random variations the same curve is found, irrespective of the nature of the group for whom the function is plotted. The curve is often defined by three parameters: a, which is proportional to the slope of the curve at the point of inflection and represents the discriminating power of the item; b, the proficiency level, θ, at the point of inflection, representing the difficulty of the item; and c, the lower asymptote—alternatively called the *pseudo-guessing parameter*—corresponding to the probability that a person completely lacking in proficiency will answer the item correctly.

Because of the unique nature of the item response curve (under the assumptions already stated), the finding that the response curve is not in fact the same for two groups is evidence that the assumptions are not satisfied for one or both groups, and statistical tests are available for testing the significance of the differences between the curves with respect to the three parameters (Thissen, Steinberg, & Wainer, 1988). There are also tests for examining the areas between the curves—that is, the degree to which the curves fail to coincide.

Unlike other methods of studying item bias, the use of the three-parameter item response model is a comprehensive one, taking into account not only differences between the groups with respect to item difficulty, but also differences with respect to discriminating power and differences with respect to the pseudo-guessing parameter. Other methods either ignore differences among items with respect to discriminating power and guessing or assume that they do not exist. The fact that such differences among items, especially in discriminating power, do exist has made the IRT model the criterion method to use for studying item bias and for identifying biased items. Its use as a standard procedure has been inhibited, however, by the large amounts of data required to yield stable findings, its attendant cost, and, more than likely, the complexity of the model itself and the frequent failure of operational tests to satisfy the assumptions of the model. Other methods, like the delta-plot method, are far less expensive, require less data, and are intuitively easier to understand and apply. However, as is described later, the delta method is now considered to be technically flawed.

The Rasch model, a one-parameter item response theory (Rasch, 1960; Wright & Panchapakesan, 1969), is one that assumes that all items are equally discriminating and that items are not answered correctly by guessing. In effect, its use for examining items for bias is limited to an examination of differences in item difficulty (after conditioning on ability). Because it assumes that there are no differences in the a- or c-parameters, any such real differences are therefore not detectable by means of the Rasch model. Even more serious is the fact that any real differences in the a- or c-parameters are likely to result in artifactual DIF values.

The foregoing is similarly true of the delta-plot (TID) method. It has been pointed out by Cole (1978), Cole and Moss (1989), Hunter (1975), Shepard (1981), and Lord (1977), and affirmed by Angoff (1982), that unless all the items in a delta plot have the same discriminating power, the method may yield misleading results, especially when the groups studied earn mean scores at widely different ability levels. The delta, it is recalled, is taken from the proportion of individuals in the two groups answering the item correctly. These proportion-correct values may be found on the item response curve corresponding to the mean ability score of the group. If one compares the difference in proportion-correct figures for the two groups under consideration for two items with different discriminating power, one sees that the difference is smaller for the less discriminating item than for the more discriminating item. (See Fig. 1.2.) This being the case, it is likely that at least some of the items identified as unbiased by the delta-plot procedure may in fact be found to be biased, if appropriate account were taken of their relatively low discriminating power. The reverse may similarly be true: Items identified as biased by the delta-plot method may in fact not be biased, but only give a biased appearance because they are more discriminating. Both types of errors would be unfortunate and costly—the first, because some biased items would go undetected; the second, because it could lead to the ultimate removal of the most useful items in the pool.

Lord (1977) was critical of proportion-correct figures for several reasons,

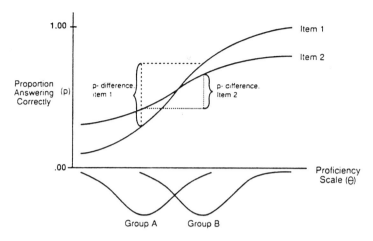

FIG. 1.2.   Item response curves for two items of different discriminating power, taken by two groups of different levels of proficiency.

among them that they are group-dependent and therefore confounded values,
sometimes leading to curious anomalies. For example, if we have two items with
different *a*-parameters and two groups of different average ability, item 1 may
turn out to be more difficult than item 2 for Group A, but less difficult than item 2
for Group B (Lord, 1980, p. 35). Unlike proportion-correct figures, the item-
difficulty parameter, derived from the three-parameter IRT model, is invariant
with respect to group.

   Shepard et al. (1981) found that the one-parameter (Rasch) index of DIF
yields a correlation higher than .99 with the TID index of DIF. This should not be
overly surprising. It can be shown that the *b*-value derived from the one-
parameter model is directly proportional to the delta. This would imply that
whatever errors of interpretation are attributed to the delta-plot procedure are
shared by the Rasch model.

   In 1979, Scheuneman published a method similar (but not identical) to chi-
square for evaluating DIF, but this method was subsequently criticized by Baker
(1981) for yielding values irrelevantly affected by sample size and with an
unknown sampling distribution—in effect, not a chi-square procedure at all. A
corrected statistic, sometimes called the "full" chi-square, appears in Bishop,
Fienberg, and Holland (1975). The full chi-square procedure calls for dividing
the groups into intervals of total score (Scheuneman [1979] suggested 4 or 5
intervals) and forming a 2 × 2 table for each interval, showing pass-fail on one
axis and the two groups on the other axis, as shown here for the *i*th interval. A
chi-square is calculated for each of the tables (intervals) and summed. The
number of degrees of freedom is the number of such intervals.

Performance on Item i

Tested	r	a_i	b_i	$N_{r_i} = a_i + b_i$
Group	f	c_i	d_i	$N_{f_i} = c_i + d_i$
		$N_{1_i} = a_i + c_i$	$N_{0_i} = b_i + d_i$	$N_i = a_i + b_i + c_i + d_i$

Nine years after Scheuneman's (1979) development, Holland and Thayer (1988) described a procedure for investigating DIF that made use of a technique designed by Mantel and Haenszel (1959) in their retrospective studies of disease. The Mantel–Haenszel procedure may be described as follows: Assume, as in the full chi-square method, that the 2×2 table shown here describes the frequencies of correct (1) and incorrect (0) performance of the focal (f) and reference (r) groups (where *focal* refers to the particular group of interest—Blacks, Hispanics, Asians, Native Americans, women, etc.—and *reference* refers to the group with whom the focal group is to be compared—Whites, males, etc.), all of whom score in the same score interval on the relevant section of the test, usually the section of the test that contains the item. In this operational sense, the focal and reference groups are matched on the ability most nearly relevant to the ability measured by the item.

The Mantel–Haenszel index is calculated at each score interval (i) of the section of the test of which the item is a part:

$$\alpha_i = \frac{p_{r_i}}{q_{r_i}} \Big/ \frac{p_{f_i}}{q_{f_i}} = \frac{\dfrac{a_i}{a_i + b_i}}{\dfrac{b_i}{a_i + b_i}} \Big/ \frac{\dfrac{c_i}{c_i + d_i}}{\dfrac{d_i}{c_i + d_i}} = \frac{a_i}{b_i} \Big/ \frac{c_i}{d_i} = \frac{a_i d_i}{b_i c_i}, \qquad (1)$$

where p_{r_i} is the proportion of the reference group in score interval i who answered the item correctly, and $q_{r_i} = 1 - p_{r_i}$. Similarly, p_{f_i} is the proportion of the focal group who answered the item correctly, and $q_{f_i} = 1 - p_{f_i}$. Thus, α_i is the ratio of the odds (p/q) that the reference group students have answered the item correctly to the odds that the focal group students have answered the item correctly. If there is no difference in the performance of the two groups on this item within this score interval, then α_i will be equal to 1. If, however, the two groups function differently—if, for example, in this score interval the focal group performs better on the item than the reference group, then $\alpha_i < 1$. If, on the other hand, the reference group performs better than the focal group, $\alpha_i > 1$.

The Mantel-Haenszel procedure estimates a common odds ratio across all matched categories. The form of its index is given as follows:

$$\hat{\alpha}_{MH} = \frac{\sum_i p_{r_i} q_{f_i} N_{r_i} N_{f_i}/N_i}{\sum_i q_{r_i} p_{f_i} N_{r_i} N_{f_i}/N_i} = \frac{\sum_i a_i d_i/N_i}{\sum_i b_i c_i/N_i}, \qquad (2)$$

which is the average factor by which the odds that a member of the reference group responds correctly to the item exceeds the odds that a member of the focal group responds correctly to the item. It is observed that the index is weighted by the number of cases in the interval; also, that the interval in which the numbers of cases in the two groups are more nearly equal receives the heavier weight.

For the sake of convenience, $\hat{\alpha}_{MH}$ is transformed to another scale, yielding an index that is referred to as *MH D-DIF,* by means of the conversion, MH D-DIF $= -2.35ln(\hat{\alpha}_{MH})$. This transformation centers the index about the value 0 (which corresponds to the absence of differential item functioning), and puts it on a scale roughly comparable to the ETS delta scale of item difficulty and *reverses* the index so that positive values of MH D-DIF indicate that the item favors the focal group; negative values indicate that the item favors the reference group and disfavors the focal group.

Holland and Thayer (1988) suggested that the Mantel–Haenszel procedure, which provides both a significance test and a measure of the effect size ($\hat{\alpha}_{MH}$, or MH D-DIF), enjoys statistical properties to be preferred over the full chi-square methods, such as those offered by Bishop et al. (1975) and by Marascuilo and Slaughter (1981), and point out, as did Angoff (1982), that statistical tests will always show significance if the sample sizes are large enough. The measure of effect size will serve to temper judgments influenced by significant results when it is seen that the effect size is actually small.

Dorans and Kulick (1986) offered a method of identifying DIF, called the *standardization method,* which makes use of the same information as does the Mantel–Haenszel procedure and is quite similar to it in other respects; indeed, the correlation between the two DIF indices, when expressed on the same scale, is .99 (Wright, 1987a). The principal differences are that, first, at each interval on the dimension of the matching variable the standardization method considers the difference in p-values for the focal and reference group (which Dorans & Kulick, 1986, call the *base group*); second, it weights these differences in terms of a specially identified *standardization group,* typically the focal group. Thus,

$$D_{STD} = \sum_i k_i(p_{f_i} - p_{b_i}) \Big/ \sum_i k_i, \qquad (3)$$

where i refers to the score interval of the matching variable and $k_i/\sum_i k_i$ is the weighting factor at score level i supplied by the standardization group and used to weight differences in performance between the focal group (p_{f_i}) and the base group (p_{b_i}). Typically, the focal group has served as the standardization group.

An important advantage of the standardization method, not shared by the

Mantel–Haenszel method except by approximation, is that it yields a direct estimate of the weighted difference in p-values between the focal and reference (base) groups. This difference can just as easily be expressed, if one wishes, in terms of deltas, the normalized equivalents of p-values expressed on a 13-4 scale (as described previously).

As has been clear in the previous discussions, the methods of identifying DIF typically focus on the correct option. But the incorrect options (distractors), and the embedded and trailing omits, also exert a major effect on the difficulty of the item, and it is likely that the source of the DIF will occasionally be found there. Dorans, Schmitt, and Bleistein (1988) and Green, Crone, and Folk (1989) recently did some developmental work on a DIF model for other-than-correct responses, and further work in this area is expected.

Like the delta method and the full chi-square method, but unlike the IRT method, the Mantel–Haenszel and standardization methods provide indices of differential item difficulty, but not of differential item discrimination. Indeed, it is possible for an item with the same difficulty parameter in the two groups but with different slope parameters to yield a DIF index of zero when analyzed by all but the IRT method. It would therefore be advisable to plot the component chi-square values, or MH indices, or standardization indices score interval by score interval, as was done by Dorans and Kulick (1986), as well as to calculate a weighted index across the entire range of score intervals. An upward or downward trend in this plot would warrant the conclusion that there is a difference between the two groups with respect to the item's discriminating power.

OTHER CONSIDERATIONS

Characteristics Common to All Methods

It is significant that all the methods available to identify DIF are designed to match the groups, either directly or indirectly, on the proficiency measured by the items. Even the delta-plot method, which does not normally use an explicit matching variable, matches the groups nevertheless, in the sense that group differences are observable, but for all practical purposes in using the method, they are ignored; what is of interest in examining the results is the off-diagonal dispersion, the appearance of anomalous, that is, aberrant, item points relative to the other item points in the swarm—in effect, the outlier items that contribute to the item × group interaction.

The sense of conditioning on a criterion variable (usually the total score on the section that contains the item or, in the case of the delta method, the collection of other items in the section) is common to nearly all methods of detecting DIF, including a method described by Stricker (1982), which calls for the correlation between item and group membership, with true scores on the total (criterion) score partialled out. The general notion of conditioning on a criterion variable in the process of examining group differences is also illustrated in the Cole (1973) model of test bias, in which, for a given score on the criterion, the average test scores of the two groups being compared are examined.

When explicit matching is carried out on an observed score, as it is for the chi-square, Mantel–Haenszel, and standardization methods, it appears that the matching variable should be stratified as finely as possible, consistent with the amount of data on hand. To use broad strata would allow group differences within the strata to dilute the effect of the matching.

It is also significant that all the methods and techniques that have been developed to identify DIF in the items assume that the group of items, or the test that contains the items, is homogeneous and unidimensional. This assumption is explicitly true of the IRT models and, as just indicated, at least implicitly true of the delta-plot method and the chi-square, Mantel–Haenszel, and standardization methods. To test this assumption conceptually, one might imagine an analysis involving matched groups of men and women, of a test containing both verbal and mathematical items. The results of such an analysis would undoubtedly show a strong tendency for the verbal items to favor women and for the mathematical items to favor men, thus providing evidence that verbal and mathematical items do indeed represent different domains.

The Golden Rule Settlement

In recent years a question has arisen at the level of social policy in connection with the settlement between the Golden Rule Insurance Company on the one hand and the Illinois Department of Insurance and Educational Testing Service (ETS) on the other (Faggen, 1987), regarding the way in which items would be considered for inclusion in the Illinois insurance licensing examinations. It was agreed as part of the settlement—there were other conditions as well—that a raw difference, favoring White applicants over Black applicants, of .15 or more in an item's p-values was to be taken as evidence that the item is to be considered biased in the social sense, that is, unfair to the lower-performing group, and identified as an item not normally to be included in the test. The virtually unanimous view of the psychometric community (Bond, 1987, referred to it as "axiomatic"), however, is that a simple raw difference in favor of the White group with respect to their average success rate on a test item is, by itself, insufficient reason for concluding that the item is biased against the Black group. The same consideration applies to mean scores on a test.

There are two lines of evidence to support this view. First is that just as we have reason to expect individuals to differ consistently among one another in test performance, so do we also have reason to expect that entire groups will differ consistently among one another in test performance. This is not to say that such differences are innate and unchanging, or that they in any sense reflect a fundamental difference in ability. Indeed, we know that individual and group differences on cognitive tests are in very large part brought about by differences in the nature, quality, and amount of education, both in school and out of school, to which people are exposed. This is particularly true of Black people in our society. We know that Blacks in America had been for many years excluded, both by law and by custom, from the normal educational stream. It should therefore come as no surprise to us that they typically score lower today, on the average, than White groups. Clearly, there is bias here, but just as clearly, the bias resides in the treatment that has been historically accorded these groups and which now reflects itself in general academic performance, including, specifically, performance on the tests. To deny the reality of the differences in test performance—at least, the likelihood that the differences are real—is to deny that there is a real difference in the academic knowledge and skills that the tests are designed to measure and to deny that some minority groups in this society are indeed educationally disadvantaged. It would say, in effect, that the educational opportunities afforded minority groups in this society are, and have consistently been, equivalent in quality to those afforded the mainstream groups. This is clearly not the case.

As already discussed, the task of the various models of DIF is to identify those items whose behavior is anomalous, inconsistent with the message of the test as a whole. All the models of DIF recognize, either directly or indirectly, the strong likelihood that some component of the observed score difference between the groups under study—including White and Black groups—is a real difference. It is in this sense that they all aim to separate bias in the item, if it exists, from the bias in society, as discussed previously, that reflects itself in group differences in school performance and in test performance as well.

Quite apart from the more general logic that supports the examination of group differences after first matching for ability, there is a specific psychometric aspect to this logic as well. Linn and Drasgow (1987) considered the position embodied in the Golden Rule settlement and have made it clear that, among other things, the settlement undermines the cause of good measurement: In calling for the considered exclusion of items that show relatively large disparities (p-value differences greater than .15) between White and Black examinees, the settlement works toward the avoidance of the most discriminating items, those that distinguish between high- and low-performing groups, in favor of the less discriminating items. The inevitable outcome of such an effort is that the resulting test will necessarily be a less reliable, less psychometrically discriminating, and ultimately less valid instrument.

It was asserted earlier that there were two arguments supporting the view that a raw difference between the two groups in item performance is not by itself sufficient reason for concluding that the item is biased against the lower-performing group. One reason, already given, is that a large difference is to be expected in view of the history of educational experiences of the lower performing Black group. The record of poverty today and the educational ills that typically accompany poverty today—low rates of school attendance and high rates of dropout, poor academic performance, low representations in national competitions (Merit scholarships, Westinghouse awards) and recognitions (e.g., Study of Mathematically Precocious Youth)—provides convincing evidence that the principal motivations of many young Black people in our society today do not run along academic and intellectual lines. The implication one would be forced to draw from the Golden Rule settlement, on the other hand, is that the entire disparity between White and Black test performance is accounted for by bias in the test, that in point of fact there is no real difference in the knowledge and skills of the two groups and that Black students are in fact not educationally disadvantaged.

The second argument is one that was alluded to early in this chapter, that statistical evidence of a large difference in the groups' performance, even evidence of DIF itself, is not by itself entirely persuasive in deciding whether or not to remove an item from the test; there may be good reason for retaining the item in spite of the statistical findings. For example, Doolittle and Cleary (1987) found that female students do worse than male students of the same general mathematical ability on geometry and mathematical reasoning items. If, then, one were to follow the results of the analysis mechanically, one would remove such items from the test. But this obviously makes little sense. The understanding of geometry and the ability to reason mathematically represent legitimate and necessary goals of mathematics education, and students, whoever they are, should be expected to cope successfully with problems of this sort. To remove such items would not only render the test incomplete, it would be disadvantageous to the students who failed them, for it would serve to conceal the particular source of their mathematics deficiency and perpetuate it. Shepard (1987a) expressed a similar view: "[T]o the extent that members of one group do more poorly on a subtest of items that are a *legitimate part of the content domain,* we would be reluctant to call the discrepancy evidence of *bias*" (p. 186, italics in original).

The process of matching the two groups for ability, although certainly a preferred procedure, nevertheless does raise, in the public's mind, some interesting questions of its own. For example, when there already exists a marked difference between the Black and White groups, what does it mean to "match"? If we select from the Black and White groups the same number (or proportion) of individuals, score level by score level, we have indeed conditioned effectively on ability (proficiency), as measured by the total test score. At the same time, however, have we not produced for study a group of Blacks who are unrepresentative of Blacks generally and a group of Whites who are similarly unrepresentative of Whites generally? And is it now possible that, when we have conducted the DIF analysis, we have in fact assembled a set of data for an irrelevant comparison, between groups who are not the original groups of interest? Does the analysis now have the intended value? In reply to this concern we can say that we have extracted the ability differences between the groups and have laid bare for comparison the remaining differences, those having to do with the students' color, culture, and group identity. In the last analysis, this is the essence of the comparison we wish to make.

Characteristics of the Matching Criterion

There is unanimous agreement that the matching criterion should be valid, reliable, and fair to be acceptable. It is also important that it be so perceived. For if the criterion is itself biased to some degree, then the application of a DIF analysis will certainly be flawed; further, if bias is pervasive in the criterion, then any attempt to identify bias in its component items will inevitably fail. This is the weakness in a circular procedure, in which the "criterion of truth" is not only a test—and therefore already suspect in the minds of some—but is also the test that comprises the very items whose possible bias we seek to determine. On the other hand, the circularity cannot be avoided; the test itself is the most relevant and reliable criterion available to help answer the important questions relating to the validity of the test and the inferences one is to draw from it. And from a statistical point of view it appears that if the studied item is not included in the matching criterion, then the Mantel–Haenszel procedure will not be optimal. Holland and Thayer (1988, p. 141) suggested a two-step procedure for examining items for DIF: "Step 1: Refine the matching criterion by eliminating items based on a preliminary DIF . . . analysis. Step 2: Use as the matching criterion the total score on all items left in the refined criterion plus the studied item— even if it is then omitted from the criterion of all other items when they are studied in turned (*sic*)." This iterative procedure, which successively refines and purifies the criterion over the course of several analyses, should satisfy the concern that the procedure is circular and therefore suspect.

Interpretation of DIF

It is to be emphasized that finding DIF in an item does not necessarily imply that the item is biased, that is, unfair to one of the groups. Considerations of unfairness would imply normative (competitive) comparisons with other individuals, in instances where, for example, the examinee earns what is considered to be a reward for a relatively high score or a demerit for a relatively low score. But there are also instances when such judgments and actions are not the issue, when, for example, two different language or cultural groups are being compared on a common measure as part of a research effort in linguistic comparisons (e.g., Alderman & Holland, 1981; Angoff & Sharon, 1974). Nor is it necessarily the case that unfairness exists in the item itself; often an item showing even substantial DIF may be judged to be quite fair, depending on its purpose. Ironson (1982) cited an example of an item asking for the temperature required for baking a cake. The item, even if statistically biased against males, may be quite appropriate if it is used in a test to select cooks and bakers.

The question then arises of how, in general, items that function differentially are to be regarded and interpreted. There appears to be general agreement that, cast most easily in the sense of the IRT model, items that do not yield the same item response function for two or more groups are violating one of the fundamental assumptions of item response theory, assumptions also implicit in the other models of DIF, namely that the item and the test in which the item is contained are measuring the same unidimensional trait (e.g., Linn et al., 1981; Shepard, 1987a). A large DIF value would suggest that the item is measuring an additional construct in one of the groups that may not be relevant to the intended construct of the test. As a consequence, the conclusion might be reached that the assumption of unidimensionality is not satisfied: The test is not unidimensional for at least one of the two groups, or does not measure the same dimension in the two groups. (This conclusion—which could be investigated in a study of the internal structure of the test, by, for example, factor analyzing the items of the test separately for the two groups (see Cole, 1981)—suggests that dimensionality is not a function of the test by itself, but a function of the test only in the context of a particular group of examinees. Moreover, the example, cited previously, of the differential difficulty in a mathematics test of mathematical reasoning items for one of the groups suggests that the general conclusion of multidimensionality might have to be further confirmed by an editorial examination of the item content.) In any case, inasmuch as the construct represented by the test may be different from one group to another, the inferences that may be drawn, and the judgments and actions taken on the basis of the scores, may similarly be different from one group to another. It is in this sense that the validity of the test as a basis for a particular inference is thrown into question, and it is in this sense that bias, as unfairness, is defined; that bias has to do with inferences, evaluations, and ethical considerations as they affect the test's use.

Use of Additional Matching Variables

It is useful to regard group differences in item (and test) performance as consisting, in theory, of two components: the "true," or unassailable, difference between the groups and an artifactual difference brought about by the use of inappropriate and irrelevant (DIF) items. These two effects, in sum, have sometimes been referred to as *impact*. The use of the total score criterion as a matching, or conditioning, variable, as a measure of the "true" proficiency of the groups, serves to separate out these two effects. But the separation can only be as effective as the relevance, or, operationally, the correlation, of the criterion variable with success on the item. Clearly, if the correlation is zero, the matching criterion is entirely ineffective in separating out these effects, and one has no alternative but to refer to the group difference as undifferentiated impact. It is therefore important to choose a matching criterion that correlates best with the item; and if the test is truly unidimensional, the total score on the test is probably the one variable that correlates optimally with the item. But item-test correlations, even for reliable, well-constructed tests, do not average much above .50, suggesting that there is still a great deal of variance in the item left untapped by the total test score. This argues for the use of additional matching variables in an effort to increase the overall correlation with the item.

It has been reported by test developers that they are often confronted by DIF results that they cannot understand; and no amount of deliberation seems to help explain why some perfectly reasonable items have large DIF values. Several investigators (e.g., Cole, 1981; Linn, 1986; Plake, 1980; Shepard, 1981, 1982; Tittle, 1982) noted that the judgment of bias is generally unreliable. This is not surprising; the judgment of item difficulty by itself is not highly reliable (see, e.g., Thorndike, 1982), and the judgment that an item will or will not be differentially difficult is expectedly even less reliable. In one attempt to account for DIF results, Bleistein and Wright (1985) found, in a study of the performance of Asian-American students on mathematical word problems, that the lack of English fluency appeared to be the cause (or at least one of them) for their poor performance. In the case of mathematics achievement tests, Wise (1985) reported that she was able to account for a significant proportion (about seven eighths) of the mean male–female difference at the twelfth grade level by conditioning on the amount of math taken in high school and on ninth grade level math achievement. Further, it is not a difficult stretch to hypothesize that the solution of geometry problems calls on spatial ability (Maccoby & Jacklin, 1974). It would be useful to know to what extent women, who typically score lower than men on spatial tests, do worse on geometry problems for this reason. As yet another example, it is more than likely that controlling on one or more aspects of socioeconomic level might well explain some of the disparity in Black–White scores. In general, then, it is certainly possible that other variables, in addition to total score, may help to explain otherwise unexplainable results. It seems reasonable to test this possibility—to identify first those items with substantial DIF values, after controlling first on total score alone, then to add variables in order (either by matching or by forming a single weighted composite criterion) that, by hypothesis, show promise of explaining more of the variance in item behavior than initially found—to determine whether, in fact, there has been a reduction in the variance of DIF values as a result of using these additional matching variables. Any further operational decision to retain, revise, or discard such items would depend on the nature of the added variables and the judgment of the educational, psychological, and social mechanisms that caused the observed change in the DIF values. A principal caution to be observed in carrying out such studies is that the added matching variables are not of a sort that would interact with—that is, that they do not have different meanings for—the two groups, a potential danger that may be particularly acute when we seek to condition on educational, occupational, or other social status variables.

The foregoing effort can also be accomplished by other means; for example, by studying groups that are matched in terms of age, grade level, and socioeconomic status, as described by Jensen (1980) and carried out by him and by Linn et al. (1981). Still other analyses could be conducted by studying differences between pseudogroups, that is, groups of the same race, but representing differences of a sort characterized by typical Black–White comparisons (Jensen, 1980).

At a more general level, a process of analysis such as this may also help us to clarify the notion of *differential opportunity to learn* in deciding on the appropriate disposition of an item. In discussions of this sort, it will be useful to avoid terms that, like this one, express an evaluation and judgment in advance of an examination of data, and to substitute a somewhat more parsimonious term, such as *differential educational exposure,* which avoids hypothesizing any mechanism that might have caused the disparity between the groups to occur.

Appropriate Criterion for the Judgment of Significance

On a previous occasion (Angoff, 1982), the suggestion was made that, when DIF is to be tested for significance, the use of random variation as a yardstick for comparison might be too stringent a source of variance for ordinary use. Instead, we might choose to identify and scrutinize only those items whose DIF values exceeded *acceptable* levels. Thus, for example, only values of DIF found in ethnic, racial, or sex studies that exceeded those found in studies of the test following its administration to two nonrandom groups—say, two groups of students choosing to take the test at different administrations, or two groups tested in geographically separated metropolitan centers—would be deemed significant, assuming that differences between such pairs of groups would be considered tolerable. The sense of this criterion is that if we are willing to tolerate a DIF of this size in other contexts, why not in the male–female (or Black–White, Hispanic–White, Asian–White, etc.) context?

Practical Considerations

One outcome of the DIF process that does promise to be troublesome has to do with the disposition of items with positive values of DIF, items that, after matching, appear to be *easier* for the focal group than for the reference group. It is recalled that the overall mean value of DIF, when the total test score is used as the matching variable, is defined as zero; therefore there will necessarily be a substantial proportion of positive values (or a small proportion of highly positive values). But the basic purpose of the DIF study is to identify items that are disadvantageous to minorities and women. The allegation is that the tests are developed from a perspective that is largely White, middle-class, and male; and that from such a perspective, item content that is socially and educationally biased is likely to be overlooked unless subjected to specific study. Yet, as just indicated, when the total test score is used as the matching variable, the DIF procedures all coerce the finding that if some items have negative DIF, others will have positive DIF; and some writers would maintain that to be even-handed one should scrutinize items with positive DIF for rejection or revision just as one scrutinizes for rejection or revision items with negative DIF. But as just indicated, this practice would fly in the face of the original purpose of DIF analyses, which is to rid the test of any items found to be biased against minorities or women.

One practical way out of this quandary is to examine positive DIF items for any obvious flaws that would clearly disadvantage the White middle-class male and revise only the most egregious among them, but otherwise devote attention only to the items with negative DIF. This proposal will certainly cause some dissent, as will virtually any other proposal. One can only hope that the debate over the dilemma will yield a solution satisfactory both to those who insist on "even-handedness" and those who argue "original purpose".

Yet another way to deal with this matter is to balance the test with different sets of items known to favor different groups; items on Black history and literature, to favor Black students; items relating to persons and personal relationships, art, music, literature, and drama, to favor women; items relating to male sports, war, science, and mathematics, to favor men; and so forth. The natural question here is: What mix of various content areas best reflects reality? And according to whose perception of reality? And would not this procedure open the door to the danger of self-serving efforts to engineer the results of the test? There is no easy answer to these questions, but here, as in many other situations, we must depend on the consensus of committees of educators who are expert in subject-matter and curriculum and closely familiar with the data of group differences. It would be left to these people to design the test content in accordance with current educational philosophies and practices as they understand them.

FURTHER APPLICATIONS OF THE DIFFERENTIAL ITEM FUNCTIONING TECHNOLOGY

Out of the methodological efforts of the last 25 years has emerged an arsenal of methods for the analysis and identification of items with DIF characteristics. An overview at this point suggests that the methods of choice are the Mantel–Haenszel procedure, which permits the examination of differential item difficulty effects, and the comprehensive three-parameter item response theory approach, which permits the observation of differences in any of the characteristics of the

IRT function. A number of questions remain, some related to the specifics of technique, others to broader, philosophical issues. It is expected that continued work on methodology and application will answer some of the present questions, and, more than likely, raise new ones.

In the meantime, we do have a respectable methodology to use in answering some pressing issues of item bias. It should not go unnoticed, however, that the same methodology is useful in other contexts, not necessarily having to do with social bias as such, and it may be useful to identify some of them and urge the continued use of the DIF methodology in those contexts and its introduction into new contexts. Examples of some of these other contexts follow:

During the early 1960s, new types of curricular organization and content were introduced into American secondary school curricula, especially in the teaching of science. For a time, some students were still being taught by means of the traditional textbooks, while others were being introduced to textbooks written to accompany the new curricula. This outcome directly affected the development of the College Board Achievement Tests in science. It was clear that these tests would have to accommodate both the students who had been enrolled in the new curricula and those who had been enrolled in the traditional curricula, and DIF studies were carried out to determine whether there was an equal balance of items of both types (Angoff, 1971).

As mentioned earlier, DIF studies have been used to identify differential response patterns on the Test of English as a Foreign Language for examinees coming from different countries and speaking different languages (e.g., Alderman & Holland, 1981; Angoff & Sharon, 1974). Presumably, information provided by studies of this sort could be valuable for students of linguistics, not to identify biased items but simply to investigate the effect of non-English linguistic differences on English expression.

In the equating of scores on different test forms it is often necessary to use a set of common items to be administered to both groups, each taking a different form. To verify that these common items are in fact common psychologically, having the same meaning (although not necessarily the same difficulty) for both groups, it is found useful to carry out a DIF study. Such studies have in fact revealed important differences (after matching) in the difficulty of these common items, especially when they have been used for equating different forms of an achievement test administered to different groups at different times in the school year (Cook & Petersen, 1987).

As already cited, Gulliksen (1964) carried out some cross-cultural attitude studies, using a procedure similar to the delta-plot (TID) method. With the improved DIF methodology now available, such studies, perhaps using a different procedure, could be carried out on a continuing basis.

On one occasion there was some concern that a for-profit "performance contracting" (as it was then called) organization, engaged to develop an educational program in reading and mathematics and to teach the courses on a trial basis to children in the elementary schools of a Southern school system, had actually been teaching the children the correct answers to items on the tests that were to be used later for evaluating the program. A DIF study, in which the children's responses on the tests were compared with the response of a control group of children not participating in the special program, confirmed the suspicion that the tests had indeed been compromised; the study made it clear that several items on the tests were inordinately easier, relative to the other items in the tests, for the group who were suspected of having been "taught the test."

Studies of language translations have been carried out by Angoff and Modu (1973), Angoff and Cook (1988), and Hulin, Drasgow, and Parsons (1983), and validated by means of DIF procedures to determine whether an item has the same meaning when expressed in two different languages.

In the mid-1970s, when interest in the SAT score decline was at its peak, it was hypothesized that some of the old items in the common-item sections used for equating the current forms may have changed in difficulty over time and may have affected the score scale in such a way as to cause an artifactual decline in scores. A DIF analysis demonstrated that this was not the case.

It has often been said that the intellectual behaviors of two children of the same mental age but different chronological ages are different—that, for example, a 6-year-old with a mental age of 8 and an 8-year-old with a mental age of 8 are different intellectually. There is not an extensive empirical literature, however, on precisely what the nature of these differences may be. Where do these differences appear and in what particular cognitive dimensions? In the context of test performance, how can they be recognized in the children's responses to test items? If they do not appear in the correct options, do they appear in the distractors; and if not there, then in what respects do these differences exist? Quite possibly, differential item functioning techniques might be of considerable assistance in research of this sort.

Thus, even where item bias as such is not the issue, it is interesting to study the behavior of items and its variation across ethnic, cultural, and linguistic groups and across groups that differ as a function of nationality, geography, time, sex, age, and educational disability. With techniques currently available, one can carry out more rigorous studies of general and specific retardation with possibly useful application in areas of educational and psychological diagnosis. It is maintained that the methods now available for examining differential item functioning can be used for studying a much broader range of problems than the problem of item bias and it is important that we investigate appropriate applications for them.

2 History and Development of DIF

Nancy S. Cole
Educational Testing Service

William Angoff has provided an overview of the development of DIF, its technical antecedents, and some of the issues and complexities that remain. As discussant, I am going to choose the route of supplementing Mr. Angoff's comments rather than responding to them, I hope still in the spirit of the "history and development of DIF."

HISTORICAL CONTEXT OF SOCIAL CONCERNS

To appreciate the issue of test and item bias, it may be useful to remind ourselves of a history through which most of us lived—the civil rights era of the 1960s. This era is important to our understanding of DIF because test and item bias concerns in their modern form grew out of this era, were responses to it, were influenced by it, and took their role as a standard part of the testing enterprise because of it.

This era was marked, of course, by enormous concern for equal opportunity, by attack on systems viewed as discriminating from education to employment to social services, by development of the popular and legal concept of affirmative action, by a racial/ethnic self-consciousness shown in ways ranging from Black power to federal reporting requirements by race. Educational differences resulting from unequal educational systems of the past, like different employment rates in good jobs, were seen as the vestiges of the old discriminatory order. Test scores reflecting those differences were viewed by many in the same light as seniority or job experience in promotion or hiring: available only to the favored group, the outward embodiment of years of wrongdoing.

In this milieu, the technical testing community was enormously confused and even hurt by the attacks on its tests as biased. It viewed the tests as neutral tools that, granted, could be used for either good or bad, but were inherently neither. The test's role was not to address the social evils of the world but to be a neutral reporter of what it found. In fact, as educators, this testing community always had assumed its tests did good, or at least, if it never really had checked carefully for that outcome, it had hoped and planned for them to do good. In fact, the community felt its test results helped point out social problems (if not helped solve them) and that it should be seen as among the good guys.

Further, the testing community's technical orientation was color-blind. Its procedures did not take racial-ethnic identity into account in any explicit, intentional way, and the community's implicit definition of fairness was essentially to be color-blind—this at a time when the world around it was increasingly color conscious. In this era, testers barely had begun to grapple with what it would mean to be both group-conscious and fair.

I paint this somewhat exaggerated picture of a technical community largely at odds with the times to lay the groundwork for understanding some of the failures of conversation between the technical community and the public, remnants of which we continue to see to this day. And I paint it, not to denigrate either the public view or the technical view of the time. Both views had legitimacy. However, the public and technical conversations about testing and test bias reflected these entirely different starting points. Therefore, when the efforts at conversation began (in the late 1960s and through the 1970s), the result was like two ships passing in the night. How we discuss and address the 1989 version of these public and technical concerns remains with us as a continuing problem.

PUBLIC VERSUS TECHNICAL
LANGUAGE ISSUES

The problem involves not only the different ways in which we the technical community and many other segments of the society come at the problem. The problem is even in the very language in which we address the problem. In reading Bill Angoff's article, I was struck again by the enormous difficulties language causes us on this issue. I note here, first, the differences between the social and technical connotations of words and, second, the differences in language between the theoretical constructs we use and the operational definitions of those constructs.

Social Versus Technical Connotations of Language. For a conversation between testers and the public to occur, there had to be a common language. Because the testers were bilingual, users of both the technical and public language, and the public was monolingual in that regard, the public language was the obvious choice for the conversation. So public terms such as *bias* and *fairness* set the language for the discussion. However, even while the conversation occurred, the testers never really recognized that their side of the conversation was not being held consistently in the public language. The testers often were using the public words but carrying with them a technical meaning.

To the public, bias was bad. It meant unfair; it meant working against equal opportunity. Things biased were grouped right along with Bull Conners and his dogs and clubs. As we testers tried to converse with the public, we kept forgetting the language we were speaking and would slip back into the technical language without realizing the difference. To us, bias was certainly not good but it was a less than optimal technical characteristic, not a social evil. So we fell into a language of test and item bias, to which we gave technical meaning, and tried to have a conversation with a public for whom the words were loaded with value-laden connotations to which we did not attend.

And we found ourselves in the strange situation of doing so-called "statistical item bias analyses," finding positive statistical results, and then having to judge the items independently of the statistics to say whether the results represented bias even in our technical sense of unfair—all without reaching the public notions of bias. Ships passing in the night.

In the Angoff article, I noticed that he tries to escape this problem by sometimes using differential item functioning as the generic label for the class of statistical procedures that grew up under the *item bias procedures* label. Oh that we had been so smart 20 years earlier!

Theoretical Versus Operational Connotations of Language.   The difficulties of language, bad enough in the differences between the public and technical connotations, unfortunately do not stop there. The technical language involves not only the theoretical meanings on which we model our efforts, but the ways we are forced (because of practicalities) to operationalize our models. This problem was clear in Angoff's chapter when he discussed the theoretical notions of judging items based on comparing groups "matched on ability." In theory, that is precisely the proper way to think about the models we are applying. In practice, of course, we must operationalize "ability." As technicians we all know that; we understand its necessity. Consequently, we can allow our meanings to move back and forth between the theoretical statement and the operational one without confusion. But in a public rather than technical conversation, the potential for confusion abounds.

We face the confounded problem of going from the public connotation of the word *ability* to the technical theoretical meaning and then to the operational meaning we give it. In so doing, in spite of the very central public concern that tests may not adequately reflect ability, we have for good reasons reduced the very word *ability* to mean operationally "test score." In fact, I think test scores are likely the best way to operationalize the theoretical procedures under discussion here.

The problem is the way we mix the public and the technical language—perhaps in our thinking as well as in our language. Maybe we would do better to create a more complete technical language so we would recognize more easily when we are shifting languages. Then, too, we might find it easier to examine when a technical solution does and does not address a social concern. Perhaps our use of the same words in both languages pushes us toward assuming the connection of the technical and the social concerns where, in fact, little connection may exist.

PROMINENT CONTEXT ISSUES TODAY

The chasm between the technical and public considerations of the 1960s was immense. It seems to me smaller today, but a major chasm nonetheless. Let us look at some of the issues that frame the public and technical considerations today, 20 years or more years since the prominent public and technical discussions of possible bias in testing began.

The Public Context.   Today, not all arenas share the spotlight of concern that existed in the 1960s. Employers seem to be viewed less as villians in many quarters, and the courts seem to be struggling to soften the employer's burden of proof in defending employment selection practices. There seems to be some backlash against affirmative action notions as well. Thus, on employment fronts, one could surmise that there is a lessening of fervor and commitment—this, in spite of the fact that the ideals of civil rights and equal opportunity today are likely more an accepted norm of the society than at any time in the past.

In education, however, the emotional fervor remains high. To the civil rights movement of the 1960s, education represented perhaps the greatest hope for social change. Now 25 years after the Civil Rights Act of 1964, the change, though real, is slow. The public, politicians, the courts, and educators themselves are dissatisfied with the educational system, not just for target groups but for all children. We have found from pronouncements of national commissions, from negative comparisons with other nations, and (ironically) from declining test scores that we are a nation at risk. And now we find that improving the educational system is a huge job requiring substantial time and resources.

Tests remain the messenger of this bad news. In this context, tests show continuing group differences that the public does not really want to believe and feels unsure whether it should believe. In addition, tests have become more than the messenger; through many state testing programs, tests have become part of the effort to change the system. In this role tests are seen in some quarters as sharing the burden of failure placed on reform efforts to date. Furthermore, tests are less mysterious and more open for everyone to see and criticize. They cannot even hide behind that old mystique.

The Technical Context.   On the technical side, there has been both change and continuation of some of the issues that created the initial chasm. Testers have been "sensitized" to issues related to race and sex just as have other citizens. Group membership is a characteristic included in technical as well as editorial and judgmental procedures of test makers. Even more fundamentally, some are willing to expand the notion of validity to consider uses and consequences or to try to judge the systemic effect of tests.

There remains, however, an appropriate concern for technical standards separate from the social concerns. There remain concerns to be symmetrical in the use of group identity regardless of the asymmetry that produced the need to identify groups. These tendencies—and others like them—may be appropriate ones for a technical community. However, the language issue that also remains with us is a huge problem we could do without. We continue to struggle with common words carrying far more baggage in popular usage than the technical meaning gives them.

SUMMARY

This conference is addressed to issues that have a complex history and around which there remain many public pitfalls. An understanding of this history and public context is important background information for the considerations being addressed. DIF is now a technical tool in ETS to help us assure ourselves that our tests are as fair as we can make them. It is a public issue as well with some of the public viewing it as solution to far greater issues than it solves and others of the public convinced it is a sham.

However, interestingly, the procedures are diverging in some ways from this history and public role. We are beginning to use the procedures to understand "the subtle differences in the content of a stimulus to which individuals react differently" (Cole, 1981, p. 1076). To paraphrase from the same article: We have begun to learn about small, not large effects that are subtle not obvious—effects that will likely have implications, when we finally understand them, for the education and testing of many individuals whether they are members of minority groups or not. We will likely come to think of this research less in terms of ethnically identified or gender groups and more in terms of individual differences in test taking and learning. This conference makes that prophecy of 1981 look good indeed.

II STATISTICAL
METHODOLOGY

It is to the benefit of a test maker to look for DIF and not find any. In statistical terminology, "not finding DIF" means "accepting the null hypothesis." That is, we assume that there is no DIF, and after considering the evidence decide that we cannot reject that hypothesis. It is very easy to accept the hypothesis that there is no DIF. To accomplish this one merely has to run poor studies with smallish sample sizes and use weak statistical methods. Thus, to be credible, a claim to have found "no DIF" must mean a careful study with as large a sample size as could be found that uses the most powerful statistical procedures available to analyze these data.

The history of DIF procedures, described in Part I, illustrates how statistical methods were developed initially to match heuristic ideas about what ought to be measured. This was, properly, the most important initial concern, with niceties such as statistical power being left for later. In chapters 3, 4, and 5, the authors describe the most powerful methods for detecting and measuring DIF now available. In chapter 3, Dorans and Holland provide a thorough description of two quite similar procedures (standardization and Mantel–Haenszel). These methods are nonparametric in that they do not attempt to model response likelihoods. Both methods are statistically efficient and inexpensive to compute. They also include a discussion of the use of standardization to identify distractors that differentially attract examinee choices.

In chapter 4, Thissen, Steinberg, and Wainer expand on their earlier work (1988) that utilized the likelihood ratio of two models to detect DIF. Statistical theory predicts that this methodology is asymptotically optimal when the IRT model that is assumed to underlie examinee responses is appropriate. Four model-based methods, all relying on likelihood ratio statistics, are described and compared. The authors also demonstrate how the methodology generalizes to study patterns of differential response among the item's distractors. This generalization is achieved through the use of a polytomous IRT model and results in what the authors call a methodology for studying *Differential Alternative Functioning* (DAF). This powerful new tool is shown to be helpful in diagnosing the misfunctioning of an item after DIF has been detected.

Darrell Bock provides, in chapter 5, an illuminating discussion of the two previous chapters. He points out that when the stratifying variable (usually the rest of the test) is very reliable (long) the two methods will yield virtually identical results. But when the test is short, the extra stability achieved through the use of a model-based procedure is important. Thus he suggests that when the raw score provides a good enough stratification among examinees, an observed score procedure is an inexpensive way to estimate DIF. Thissen, Steinberg, and Wainer's results indicate that model-based methods using likelihood ratio tests will work effectively for tests as short as four items. Bock points out that another advantage of IRT methods is that they potentially can detect differences in the slopes of ICCs. This property is useful in a variety of special circumstances. He also suggests another observed-score variant for DIF detection that he believes is promising because it is noniterative and can detect "cross-over."

In chapter 6, Wainer points out how a model-based generalization of the standardization procedure can measure how much DIF there is after one of the other procedures has detected that some is there. Donoghue, Holland, and Thayer expand the work on the Mantel–Haenszel and the standardization procedures for detecting DIF in chapter 7, providing analytic and empirical evidence about the effects of nuisance factors on these procedures in practical circumstances. The design of their Monte Carlo study should be helpful to future comparative studies of DIF methods. J. O. Ramsay, in chapter 8, provides a commentary of their findings and introduces a generalization that appears to broaden the prospective usefulness of the Mantel–Haenszel procedure.

The rest of Part II consists of three articles not directly given at the conference, but that expand on the topics in chapters 3 and 8 in important ways. In chapter 9, Longford, Holland, and Thayer show how to use random effect or variance components models to aggregate DIF results for groups of items to achieve various objectives. In particular, they show how to combine DIF estimates from several administrations to obtain variance components for administration differences in DIF within an item, and show in their examples that this effect is quite small. In addition, they show how to use these models to improve DIF estimation in single administrations, and how to combine evidence across items in randomized DIF studies. In chapter 10, Shealy and Stout use multidimensional IRT models to develop a theory of the causes of DIF and show how DIF in individual items combines to affect the whole test. Allen and Holland, in chapter 11, address the problem of nonresponse in DIF analyses when "no response" to group identification questions is substantial, as it is for many testing programs. They show how the parameters estimated by the Mantel–Haenszel and the standardization procedures are affected by different assumptions about nonresponse to group identification.

3 DIF Detection and Description: Mantel–Haenszel and Standardization

Neil J. Dorans
Paul W. Holland
Educational Testing Service

Differential item functioning (DIF) refers to a psychometric difference in how an item functions for two groups. DIF refers to a difference in item performance between two comparable groups of examinees, that is, groups that are matched with respect to the construct being measured by the test. The comparison of matched or comparable groups is critical because it is important to distinguish between differences in item functioning from differences between groups.

In the first chapter of the book *Handbook of Methods for Detecting Test Bias*, Shepard (1982) defined what then was called *item bias* and now is referred to as DIF as psychometric features of the item that can misrepresent the competence of one group. She provided an understanding of the meaning of DIF by presenting some conceptual definitions of the term, including: "An item is unbiased if, for all individuals having the same score on a homogeneous subtest containing the item, the proportion of individuals getting the item correct is the same for each population group being considered" (Scheuneman, 1975, p. 2). This definition by Scheuneman may be the earliest contingency table definition of DIF. It is the definition underlying the observed-score DIF approaches described in this chapter.

Lord (1980) provided the item response theory (IRT) definition of DIF:

> If each test item in a test had exactly the same item response function in every group, then people of the same ability or skill would have exactly the same chance of getting the item right, regardless of their group membership. Such a test would be completely unbiased. If on the other hand, an item has a different item response function for one group than for another, it is clear that the item is biased. (p. 212)

This IRT definition underlies the DIF procedures described in the companion chapter by Thissen, Steinberg, and Wainer (chapter 4 of this volume).

Thissen (1987), in his discussion of a series of DIF papers dealing with DIF on the Scholastic Aptitude Test (SAT) that are contained in Schmitt and Dorans (1987b), added to these definitions by referring to DIF as:

> . . . an expression which describes a serious threat to the validity of tests used to measure the aptitude of members of different populations or groups. Some test items may simply perform differently for examinees drawn from one group or another or they may measure "different things" for members of one group as opposed to members of another. Tests comparing such items may have reduced validity for between-group comparison, because their scores may be indicative of a variety of attributes other than those the test is intended to measure. (p. 1)

Statistical methods used to identify DIF are defined by Shepard (1982) as "internal methods designed to ensure that the meaning, which individual items attribute to the total test, is the same for all subgroups" (p. 23). A variety of methods have been used since the 1950s. Two methods presently employed at the Educational Testing Service for DIF assessment are the standardization approach (Dorans & Kulick, 1986) and the Mantel–Haenszel approach (Holland & Thayer, 1988). Both procedures compare matched or comparable groups. This chapter describes these two procedures in some detail.

The structure of the chapter is as follows. DIF is contrasted with impact via Simpson's paradox, which demonstrates the importance of matching in DIF studies. Then a definition of DIF is offered. The Mantel–Haenszel (MH) procedure is described as a statistically powerful method for detecting DIF, and the standardization approach is described as a flexible procedure for describing DIF. A common framework from which to view these two related procedures then is presented. Then, the relationship between the MH procedure and the Rasch model under the condition that the Rasch model is appropriate for the data is discussed. Next, the utility of the standardization approach for assessing differential distractor functioning is described. Some issues in applied DIF analyses are discussed. Finally, future directions in DIF analyses are considered.

DIF NOT IMPACT

It is important to make a distinction between DIF and impact. Impact refers to a difference in performance between two intact groups. Impact is everywhere in test and item data because individuals differ with respect to the developed abilities measured by items and tests, and intact groups, such as those defined by ethnicity and gender, differ with respect to the distributions of developed ability among their members. For example, on a typical SAT-Mathematics item it is usually the case that Asian-Americans, as a group, score higher than Whites, men score higher than women, and juniors and seniors score higher than junior high school students. This difference in performance is called impact. Frequently, impact on any given item is consistent with impact on other items of the same type. In fact, impact at the item level frequently is explained by impact across all items of similar type or impact at the total score level.

In contrast to impact, which often can be explained by stable consistent differences in examinee ability distributions across groups, DIF refers to differences in item functioning *after* groups have been matched with respect to the ability or attribute that the item purportedly measures. Unlike impact, where differences in item performance reflect differences in overall ability distributions, DIF is an *unexpected* difference among groups of examinees who are supposed to be comparable with respect to the attribute measured by the item and test on which it appears.

Simpson's Paradox

Simpson's paradox (Simpson, 1951) illustrates why we should compare the comparable, as is done in DIF analyses. Table 3.1 summarizes the performance of two hypothetical groups, A and B, on an imaginary item. This table contains four rows and six columns of numbers The first three columns pertain to Group A, whereas the last three pertain to Group B. The first three rows pertain to three different ability levels ranging from the lowest to the highest, whereas the fourth row sums across ability levels. (In the case of the third and sixth columns, the sum in the fourth row is a weighted sum.) The symbols N_m, N_{cm}, and N_{cm}/N_m refer to the number of people at the ability level m, the number of people at ability level m who answered the item correctly, and the proportion at ability level m who answered the item correctly, respectively.

Of the 2,400 examinees in Group A, 1,440 or 60% answered the item correctly. In contrast, only 50%, 1,200 of 2,400, of Group B answered the item correctly. The impact on this item is $.6 - .5 = .1$ in favor of Group A.

Upon closer examination, however, the ratio N_{cm}/N_m at each of the three

TABLE 3.1
Summary of the Performance of Two Hypothetical Groups
on an Imaginary Item

Group A			Group B		
N_m	N_{cm}	N_{cm}/N_m	N_m	N_{cm}	N_{cm}/N_m
400	40	.10	1000	200	.20
1000	500	.50	1000	600	.60
1000	900	.90	400	400	1.00
2400	1440	.60	2400	1200	.50

ability levels for Group A is actually .1 lower than the corresponding ratio for Group B. These conditional proportions are .1, .5, and .9 for Group A, and .2, .6, and 1.0 for Group B. Hence, when we compare the comparable at each ability level m, we find that this item actually favors Group B over Group A, not vice versa as suggested by impact. This contradiction between impact and DIF is due to unequal distributions of ability in Groups A and B, as seen in the N_m columns. This imaginary item actually disadvantages Group A, but because Group A is more able than Group B, the overall impact suggests that the item favors Group A.

Simpson's paradox (1951) has a rich history in the statistical literature (e.g., Blyth, 1972; Wagner, 1982; Yule, 1903). Recently, Wainer (1986) illustrated how this paradox affects the interpretation of changes in SAT mean scores over time. Simpson's paradox illustrates the importance of comparing the comparable. Both the standardization approach (Dorans & Kulick, 1983a, 1986), which has been used on the SAT since 1982, and the Mantel–Haenszel method (Holland & Thayer, 1988), which has been used with most ETS testing programs since 1987, emphasize the importance of comparing the comparable. In practice, both approaches use equal ability as measured by total test score as a measure of comparability. They share a common definition of Null DIF, namely that there is no differential item functioning between groups *after* they have been matched on total score. In theory, both procedures are flexible enough to match on more than total score (see last portion of this chapter for a discussion of this issue). In practice, matching typically is based on a single total score.

These two DIF assessment procedures are highly related and complement each other well. The Mantel–Haenszel method is a statistically powerful technique for detecting DIF. Standardization is a very flexible, easily understood descriptive procedure that is particularly suited for assessing plausible and implausible explanations of DIF.

MANTEL–HAENSZEL: TESTING THE CONSTANT ODDS RATIO HYPOTHESIS VERSION OF DIF

In their seminal paper, Mantel and Haenszel (1959) introduced a new procedure for the study of matched groups. Holland (1985) and later Holland and Thayer (1988) adapted the procedure for use in assessing differential item functioning. This adaptation is used at the Educational Testing Service (ETS) as the primary DIF detection device. The basic data used by the MH method are in the form of M 2×2 contingency tables or one large three-dimensional 2-by-2-by-M table.

TABLE 3.2
The 2(Groups-b-2(Item Scores)-by-M(Score Levels)
Contingency Table Viewed in 2-b-2 Slices

| | Item Score | | |
Group	Right	Wrong	Total
Focal Group (f)	R_{fm}	W_{fm}	N_{fm}
Reference Group (r)	R_{rm}	W_{rm}	N_{rm}
Total Group (t)	R_{tm}	W_{tm}	N_{tm}

The 2-by-2-by-M Contingency Table

Under rights scoring for the items in which responses are coded as either correct or incorrect (including omissions), counts of rights and wrongs on each item can be arranged into a 2-by-2-by-M contingency table for each item being studied. There are two levels for group: the *focal* group that is the focus of analysis and the *reference* group that serves as a basis for comparison for the focal group. At ETS, the current practice is to do analyses in which Whites are the reference group, and Blacks, Hispanics, Asian-Americans, and Native Americans serve as the focal groups, and analyses in which women are the focal group and men are the reference group. There are two levels for item response, right or wrong, and there are M score levels on the matching variable, for example, total score. Finally, the item being analyzed is referred to as the *studied item*. The 2(groups)-by-2(item scores)-by-M(score levels) contingency table for each item can be viewed in 2-by-2 slices (there are M slices per item) as shown in Table 3.2.

The null DIF hypothesis[1] for the Mantel–Haenszel method can be expressed as

$$H_0: [R_{rm}/W_{rm}]/[R_{fm}/W_{fm}] = 1 \quad m = 1, \ldots, M, \tag{1}$$

or alternatively,

$$H_0: [R_{rm}/W_{rm}] = [R_{fm}/W_{fm}] \quad m = 1, \ldots, M. \tag{2}$$

In other words, the odds of getting the item correct at a given level of the matching variable is the same in both the focal group and the reference group, across all M levels of the matching variable.

---

[1]Note that in stating hypotheses we have not distinguished between population and sample quantities. All of our hypotheses should read as relations among the expectations of the indicated statistics.

The Constant Odds Ratio Hypothesis

In their original work, Mantel and Haenszel (1959) developed a chi-square test of the null DIF hypothesis against a particular alternative hypothesis known as the constant odds ratio hypothesis,

$$H_a: [R_{rm}/W_{rm}] = \alpha \, [R_{fm}/W_{fm}] \quad m = 1, \ldots, M \text{ and } \alpha \neq 1. \tag{3}$$

Note that when $\alpha = 1$, the alternative hypothesis reduces to the null DIF hypothesis. The parameter α is called the *common odds ratio* in the M 2-by-2 tables because under H_a, the value of α is the odds ratio that is the same for all m,

$$\alpha_m = [R_{rm}/W_{rm}]/[R_{fm}/W_{fm}] = [R_{rm}W_{fm}]/[R_{fm}W_{rm}]. \tag{4}$$

Chi-Square Test Statistic

There is a chi-square test associated with the MH approach, namely a test of the null hypothesis, H_0: $\alpha_m = 1$,

$$MH-\chi^2 = \left[\left| \sum_m R_{rm} - \sum_m E(R_{rm}) \right| - .5 \right]^2 \Big/ \sum_m Var(R_{rm}), \tag{5}$$

where,

$$
\begin{aligned}
E(R_{rm}) &= E(R_{rm} \mid \alpha = 1) = N_{rm}R_{tm}/N_{tm}, \\
Var(R_{rm}) &= Var(R_{rm} \mid \alpha = 1) \\
&= [N_{rm}R_{tm}N_{fm}W_{tm}]/[N_{tm}^2(N_{tm} - 1)],
\end{aligned} \tag{6}
$$

and where the $-.5$ in the expression for $MH-\chi^2$ serves as a continuity correction to improve the accuracy of the chi-square percentage points as approximations to the observed significance levels. The quantity $MH-\chi^2$ is distributed approximately as a chi-square with one degree of freedom.

Holland and Thayer (1988) reported ". . . that a test based on $MH-\chi^2$ is the uniformly most powerful unbiased test of H_o versus H_a. Hence no other test can have higher power somewhere in H_a than the one based on $MH-\chi^2$ unless the other test violates the size constraint on the null hypothesis or has lower power than the test's size somewhere else on H_a" (p. 134). In other words, the MH approach is the statistical test possessing the most statistical power for detecting departures from the null DIF hypothesis that are consistent with the constant odds ratio hypothesis.

Estimate of Constant Odds Ratio

Mantel and Haenszel (1959) also provided an estimate of the constant odds ratio,

$$\alpha_{MH} = [\Sigma_m R_{rm}W_{fm}/N_{tm}]/[\Sigma_m R_{fm}W_{rm}/N_{tm}]. \tag{7}$$

This estimate is an estimate of DIF effect size in a metric that ranges from 0 to ∞ with a value of 1 indicating null DIF. This odds ratio metric is not particularly meaningful to test developers who are used to working with numbers in an item difficulty scale. In general, odds are converted to log odds because the latter are symmetric around zero and easier to interpret.

MH DIF in Item Difficulty Metrics

At ETS, test developers are used to working with item difficulty estimates in the *delta metric,* which has a mean of 13 and a standard deviation of 4. To obtain a delta, the proportion correct (p) is converted to a z score via a p-to-z transformation using the inverse of the normal cumulative function, followed by a linear transformation to a metric with a mean of 13 and a standard deviation of 4 via:

$$\Delta = 13 - 4\{\Phi^{-1}(p)\} \tag{8}$$

such that large values of Δ correspond to difficult items, whereas easy items have small values of delta. Holland and Thayer (1985) converted α_{MH} into a difference in deltas via:

$$MH\ D\text{-}DIF = -2.35\ \ln[\alpha_{MH}]. \tag{9}$$

Note that positive values of *MH D-DIF* favor the focal group, whereas negative values favor the reference group.

Another metric that is used more universally to describe item difficulty is the p-metric, percent correct or proportion correct metric. The α_{MH} can also be expressed in this metric,

$$MH\ P\text{-}DIF = P_f - P_r\dagger, \tag{10}$$

where,

$$P_r\dagger = [\alpha_{MH}P_f]/[(1 - P_f) + \alpha_{MH}P_f], \tag{11}$$

which can be thought of as a predicted proportion correct in the reference group based on the MH odds ratio, and P_f is the proportion correct observed in the focal group.

Standard Error of the Mantel–Haenszel DIF Indices

A useful, approximate standard error for the log of the Mantel–Haenszel odds ratio estimator was developed by Robins, Breslow, and Greenland (1986) and, in the equivalent form used here, by Phillips and Holland (1987). This expression may be multiplied by 2.35 to yield an estimated standard error for *MH D-DIF,*

$$SE(MH\ D\text{-}DIF) = \{2.35/C\}*\left\{ \sum_m [(R_{rm}W_{fm} + \alpha_{MH}W_{rm}R_{fm})\right.$$

$$\left. *[R_{rm} + W_{fm} + \alpha_{MH}(W_{rm} + R_{fm})]/(2N_{tm}^2)] \right\}^{.5}, \qquad (12)$$

where,

$$C = \Sigma_m R_{rm}W_{fm}/N_{tm}. \qquad (13)$$

The standard error for $MH\ P\text{-}DIF$, derived in Holland (1989), is

$$SE\ (MH\ P\text{-}DIF) = \{(1 - K)^2 P_f(1 - P_f)/N_f + 2K(1 - K)P_f(1 - P_f)/N_f$$
$$+ K^2[P_f(1 - P_f)\}]^2 [SE(MH\ D\text{-}DIF)/(2.35)]^2\}^{.5}, \qquad (14)$$

where,

$$K = \alpha_{MH}/(1 - P_f + \alpha_{MH}P_f)^2, \qquad (15)$$

and N_f is the total number of examinees in the focal group.

ETS DIF Classification Rules

To use the $MH\ D\text{-}DIF$ measure to identify test items that exhibit varying degrees of DIF a classification scheme was developed at ETS for use in test development that puts items into one of three categories: negligible DIF (A), intermediate DIF (B), and large DIF (C). Items are classified as A for a particular combination of reference and focal groups if either $MH\ D\text{-}DIF$ is not statistically different from zero or if the magnitude of the $MH\ D\text{-}DIF$ values is less than one delta unit in absolute value. Items are classified as C if $MH\ D\text{-}DIF$ both exceeds 1.5 in absolute value and is statistically significantly larger than 1.0 in absolute value. All other items are classified as category B. In both categories A and C statistical significance is at the 5% level for a single item. Presently, an item can have up to five different $MH\ D\text{-}DIF$ values associated with it, one for each of five possible combinations of focal and reference groups. An item currently is assigned the lowest letter grade from all the DIF analyses performed on it.

The MH Procedure and the Rasch Model

Holland and Thayer (1988) pointed out a close connection between chi-square types of DIF procedures, such as the MH procedure, and "theoretically pre-ferred" methods based on IRT models, such as those described by Thissen, Steinberg, and Wainer (this volume, chapter 4). They draw this close connection in fairly abstract terms using a very general class of IRT models. The interested reader should consult the original source for the mathematical details. To make matters concrete Holland and Thayer showed how the Rasch model and the MH procedure are related when the assumptions underlying the Rasch model fit the data. In particular, they demonstrated that under the Rasch model the constant odds ratio hypothesis holds exactly in the population if: (a) All items in the matching criterion, with the possible exception of the studied item, are free of DIF; (b) the criterion for matching is a number-right score that includes the studied item; and (c) the data are random samples from the reference and focal populations. It is only under these special conditions, some of which are strong, particularly the assumption that the Rasch model fits the data, that the MH procedure and the Rasch model have a special relationship. It is important to realize that the Holland and Thayer analysis does not imply that the Rasch model and MH procedure always are related intimately. Instead, Holland and Thayer used the MH procedure and the Rasch model to relate the chi-square procedures and the IRT procedures under special conditions. In the process, they determined the need to include the studied item in the matching criterion, which has implications for DIF applications and future research, both of which are discussed later.

STANDARDIZATION: A FLEXIBLE METHOD
FOR DESCRIBING DIF

In the early 1980s, Dorans (1982) reviewed a number of item bias studies that had been conducted on SAT data in the late 1970s. These studies had used the Angoff and Ford (1973) delta-plot methodology and, in some cases, a log-linear method. The delta-plot method can be justified from a one-parameter normal ogive IRT model, and as such, is of as limited applicability to multiple-choice item data as is the Rasch model. DIF detection with either the Rasch model or the delta-plot model is confounded with lack of model fit, a confounding that occurs frequently because items do not have a common discrimination parameter. The log-linear approach employed in those early SAT studies was flawed because the conditioning variable was too coarsely grouped, a practice we refer to as *fat matching*. Taken to its extreme, fat matching leads to a single level for the matching variable, which converts DIF studies into impact studies. Dorans concluded that a new method was needed.

Large data sets often are associated with SAT test forms. Given large SAT data sets and a desire to avoid contamination caused by model misfit, Dorans and Kulick (1983a) decided to not employ IRT models. Instead, they opted for an IRT-like approach that compared empirical item response curves in which a total score was used as an estimate of ability. Summarizing these numerous nonparametric item test regressions via some numerical index seemed to be essential if this procedure was to become practical. They were steered in the direction of standardization via the Alderman and Holland (1981) report on DIF assessment or the Test of English as a Foreign Language (TOEFL).

According to the standardization method, an item is exhibiting DIF when the expected performance on an item differs for examinees of equal ability from different groups. Expected performance on an item can be operationalized by nonparametric item test regressions. Differences in empirical item test regressions are indicative of DIF.

One of the main principles underlying the standardization approach to DIF assessment is to use all available appropriate data to estimate the conditional item performance of each group at each level of the matching variable. The matching done by standardization and Mantel–Haenszel does not require the use of stratified sampling procedures that yield equal numbers of examinees at a given score level across groups. In fact, throwing away data in this fashion just leads to poorer estimates of effect sizes that have larger standard errors associated with them than effect sizes based on all the data.

The first step in the standardization analysis is to use all available data to estimate nonparametric item test regressions in the reference group and in the focal group. Let $E_f(I \mid M)$ define the empirical item test regression for the focal group f, and let $E_r(I \mid M)$ define the empirical item test regression for the reference group r, where I is the item score variable and M is the matching variable. The definition of DIF employed by the standardization approach implies that $E_f(I \mid M) = E_r(I \mid M)$.

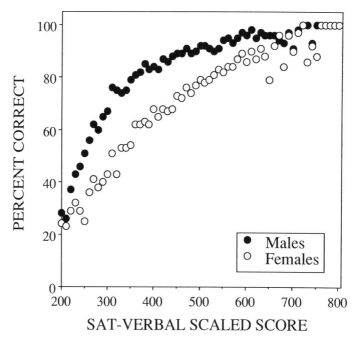

FIG. 3.1.   Empirical item response functions for female students and male students on an SAT analogy item that exhibits substantial negative DIF for women.

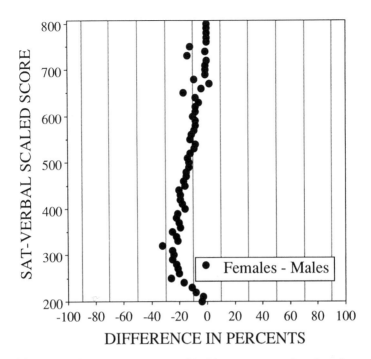

FIG. 3.2. Difference between empirical item response functions for female students and male students on an SAT analogy item that exhibits substantial DIF.

The most detailed definition of DIF is at the individual score level, m,

$$D_m = E_{fm} - E_{rm} \qquad (16)$$

where, E_{fm} and E_{rm} are realizations of the item test regressions at score level m. The D_m are the fundamental measures of DIF according to the standardization method because these quantities are differences in item performance between focal group and reference group members who are matched with respect to the attribute measured by the test. Any differences that exist after matching cannot be explained or accounted for by ability differences. These are unexpected differences as opposed to those expected given ability differences. Plots of these differences, as well as plots of $E_f(I \mid M)$ and $E_r(I \mid M)$, provide visual descriptions of DIF in fine detail. Figures 3.1 and 3.2 are sample plots of nonparametric item test regressions and differences for an actual SAT item that exhibits considerable DIF. In contrast, Figures 3.3 and 3.4 are item test regressions for an actual SAT item that exhibits minimal DIF.

Visual analysis is an important component of the standardization approach. Figure 3.1 comes from the first study to use standardization to do DIF analyses on the SAT (Dorans & Kulick, 1983a). In that study, there were 21,209 female

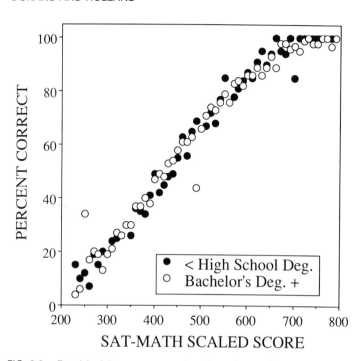

FIG. 3.3. Empirical item response functions for students whose fathers had not completed high school (< High School Deg.) and students whose fathers had at least a bachelor's degree (Bachelor's Deg. +) on an SAT mathematics item that exhibits negligible DIF.

examinees in the focal group and 21,285 male examinees in the reference group. In Fig. 3.1, E_{fm} and E_{rm} are presented in a percent correct metric, ranging from 0 to 100, whereas the matching variable is scored on the familiar 200 to 800 College Board scale. Each point in the plot represents the conditional item mean score (under rights scoring) at each scaled score level. This plot and the corresponding difference plot in Fig. 3.2 provide detailed visual descriptions of difference and similarities of focal and reference group performance on the item at each of the 61 scale score levels ranging from 200 to 800 in 10-point increments.

The content for this item, which appeared on the December 1977 form of the SAT, reveals why there is such large DIF on this item. It is a verbal analogy item: *DECOY : DUCK* :: (A) *net : butterfly* (B) *web : spider* (C) *lure : fish* (D) *lasso : rope* (E) *detour : shortcut*. This edition of the SAT was assembled prior to the institution of the ETS Test Sensitivity Guidelines (see Ramsey, this volume, chapter 19), which screen items for content or language that is offensive or could be detrimental to the performance of ethnic or gender subgroups. Had such guidelines been in place, this item may never have appeared in a final edition of the SAT because a casual examination of the item reveals that knowledge of

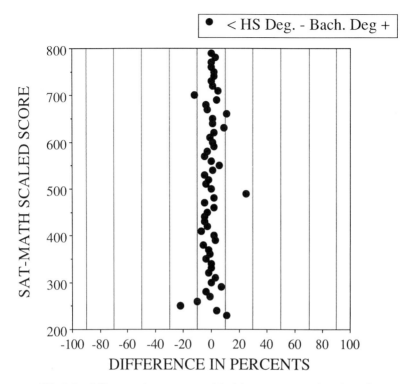

FIG. 3.4. Difference between empirical item response functions for students whose fathers had not completed high school (< High School Deg.) and students whose fathers had at least a bachelor's degree (Bachelor's Deg. +) on an SAT mathematics item that exhibits negligible DIF.

hunting and fishing jargon probably influence performance on this item. Sex differences with respect to familiarity with this jargon probably accounts for why men outperform matched women at difference of 15% to 20% at each SAT-Verbal scaled score level between 250 and 500. For example at a scaled score level of 300, over 60% of the men answer the item correctly, whereas only 40% of the women choose the correct response option. Clearly, this is a very easy item for men that is somewhat harder for women, an item that exhibits substantial DIF, and a high DIF item that is biased against women.

In contrast, the plots in Figs. 3.3 and 3.4 depict an item that exhibits negligible DIF. This item came from the second study that used standardization on the SAT (Kulick & Dorans, 1983a), in which father's level of education was used to compare groups from different socioeducational groups. Examinees whose fathers had not completed high school (the focal group, $N = 7,053$) performed on this SAT-Mathematics item in much the same way as students whose fathers had attained at least a bachelor's degree (the reference group, $N = 24,910$). Whereas the decoy : duck item had atypical DIF for its test edition, the DIF for this SAT-Mathematics item was more typical of items on that March 1980 form of the SAT.

Standardization's Item Discrepancy Indices

The sheer volume of the SAT item pool precludes sole reliance on item test regression plots and difference plots for DIF assessment. There is a clear need for a numerical index that targets items like that depicted in Figs. 3.1 and 3.2 for closer scrutiny, while allowing items such as that depicted in Figs. 3.3 and 3.4 to pass swiftly through the screening process. Standardization has two such flags: the standardized p-difference (*STD P-DIF*) and the root-mean-weighted squared difference (*RMWSD*). Both indices use a weighting function supplied by the standardization group to average differences (or squared differences) across levels of the matching variable. The function of the standardization group, which may be a real group or a hypothetical group, is to supply a set of weights, one for each score level, for use in weighting each individual D_m (or $D_m{}^2$) before accumulating these weighted differences (or squared differences) across score levels to arrive at a summary item discrepancy index.

The Standardized P-Difference.   The standardized p-difference is defined as:

$$STD \ P\text{-}DIF = \sum_m w_m(E_{fm} - E_{rm}) \Big/ \sum_m w_m = \sum_m w_m D_m \Big/ \sum_m w_m, \qquad (17)$$

where $(w_m/\Sigma w_m)$ is the weighting factor at score level m supplied by the standardization group to weight differences in item performance between the focal group (E_{fm}) and the reference group (E_{rm}). The standardized p-difference is so named because the original applications of the standardization methodology defined expected item score in terms of proportion correct at each score level,

$$STD \ P\text{-}DIF = \sum_m w_m(P_{fm} - P_{rm}) \Big/ \sum_m w_m = \sum_m w_m D_m \Big/ \sum_m w_m, \qquad (18)$$

where P_{fm} and P_{rm} are the proportions correct, number of examinees who answer correctly over total number of examinees, in the focal and reference groups at score level m,

$$P_{fm} = R_{fm}/N_{fm}; \ P_{rm} = R_{rm}/N_{rm}. \qquad (19)$$

In contrast to impact, in which each group has its relative frequency serve as a weight at each score level,

$$IMPACT = P_f - P_r$$

$$= \sum_m N_{fm}P_{fm} \bigg/ \sum_m N_{fm} - \sum_m N_{rm}P_{rm} \bigg/ \sum_m N_{rm}, \qquad (20)$$

STD P-DIF uses a standard or common weight on both P_{fm} and P_{rm}, namely, $(w_m/\Sigma w_m)$. The use of the same weight on both P_{fm} and P_{rm}, or more generally E_{fm} and E_{rm}, is the essence of the standardization approach. In Equation 20, P_r is proportion correct observed in the reference group, whereas P_f is the proportion correct observed in the focal group.

The particular set of weights employed for standardization depends on the purposes of the investigation. Some plausible options are the following:

1. $w_m = N_{tm}$, the number of examinees as m in the total group;
2. $w_m = N_{rm}$, the number of examinees at m in the reference group;
3. $w_m = N_{fm}$, the number of examinees at m in the focal group;
4. $w_m =$ the relative frequency at m in some reference group.

In practice, $w_m = N_{fm}$ has been used because it gives the greatest weight to differences in P_{fm} and P_{rm} at those score levels most frequently attained by the focal group under study. Use of N_{fm} means that *STD P-DIF* equals the difference between the observed performance of the focal group on the item and the predicted performance of selected reference group members who are matched in ability to the focal group members. This can be derived very simply,

$$STD\ P\text{-}DIF = \sum_m N_{fm}(P_{fm} - P_{rm}) \bigg/ \sum_m N_{fm}$$

$$= \sum_m N_{fm}P_{fm} \bigg/ \sum_m N_{fm} - \sum_m N_{fm}P_{rm} \bigg/ \sum_m N_{fm}$$

$$STD\ P\text{-}DIF = P_f - P_f^*, \qquad (21)$$

where P_f^* can be thought of as the performance of the focal group predicted from the reference-group item test regression curve, P_{rm}, or as suggested previously, the predicted performance of selected reference group members who are matched in ability to the focal group.

STD P-DIF is an index that can range from -1 to $+1$ (or -100% to 100%). Positive values of *STD P-DIF* indicate that the item favors the focal group, whereas negative *STD P-DIF* values indicate that the item disadvantages the focal group. *STD P-DIF* values between $-.05$ and $+.05$ are considered negligible. *STD P-DIF* values between $-.10$ and $-.05$ and between $.05$ and $.10$ are inspected to ensure that no possible effect is overlooked. Items with *STD P-DIF* values outside the $\{-.10, +.10\}$ range are more unusual and should be examined very carefully.

A delta metric version of the *STD P-DIF* index is:

$$STD\ D\text{-}DIF\ =\ -2.35\ln\{[P_f^*/(1 - P_f^*)]/[P_f/(1 - P_f)]\}. \tag{22}$$

STD D-DIF tends to have a smaller variance than *MH D-DIF* across items, and correlates higher with *MH D-DIF* than does *STD P-DIF* across items.

Standard Errors for Standardization's DIF Indices

The standard errors for the standardization method DIF indices also were developed by Holland. The standard error for the focal group weighting version of *STD P-DIF* is

$$SE(STD\ P\text{-}DIF)\ =\ \{P_f(1 - P_f)/N_f + \text{VAR}(P_f^*)\}^{.5}, \tag{23}$$

where,

$$VAR(P_f^*)\ =\ \sum_m N_{fm}^2 P_{rm}(1 - P_{rm})/(N_{rm}N_f^2) \tag{24}$$

The standard error for the focal group weighting version of *STD D-DIF* is

$$SE(STD\ D\text{-}DIF)\ =\ (2.35)\{[(P_f(1-P_f)N_r)^{-1} \\ +\ VAR(P_f^*)/P_f^*(1 - P_f^*)\}^{.5}, \tag{25}$$

where N_r is the number of examinees in the reference group.

Differential Distractor Functioning, Speededness, and Omission

DIF assessment does not stop with the flagging of an item for statistical DIF. In fact, the flagging step can be viewed as just the beginning. The next step is to try to understand the reason or reasons for the DIF. Green, Crone, and Folk (1989) developed a log-linear approach for assessing what they called *differential distractor functioning* (DDF). The standardization approach to distractor analysis also can be quite helpful. Some of the items identified by Green et al. are analyzed from the standardization framework described later; some of these items also are analyzed in chapter 4 for *differential alternative functioning* (DAF).

Differential Distractor Functioning.   The generalization of the standardization methodology to all response options including omission and not reached is straightforward and is known as *standardized distractor analysis* (Dorans, Schmitt, & Bleistein, 1988, 1989). It is as simple as replacing the keyed response with the option of interest in all calculations. For example, a standardized response rate analysis on option A would entail computing the proportions choosing A (as opposed to the proportions correct) in both the focal and reference groups,

$$P_{fm}(A) = A_{fm}/N_{fm}; \ P_{rm}(A) = A_{rm}/N_{rm}, \tag{26}$$

where A_{fm} and A_{rm} are the number of people in the focal and reference groups, respectively, at score level m who choose option A. The next step is to compute differences between these proportions,

$$D_m(A) = P_{fm}(A) - P_{rm}(A). \tag{27}$$

Then, these individual score level differences are summarized across score levels by applying some standardized weighting function to these differences to obtain *STD P-DIFF(A)*,

$$STD \ P\text{-}DIF(A) = \sum_m w_m D_m(A) \Big/ \sum_m w_m, \tag{28}$$

the standardized difference in response rates to option A. In a similar fashion, one can compute standardized differences in response rates for options B, C, D, and E, and for nonresponses as well.

The plots produced by the standardized distractor analyses can be quite helpful in trying to interpret DIF data. As an example, consider the plots in Figs. 3.5 through 3.10. Portrayed are selected empirical option response curves for an SAT antonym item from a disclosed 1984 test form for which the key, distractors, and DIF information are provided in Table 3.3. As can be seen in the table, standardization identifies DIF on the key, the opposite of *practical* is (D) *having little usefulness,* for Blacks (BLK *STD P-DIF* = −16%) and Puerto Ricans (PR *STD P-DIF* = −11%), but only marginally for Mexican Americans (MA *STD P-DIF* = −5%). In addition, the *STD P-DIF(option)* values indicate where the

TABLE 3.3
The Key, Distractors, and DIF Information for an SAT
Antonym Item, the Response Curves to Which Are
Displayed in Figs. 3.5 through 3.10

STD P-DIF (Option)				
MA	PR	BLK		PROBLEM
				PRACTICAL:
4	9	12	(A)	difficult to learn
0	0	0	(B)	inferior in quality
1	1	1	(C)	providing great support
−5	−11	−16	(D)	having little usefulness
0	0	0	(E)	feeling great regret

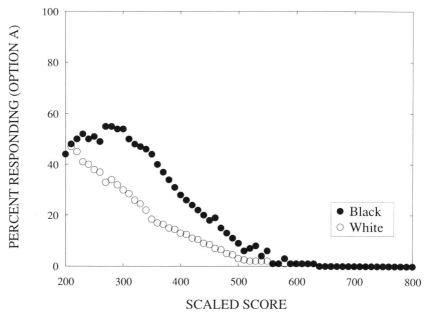

FIG. 3.5. Empirical option curves for Black students and White students for option (A) of an SAT antonym item.

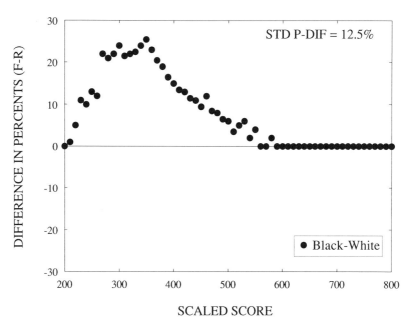

FIG. 3.6. Differences in response rates between Black students and White students on option (A) of an SAT antonym item.

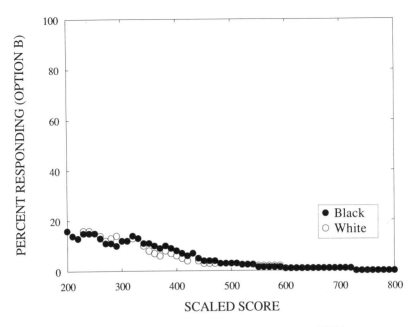

FIG. 3.7. Empirical option curves for Black students and White students for option (B) of an SAT antonym item.

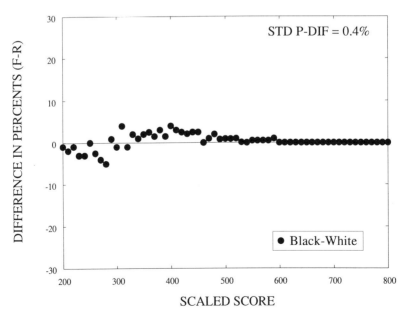

FIG. 3.8. Differences in response rates between Black students and White students on option (B) of an SAT antonym item.

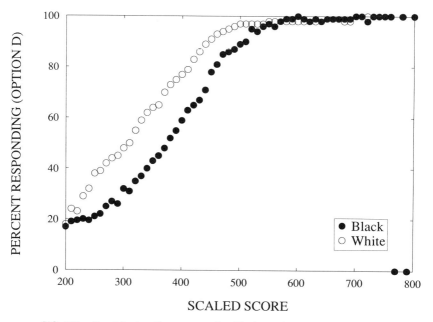

FIG. 3.9. Empirical option curves for Black students and White students for option (D), the key, of an SAT antonym item.

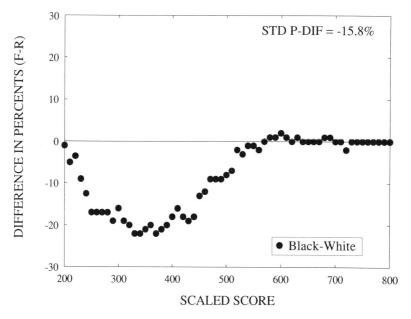

FIG. 3.10. Differences in response rates between Black students and White students on option (D), the key, of an SAT antonym item.

TABLE 3.4
Standardized Distractor Information
with Relatively Small Differential Distractor Functioning

STD P-DIF (Option)			
AA	HISP	BLK	PROBLEM
			DECADENT:
−1	0	1	(A) enormously wealthy
−4	−1	−1	(B) remarkably charming
−3	−2	−2	(C) ruthless
−1	0	0	(D) distinctive
5	5	3	(E) flourishing
.63	.76	.44	MH D-DIF

"anti-DIF" may lie, and the plots for the Black group corroborate these indications. Clearly, the Black and Puerto Rican focal groups are drawn toward (A) *difficult to learn,* which suggests that they have confused the word *practical* with the word *practice.*

For additional examples, we use the two SAT items reported by Green et al. (1989) to exhibit relatively small differential distractor functioning, and substantial differential distractor functioning. The standardized distractor information for the item with relatively small differential distractor functioning is shown in Table 3.4. This item exhibits marginal positive DIF for all three focal groups, Asian Americans (AA), Hispanics (HISP), and Blacks (BLK). Likewise, there is very little differential distractor functioning, as measured by the standardization method./

The data for the second item identified by Green et al. (1989) are more interesting, as can be seen in Table 3.5. There is a moderate level of DIF for all

TABLE 3.5
Standardized Distractor Information
with Substantial Differential Distractor Functioning

STD P-DIF (Option)			PROBLEM
AA	HISP	BLK	In some animal species, differences between opposite sexes are so _____ that it is difficult to tell that the male and female are _____.
2	10	3	(A) measurable . . . . distinct
1	−2	−3	(B) minute . . . . similar
2	2	4	(C) obvious . . . . indistinguishable
−8	−12	−9	(D) extreme . . . . related
2	1	3	(E) trivial . . . . identical
−1.09	−1.40	−1.05	MH D-DIF

three focal groups on this item; for Hispanics, the DIF level is particularly noticeable. The standardized distractor information is particularly informative for this focal group, who are drawn toward option (A) *measurable . . . . distinct* in much greater proportions than the matched group of Whites, who are drawn to option (D) *extreme . . . . related.* It is not clear to us why Hispanics are drawn toward (A), nor why all three focal groups exhibit negative DIF on this item. Although the distractor analysis tells where the "anti-DIF" is, it does not tell us why it is there. See Thissen, Steinberg, and Wainer (this volume, chapter 4) for a *daf* analysis of this item. See Schmitt, Holland and Dorans (this volume, chapter 14), for examples in which the standardized distractor analysis corroborates DIF hypothesis for Hispanics.

Differential Speededness.   Application of the standardization methodology to counts of examinees at each level of the matching variable who did not reach the item results in a standardized not-reached difference,

$$STD\ P\text{-}DIF(NR) = \sum_m w_m(P_{fm}(NR) - P_{rm}(NR)) \bigg/ \sum_m w_m. \qquad (29)$$

For items at the end of a separately timed section of a test, these standardized differences provide measurement of the *differential speededness* of a test. Differential speededness refers to the existence of differential response rates between focal group members and matched reference group members to items appearing at the end of a section. Schmitt and Bleistein (1987) found evidence of this phenomenon for Blacks, as compared to a matched group of Whites, on analogy items. Schmitt and Dorans (1990) reported that this effect also was found for Hispanics. In Dorans, Schmitt, and Bleistein (1988), differential speededness results for Black, Hispanic, and Asian-American focal groups, compared to a White reference group, are presented and their implications are discussed. In Dorans, Schmitt, and Curley (1988), the effects of item position on differential speededness and on DIF assessment were investigated. This study, which is described in more detail in chapter 14, found that excluding examinees who do not reach an item from the calculation of the DIF statistic for that item partially compensates for the effects of item location on the DIF estimate.

One implication that the existence of differential speededness has for analyzing DIF or DDF is that the matching variable, total score, may be contaminated due to differential speededness. Research presently being conducted by A. Schmitt and her colleagues may shed light on the seriousness of this potential contamination and the efficacy of potential solutions to the problem, such as matching on a shortened unspeeded portion of the total test. Simulation studies should prove useful here.

Differential Omission.   It should be obvious that standardization also can be applied to the study of differential omission. In fact, Schmitt and Dorans (1990) reported on some of these studies, including one by Rivera and Schmitt (1988) who found that although Hispanics as a group omit more than Whites on the SAT, Hispanics tend to omit less than Whites of comparable ability. This is a clear example of Simpson's paradox in terms of omitting behavior, an example that had immediate implications for the type of advice that was being offered to Hispanic test takers. On the basis of the marginal distributions, it appeared that Hispanics were omitting more than Whites. After conditioning on total test score, it became clear that the opposite was true. So, we close our discussion of the Mantel–Haenszel and standardization methods with another illustration of the need to compare the comparable.

MANTEL–HAENSZEL AND STANDARDIZATION FROM A COMMON FRAMEWORK

Up to now, the Mantel–Haenszel method and the standardization method have been described from the frameworks from which they evolved: Mantel–Haenszel as a powerful statistical test of the constant odds ratio model, and standardization as a nonparametric alternative to IRT for describing item ability regressions. The two procedures, however, share a common framework spelled out in Dorans (1989).

For rights-scored tests, the standardization definition of null DIF is in terms of zero p-differences at all levels of the matching variable,

$$R_{fm}/N_{fm} - R_{rm}/N_{rm} = 0 \qquad m = 1, \ldots, M. \tag{30}$$

The definition of null DIF for Mantel–Haenszel is

$$[R_{rm}/W_{rm}]/[R_{fm}/W_{fm}] = 1 \qquad m = 1, \ldots, M. \tag{31}$$

When null DIF holds, the standardization definition can be rearranged as:

$$R_{fm}/N_{fm} = R_{rm}/N_{rm},$$

$$R_{fm}N_{rm} = R_{rm}N_{fm},$$

$$R_{fm}(W_{rm} + R_{rm}) = R_{rm}(W_{fm} + R_{fm}),$$

$$R_{fm}W_{rm} + R_{fm}R_{rm} = R_{rm}W_{fm} + R_{fm}R_{rm},$$

$$R_{fm}W_{rm} = R_{rm}W_{fm},$$

$$R_{rm}/W_{rm} = R_{fm}/W_{fm}, \tag{32}$$

which becomes the Mantel–Haenszel definition of null DIF,

$$[R_{rm}/W_{rm}]/[R_{fm}/W_{fm}] = 1 \qquad m = 1, \ldots, M. \tag{33}$$

Mantel–Haenszel and standardization share a common definition of null DIF that is stated in different metrics. The two procedures differ with respect to how they measure departures from null DIF.

Under rights scoring for the items in which responses are coded as either correct or incorrect (including omissions), both the standardization procedure and the Mantel–Haenszel procedure use the same basic data to focus on differences in conditional item performance, which can be operationalized as differences in nonparametric item test regressions (standardization) or in terms of a constant odds ratio model (Mantel–Haenszel). As we have seen earlier, counts of rights and wrongs on each item can be arranged into a 2(groups)-by-2(item scores)-by-M(score levels) contingency table for each item being studied.

The Mantel–Haenszel and standardization procedures operate on the basic data of the 2(groups)-by-2(item scores)-by-M(score levels) contingency table in different ways. As a consequence, they measure departures from the null DIF condition in slightly different ways.

The first difference in how the two procedures measure departures from null DIF is in the metric for defining DIF. Standardization uses differences in conditional proportions correct,

$$D_m = P_{fm} - P_{rm}, \qquad (34)$$

whereas Mantel–Haenszel uses conditional odds ratios,

$$\alpha_m = [R_{rm}/W_{rm}]/[R_{fm}/W_{fm}] = [R_{rm}W_{fm}]/[R_{fm}W_{rm}]. \qquad (35)$$

The second difference in DIF measurement is in the choice of weights used to average the D_m or the α_m across levels of the matching variable. The Mantel–Haenszel approach uses weights that are nearly optimal statistically for testing a constant odds ratio model. These weights are:

$$MH_m = W_{rm}R_{fm}/N_{tm}, \qquad (36)$$

such that

$$\alpha_{MH} = \sum_m MH_m\, \alpha_m \bigg/ \sum_m MH_m. \qquad (37)$$

In contrast, the weights employed in the standardization approach are not defined statistically. Instead, they may be chosen to suit the needs of a particular investigator. This flexibility has not been utilized often. Rather, the intuitively appealing focal group frequency distribution, which was employed by Dorans and Kulick (1983a) in their original work on the SAT, typically is used to describe departures from null DIF,

$$STD\ P\text{-}DIF = \sum_m N_{fm}(P_{fm} - P_{rm}) \bigg/ \sum_m N_{fm}. \qquad (38)$$

Holland and Thayer (1988) pointed out that Cochran (1954) developed a set of weights for the p-difference metric that are statistically motivated; that is, they are appropriate for testing a constant difference model across score levels. These weights are:

$$C_m = N_{rm}N_{fm}/N_{tm}. \tag{39}$$

The third difference in DIF measurement between the two methods is the metric in which the final statistic is portrayed. Although a delta metric version of the standardization DIF statistic has been developed, the primary, almost exclusive, metric used by standardization has been the p-metric, even for formula-scored tests where an item formula-scored metric would seem superior on logical grounds. In contrast, the delta metric has been the metric of choice for the Mantel–Haenszel method. One consequence of this difference in choice of metrics is that standardization tends to downplay DIF in easy and hard items because the p-metric is bounded at both the top and bottom. In contrast, the delta metric is unbounded at the extremes, and consequently differences for easy and hard items are played up.

Despite these differences in choice of metric and weighting, standardization and Mantel–Haenszel agree very closely with respect to measurement of departures from null DIF for the vast majority of items. In fact, correlations across items between the two DIF methods in the same metric, for example, delta, are typically close to unity, and slightly higher than within-method correlations between metrics, which are in the high nineties. Cross-metric cross-method correlations across items are usually in the mid-nineties. These correlations indicate that the two methods are measuring essentially the same thing, DIF, in slightly different ways; intuitively appealing weighting of conditional differences in proportions correct versus statistically driven weighting of conditional odds ratios. The correlations also indicate that the choice of metric for describing the DIF effect may be more critical from a practical point of view than is the choice of method.

IMPLEMENTATION ISSUES

DIF implementation at ETS occurred quickly once Mantel–Haenszel was selected as the method for DIF detection and standardization was selected as the method for DIF description. With implementation came an assortment of issues that required temporary if not permanent resolution. In this section of the chapter, several of these issues are discussed. In the next section, future research associated with issues that remain either unsolved or only partially solved are discussed.

Inclusion of Studied Item

Holland and Thayer's (1988) analysis of the interrelationship between Mantel–Haenszel and the Rasch model led to some counterintuitive conclusions about whether an item should be included as part of the criterion when DIF analysis is performed on the item. Holland and Thayer concluded on theoretical grounds that an item should be included as part of the matching variable:

> If it is not included, then the MH procedure will not behave correctly when there is no dif according to an IRT model. However the Rasch analysis suggests that the inclusion of the studied item in the matching criterion does not mask the existence of dif, rather it is the inclusion of other items exhibiting dif in the criterion that could lead to the finding that no dif exists for the studied item when in fact it does. (p. 141)

The need to ensure that other items in the matching criterion are free of DIF is one argument for criterion refinement, a procedure described in the next section.

The mathematical argument for inclusion of the item in the matching variable is presented in Holland and Thayer (1988), who also showed how trivial it is to correct the M 2-by-2 tables for rights-scored tests in which number-right score is the matching criterion. The correction for formula-scored tests, however, is not so trivial.

Criterion Refinement or Purification

An argument that often is voiced against the Mantel–Haenszel procedure, the standardization procedure, and other DIF assessment techniques that use an internal criterion is the circularity involved in using total test score as a criterion for matching. Although not a perfect matching criterion because all tests contain a certain amount of statistical noise, scores on a test are often the best available matching criterion for several reasons. First, the total test score is often a much more reliable measure of what any individual item purports to measure. Second, many test scores have demonstrated validity for their intended purposes. Third, test scores typically are obtained under the same conditions for all examinees.

Despite these advantages of reliability, validity, and standardized administration, tests scores are criticized because items are part of the score, and there is a concern about the circularity of using potentially biased test scores as a criterion for DIF analyses. The most direct way of demonstrating that the total test score is acceptable as a matching variable is to demonstrate that it is valid for its intended purposes, and that it is equally valid for all focal and reference groups. DIF analysis is not a substitute for validity studies. In fact, the DIF analysis assumes that the criterion is valid and fair.

Because all tests are imperfect, they in fact may contain some items that do have DIF. Otherwise, the DIF analysis would be a meaningless exercise. In an attempt to ensure that the matching criterion is in fact DIF-free, DIF analyses at ETS occur in two steps. The first step is called the *criterion refinement* or *purification* step. Here, items on the matching variable are analyzed for DIF, and any items that exhibit sizeable DIF are removed regardless of the sign of the DIF. Then, this refined criterion is used for another DIF analysis of the same items and any other items that were not included in the criterion refinement step.

FUTURE DIRECTIONS

DIF implementation is in a nascent stage. Much basic research has been done, but much more needs to be done. Our methodologies for DIF assessment are good, but could be better. In this section, areas for further methodological research are identified. These areas fall into three major classes: the matching variable, the studied variable, and the group variable.

The Matching Variable

Dimensionality and DIF: The Need for Multivariate Matching. Items with sizable DIF are items that behave differently for one group. This difference indicates that the identified item does not appear to measure the same construct as the total test. Thus, DIF measures violations from unidimensionality. The unidimensionality of the matching variable is central to the DIF assessment process. Shepard (1982) stressed this by saying: ". . . it should be clear that the assumption of unidimensionality underlying all of the [DIF] methods is not merely a statistical prerequisite but it is central to the way in which item bias is defined" (p. 25). Later, Shepard (1987b) discussed how multidimensionality and DIF interact:

> It is also generally understood that the various [DIF] procedures function by sig-nalling multidimensionality. Therefore, the statistical indices can detect when sub-parts of the test are measuring differently for different groups, but are not automat-ically evidence of bias. To address the issue of bias requires re-examination of the original construct; is the source of multidimensionality some irrelevant difficulty (hence bias) or a valid subdimension of the intended construct. (p. 1)

From a factor analytic point of view, multidimensionality abounds in item data. Each item is a measure of what the total test measures; that is, what it has in common with other items, and what it alone measures, its unique item factor. When a test is composed of unidimensional items, as is the case for the mathe-matical portion of the Scholastic Aptitude Test, DIF occurs when subgroup differences along the unique item dimension do not reflect subgroup differences in developed mathematical ability. When a test is measuring multiple dimen-sions, as is likely to be the case with a science achievement test, DIF may reflect unique item factor differences between subgroups or the fact that subgroups vary in different ways on the different dimensions measured by the test. DIF is a violation of unidimensionality, but simple interpretation of DIF requires a uni-dimensional matching variable. See Bleistein and Schmitt (1989), Dorans and Schmitt (1989), Hu and Schmitt (1989), Mazzeo (1989), and Morgan (1989) for a series of papers on the interplay between DIF assessment and dimensionality.

A multidimensional matching variable complicates DIF assessment. Multi-variate matching, however, may provide a solution to the problem of multidi-mensionality. In multivariate matching, examinees are matched on more than one variable. For example, a general developed ability test might be composed of verbal reasoning and mathematics items. Matching on a total score might reveal that the verbal items exhibit positive DIF for women, whereas the mathematics items exhibit negative DIF. One option is to perform separate DIF analyses for the verbal items and for the mathematics items, as is now done with the SAT. Another option is to match on both the verbal score and the mathematics score prior to comparing how the items function in both groups.

Multivariate matching can have heavy data requirements because of need to cross the levels of all the variables that go into the match. In addition, data may be sparse for many combinations of the two or more variables, especially if they are highly correlated. Where data are sparse, separate analyses against more unidimensional criteria, for example, math items against a math score, and verbal items against a verbal score, may be the only practical option. Methods such as propensity score matching (Rosenbaum & Rubin, 1985) may be a useful solution when data are sparse.

Inclusion of Studied Item for Formula-Scored Tests.   As mentioned earlier, Holland and Thayer (1988) demonstrated how easy it is to adjust the MH calcula-tions for inclusion of the studied item in the matching criterion when the match-ing criterion is a number-right score. Inclusion of the studied item with a formula-scored criterion is not at all straightforward because it is not a simple matter to adjust the matching variable after the formula score has been rounded to integer format. As a consequence, some peculiar practices have evolved with DIF analyses for formula-scored tests. For example, analyses of studied items that are external to the matching variable, for instance, pretest items collected in the nonoperational section of the SAT, are done against a rights-scored criterion despite the fact that the test was administered under formula-scored conditions. Under formula-scored conditions, omitting an item is different than getting it incorrect. Under rights-scored conditions, omitting an item is treated the same as getting the item incorrect. So, in order to include the pretest item in the criterion, the matching variable is scored in a manner that is inconsistent with test admin-istration conditions.

One potential solution to this problem is to employ multivariate matching on rights, wrongs, omits, and not reached (presently examinees who do not reach the item are excluded from the calculation of the DIF statistic). Another option is to use a version of formula scoring in which a correct response is assigned a score equal to the number of response options, an omit or not reached is assigned a one, and a wrong is assigned a zero. Under this type of formula scoring, there are no fractions, and hence no need to round to integer format. Hence, the adjustment for inclusions may be as simple as it is for rights-scored tests.

Studied Variable

Formula Score DIF.   It has been a common practice to rights score items for the purpose of item analysis regardless of the conditions under which the item was administered. For rights-scored tests, this is a perfectly reasonable practice. For formula-scored tests, however, rights scoring of the item is not consistent with the conditions under which the item was administered. Had the examinee known an item was to be rights scored, it is unlikely he would have omitted that item because omitting is tantamount to getting the item wrong on a rights-scored test.

The DIF computer programs used at ETS employ rights scoring of items for both Mantel–Haenszel and standardization to obtain *MH D-DIF, MH P-DIF, STD P-DIF,* and *STD D-DIF.* In addition, the program can be asked to compute a little-used standardization statistic, which may in fact be the best standardization statistic to use for formula-scored tests, such as the SAT,

$$STD \text{ } FS\text{-}DIF = \sum_m w_m(E_{fm} - E_{rm}) \Big/ \sum_m w_m = \sum_m w_m D_m \Big/ \sum_m w_m, \quad (40)$$

where instead of scoring the item 1 if correct and 0 if incorrect or omit, which yields *STD P-DIF,* the item is scored 1 if correct, 0 if omit, and $-1/(k - 1)$ if incorrect, where k is the number of response options. Under this type of scoring, the expected item performance in the focal group at score level m is

$$E_{fm} = \{R_{fm}*(1) + O_{fm}*(0) + W_{fm}*(-1/(k - 1))\}/N_{fm}, \quad (41)$$

where R_{fm}, W_{fm}, and O_{fm} are counts of the number right, the number wrong, and the number of omits, respectively at score level m in the focal group and N_{fm} is the sum of R_{fm}, W_{fm}, and O_{fm}. Likewise, for the reference group, we have

$$E_{rm} = \{R_{rm}*(1) + O_{rm}*(0) + W_{rm}*(-1/(k - 1))\}/N_{rm},$$

Unlike *STD P-DIF, STD FS-DIF* does not range from -1 to $+1$. Instead, its theoretical range is $-k/(k - 1)$ to $+k/(k - 1)$. Under no omitting, which is likely for easy items, *STD FS-DIF* $= k/(k - 1)$ *STD P-DIF.* These two standardization indices are more likely to diverge when items are difficult and omitting becomes a dominant behavior.

Testlet DIF.   Most DIF assessment procedures are just differential item functioning procedures; the item is the unit of analyses. Some differential functioning issues are better answered at a larger level of analysis, such as performance on a set of reading passage items, or performance on a set of items of comparable content. Here, the unit of analysis shifts to the testlet (Wainer & Kiely, 1987). Special types of testlets called *item parcels* have been useful in dimensionality assessment (Dorans & Lawrence, 1987). Wainer and Lewis (1990) showed other areas where testlet-level analysis also has proved superior to item-level analysis. Dorans and Lawrence (1987) argued that parcel (testlet) analysis may be preferable to item analysis because testlets are more reliable indicators than are single items. There exists a need to develop and try out procedures for Testlet DIF, or DTF to be exact. Some promising possibilities are the flexible standardization method (Dorans & Kulick, 1986), IRT-based models developed by Thissen and his colleagues, and linear regression procedures.

The standardization approach could be adapted readily to testlet DIF by replacing expected item performance with expected testlet performance in the basic standardization equation. This would result in a comparison of empirical testlet–test regressions, using a standard weighting function to produce numerical indices that describe how far apart these regressions are for some standardization population.

As the number of items in a testlet increases, the more likely it is that the testlet–test regression will be linear, provided item difficulties are somewhat spread out among items defining the testlet. In that case, a comparison of linear regressions would be possible.

Group Variable

Melting-Pot DIF.   Hu and Dorans (1989) recently found that removal of an item that was flagged for positive gender DIF lowered women's scores slightly and raised men's scores slightly, as expected. It also had some unintended consequences. It raised the scores of Hispanics and Asian-Americans more than it raised male scores. In addition, it raised the scores of Hispanic and Asian-American women despite the fact that deletion of this item with positive gender DIF reduced the overall female mean score. In addition to pointing out that deleting items for DIF can have unintended consequences for the groups that were not the focus of analysis, this finding demonstrates a flaw with the *marginal DIF analysis* that we do now. Instead of crossing gender with ethnicity/race to study DIF, we look at the margins; that is, we do DIF analyses on gender and we do DIF analyses on ethnicity/race. This marginal DIF analysis ignores potential interactions between gender and ethnicity/race, interactions that may be important. One possible solution to this problem is to do Melting-Pot DIF analyses in which the reference group is the population of all test takers who meet the appropriate grade level and language proficiency criteria, the melting-pot group. Each gender/ethnic group is a focal group. Melting-Pot DIF would permit one to do gender comparisons within ethnic group, as well as ethnic group comparisons with gender group. Marginal DIF analyses could be obtained, of course, by collapsing across the other margin. One advantage of Melting-Pot analysis is that everybody is a focal group member once and a reference group member once. Another advantage is that more DIF is more likely to be found in the smaller subpopulations because they are a smaller part of the melting pot. On the negative side, DIF will be harder to find in the larger groups, such as White women and White men. One possible solution to the problem would be to borrow Wainer's (this volume, chapter 6) notions of *standardized impact*, similar to the standardization index, and *total standardized impact*, which can be obtained by weighting the standardized impact by the number of individuals in the focal group. This practice, however, might introduce the opposite problem: Small groups would be ignored.

Educational Advantage Construct.   As DIF implementation moves swiftly along at ETS and elsewhere, it is clear that several fundamental issues require more attention. Several of these issues have been discussed in this section of the chapter. One very important issue that remains to be discussed is that of focal group definition. To date, focal groups have been intact, easily defined groups such as Asians, Blacks, Hispanics, and women. References groups have been Whites or men. It could be argued, however, that these intact ethnic groups are merely surrogates for an educational disadvantage attribute that should be used in focal group definition. In fact, within any of these groups, there is probably a considerable degree of variability with respect to educational advantage or disadvantage. Perhaps we should be focusing our group definition efforts toward defining and measuring educational advantage or disadvantage directly. This argument echoes that made more than a decade ago in the *American Psychologist* by Novick and Ellis (1977), where a strong case was made for "the explicit identification of those attributes that constitute disadvantage, rather than accepting group membership as a surrogate for disadvantage" (p. 318), and more recently by Schmitt and Dorans (1990). Novick and Ellis acknowledged that the problems of understanding what constitutes disadvantage and being able to measure it adequately were formidable. They still are. Significant advances in DIF implementation, however, may depend on serious efforts that address this issue.

CLOSING COMMENTS

The major purpose of this chapter was to present the Mantel–Haenszel technique for DIF detection and the standardization technique for DIF description. We began by making the important distinction between DIF and Impact, pointing out the need to compare the comparable. Then the Mantel–Haenszel procedure and the standardization procedure were described in some detail in that order. A common framework was used to present similarities and dissimilarities between the two methods. Then we discussed relationship of the MH procedure to IRT methods for DIF detection in general, and the Rasch model, in particular. Then the use of standardization for assessing differential distractor functioning, differential speededness, and differential omission was presented.

Several issues in applied DIF analyses were discussed, including inclusion of the studied item in the matching variable, and the refinement of the matching variable. Future research topics dealing with the matching variable, the studied variable, and the group variable were discussed.

Large-scale DIF implementation is a relatively new phenomenon in the field of measurement. Low-cost, practical, statistically sound techniques, like the Mantel–Haenszel and standardization approaches, have made large-scale implementation a reality. These are powerful techniques for DIF detection and description. As the implementation issues and future direction sections of this chapter indicate, these procedures could be improved, made more applicable to the actual testing situation. Although they are sound methods for DIF assessment, enhancements can and should be made. The major focus of future DIF research efforts, however, should not be on methodological enhancements. Although it could be improved, the methodology is quite sound. Future research should focus on trying to uncover testable, verifiable, robust explanations for why DIF occurs when it does. As chapter 14 by Schmitt, Holland, and Dorans reveals, this will not be an easy task, partly because DIF is usually small relative to other item properties such as difficulty, partly because DIF research is constrained by many practical and ethical constraints, and partly because DIF, like bias, is a political issue, as well as an issue that is laden with emotional overtones. The major challenge facing the DIF field is to take the methods described in this chapter or the methods described in the companion chapter 4 and use them to identify replicable DIF, generate sound hypotheses about this replicable DIF, test these hypotheses under controlled conditions, and develop guidelines for producing future tests that are free from these irrelevant sources of group differences.

ACKNOWLEDGMENT

An earlier version of this chapter was presented at ETS/AFHRL Conference, *Differential Item Functioning: Theory and Practice,* Educational Testing Service, Princeton, NJ, October 6, 1989. The opinions expressed in this chapter are those of one or both of the authors and should not be misconstrued to represent official policy of the Educational Testing Service. The authors are grateful to Alicia Schmitt and Howard Wainer for their careful reviews of earlier versions of this chapter.

4

Detection of Differential Item Functioning Using the Parameters of Item Response Models

David Thissen
University of North Carolina at Chapel Hill

Lynne Steinberg
Syracuse University

Howard Wainer
Educational Testing Service

Item response theory (IRT) provides a class of models describing the relationship between individual item responses and the construct(s) measured by the test. The central elements of an IRT model are that there is an unobservable (latent) variable such as *ability* or *proficiency,* usually called θ, that varies in the population of examinees (Lord, 1952), and that there is a *trace line* (Lazarsfeld, 1950) for each item response. The trace line is a function of θ; for dichotomously scored items (correct/incorrect), the trace line for the correct response is usually monotonically increasing as θ increases, and gives the varying probability of that response across the θ (ability/proficiency) continuum. Figure 4.1 shows trace lines (sometimes also called the *item characteristic curves*) for the correct response to several items.

In practical applications of IRT, the trace lines take some specified functional form. One of the most commonly used trace line models is the three-parameter logistic (Birnbaum, 1968), in which the probability of a correct response to item i ($x_i = 1$) as a function of θ is

$$T(x_i = 1) = c_i + \frac{1 - c_i}{1 + \exp[-a_i(\theta - b_i)]};\qquad (1)$$

the item parameters a_i, b_i, and c_i are the discrimination, difficulty, and guessing levels, respectively. (See Lord, 1980, or Hambleton & Swaminathan, 1985, for an extensive discussion of this model, as well as IRT in general). The trace line model has many uses; but Lord (1977, 1980) observed that the trace line is ideally suited to defining *differential item functioning* (DIF), or the lack thereof.

The value of the trace line at each level of θ is the conditional probability of a correct response given that level of ability or proficiency. If we are considering the possibility that an item may function differently (exhibit DIF) for some *focal* (F) group relative to some (other) *reference* (R) group, then in the context of IRT we are considering whether the trace lines differ for the two groups. If the trace lines are the same, there is no DIF; if the trace lines differ, there is DIF. In the language of the time, when the phrase *item bias* was used for DIF, Lord (1980) wrote, "If an item has a different item response function for one group than for another, it is clear that the item is biased" (p. 212).

Because the trace line for an item is determined by the item parameters (in the case of the three-parameter logistic, a_i, b_i, and c_i), Lord (1977, 1980) noted that the question of DIF detection could be approached by computing estimates of the item parameters within each group. After a suitable adjustment to correct for possible differences in the distribution of θ within the two groups, a statistical test of whether the item parameters differed significantly between the two groups provided evidence of DIF. Lord proposed two tests for evaluating the significance of DIF; the simpler of the two compared the difficulty parameters for the two groups in

$$d_i = \frac{\hat{b}_{Fi} - \hat{b}_{Ri}}{\sqrt{\text{Var } \hat{b}_{Fi} + \text{Var } \hat{b}_{Ri}}}, \tag{2}$$

in which $\hat{b}_{gi}$ is the maximum likelihood estimate of the parameter b_i in group g and Var $\hat{b}_{gi}$ is the corresponding estimate of the sampling variance of $\hat{b}_{gi}$. Lord (1977, 1980) noted that a similar test could be done for differences between the a_is, and that probability statements could be made by referring d_i to tables of the standard normal distribution.

Lord (1977, 1980) further proposed a more general test of the joint difference between $[a_i, b_i]$ for the two groups,

$$D_i^2 = \mathbf{v}_i' \Sigma_i^{-1} \mathbf{v}_i, \tag{3}$$

where $\mathbf{v}_i'$ is $[\hat{b}_{Fi} - \hat{b}_{Ri}, \hat{a}_{Fi} - \hat{a}_{Ri}]$, Σ_i^{-1} is the estimate of the sampling variance-covariance matrix of the differences between the item parameter estimates, and D_i^2 is distributed as χ^2 on 2 d.f. for large samples.[1] Lord did not consider the guessing parameters (c_i) in such hypothesis tests; he specified that they should be constrained to be equal for both groups.

---

[1]Lord did not call the statistic in Equation 3 D^2; he called it χ^2. However, in this chapter we consider several different statistics that are all distributed as χ^2 under certain assumptions; it is better in such a context to reserve the notation χ^2 for the theoretical distribution, and use other notation for the sample statistics. We use the notation D^2 for the generalized distance statistic, such as that in Equation 3, because it is frequently called Mahalanobis D^2 in the multivariate statistical literature after early work on its usefulness by Mahalanobis (1930, 1936). The generalized distance is also sometimes called the Wald statistic in reference to important work on its distributional properties by Wald (1943, 1944). For the conditions under which both D^2 and the likelihood ratio (LR) statistic (Neyman & Pearson, 1928) are distributed as χ^2, see Rao (1973, pp. 418–420).

A problem arising in the practical application of Lord's (1977, 1980) procedure for DIF detection, as originally implemented, is that the estimates of the standard errors of the item parameters obtained from the so-called *joint maximum likelihood* algorithm (as implemented in LOGIST [Wood, Wingersky, & Lord, 1976]) are not entirely accurate. In a simulation study, McLaughlin and Drasgow (1987) found that this inaccuracy of the standard errors resulted in overall proportions of significant DIF (in the null case) as high as 11 times the nominal α level. However, item parameter estimation procedures have been improved a great deal in recent years.

In this chapter, we follow Lord's (1977, 1980) view that an item exhibits DIF if the trace lines for the reference and focal groups differ. Because IRT trace lines are determined by the item parameters, this implies that the statistical question in DIF detection is whether the item parameters for the reference and focal groups differ reliably (or significantly). Millsap (1989) made a sharp distinction between methods of DIF detection based on latent-variable item response models and those based directly on observable statistics. Here we do not consider methods based entirely on observable statistics, such as the Mantel–Haenszel procedure (Holland & Thayer, 1988), standardization (Dorans & Kulick, 1986), or related methods based on logistic regression (Rogers & Swaminathan, 1989); Dorans and Holland (chapter 3, this volume) discuss some of these methods.

For the most part, the topic of this chapter is limited to DIF *detection*— statistical tests of the reliability or significance of differences between trace lines. There are also IRT-based methods that are entirely descriptive of the effects of DIF in the scale of response-probability, sometimes called "area-between-the-curves" techniques (Hambleton & Swaminathan, 1985, pp. 285–289; Linn, Levine, Hastings, & Wardrop, 1981; Raju, 1988). Although these descriptive techniques may be useful in some contexts, they are not associated with inferential statistics directly useful for DIF detection, and they are not considered here.

In a sense, only one DIF detection procedure is considered in this chapter. That procedure is to fit an item response model to the data for the reference and focal groups, and test the significance of the difference between the item parameter estimates for the two groups; if the difference is significant, the item is said to exhibit DIF. In broad outline, this procedure was specified by Lord (1977, 1980). However, there have been substantial advances in the statistical technology involved in model-fitting and hypothesis-testing in the context of item response models in the past decade; as a result, the computational procedures discussed here differ from those proposed by Lord more than a decade ago. Also, somewhat different approaches to parameter-estimation and hypothesis-testing are optimal for different models and different sets of data; therefore, in this chapter we discuss four variants on our single theme. The four approaches to IRT DIF detection we consider in this chapter are:

• *General IRT-LR* uses the Bock–Aitkin (Bock & Aitkin, 1981) marginal maximum likelihood estimation algorithm to estimate the parameters of a wide variety of item response models, and likelihood ratio tests to evaluate the significance of observed differences (Thissen, Steinberg, & Gerrard, 1986; Thissen, Steinberg, & Wainer, 1988).

• *Loglinear IRT-LR* uses maximum likelihood estimation for loglinear item response models and likelihood ratio tests to evaluate the significance of observed differences (Kelderman, 1990; Thissen & Mooney, 1989).

• *Limited-information IRT-LR* uses generalized least squares (GLS) estimation for normal-ogive item response models and likelihood ratio tests to evaluate the significance of observed differences (Muthén & Lehman, 1985).

• *IRT-D²* uses marginal maximum likelihood estimation and ratios of parameter estimates to their standard errors to evaluate the significance of observed differences (Bock, Muraki, & Pfeiffenberger, 1988; Muraki & Engelhard, 1989).

Previous work with these techniques has concentrated on DIF detection using models for binary (correct/incorrect) responses. A promising area for future research directed toward understanding (and ultimately controlling) DIF involves the investigation of differential *alternative* functioning (DAF). Can DIF be "located" in differential selection of certain response alternatives on a multiple-choice item? Using standardized distractor analysis, Schmitt and Dorans (1988) showed that this may be the case; Green, Crone, and Folk (1989) described the effectiveness of an observed-score method of evaluating differential *distractor* functioning (DDF). Later in this chapter, we discuss the application of IRT-based methods to the examination of differential functioning of the individual alternatives of a multiple-choice item.

We are concerned here primarily with tests of the statistical significance of DIF. As is always the case with tests of statistical significance, there is a distinction between that which is significant and that which is important. The test of significance of DIF, in an IRT framework, tells us that the differences observed between the trace line parameters for the reference and focal groups are reliably measured. Such reliable differences between item parameters may be of paramount importance in research settings, because they reflect differences between items-for-groups on a well-behaved scale. In principle, items of any degree of difficulty for either group may exhibit equal DIF, when DIF is measured in terms of the parameters; such potential invariance may be very useful to researchers who seek to explain DIF in terms that transcend individual items.

On the other hand, in the operational test-construction setting, some items exhibiting significant DIF may have no differential consequences for the test scores of those in the reference and focal groups, perhaps because the items are so difficult (or easy) that, regardless of DIF, very few respond correctly (or incorrectly) in either group. Such items may show significant DIF in the item parameter metric but little *differential impact* in the scale of probability-correct. See Wainer (chapter 6, this volume) for a discussion of the concept of differential impact.

FOUR METHODS OF TESTING THE DIFFERENCE
BETWEEN ITEM PARAMETERS FOR TWO GROUPS:
AN ILLUSTRATION

The items we use in our introductory illustrations were included in a conventional orally administered spelling test, with data obtained from 659 undergraduates at the University of Kansas. The reference group for this analysis includes the male students ($N = 285$), and the focal group is made up of the female students ($N = 374$). The original test comprised 100 words, but only 4 have been selected for use here. The four words to be spelled are *infidelity, panoramic, succumb,* and *girder*. These four items were selected because preliminary analyses suggested that they have very nearly equal discrimination parameters; this is convenient for purposes of illustration. The data were free-response, so there is no guessing to be considered. The words *infidelity, panoramic,* and *succumb* were selected to comprise an "anchor" (a set of items believed to involve no DIF) with information over a range of the θ-continuum. The word *girder* is the *studied* item; it was selected because it shows substantial differential difficulty for the two groups in these data. The Mantel–Haenszel χ^2 statistic for *girder* is 18. The data are shown in Table 4.1.

TABLE 4.1
Observed Frequencies and Percentages of the Male and Female Examinees
for the Sixteen Response Patterns for Spelling *Infidelity, Panoramic, Succumb,*
and *Girder*; 1 = correct, 0 = incorrect

Anchor Response Pattern	Studied Item (girder)	N		%		
		Males	Females	Males	Females	Male–Female
000	0	22	29	7.7	7.8	−0.1
100	0	30	50	10.5	13.4	−2.9
010	0	13	15	4.6	4.0	0.6
001	0	1	6	0.4	1.6	−1.2
110	0	24	67	8.4	17.9	−9.5
101	0	5	12	1.8	3.2	−1.4
011	0	1	2	0.4	0.5	−0.1
111	0	10	22	3.5	5.9	−2.4
000	1	10	7	3.5	1.9	1.6
100	1	27	30	9.5	8.0	1.5
010	1	14	4	4.9	1.1	3.8
001	1	1	0	0.4	0.0	0.4
110	1	54	63	18.9	16.8	2.1
101	1	8	10	2.8	2.7	0.1
011	1	8	6	2.8	1.6	1.2
111	1	57	51	20.0	13.6	6.4
Total		285	374	100	100	0

General IRT-LR

As described in the introduction, an item response model is based on the assumption that the probability of any particular item response is a function of a latent variable (θ); the curve describing the probability of item response x_i to item i is the trace line, $T(x_i; \beta_i)$, which is a function of one or more item parameters collected in the vector β_i. Under the assumption of *local independence*, meaning that all covariation among the item responses is attributable to the items' individual relationships with θ, the probability of observing response pattern $\mathbf{x}$ is

$$P(\mathbf{x}) = \int \prod_{i=1}^{n} T(x_i; \beta_i) \, \phi(\theta; \xi) \, d\theta, \tag{4}$$

where $\phi(\theta; \xi)$ is the population distribution of θ, depending on parameters collected in the vector ξ. In DIF detection, there are two groups indexed by g, the reference group ($g = R$) and the focal group ($g = F$), and the probability of observing response pattern $\mathbf{x}_g$ in group g is

$$P(\mathbf{x}_g) = \int \prod_{i=1}^{n} T(x_{gi}; \beta_{gi}) \, \phi(\theta; \xi_g) \, d\theta, \tag{5}$$

because the groups represent samples from different populations, we usually assume that the population-distribution parameters ξ_g differ for the two groups. The question to be answered in DIF detection is whether the item parameters β_{gi} differ significantly between the two groups. To answer this question in the framework of statistical hypothesis testing under the IRT model, we estimate the parameters using the data from both groups, and test the significance of the difference between β_{Ri} and β_{Fi}.

In this section we consider the general IRT-LR approach to DIF detection (Thissen et al., 1986; Thissen et al., 1988). In principle, any trace line model may be substituted in Equation 5; for a taxonomy of some well-established item response models, see Thissen and Steinberg (1986). In this section we illustrate the procedure using the one-parameter logistic model, which is appropriate for tests comprising equally discriminating binary-response items with no guessing; in subsequent sections, we illustrate the procedure for the three-parameter logistic model (Birnbaum, 1968) and the multiple-choice model (Thissen & Steinberg, 1984). For any of these models, we estimate the parameters using *marginal maximum likelihood* (MML), with algorithms described by Bock and Lieberman (1970), Bock and Aitkin (1981), Thissen (1982), and Thissen and Steinberg (1984). We compute the parameter estimates using the computer program MULTILOG (Thissen, 1988), which implements the Bock and Aitkin algorithm for a wide variety of logistic trace line models; see the chapter Appendix for details about the use of the computer program.

Tests of statistical significance in IRT-LR procedures always involve the comparison of two models, a *compact* model (C) and an *augmented* model (A), to use the terminology of Judd and McClelland (1989). The augmented model includes all of the parameters of the compact model, as well as additional parameters; thus, it is frequently said that the compact model is hierarchically nested within the augmented model. The goal of the procedure is to test whether the additional parameters in the augmented model are significantly different from zero. More generally, the goal of the test of significance is to determine whether there are sufficient data to determine that it is unlikely that the true values of these parameters are actually on the opposite side of zero from their estimated values (see Bock, 1975, pp. 15–16).

The form of the LR tests is always

$$G^2(d.f.) = 2 \log \left[\frac{\text{Likelihood[A]}}{\text{Likelihood[C]}} \right], \tag{6}$$

where Likelihood [·] represents likelihood of the data given the maximum likelihood estimates of the parameters of the model, and *d.f.* is the difference between the number of parameters in the augmented model and the number of parameters in the compact model. Under very general assumptions, the value of $G^2(d.f.)$ is distributed as $\chi^2(d.f.)$ under the null hypothesis (Rao, 1973, pp. 418–420). Thus, if the value of $G^2(d.f.)$ is large, representing an unlikely value from a $\chi^2(d.f.)$ distribution, we reject the null hypothesis—and the compact model.

There are two uses of LR tests in the context of DIF analysis. The first use of such a test arises only when few items are being considered, and the table cross-classifying the examinees on the basis of their response patterns has few, if any, observed zeros. Under these circumstances, there is an overall goodness-of-fit LR statistic for the item response model: The compact model is the item response model being tested, and the augmented model is the general multinomial model including all parameters that could possibly augment the compact model, giving the result that the observed and expected frequencies in each cell are equal. The LR test of the IRT model against the general multinomial alternative is called a *goodness-of-fit* test because, if this test is *not* significant, we infer that none of the (possibly) augmenting parameters are significantly different from zero, and we say that the model appears to fit the data. It is desirable to test the overall goodness-of-fit of the model before proceeding with the tests of DIF; however, when the number of items is large and there are many observed zeros in the very large table cross-classifying the data according to the item responses, the general multinomial alternative hypothesis is itself unreasonable and no satisfactory goodness-of-fit test is currently available.

The second use of LR tests is to test DIF. As we noted in the previous section, the null hypothesis of no DIF is defined here to be that there is no significant, or reliable, difference between the item parameter(s) for the reference and focal groups. Thus, to test DIF for item i, we compute the ML (Maximum Likelihood) estimates of the parameters of the compact model (with no DIF for item i) and the likelihood under that model, and the ML estimates and likelihood of the model augmented by some parameters representing differences between the item i parameters for the reference and focal groups. Then the likelihood ratio statistic provides a test of the significance of DIF on k degrees of freedom, where k is the number of item parameters differing between the reference and focal groups.

To fix ideas, we make our first use of a very simple illustration: Using the data in Table 4.1, we test the significance of DIF for the spelling word *girder*. Data were carefully selected for this illustration so we could use one of the simplest item response models, in which the trace lines follow the logistic model

$$T(x_i = 1) = \frac{1}{1 + \exp[-a(\theta - b_i)]}, \tag{7}$$

where the discrimination parameter a is the same for all items, and the difficulty parameter b_i is estimated for each item i. The population distributions $\phi(\theta)$ are assumed to be $N(0,1)$ for the reference group and $N(\mu_F,1)$ for the focal group. We consider the model testing DIF for item 4 (*girder*); the augmented model has item parameters $\{a, b_1, b_2, b_3, b_{R,4}, b_{F,4}\}$ and population parameter μ_F; the compact model constrains $b_{R,4} = b_{F,4} = b_4$. The parameter estimates for the augmented model, including DIF for item 4, are shown in Table 4.2.

For the tests of significance, the goodness-of-fit is $G^2(23) = 25, p = .35$, for this model (with DIF for item 4, *girder*); thus, we conclude that the model using the one-parameter logistic and the normal population distribution fits the data satisfactorily. For the model constraining $b_{F,4} = b_{R,4}$, the goodness-of-fit is $G^2(24) = 44, p = .007$. For the null hypothesis of no DIF, we compute $G^2(1) = 19, p < .001$, and conclude that item 4 exhibits DIF. The trace lines for these items are shown in Fig. 4.1.

Loglinear IRT-LR

The one-parameter logistic trace-line model, attributed to Rasch (1960), may also be written

$$T(x_i = 1) = \frac{1}{1 + \exp[-(\theta - \beta_i)]}; \tag{8}$$

the probability of observing response pattern x is

$$P(\mathbf{x}) = \int \prod_{i=1}^{n} T(x_i = 1)^{x_i} T(x_i = 0)^{1-x_i} f(\theta) \, d\theta. \tag{9}$$

In the model as defined by Equations 8 and 9, the population distribution $f(\theta)$ is unspecified, and the slope-parameter a is absorbed in the scale of θ.

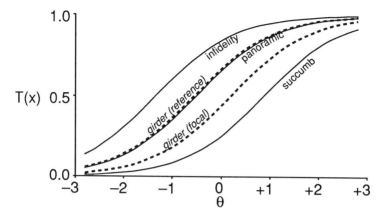

FIG. 4.1. Trace lines for the correct response to the four spelling items. The heavy dashed lines represent the trace lines for *girder* for the reference group (on the left) and the focal group (on the right). The light solid lines represent the trace lines for *infidelity, panoramic,* and *succumb* (in left-to-right order); note that the trace line for *panoramic* is adjacent to (and obscured by) the trace line for *girder* for the reference group.

Table 4.2
Parameter Estimates from MULTILOG
for the Data in Table 4.1

Parameter	Estimate
μ_F	0.02
a	1.25
b_1	-1.34
b_2	-0.51
b_3	0.88
$b_{R,4}$	-0.55
$b_{F,4}$	0.20

It has long been understood that maximum likelihood parameter estimation for the Rasch (1960) model is unique; a series of papers published in the 1980s has made it clear that this is due to the fact that it is a *loglinear* model for the probabilities of each response pattern (Clogg, 1988; Cressie & Holland, 1983;

de Leeuw & Verhelst, 1986; Duncan, 1984; Hout, Duncan, & Sobel, 1987; Kelderman, 1984; Thissen & Mooney, 1989; Tjur, 1982). The combination of Equations 8 and 9 may be written

$$\log[P(\mathbf{x})] = \sum_{i=1}^{n} \beta_i x_i + \gamma_t, \tag{10}$$

in which $t = \Sigma x$ and the parameters γ_t represent the score-group, and thereby the population, distribution. It is conventional in the loglinear Rasch model literature to resolve the indeterminacy of the scale of θ by fixing $\beta_1 = 0$ and $\gamma_0 = 0$. This convention results in parameter estimates on a different scale from that used when θ is assumed to be distributed $N(0,1)$, as in the preceding section; however, the parameters of the $N(0,1)$ population model may be transformed to $b_i^* = ab_i - ab_1$, where the b_i^* are on the same scale as the βs and the population distribution is $N(-ab_1, a^2)$.

For two groups, the additional index g (for instance, coded $+1$ for the reference group and -1 for the focal group) may be introduced, and the unconstrained loglinear Rasch model becomes

$$\log[P(\mathbf{x})] = \sum_{i=1}^{n} \beta_i x_i + \sum_{i=1}^{n} \beta_{g \times i} g x_i + \gamma_t + g \gamma_{g \times t}; \tag{11}$$

this is of particular interest here, in the context of DIF detection, because the parameters $\beta_{g \times i}$ represent interactions between group membership and the item parameters. If $\beta_{g \times i} = 0$, there is no DIF; Kelderman (1990) suggested the use of this fact in DIF detection (see also Thissen & Mooney, 1989). The only difference between this approach to DIF detection and that described in the previous section is that, in the loglinear parameterization, the *difference* between the item parameters for the two groups is represented explicitly as a parameter (i.e., $\beta_{g \times i}$); so we discuss tests of the hypothesis that the difference-parameter is zero in place of tests of equality constraints.

Only the Rasch (1960) family of models appears to be amenable to representation as a loglinear model; the widely used two- and three-parameter logistic models, and most models for multiple-categorical responses, cannot be so represented. This restriction limits the usefulness of this approach to tests for which Rasch-family models may be appropriate. However, an advantage of the loglinear representation is the concomitant ease with which the parameters of these models are readily estimated with any standard loglinear analysis program. For the example presented here, we used SPSS-X LOGLINEAR to compute the item parameters and test statistics (see the chapter Appendix); other computer programs, such as MULTIQUAL (Bock & Yates, 1973) that use the direct approach to loglinear parameter estimation (Bock, 1975, chapter 8; Haberman, 1979) would work equally well. For larger numbers of items, the general approach becomes inefficient. Kelderman and Steen (1988) developed a computer program, called LOGIMO, specifically designed for parameter estimation and hypothesis testing in the context of loglinear IRT.

It is convenient for some purposes to reparameterize the γ-space in the loglinear model; here we use

$$\log[P(\mathbf{x})] = \sum_{i=1}^{n} \beta_i x_i + \sum_{i=1}^{n} \beta_{g \times i} g x_i + \sum_{p=1}^{P} \eta_p t^p + \sum_{p=1}^{P} \eta_{g \times p} g t^p, \tag{12}$$

in which the γs are replaced by polynomials in t; the polynomial coefficients η are interpretable under some circumstances (see Holland, 1987; Thissen & Mooney, 1989).

The particular parameterization of the loglinear IRT model used here, for our four-item example for the no-DIF (null) hypothesis, is

$$\log[P(\mathbf{x})] = \sum_{i=1}^{4} \beta_i x_i + \sum_{p=1}^{4} \eta_t t^p + \sum_{p=1}^{4} \eta_{g \times p} g t^p; \tag{13}$$

and the parameterization for the DIF hypothesis for item 4 is

$$\log[P(\mathbf{x})] = \sum_{i=1}^{4} \beta_i x_i + \beta_{g \times 4} g x_i + \sum_{p=1}^{4} \eta_t t^p + \sum_{p=1}^{4} \eta_{g \times p} g t^p. \tag{14}$$

The maximum likelihood parameter estimates for the model in Equation 14 are shown in Table 4.3. Also shown, for comparison, are the values of the item parameters estimated under the assumption that the population distributions are Gaussian, transformed to the loglinear-scale conventions that $a = 1$ and $\beta_1 = 0$; these are computed as $ab_i - ab_1$.

The goodness-of-fit statistics are $G^2(18) = 22$, $p = .25$ for this model and $G^2(19) = 41$, $p = .003$ for the model constraining $\beta_{Sex \times 4} = 0$; so $G^2(1) = 19$, $p < .001$ for the null hypothesis of no DIF for *girder*.

The full rank loglinear model, with parameters shown in Table 4.3, has the advantage that it involves no assumptions about the population distributions. However, a relatively large number of parameters, the ηs, are implicitly used to characterize those unspecified distributions. The value of the likelihood-ratio test statistics for the loglinear model specifying no particular population distribution, $G^2(18) = 22$, in combination with that found in the preceding section with the assumption of Gaussian population distributions, $G^2(23) = 25$, may be used to produce a χ^2 test of non-normality of the underlying distribution. In this case, that test is $G^2(5) = 3$, $p = .60$, which means that we cannot reject the hypothesis that the underlying θ distributions are normal. (It also indicates that the loglinear model is using at least five more parameters than are really needed!)

Holland (1987) showed that a quadratic parameterization associated with the

TABLE 4.3
Loglinear Parameter Estimates for the Data in Table 4.1

Parameter	Loglinear Estimate	Normal Pop. $ab_i - ab_1$
β_1	0.0	0.0
β_2	1.03	1.03
β_3	2.78	2.77
$\beta_4 - \beta_{Sex \times 4} = \beta_{R,4}$	0.96	0.99
$\beta_4 + \beta_{Sex \times 4} = \beta_{F,4}$	1.91	1.93
η_1	0.11	
η_2	0.32	
η_3	-0.004	
η_4	0.003	
$\eta_{Sex \times 1}$	0.02	
$\eta_{Sex \times 2}$	-0.20	
$\eta_{Sex \times 3}$	0.07	
$\eta_{Sex \times 4}$	-0.007	

score-groups, as is obtained by setting η_3, η_4, $\eta_{Sex \times 3}$, *and* $\eta_{Sex \times 4}$ equal to zero, is equivalent to assuming that the posteriors are normally distributed. This result is a corollary of Holland's theorem 1, which he called the *Dutch identity;* therefore, we call it the Dutch identity model. It is not the same model as that of the previous section, where we assumed that the *population distributions* are normally distributed. The Dutch identity model fits the data if the model includes the $\beta_{Sex \times 4}$ interaction term: $G^2(22) = 23, p = .41$. Using the Dutch identity model, the likelihood ratio χ^2 for the model setting the $\beta_{Sex \times 4}$ interaction term to zero is $G^2(23) = 41, p = .01$, and the test of significance of DIF for the studied item (*girder*) is $G^2(1) = 18, p < .001$.

A functionally equivalent alternative estimation procedure for the parameters of loglinear models is based on *iterative proportional fitting* (IPF), sometimes called the Deming–Stephan (Deming & Stephan 1940) algorithm (see Bishop, Fienberg, & Holland, 1975, pp. 84ff). In the direct parameter estimation described previously, the parameters of the loglinear model (the βs and the ηs) are estimated directly from the observed data, usually with an iterative algorithm such as Newton–Raphson. In IPF, the expected values under the model in each cell of the *Groups $\times$ Item 1 $\times$ Item 2 . . .* table are obtained iteratively, and the parameters of the model are subsequently computed as closed-form functions of the expected values. For the maximum likelihood estimates of the parameters, the expected values in the table are subject to a series of constraints that are usually described by saying that certain expected marginal totals must be equal to the corresponding observed totals. For instance, if the loglinear model includes a main effect for item i, then the expected marginal totals (correct and incorrect) for item i must equal the observed frequencies; and, if the loglinear model includes main effects corresponding to raw-score-group membership, then the expected marginal totals must equal the observed frequencies for each raw score. These constraints uniquely determine the expected values, which, in turn, uniquely determine the values of the maximum likelihood estimates of the parameters.

IPF can be a very efficient method for computing the maximum likelihood estimates of the parameters of loglinear models and the associated goodness-of-fit statistics; but the loglinear model is usually written in a slightly different form, and a different set of parameters, called u-terms, are estimated (Bishop et al., 1975). Kelderman (1984, 1987, 1990; Kelderman & Macready, 1988) made extensive use of IPF in the context of loglinear IRT models, and Kelderman and Steen (1988) developed a computer program based on IPF specifically for fitting loglinear models in the context of IRT. The loglinear model in Equation 10 may be written

$$\log[P(\mathbf{x})] = u + u_{1x_1} + u_{2x_2} + \ldots + u_{nx_n} + u_t ; \qquad (15)$$

where $t = \Sigma x$. There are many more u-terms in Equation 15 than there were parameters in Equation 10; the u-terms in Equation 15 are subject to a number of restrictions, usually that linear combinations of the us must be zero. Nevertheless, the models described by Equations 10 and 15 are equivalent, and Table 4.4 shows the relationship between the item parameters in the model in Equation 10 and the u-terms in Equation 15 for four items.

The model for groups indexed by g and DIF for item i, in u-terms, is written

$$\log[P(\mathbf{x})] = u + u_{1x_1} + u_{2x_2} + \ldots \\ + u_{nx_n} + u_{g \times ix_i} + u_t + u_{g \times t} ; \qquad (16)$$

and the hypothesis of no DIF becomes the hypothesis that $u_{g \times i1} = u_{g \times i0} = 0$. The use of LOGIMO to compute the estimates and test statistics for the *girder* example is described in the chapter Appendix; the results are identical to those obtained previously using SPSS-X LOGLINEAR.

TABLE 4.4
The Relationship Between the Item
Parameters in the Model in Equation 10
and the U-Terms in Equation 15

Equation 10	Equation 15
β_1	$(u_{10} - u_{11}) - (u_{10} - u_{11})$
β_2	$(u_{20} - u_{21}) - (u_{10} - u_{11})$
β_3	$(u_{30} - u_{31}) - (u_{10} - u_{11})$
β_4	$(u_{40} - u_{41}) - (u_{10} - u_{11})$

Limited-Information IRT-LR

An alternative statistical estimation procedure to the full-information maximum likelihood approach described in the previous two sections has been called the *limited information* approach (Mislevy, 1986, p. 17), because it uses information in lower order margins of the response-pattern cross-classification of respondents, rather than the complete table of response pattern frequencies. Here we consider generalized least squares (GLS) parameter estimation; GLS is asymptotically equivalent to ML, and the same statistical theory applies (in large samples) to tests of significance with either type of estimation. Muthén and Lehman (1985) described the use of the GLS approach in DIF detection; the required computational procedures have been implemented in the computer program LISCOMP (Muthén, 1987).

LISCOMP is a general-purpose structural equation modeling program; here we describe only the small subset of its general model that is applicable to the DIF detection problem in the case of a unidimensional latent variable.[2] The estimation procedure implemented in LISCOMP is based on the normal ogive model, where

$$T(x_i = 1) = T(y_i^* > \tau) = \Phi[E(y_i^*) - \tau_i] , \qquad (17)$$

and $\Phi[\cdot]$ is the cumulative normal integral. The latent response variable y_i^*, in turn, is a linear function of the latent variable θ:

$$y_i^* = \lambda_i \theta + \epsilon_i . \qquad (18)$$

This is the classic normal ogive model in item response theory, in which

$$T(x_i = 1) = \Phi[a_i(\theta - b_i)] . \qquad (19)$$

The parameters a_i and b_i are related to the structural model parameters (Muthén & Lehman, 1985) by

$$a_i = \frac{\lambda_i}{\sqrt{1 - \lambda_i^2}} \qquad (20)$$

and

$$b_i = \tau_i / \lambda_i ; \qquad (21)$$

see Lord and Novick (1968, pp. 374–375) for a complete explication of these relationships. The normal ogive model has been largely superseded in IRT by the logistic model described in the previous two sections, because there is little difference between the two: The value of the normal integral is never more than

---

[2]In our description of the model, we use somewhat different notation than that used in the *LISCOMP User's Guide* (Muthén, 1987), to increase consistency with the notation used elsewhere in this chapter. We refer to the observed dichotomous response as x, and the latent variable as θ; they are called y and η, respectively in the *LISCOMP User's Guide*.

.01 different from that of the logistic with the same value of b_i, when the value of a_i for the normal ogive is multiplied by the constant 1.7 (Birnbaum, 1968, p. 399; attributed to Haley, 1952). Usually, the logistic function leads to simpler computations; however, the use of the normal ogive model simplifies the computations in the structural-equations context, so the normal ogive forms the basis for the GLS analysis in LISCOMP.

The normal ogive model has direct implications for the proportions responding correctly to each item (the first-order statistics) and the tetrachoric correlations among pairs of items (the second-order statistics); again, these implications are treated in detail by Lord and Novick (1968, pp. 376–379). Following procedures described by Muthén (1987), GLS estimation of the parameters makes use only of the information contained in the first- and second-order statistics.

The general-purpose estimation and model-testing algorithm implemented in LISCOMP has all of the features necessary to evaluate DIF: Data from more than one group (indexed by g) may be considered, and individual parameters may be constrained to be equal. Including the group index g, the trace line model is

$$T(x_{gi} = 1) = T(y_{gi}^* > \tau) = \Phi[E(y_{gi}^*) - \tau_{gi}] , \qquad (22)$$

and

$$y_{gi}^* = \lambda_{gi}(\theta + \alpha_g) + \epsilon_{gi} , \qquad (23)$$

where α_g is the latent mean for group g. To identify the model, α_g is fixed at zero for the reference group. The value of α_g is estimated as the mean of the population distribution for θ for the focal group. The use of the tetrachoric correlations, and GLS estimation, involves the assumption that the latent distribution is $N(\alpha_g, 1)$.

In our analysis of the spelling data, we constrain all of the loadings λ_{gi} to be equal to a single value λ; this gives an equal-slope analysis parallel to the one-parameter logistic analyses in the preceding two sections. To evaluate DIF for item 4, we fit the model with the constraints that $\tau_{11} = \tau_{21}$, $\tau_{12} = \tau_{22}$, and $\tau_{13} = \tau_{23}$ (those constraints have the effect of establishing items 1–3 as the no-DIF anchor); and we estimate the parameters to obtain the goodness-of-fit statistics with the constraint $\tau_{14} = \tau_{24}$ and then without that constraint. The estimates for the unconstrained (DIF) model are shown in Table 4.5.

For the goodness-of-fit of this model, $G^2(13) = 15$, $p = .31$. $G^2(14) = 35$, $p = .002$ for the model constraining $\tau_{R,4} = \tau_{F,4}$; so $G^2(1) = 20$, $p < .001$ for the null hypothesis of no DIF for *girder*. The goodness-of-fit tests have fewer degrees of freedom than do those reported in the preceding sections because they summarize the fit of the model *only* to the first- and second-order statistics. Specifically, there are four proportions and six correlations for each group, for a total of 10 values from the data, as opposed to the 16 response-pattern frequencies in the data for the full-information methods.

To further illustrate the fact that the answers obtained here are essentially

TABLE 4.5
Structural Parameter Estimates
from LISCOMP for the Data in Table 4.1

Parameter	Estimate
α_F	0.03
λ	0.60
τ_1	−0.79
τ_2	−0.30
τ_3	0.52
τ_{R4}	−0.32
τ_{F4}	0.12

those obtained in the previous two sections, in Table 4.6 we transform the normal ogive parameters to the scale of the logistic parameters from MML estimation (MULTILOG). Comparison of those values with the estimates in Table 4.2 shows that they differ only very slightly; most of the difference is due to the slight difference in shape between the normal ogive and logistic models.

IRT-D^2

Bock et al. (1988) developed a procedure for the maintenance of large-scale item pools over time in the presence of *item parameter drift*. A problem with long-term usage of test items, for example, in a continuing adaptive testing program, is that over time the difficulty of the items may change—that is, the location of the items on the θ scale may "drift." Changes in educational curricula, for instance, are likely to induce such changes, and Bock et al. illustrated the method with data about change over time in the parameters of certain items in the College

TABLE 4.6
Parameter Estimates from LISCOMP
for the Data in Table 4.1, Transformed
to be Comparable to the MML Estimates
in Table 4.2

Parameter	Estimate
α_F	0.03
$\dfrac{1.7\lambda}{\sqrt{1 - \lambda^2}}$	1.28
τ_1/λ	−1.31
τ_2/λ	−0.49
τ_3/λ	0.87
$\tau_{R,4}/\lambda$	−0.53
$\tau_{F,4}/\lambda$	0.21

Board Physics Achievement Test. The Bock et al. procedure, implemented in the computer program BIMAIN (Muraki, Mislevy, & Bock, 1987), is primarily designed to characterize the amount of drift in the item locations over time. To do this, data from several different groups of examinees, who responded to the items at different times, usually one or more years apart, are considered; and the trend in difficulty of each item is represented as a polynomial function of time.

Item parameter drift is, of course, a special case of DIF: There are two (or more) groups of examinees, and the research question is whether the item parameters, and therefore, the trace lines, differ between or among the groups. The only real difference between the drift question and the DIF question is that the drift question involves time, and that strongly suggests trend analysis. The drift question is also primarily concerned with item location, suggesting that the primary concern of the analysis is with the item difficulty parameter. So the BIMAIN procedure has been designed to consider group differences only in the difficulty parameter. (Muraki and Engelhard [1989] discussed the use of the BIMAIN program in examining DIF.)

The drift and DIF detection procedure implemented in BIMAIN uses the three-parameter logistic item response function (Birnbaum, 1968), in which the probability of a correct response from a person in group g to item i ($x_{gi} = 1$) as a function of θ is

$$T(x_{gi} = 1) = c_i + \frac{1 - c_i}{1 + \exp[-a_i(\theta - b_{gi})]}. \tag{24}$$

Note that only the difficulty parameter, b_{gi}, is doubly subscripted for groups and items. In the procedure as currently implemented, the parameters a_i and c_i are not permitted to differ between groups. There are facilities in BIMAIN for constraining c_i to equal zero for all items, yielding a two-parameter logistic analysis, and for constraining $a_i = a$, yielding a one-parameter logistic. When we illustrate the procedure with the four spelling items, we use the one-parameter logistic specification.

In the context of DIF detection, the Bock et al. (1988) procedure begins by estimating the item parameters using a combination of the Bock and Aitkin (1981) EM algorithm followed by one or more iterations of the Bock and Lieberman (1970) direct Newton–Raphson algorithm. The latter serves to produce accurate estimates of the standard errors of the parameters, accounting for the fact that θ is a random variable. In the item parameter estimation, the population distributions of both groups are assumed to be Gaussian; however, the mean and variance of the focal group distribution are estimated, relative to the $N(0,1)$ scale of the reference group.

After the item parameters have been estimated, an adjustment factor, $\hat{\delta}_F$, for the focal group is computed as an average of the differences between $\hat{b}_{Fi}$ and $\hat{b}_{Ri}$. The current version of the procedure offers three options in weighting the differences between the $\hat{b}_{gi}$ in computing $\hat{\delta}_F$, corresponding to different weighting procedures. The first is described by Bock et al. (1988), the second by Muraki and Engelhard (1989), and the third uses an unweighted average. In the spelling example, we used the unweighted average, so

$$\delta_F = \frac{1}{n} \sum_{i=1}^{n} \hat{b}_{Fi} - \hat{b}_{Ri}, \tag{25}$$

and the adjusted values of $\hat{b}_{Fi}$ are

$$\hat{b}'_{Fi} = \hat{b}_{Fi} - \delta_F. \tag{26}$$

The mean of the focal group population distribution is also adjusted using δ_F.

Muraki and Engelhard (1989) described the use of what they called the *standardized index of bias (SIB)*:

$$SIB_i = \frac{|\hat{b}'_{Fi} - \hat{b}'_{Ri}|}{\sqrt{\text{Var } \hat{b}_{Fi} + \text{Var } \hat{b}_{Ri}}}. \tag{27}$$

Muraki and Engelhard noted that a criterion of about 2 may be used to judge an item to exhibit DIF. Of course, this is essentially Lord's (1977, 1980) procedure, updated to include contemporary, optimal item parameter estimation with real constraints that the a_is and c_is are equal for the two groups, and accurate standard errors. The results obtained by applying this procedure to the spelling data are shown in Table 4.7. In agreement with the three IRT-LR procedures, the BIMAIN analysis strongly suggests that there is evidence of DIF for item 4: The SIB is 3.62, well above the cutoff level of 2 suggested by Muraki and Engelhard (1989). SIB^2 is more straightforwardly comparable to the χ^2 statistics used in the IRT-LR procedures; the value is 13.1.

The results in Table 4.7 also suggest that item 1 may exhibit DIF. This is due to the fact that the algorithm implemented in BIMAIN computes the (weighted) average difference between the b parameters as an estimate of the difference between the latent group means, and uses that average to adjust both the means and the focal group bs. When there are only a few items, that presents a problem:

TABLE 4.7
Item Parameter Estimates from BIMAIN for the Data in Table 4.1

Parameter	Reference Estimate (s.e.)	Focal Estimate (s.e.)	SIB	SIB²
a	1.29 (.10)	1.29 (.10)		
b_1	−1.16 (.13)	−1.61 (.12)	2.57	6.6
b_2	−0.59 (.12)	−0.63 (.10)	0.26	0.1
b_3	0.78 (.13)	0.71 (.11)	0.43	0.2
b_4	−0.56 (.12)	0.01 (.10)	3.62	13.1

Here, one of the four items (or 25%) shows DIF. When it considers all four items, BIMAIN concludes that the mean for the focal group latent distribution is $-.16$, because the item exhibiting DIF (item 4) is included in that estimate. BIMAIN then adjusts all of the bs for the focal group; the result is that part of the item 4 DIF appears as DIF-in-the-opposite-direction for item 1. We note in passing that the combined values of SIB^2 for items 1 and 4 in the BIMAIN analysis total 19.7; that is very close to the value obtained for item 4 alone for the three IRT-LR procedures, all of which tested DIF for item 4 under the explicit assumption that there is no DIF on the first three items.

If item 4 is eliminated from the analysis, BIMAIN detects no DIF in the remaining three items, and the estimate of the focal group population mean becomes .03, in agreement with MULTILOG and LISCOMP. The results for the three anchor items alone are shown in Table 4.8.

In the IRT-D^2 method, the estimate of the mean difference is obtained from the (weighted) average difference between difficulty parameters for all of the items; no distinction is made between anchor items and items to be examined for potential DIF. This differs from the IRT-LR approaches, in which the anchor items are pre-specified and the population mean difference is established by the anchor items alone. If there are many items, we might reasonably presume that average difference between the item difficulty parameters will accurately reflect population mean differences. With few items, as in this overly-simple didactic example, a single item exhibiting DIF may seriously disturb the estimate of the focal group population mean. On the other hand, the fact that BIMAIN does not require prespecification of the anchor is an attractive feature for situations in which no prespecified anchor is readily available.

A SECOND ILLUSTRATION: SAT SENTENCE COMPLETION ITEMS

Most major testing programs currently rely on multiple-choice items. The DIF detection problem is more complex for multiple-choice item response data than it

TABLE 4.8
Item Parameter Estimates from BIMAIN for the Data in Table 4.1,
Considering Only the Three No-DIF Anchor Items

Parameter	Reference Estimate (s.e.)	Focal Estimate (s.e.)	SIB	SIB²
a	1.22 (.12)	1.22 (.12)		
b_1	-1.20 (.14)	-1.49 (.13)	1.56	2.4
b_2	-0.60 (.13)	-0.45 (.11)	0.90	0.8
b_3	0.81 (.13)	0.95 (.11)	0.81	0.7

is for free response data, because the analysis must consider the effects of guessing as well as unequal discrimination parameters. In this section, we consider DIF detection for binary-scored multiple-choice items. The focus of our illustration is item 20, section 1, of Form 6K of the Scholastic Aptitude Test (SAT), administered in December 1986.[3] Green et al. (1989) found that this item exhibited substantial differential distractor functioning (DDF) among groups of White, Black, and Hispanic examinees, indicating that the item somehow functions differently for the three groups. We consider the differential functioning of the distractors for this item in detail in a subsequent section. Green et al. did not consider the question of DIF (i.e., is the trace line for the correct response different for the three groups?). We examine item 20 for DIF in this section.

Item 20 is in the sentence completion format; the item is:

20. In some animal species, differences between opposite sexes are so———
that it is very difficult to tell that the male and female are———.

  (A) measurable . . distinct
  (B) minute . . similar
  (C) obvious . . indistinguishable
  (D)*extreme . . related
  (E) trivial . . identical

We consider the responses of 33,376 White examinees (the reference [R] group) and 2,962 Black examinees (the focal [F] group) to item 20 and four other items (16, 17, 19, and 21) of the same sentence completion section of SAT Form 6K. Items 16, 17, 19, and 21 were selected to serve as the anchor for our DIF analysis because Green et al. (1989) did *not* find that these items exhibited DDF. The sample of examinees represents all of those among the first 50,000 examinees in the records for the December 1986 administration of the test with complete data on the ethnic background question of the SAT Student Descriptive Questionnaire (SDQ) and the five items (omits were considered missing data). In order to simplify the illustration, we did not consider the data from the Hispanic sample (although Green et al. did).[4]

Because the item is in multiple-choice format, we use the three-parameter

---

[3]Form 6K is a "released" form of the SAT; however, we note that it is still protected by copyright.

[4]Among the first 50,000 examinees, there were 38,052 who described themselves as *white*, 3,556 who selected *black*, 1,984 who selected one of the three alternatives included in *hispanic background*, 3,165 who chose one of the other alternatives, and 3,243 who did not respond. The sample sizes are further reduced in this analysis by the number who omitted one or more of the five items considered here. Allen and Wainer (1989) discussed the effects of such missing data on analyses such as these.

logistic (3-PL) model (Birnbaum, 1968) in the general IRT-LR and IRT-D^2 procedures; the trace line for the correct response is

$$T(x_i = 1) = c_i + \frac{1 - c_i}{1 + \exp[-1.7a_i(\theta - b_i)]}. \tag{28}$$

The astute reader will also note that, at this point, we have introduced the constant 1.7 into the logistic model to place the parameters in the metric of the normal ogive model (see Birnbaum, 1968, p. 399); we did not use the 1.7 in the previous section because that analysis used the one-parameter logistic model, and it is not conventional to parameterize the 1-PL model in the normal metric. It is almost universally conventional to show the parameters of the 3-PL model in the normal metric, and we follow that convention here.

General IRT-LR

The general IRT-LR analysis is as it was described in the preceding section, except that the 3-PL model in Equation 28 is substituted in Equation 5 to give the probability of each response pattern, and each item has three parameters $\{a, b, c\}$ for each group. Using the computer program MULTILOG (Thissen, 1988), we fitted the model under the constraint that the item parameters for the anchor (items 16, 17, 19, and 21) are equal for the reference and focal groups, and the item parameters for item 20 differ. Following our previous description of the 3-PL procedure (Thissen, Steinberg, & Wainer, 1988), we imposed a $N(-1.4, .5)$ Bayesian prior on logit[c]. The value of the goodness-of-fit statistic for this model is significant, $G^2(43) = 111$, indicating that the model may not fit.

There are several possible reasons for the inadequacy of the model. One is that the sample size is very large—over 30,000 for the reference group and about 3,000 for the focal group. With such a large sample, relatively small deviations from the model are significant. It could be that the logistic trace lines are not the "correct" shape, or it could be that the assumed Gaussian population distribution is detectably wrong in this example.[5] Regrettably, it is not yet within the state of the art to partition the goodness-of-fit statistic into components attributable to these separate sources of lack of fit for the 3-PL model, although Glas (1988) developed some such diagnostic statistics for the 1-PL model. The model may be imperfect; but it is not clear how to correct it.

It is also possible that the significant value of the goodness-of-fit statistic is not caused by mis-specification of either the trace lines or the population distribution, but rather by mis-specification of the sampling process. The goodness-

---

[5]It is also possible, in principle, that the lack of fit is due to multidimensionality; however, item factor analysis using TESTFACT (Wilson, Wood, & Gibbons, 1987) indicated that the second factor is not significant.

of-fit statistic assumes simple random sampling; it is possible that there is some element of cluster sampling in operational SAT data arising from the fact that data are obtained from relatively homogeneous groups in testing centers. The administration of the SAT is not designed as a sample survey, because that is not its purpose; it is therefore difficult, if not impossible, to determine what the degree of cluster sampling might be. If there is some degree of clustering in the data, all of the χ^2 statistics will be somewhat inflated; it is not unreasonable to suppose that the inflation may take the form of a design effect of about two. (That value was used by Bock & Mislevy [1981] in their analysis of a stratified national sample.) That degree of clustering would make all of the χ^2 statistics twice as large as they should be, and explain the lack of fit even if the model is essentially correct. In any event, it is not clear what options might be available to us to correct the apparent lack of fit; therefore, we proceed as though the model is satisfactory.

In the general IRT-LR analysis, we test the significance of the difference between the reference and focal groups for the three parameters of the model separately, in order: c, a, b. The order is not arbitrary: It only makes sense to test the hypothesis of equal slope parameters (a) if we are willing to assume that the guessing levels (c) for the two groups are equal; otherwise the two slopes would be between different asymptotes, and there would be no reason for them to be equal. And it is only sensible to test the difference between the location parameters (b) in the context of equal slope parameters.

Fitting the model with c_F constrained to equal c_R, we find that the goodness-of-fit statistic is $G^2(44) = 111$, and the test of significance of the difference between the guessing-level parameters is $G^2(1) = 0$. Upon constraining $a_F = a_R$, we find that the goodness-of-fit statistic increases to $G^2(45) = 124$, and the test for the significance of the difference between a_F and a_R is $G^2(1) = 13, p < .001$. For completeness in the illustration, we add the constraint $b_F = b_R$, and find that

TABLE 4.9
MULTILOG Parameter Estimates
for Five SAT Sentence Completion Items

Item	c	a	b
20, R	0.27	0.96	−0.29
20, F	0.27	1.90	0.12
16	0.15	0.85	−1.50
17	0.37	0.74	−0.80
19	0.31	0.72	−0.94
21	0.14	0.90	0.27

Note: Populations: Reference: $N(0,1)$; Focal: $N(-.71,1)$.

the goodness-of-fit statistic increases to $G^2(46) = 220$, and the test for the significance of the difference between b_F and b_R is $G^2(1) = 96$, $p < .001$.

We conclude that item 20 exhibits substantial DIF; the item parameters (with $c_F = c_R$, but no further constraints) are shown in Table 4.9. The slope (a) is much higher and the item is also more difficult (b) for the focal group. The two trace lines are shown in Fig. 4.2; it is clear that low-proficiency examinees in the reference group have a substantially higher probability of a correct response than do low-proficiency examinees in the focal group. With the population distribution of the reference group assumed to be standard normal, the estimate of the mean for the focal population is $-.71$; combined with the form of the trace lines, this results in substantial differential impact of this item against the focal group (see Wainer, chapter 6, this volume).

IRT-D²

The implementation of the IRT-D² procedure in BIMAIN (Muraki et al., 1987) is the only other procedure among the four considered here that includes the 3-PL model, accounting for guessing on the multiple-choice items. As noted in the previous section, no anchor is explicitly specified in the BIMAIN analysis. When the 3-PL model is used, the program automatically constrains the guessing parameters c and the slopes a for the focal and reference groups to be equal. Distinct values of b are estimated for the focal and reference groups for each

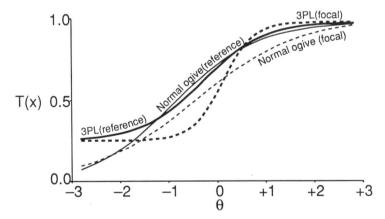

FIG. 4.2. Trace lines for the correct response to SAT sentence completion item 20. The heavy solid line is the 3-PL trace line for the reference group; the heavy dashed line is the 3-PL trace line for the focal group. The light solid line is the two-parameter normal ogive trace line for the reference group; the light dashed line is the two-parameter normal ogive trace line for the focal group.

item. Both population distributions are assumed to be Gaussian; however, during the estimation process, the standard deviation of the focal group is adjusted to provide a separate estimate of the standard deviation of that population relative to unity for the reference group. At the end, δ (From equation 25) is used to provide an estimate of the mean of the focal group relative to zero for the reference group, and to adjust the b-parameters for the focal group accordingly (Equation 26). Values of the standardized index of bias (SIB; Equation 27) are then computed.

The parameter estimates from BIMAIN are shown in Table 4.10. They differ (albeit slightly) from the MULTILOG estimates in Table 4.9 for two reasons. One reason for the difference is that a different set of parameters was estimated in the two procedures: The slope parameter (a) for item 20, which was estimated separately for the two groups with MULTILOG, is constrained equal for the two groups here; and the location parameters (b) for items 16, 17, 19, and 21, which were constrained equal for the focal and reference groups in MULTILOG, are estimated separately by BIMAIN. The different parameterization leads to somewhat different parameter estimates. A second source of the differences between the estimates in Tables 4.9 and 4.10 is the difference in the Bayesian prior distributions assumed for the item parameters. We used the default priors provided in BIMAIN, which are $N(0, .5)$ for the logs of the a parameters, $N(0,2.0)$ for the b parameters, $\beta(5,17)$ for the c parameters. These priors are different from the uniform (improper) priors for a and b, and the $N(-1.4, .5)$ for logit[c] used with MULTILOG.

BIMAIN provides a test of DIF only with respect to the b parameter. In this

TABLE 4.10
BIMAIN Parameter Estimates
for Five SAT Sentence Completion Items

Item	c	a	b
20, R	0.22	0.85	−0.43
20, F	0.22	0.85	0.06
16, R	0.23	0.81	−1.47
16, F	0.23	0.81	−1.40
17, R	0.33	0.69	−0.94
17, F	0.33	0.69	−1.19
19, R	0.28	0.69	−1.01
19, F	0.28	0.69	−1.26
21, R	0.11	0.81	0.23
21, F	0.11	0.81	0.16

Note: Populations: Reference: $N(0,1)$; Focal: $N(-.83,1.06)$.

case, the value of SIB for item 20 is 3.84, well above the critical value of about 2 (Muraki & Engelhard, 1989). The values of SIB for the other four items—the anchor for IRT-LR procedures—are all less than one, indicating that although there is DIF for item 20, there is no evidence of DIF for the other four items. As in the previous section, we use the unweighted average of the b-differences as δ; that produces an estimate of the mean for the focal population of $-.83$, which is fairly similar to that obtained with the four-item anchor with MULTILOG.

Limited-Information IRT-LR

The model implemented in LISCOMP (Muthén, 1987) is not really appropriate for these data, because it includes only the two-parameter normal ogive model. Although LISCOMP effectively fits item response curves, the trace lines for the correct response are required to have (left) lower asymptotes of zero; that is unlikely to represent the data from multiple-choice items well, due to the effects of guessing. We report the results obtained applying the limited-information IRT-LR procedure to these data for the sake of completeness, and to illustrate the effects of model mis-specification.

The parameter estimates for the SAT sentence completion data obtained with LISCOMP are shown in Table 4.11. There are no c parameters; the model is the two-parameter normal ogive, as described in the preceding section. Using the facilities of LISCOMP to impose equality constraints on the parameters, the same basic arrangement of the analysis was used as with MULTILOG: Items 16, 17, 19, and 21 served as an anchor, with their parameters constrained to be the same for both the focal and reference groups. The two parameters of item 20 (λ and τ) were estimated separately for the data from the focal and reference samples. The goodness-of-fit statistic was $G^2(17) = 75$; this value indicates a substantially

TABLE 4.11
LISCOMP Parameter Estimates
for Five SAT Sentence Completion Items

Item	c	$\dfrac{\lambda}{\sqrt{1-\lambda^2}}$	$\dfrac{\tau}{\lambda}$
20, R		0.69	−0.90
20, F		0.56	−0.43
16		0.70	−1.85
17		0.54	−1.79
19		0.55	−1.73
21		0.68	−0.03

Note: Populations: Reference: $N(0,1)$; Focal: $N(-.71,1)$.

worse fit to the data than that obtained with MULTILOG. The model does not fit as well because it ignores the substantial effects of guessing.

If we proceed (regardless) with the tests of DIF, we find that the goodness-of-fit statistic increases to $G^2(18) = 80$ when we constrain $\lambda_F = \lambda_R$; the one degree-of-freedom test for H:$\lambda_F = \lambda_R$ is $G^2(1) = 5$, $p < .05$. And when we constrain $\tau_F = \tau_R$, the goodness-of-fit statistic increases to $G^2(19) = 168$ and the one degree-of-freedom test for H:$\tau_F = \tau_R$ is $G^2(1) = 88$, $p < .001$. If we ignore the lack of fit due to guessing, the limited-information IRT-LR analysis confirms DIF for item 20.

At first glance, the test statistics seem to agree with those produced using the general IRT-LR procedure (MULTILOG). Both analyses indicate significant differences between both slopes and thresholds for the two groups. However, inspection of the estimates in Tables 4.9 and 4.11 reveals a problem: The limited-information IRT-LR analysis provides estimates in which the slope parameter is smaller for the focal group, whereas general IRT-LR analysis included a significantly larger slope for the focal group. Inspection of the trace lines themselves reveals the source of the discrepancy; the two-parameter normal ogive trace lines (from LISCOMP) are shown as thin lines along with the 3-PL trace lines (from MULTILOG) in Fig. 4.2. Although it has an asymptote at zero, the two-parameter normal ogive trace line for the reference group approximates the 3-PL curve well above $\theta = -1.5$; that region includes most of the data for that group. However, the 3-PL curve for the focal group is sharply sigmoid just below $\theta = 0$, where most of the data from that group lie; no two-parameter normal ogive can approximate that well. The fitted two-parameter curve has a very low slope, passing first under, then over, then under the 3-PL curve. The effect of the model mis-specification is to confuse the effects of guessing with the slope; instead of the 3-PL model's guessing-and-a-steep-slope, the two-parameter normal ogive's approximation is no-guessing-and-a-shallow-slope. And the approximation is not very good.

Further comparison of the parameter estimates in Table 4.11 with those in Tables 4.9 and 4.10 shows pervasive effects of the shift of guessing into the slope and threshold parameters. All of the LISCOMP slope estimates are much lower than those produced for the 3-PL model (by either MULTILOG or BIMAIN), and all of the LISCOMP thresholds are lower as well. The two-parameter normal ogive model must express guessing as either a low slope, or a low threshold (easiness), or both.

As we saw in the preceding section on the spelling data, the limited-information IRT-LR procedure implemented in LISCOMP performed well for DIF detection in a situation in which its model was appropriate—where there was no guessing. However, the procedure does not handle multiple-choice data, with guessing, well. Muthén, Shavelson et al. (1988) reported using LISCOMP for item factor analysis of multiple-choice items, using guessing-corrected tetrachoric correlations obtained using TESTFACT (Wilson et al., 1987) as input. However, Muthén, Shavelson et al. used unweighted least squares (ULS) estimation; ULS does not provide the χ^2 statistics necessary for a DIF detection study. A parallel approach to DIF detection would require guessing-corrected estimates of the sample thresholds, as well as the tetrachoric correlations; and all of those data would have to be constructed in such a way as to give a positive-definite weight matrix so the GLS procedure could be used and the goodness-of-fit statistics computed. It is not clear at this writing that all of that can be done.

Loglinear IRT-LR

If the two-parameter normal ogive model is inappropriate for the SAT sentence completion data, the loglinear IRT model (as implemented in LOGIMO, for instance [Kelderman & Steen, 1988]) is doubly inappropriate, because it involves only the one-parameter logistic (Rasch, 1960) model. The Rasch model requires the trace lines for the correct response to have lower asymptotes of zero and equal slopes; neither of those conditions seem to be met by the sentence completion data. As was the case with the limited-information approach, we report the results obtained applying the loglinear IRT-LR procedure to these data for the sake of completeness, and to further illustrate the effects of model misspecification.

Using the facilities of LOGIMO to impose equality constraints on the parameters, the same basic arrangement of the analysis was used as with MULTILOG and LISCOMP: Items 16, 17, 19, and 21 served as an anchor, with their parameters constrained to be the same for both the focal and reference groups. The threshold for item 20 was estimated separately for the data from the two groups. The goodness-of-fit statistic is $G^2(47) = 223$; this value indicates a substantially worse fit to the data than that obtained with the more complex models. The Rasch model is simply inappropriate for these data.

If we proceed (regardless) with the tests of DIF, we find that the goodness-of-fit statistic increases to $G^2(48) = 340$ when we constrain $\beta_F = \beta_R$; the one degree-of-freedom test for H: $\beta_F = \beta_R$ is $G^2(1) = 117, p < .001$. The parameter estimates for the SAT sentence completion data obtained with LOGIMO are shown in Table 4.12. There are no a or c parameters. The threshold parameters are shown in the form $u_0 - u_1$; the overall location of the item parameters is not only arbitrary, it is difficult to establish in the loglinear context. Unlike the other three procedures discussed here, the loglinear analysis does not explicitly include the mean of the reference population as a (fixed) parameter; the form of the population distribution is unspecified and its location is not clearly defined in terms of the parameters. It happens, for these data, that the scale established by $u_0 - u_1$ is quite similar to LISCOMP's normal ogive scale, so we tabulated the parameters in that form to show the basic similarity of the results to the other (no-guessing) analysis.

TABLE 4.12
LOGIMO Parameter Estimates
for Five SAT Sentence Completion Items

Item	c	a	$u_0 - u_1$
20, R			−0.73
20, F			−0.21
16			−1.86
17			−1.43
19			−1.40
21			0.25

Note: Populations: ?

Discussion: 3-PL DIF Detection

A summary of the tests of DIF for item 20 is shown in Table 4.13. Among the four DIF detection procedures considered in this chapter, only the general IRT-LR procedure (implemented in MULTILOG) is capable of providing tests of differential guessing (different c parameters), and differential slopes (different a parameters) after suitably correcting for guessing. The IRT-D^2 procedure could, in principle, provide parallel tests; but these are not currently implemented in BIMAIN. It happens that item 20 exhibits no c-DIF, but some a-DIF; other items may show other patterns, and those could be of interest to the data analyst.

Regardless of the violation of their various assumptions, all four procedures provide strong evidence of DIF for item 20. This is, in itself, interesting; we chose to analyze item 20 because Green et al. (1989) reported that it showed differential *distractor* functioning (DDF), and therefore they concluded that the item functioned differently for their three samples. Green et al. did not consider the correct responses in their analyses; we have here confirmed that the item also exhibits substantial DIF. In the following section, we integrate our analysis of DIF with DDF, to form an analysis of DAF: differential alternative functioning.

TABLE 4.13
Test Statistics for the SAT Sentence Completion Items:
Anchor: Items 16, 17, 19, and 21; Studied item: 20

	MULTILOG	LISCOMP	BIMAIN	LOGIMO
Anchor F = R, plus . . .				
. . . Item 20 parameters F ≠ R	$G^2(43) = 111$			
H_0: $c_{F,20} = c_{R,20}$	$G^2(1) = 0$			
. . . $a_{F,20} \neq a_{R,20}$; $b_{F,20} \neq b_{R,20}$	$G^2(44) = 111$	$G^2(17) = 75$		
H_0: $a_{F,20} = a_{R,20}$	$G^2(1) = 13$	$G^2(1) = 5$		
. . . $b_{F,20} \neq b_{R,20}$	$G^2(45) = 124$	$G^2(18) = 80$		$G^2(47) = 223$
H_0: $b_{F,20} = b_{R,20}$	$G^2(1) = 96$	$G^2(1) = 88$	$SIB^2 = 15$	$G^2(1) = 117$
. . . Item 20 parameters F = R	$G^2(46) = 220$	$G^2(19) = 168$		$G^2(48) = 340$

EXTENSIONS

Using the Multiple-Choice Model to Detect Differential Alternative Functioning (DAF)

If an item exhibits DIF, it follows that different proportions of examinees in different groups respond incorrectly; on a test composed of multiple-choice items, that means they select one of the incorrect alternatives, or *distractors*. Might differential alternative- or distractor-choice be informative about the reasons for groups' differences underlying DIF? A number of researchers have said it might be so, and some have described analysis directed toward the analysis of alternative-choice. For instance, Schmitt and Dorans (1988) used *standardized distractor analysis,* a variant of the standardization technique, to understand instances of DIF appearing on SAT items.

Might differential alternative-choice be interesting in its own right, as we seek to understand the responses of examinees to test items? Green et al. (1989) described the idea as follows: "Some interesting clues about group differences in the testing process are afforded by the particular incorrect responses that people make to test items. If different groups prefer different incorrect responses to an item, often called foils or distractors, then the item probably means something different to the different groups. Items that have different meanings to different groups would seem to be biased in a very fundamental sense" (p. 147).

Green et al. (1989) described a procedure, closely related to standardization methods, for detecting differential distractor functioning (DDF), and presented results obtained with their method when used with a form of the verbal SAT. Considering self-reported White, Black, and Hispanic groups, they found that 14 of the 85 items showed significant DDF. Item 20, considered in the preceding section, produced the largest value of their test statistic.

In the context of item response theory, we have proposed that the multiple-choice model might be used to provide more informative analysis of the structure of DIF (Thissen, Steinberg, & Fitzpatrick, 1989). In this section, we use the multiple-choice model (Thissen & Steinberg, 1984) in the context of a general IRT-LR analysis, comparing the alternative choices by Black and White examinees for item 20. Our analysis differs somewhat from that of Green et al. (1989), in that we consider differential *alternative* functioning (DAF): We fit trace lines to all of the alternatives (correct and incorrect) of the multiple-choice item; if those trace lines differ between groups, the item is said to exhibit DAF.

For a multiple-choice item i with m_i alternatives, the multiple-choice model includes a trace line for each alternative k defined as

$$T_i(k) = \frac{\exp(a_k\theta + c_k) + d_k \exp(a_0\theta + c_0)}{\sum_{h=0}^{m_i} \exp(a_h\theta + c_h)}, \qquad (29)$$

in which there are:

$(m_i + 1)$ alternative-discrimination parameters a_k,
$(m_i + 1)$ alternative-intercept parameters c_k, and
m_i alternative-guessing parameters d_k.[6]

The alternatives $k = 1, \ldots, m_i$ represent the response alternatives for the item; the response category $k = 0$ is a latent response category, in which the respondents *don't know* (DK), but choose one of the available observable responses (with probability d_k) by guessing. Identifiability of the model requires that one linear constraint must be imposed on each of the sets of parameters; we usually use the constraints

$$\sum_{k=0}^{m_i} a_k = \sum_{k=0}^{m_i} c_k = 0 \tag{30}$$

and

$$\sum_{k=1}^{m_i} d_k = 1. \tag{31}$$

After the identifiability constraints are imposed, there are a total of $3m_i - 1$ free parameters for each item: 14 for the five-alternative multiple-choice format. For a detailed treatment of maximum likelihood estimation of the parameters of the multiple-choice model, see Thissen and Steinberg (1984); for a more extended discussion of an application of the model and the interpretation of the parameters, see Thissen et al. (1989).

Here we illustrate the use of the multiple-choice model for DAF detection for SAT Form 6K, item 20, described in the preceding section. Using the previously described sample of 33,376 White examinees (the reference [R] group) and 2,962 Black examinees (the focal [F] group), now cross-classified into two 5^5 tables according to their responses to item 20 and the four anchor items, we followed the (completely) general IRT-LR procedure using MULTILOG (Thissen, 1988): We fitted the model to the data for both groups with different parameters for item 20 for the focal and reference groups; then we fitted the model under the constraint that the item parameters for item 20 must be the same for the two groups. The likelihood ratio test of the equality of the item 20 parameters is $G^2(14) = 145$.[7] We conclude, in agreement with the results ob-

---

[6]Note that the parameters denoted c in the multiple-choice model are not the same as the c-parameters of the 3-PL model.

[7]In this case, there is no overall goodness-of-fit test of the model; the two 5^5 tables each contain 3,125 cells, and there are many observed zeros and small expected values. Thus, there is no test against the general multinomial alternative.

TABLE 4.14
Parameter Estimates for the Multiple-Choice Model
for SAT Sentence Completion Item 20

Reference Group			*Response Category*			
Parameter	DK	A	B	C	D*	E
a	−4.42	1.00	0.57	0.37	2.03	0.45
c	−4.51	0.72	1.17	−0.20	2.98	−0.17
d		0.11	0.21	0.18	0.35	0.13
Focal Group			*Response Category*			
Parameter	DK	A	B	C	D*	E
a	−1.79	1.65	1.20	−2.07	3.27	−2.26
c	−0.21	1.01	1.14	−1.89	2.52	−2.57
d		0.14	0.19	0.14	0.40	0.13

tained by Green et al. (1989), that the distribution of response-alternative choices
is different for the two groups.

The estimated multiple-choice model parameters for the two groups for item
20 are shown in Table 4.14, and the alternative trace lines are in Fig. 4.3. In the
panel for alternative D (the keyed alternative) in Fig. 4.3, we see essentially the
same DIF found in the 3-PL analysis in the preceding section: The item is more
difficult and discriminating for the focal group. The trace lines for D from the
multiple-choice model also suggest different guessing levels for the two groups.

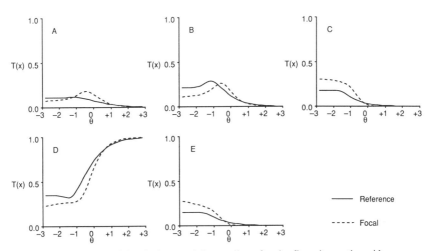

FIG. 4.3.   Multiple-choice model trace lines for the five alternatives (A,
B, C, D, E) for SAT sentence completion item 20. The solid lines are for
the reference group; the dashed lines are for the focal group.

To some extent, this may be due to the more sophisticated model for guessing incorporated in the multiple-choice model; however, it also occurs in a region of the trace lines beyond most of the data, so it may also be unreliable extrapolation.

The trace lines for the distractors show that reference-group examinees of relatively low proficiency (θ) are more attracted to alternative B, whereas focal-group examinees of relatively low proficiency are more likely to choose alternatives C and E, and there is some differential attractiveness of alternative A for focal-group examinees of moderate θ. The curves in Fig. 4.3 correspond closely to the plots of alternative-choice against raw summed score shown in Figure 2 of Green et al. (1989). It is not at all clear to us why item 20 shows such prominent DAF. Green et al. found that DDF was unusually concentrated in the sentence completion parts of the test; and item 20 is an example of a kind of semantically peculiar sentence that may only appear on difficult tests like the SAT. An interesting research question might be whether some (social/ethnic/linguistic) groups are better than others at handling the occurrence of semantic oddities on such tests; pursuit of this idea would require consideration of many more items like item 20. Or the effect may be something we do not understand at all; there are many of those in psychology. The analysis of DAF provides the item analyst or test researcher with a more powerful microscope with which to examine the structure of the responses of different groups to test items.

There are also loglinear IRT models for items with multiple response alternatives (see Kelderman, 1988); thus, there is loglinear IRT-LR DAF detection using those models and loglinear estimation systems such as LOGIMO (Kelderman & Steen, 1988). And the general model implemented in LISCOMP (Muthén, 1987) provides for multiple (ordered) response alternatives, so there is limited-information IRT-LR DAF detection using LISCOMP. Neither of these approaches is suitable for application to the SAT sentence completion data, because neither class of models accommodates guessing. However, in other applications, such as some of those discussed in the next section, one or both of these alternative procedures may be useful.

The Use of DIF Detection in Educational and Psychological Research

The development of DIF detection techniques has been primarily motivated by the desire to understand (and eliminate) bias in psychological tests. However, the recent change in nomenclature (from *item bias* to *differential item functioning*) should serve to remind us that DIF detection is, more neutrally, the detection of any difference between any groups in their responses to any kind of item. Experimental research may be designed in such a way that the outcome of different treatments (e.g., training or instructional manipulations) is differential functioning of prespecified items. Several studies using DIF as the measurable experimental outcome have been reported: Tatsuoka, Linn, Tatsuoka, and Yamamoto (1988) described research in which the Mantel–Haenszel approach to DIF detection was used to evaluate consequences on item performance for different instructional groups. Tatsuoka et al. presented a very clear argument for the usefulness of DIF detection techniques in the purely experimental context. Kelderman and Macready (1988) reported a very similar study as an illustration of the usefulness of the loglinear IRT-LR approach to DIF detection; although Kelderman and Macready's presentation of the material indicated that they were using the experimental research to validate the DIF detection procedure, the entire analysis could equally well be viewed as using DIF detection to evaluate the outcome of the different instructional procedures used in the experiment. Ellis (1989) described the use of IRT-D^2 DIF detection in the experimental evaluation of test translations.

Curiously enough, the hypotheses in the study reported by Tatsuoka et al. (1988) specified that there should be no DIF for a subset of the items—thus, the hypotheses specified an anchor. The Mantel–Haenszel analysis by Tatsuoka et al. did not use the anchoring aspects of their hypothesis; all of the items were evaluated evenhandedly for DIF. Any of the three IRT-LR procedures described here could have used the anchor as specified by the theory behind the research, and would probably have provided more powerful tests of DIF for the items that were hypothesized to exhibit DIF as a consequence of the experimental manipulations. The anchored IRT-LR DIF detection procedures are not only most suitable for the evaluation of experimental outcomes; they may provide the means to do experimental research in contexts not heretofore considered.

CONCLUDING REMARKS, AND A LOOK TO THE FUTURE

Although all of the DIF detection procedures discussed here involve tests of the significance of the difference between item parameters (and thereby, trace lines) for two or more groups, the procedures differ in some respects. Being different, they have various strengths and weaknesses; what are those strengths and weaknesses, and what do they imply about the current usefulness of the methods and needed future developments? We consider each of the procedures in turn:

General IRT-LR, as Implemented in MULTILOG

The only relatively rigid assumption, enforced by the current version of the program, not underlying theory, is that the population distributions must be assumed Gaussian. The greatest strength of this procedure is also its greatest weakness: It can do anything. As currently implemented in MULTILOG, this approach may be used to test the significance of the difference between two (or more) groups on any IRT-model parameters, or any combination of parameters. This flexibility is achieved at substantial cost: Each hypothesis tested requires two complete "runs," to obtain the estimates and loglikelihoods for the model reflecting the constraint imposed by the null hypothesis and the model without that constraint. And the nature of the hypotheses tested requires that the user specify an anchor—a subset of the items that are constrained to have equal parameters (and therefore, identical trace lines) for all groups. The whole process is therefore both labor-intensive for the data analyst and computationally intensive.

At present, this probably implies that general IRT-LR, as implemented in MULTILOG using marginal maximum likelihood estimation, is best suited for research settings, testing hypotheses about DIF in planned (or even designed) contexts where the nature of the hypotheses is well-specified in advance. Without further work on both the automation of the process and its computational speed, it is probably not practical for general "sweeps" through item pools to determine which items might exhibit DIF; for that purpose, consider the Mantel–Haenszel or standardization procedures discussed by Dorans and Holland in Chapter 3 of this volume, or the IRT-D^2 procedure incorporated in BIMAIN. For the future, it is likely that algorithms specifically optimized to use the general IRT-LR procedure for many items, possibly endowed with some degree of artificial intelligence to choose hypotheses, may be developed. We endorse future work in that area. The general IRT-LR approach offers a clear approach to future work in the detection and analysis of DAF.

Loglinear IRT-LR, as Implemented in SPSS-X LOGLINEAR and LOGIMO (or Any Other General Loglinear Program)

The relatively rigid assumption enforced by any version of this approach is that some Rasch-family model is appropriate for the data. The benefit accrued from the assumption that the trace lines are equal-slope logistic functions is that only minimal assumptions about the form of the underlying population distributions are required: Some valid population distribution must *exist;* criteria for its existence were given by Cressie and Holland (1983) in the form of moment inequalities that must be met by some of the parameters. Therefore, loglinear IRT-LR could be characterized as a limited-trace-line/free-population implementation of IRT-LR and the implementation in MULTILOG is a system for relatively free trace-lines and a limited class of population distributions.

The steps in the loglinear IRT-LR procedure parallel those for the general IRT-LR procedures: Each hypothesis tested requires two complete runs to obtain the estimates and loglikelihoods for the model reflecting the constraint imposed by the null hypothesis and the model without that constraint, and the nature of the hypotheses tested requires that the user specify the anchor. The process remains both labor-intensive and computationally intensive; but it is less computationally intensive than the general-trace-line version because parameter estimation is somewhat less burdensome, especially in a computer program optimized for the item-response situation, like LOGIMO.

The loglinear models do not account for guessing or differing discrimination among the items; therefore, loglinear procedures are not at their best with commonly used multiple-choice tests. However, in the future, computerized testing offers the possibility of more widespread use of free-response tests; in a well-constructed test with items in a free-response format, guessing may be sharply limited and discrimination may vary little among items. In the context of such tests, the loglinear procedures exhibit very desirable properties. Algorithms specifically optimized to use the loglinear procedure to examine many items for DIF, possibly endowed with some degree of artificial intelligence to choose hypotheses (as suggested previously), may ease the computational burden.

Limited-Information IRT-LR, as Implemented in LISCOMP

The assumptions of this approach are that the population distributions are Gaussian, that guessing is minimal, and that there is sufficient information in the data for the weight of the analysis to rest on the first- and second-order summary statistics. Effectively, this last assumption means that the samples must be larger than for any of the other three procedures considered here.

The voracious appetite for data of the GLS procedure actually works out quite smoothly in presenting alternatives for practical work. Although the other three procedures considered here (all based on full-information MML parameter estimation) do not *need* as much data as limited-information GLS, when there is a great deal of information—a very large sample size—the MML procedures become computationally burdensome. In contrast, although GLS *needs* a great deal of data, the effect of an increase in sample size on the amount of computation is very slight. So the GLS and MML procedures fill complementary niches: If you have moderate sample sizes, MML (in one of the three other procedures discussed here) will be fine, and there may not be sufficient information for GLS; but if you have very large sample sizes, the MML procedures may become too costly, and GLS may give useful results at much lower cost.

A unique advantage at this time of the GLS procedure (in LISCOMP) is that it can handle hypothesis tests about DIF in the context of a multidimensional test. A weakness of the GLS procedure is that guessing is not modeled. Future research is required for the integration of guessing-parameter estimation in the context of multidimensional models in general.

IRT-D², as Implemented in BIMAIN

The only relatively rigid assumption enforced by the current version of the program is that any DIF must be reflected in differences between the b parameters; no other parameters may be tested. The implementation of the MML algorithm in BIMAIN permits non-Gaussian population distributions; but such distributions must be prespecified—they are not estimated from the data. The greatest strength of this procedure is its speed: Only a single MML estimation of the parameters is required; the whole process takes approximately as long as a BILOG (Mislevy & Bock, 1986) item calibration for the same data. This is the only one of the four algorithms considered in this chapter that may be useful in routine test development, for sweeps through item calibration data, evaluating DIF for each item in a pool in turn before it may be included in an operational test.

Like the other procedures, IRT-D^2 in BIMAIN has a strength that is also a weakness: It automatically tests DIF for every item in the test. That is a strength in the operational test-development context, where a large item pool may need to be evaluated for items with potential DIF. It is a weakness in the research context, where specific hypotheses exist; such specific hypotheses may be tested with more power using any of the other three procedures discussed in this chapter. A related problem with IRT-D^2 as implemented in BIMAIN is its need for a relatively ad hoc method for "adjustment" of the scales of the reference and focal groups, using some estimate of the location of $b_F - b_R$. Different adjustments give different results. Future work is required to establish the optimal procedure for practical use.

Another weakness of this procedure is one it shares with the standard technique for item-by-item evaluation of item pools (Mantel–Haenszel): It is primarily sensitive to DIF evident in the b parameter, or marginal difficulty. However, the procedure could straightforwardly be generalized to provide similarly constructed tests of the differences between slopes (and even guessing levels), or multivariate tests of DIF in any two or three parameters of the three-parameter logistic. Future development along those lines may make the approach implemented in BIMAIN most practical for large-scale test development settings.

The "Designated Anchor"

It is common practice in large-scale test-development settings to use all of the other items in a test, experimental section, or tryout form as the anchor when procedures such as Mantel–Haenszel or standardization are used to evaluate each item in turn for DIF. The most significant obstacle to the use of any of the three IRT-LR procedures in such settings is the computational burden involved in recomputing the MML or GLS estimates for the long anchor twice for each item, to obtain the values of the loglikelihood used in the test statistic. However, we have illustrated here (and in Thissen et al., 1988, for general IRT-LR as implemented in MULTILOG) that the IRT-LR procedures may perform acceptably with an anchor comprised of a very few items. In the examples in this chapter, we used three- and four-item anchors; in the analysis of artificial data reported in Thissen et al. we considered the use of one- and four-item anchors.

Aside from the computational burden, there is also a perplexing data-analytic problem involved in the use of all of the other items (whatever they may be) as the anchor in DIF detection: We cannot be sure that the other items do not themselves function differently between groups. This problem has led to suggestions that the anchor be iteratively *purified* (Lord, 1980, p. 220): Items showing DIF with the whole test used as an anchor are removed, and the process is repeated until DIF appears to be gone. It is not really clear that such a procedure results in no DIF; it may simply result in a test with *majority rule* DIF, where the average level of DIF in the original test, experimental section, or tryout form is made indistinguishable from the group-mean difference.

Here we introduce the concept of the *designated anchor* in an attempt to solve both of those problems simultaneously, and permit the use of IRT-LR procedures for DIF detection in routine test construction at reasonable cost. The idea is that some small number of items (in the range from three to about six) would be selected for each test section, to serve the sole purpose of being the DIF detection anchor. After extensive data analytic and expert review, these few items would be declared free of DIF. Then these few items would be included in the data-collection design for pretesting all new items for the test, for the sole purpose of being used as the anchor in the evaluation of each of the new items for DIF. Any of the three IRT-LR procedures described in this chapter could easily be run for the dozens (or even hundreds!) of items involved in large-scale pretesting, if the anchor was fixed and short. This procedure could be used to produce a highly standard test of DIF for each new item among the routinely computed item analysis statistics. The savings of computational time from the use of a short designated anchor would also contribute to the practicality of DAF detection, discussed in the preceding section.

The selection of the designated anchor would involve an explicit decision about the relative means of various population subgroups on the particular test or subtest involved. This selection task could be difficult. However, current large-scale DIF detection methods that simply use any collection of items as the anchor, or that iteratively purify the test, are similarly making a determination of the difference between the population means; it is just that they do so in a much less thoughtful manner than is proposed here. How would we select the designated anchor? To maximize validity, or by using an explicitly specified domain reference. We would choose the focal group- and reference group-means that make the test most valid.

In the case of the spelling test from which we obtained our introductory example (*girder*), selection of the three-item designated anchor was made relatively easy by the nature of the test. The 100 words comprising the original test were a random sample from a standard word list. The word list was the item domain, and the words in the test were a simple random sample from that domain. The average score on the test is interpreted as reflecting true population differences between males and females in their proficiency at spelling words such as those on the list. There was no difference in scores on the entire 100-item test between males and females; thus, we concluded that there was no mean difference in spelling proficiency for males and females. We simply chose a three-item anchor that also produced a negligible difference between the male and female means.

Is the selection of a designated anchor really practical for large-scale testing programs? How few (or many) items are required for the designated anchor to give the statistical tests adequate power? These are questions that would have to be answered before such a procedure could be implemented; the first question by data analysts and subject-matter experts involved in the construction of each test and the use of its results, and the second question by statistical analysis or, failing that, simulation.

Conclusion

In this chapter we have described four contemporary procedures that implement Lord's (1977, 1980) suggestion that, within the framework of item response theory, differential item functioning should be evaluated using statistical tests of hypotheses involving the difference between item parameters for reference and focal groups. The four approaches we have discussed (general IRT-LR, loglinear IRT-LR, limited-information IRT-LR, and IRT-D^2) all provide asymptotically optimal parameter estimates, and statistically sound tests of the hypotheses involved in DIF. Each of the four procedures implements estimation and hypothesis testing for a distinct subset of item response models. Because different models, and therefore different approaches to statistical estimation and hypothesis testing, are appropriate for different sets of item response data, the choice among these four procedures must be made within the specific data-analytic context. In the illustrations presented here, we have shown that all four procedures perform as expected when the model is appropriate for the data. And we have illustrated the extension of the general IRT-LR procedure to the detection of differential alternative functioning, and observed that DAF detection is also possible in some contexts using the other three procedures. The analysis of DAF substantially increases the detail with which an item's performance within different groups may be examined.

We have also noted that the usefulness of DIF detection is not limited to screening potential test items to reduce test bias; hypotheses that DIF exists may follow from experimental research questions in a variety of contexts. DIF detection procedures have been used to evaluate the outcome of experimental manipulations, and we anticipate that they will be increasingly used in that role in the future. The focused nature of the hypotheses tested in the approaches described here, using the parameters of item response models, makes these procedures clear favorites for application in the context of experimental data analysis.

ACKNOWLEDGEMENTS

We thank R. D. Bock and E. Muraki for making available the BIMAIN computer program, H. Kelderman for LOGIMO, and B. Muthén for LISCOMP. We are grateful to N. Burton and others of the SAT program staff for making available to us the data used in the second illustration, and we thank ETS for its support of this research. R. D. Bock, P. Holland, and H. Kelderman provided helpful comments on an earlier draft, for which we are grateful; of course, any flaws that remain are our own. This research was also supported in part by NIMH Training Grant No. PHS T32 MH 15789-10 while L. Steinberg held a postdoctoral fellowship in the Program in Measurement, Department of Sociology, Indiana University.

APPENDIX: HOW TO DO IT
(OR, MORE EXACTLY, WHAT WE DID)

A frequently asked question is, Just exactly how is this done? Because the various computational procedures summarized briefly in this chapter are all implemented in widely available computer programs, a practical answer to this question takes the form of a description of the data and control-line files for the various programs. In this appendix, we reproduce the data and control-line files we used to compute the parameter estimates and test statistics for our first example (considering DIF for spelling *girder*). An advantage of this form of presentation is clarity. However, a disadvantage is that it is considerably less timeless than the presentation in the form of equations in the main body of the chapter; all of these computer programs frequently change versions, and, by the time you read this, it is quite possible that these instructions will no longer function exactly as they did when we used them. It should also be remembered that newer (and often better) computer programs are continually introduced, and superior alternatives to these programs may be available.

MULTILOG

The input-data file for MULTILOG (version 5.11) follows; the item responses (1 = correct, 0 = incorrect) for the four items are in columns 1–4 for the males (the first 16 lines of the file) and 5–8 for the females (the second 16 lines of the file). This arrangement permits MULTILOG to refer to the responses of the males as items 1–4 and those of the females as items 5–8, and impose (or not) any desired equality constraints between the item parameters for the two groups. In columns 10–11, the males are coded 90 and the females are coded 09; the frequency for each response pattern is in columns 13–14. See the *MULTILOG User's Guide* (Thissen, 1988) for further information concerning this arrangement of the data.

0000	90	22
0001	90	10
1000	90	30
1001	90	27
0100	90	13
0101	90	14
0010	90	1
0011	90	1
1100	90	24
1101	90	54
1010	90	5
1011	90	8
0110	90	1
0111	90	8
1110	90	10
1111	90	57
0000	09	29
0001	09	7
1000	09	50
1001	09	30
0100	09	15
0101	09	4
0010	09	6
0011	09	0
1100	09	67
1101	09	63
1010	09	12
1011	09	10
0110	09	2
0111	09	6
1110	09	22
1111	09	51

After the data are available in a file, command lines for MULTILOG are entered using the command preprocessor INFORLOG. The INFORLOG exchange follows, setting up the computation of the estimates and G^2 for the model in which the anchor items (1–3) are constrained to have equal parameters for the reference and focal groups, but item 4 (the studied item) is unconstrained. The user's input is reproduced in **bold.** See the *MULTILOG User's Guide* (Thissen, 1988) for the definitions of the command lines and keywords used here.

```
-INFORLOG-----FOR MULTIPLE CATEGORICAL ITEM RESPONSE DATA----VERSION 2.12--

    ENTER TITLE LINE
    "Girder" dif; 3-item anchor (items 5,4,25), 1PL
    ENTER >PROBLEM (WITH OR WITHOUT ARGUMENTS), FOLLOWED BY >TEST
    LINE(S), FOLLOWED BY ANY OTHER COMMAND LINES (>ESTIMATE, >FIX, >EQUAL,
    >START, >SAVE, >LABELS, >TGROUPS, >PRIOR, >TMATRIX); >END TO FINISH.
    >PRO  RA  PA  NI=8  NG=2  NP=32
    >TEST ALL L1;
    >EQUAL BJ  IT=(5,6,7)  WI=(1,2,3);
    >END;
    HOW MANY RESPONSE CODES IN RAW DATA?
    2
    ENTER CODES 2A1
    01
    ENTER VECTOR OF CORRECT RESPONSES,  79A1
    11111111
    IS ANY CODE MISSING?  (Y OR N)
    N
    ENTER FORMAT FOR DATA
    (8A1,1X,2F1.0,F3.0)
    MULTILOG INPUT WRITTEN ON FILE 10
```

At this point, MULTILOG is executed, producing the results shown in Table 4.2. To obtain the value of G^2 for the model in which the bs for item 4 are constrained to be equal, INFORLOG is rerun to add the constraint; that interaction is as follows:

```
--INFORLOG-----FOR MULTIPLE CATEGORICAL ITEM RESPONSE DATA----VERSION 2.12--

    ENTER TITLE LINE
    Constraining "girder" to be equal for the sexes
    ENTER >PROBLEM (WITH OR WITHOUT ARGUMENTS), FOLLOWED BY >TEST
    LINE(S), FOLLOWED BY ANY OTHER COMMAND LINES (>ESTIMATE, >FIX, >EQUAL,
    >START, >SAVE, >LABELS, >TGROUPS, >PRIOR, >TMATRIX); >END TO FINISH.
    >PRO OLD;
    >EQUAL BJ  IT=(4,8);
    >END;
    MULTILOG INPUT WRITTEN ON FILE 10
```

Then MULTILOG is run a second time.

LISCOMP

For LISCOMP (MS-DOS version 1.1), the following two files contained the data, entered as response-pattern frequencies; the frequencies are assumed to be in the increasing binary order of the patterns taken-as-binary-numbers, without the patterns themselves:

SPELLM.DAT contained the data for the males:
    22 10   1   1 13 14   1   8 30 27   5   8 24 54 10 57

SPELLF.DAT contained the data for the females:
    29   7   6   0   15   4   2   6 50 30 12 10 67 63 22 51

With LISCOMP, as with MULTILOG (in the preceding section), the program is run twice; the first run provides the parameter estimates for the DIF model (with the parameters—here only the threshold τ_4) for the studied item (item 4) unconstrained (different for the reference and focal groups). The following command file was used; for an explanation of the meaning and use of the command lines and keywords, see the *LISCOMP User's Guide* (Muthén, 1987).

```
TI GIRDER DIF, MALES
DA NO=285 IY=4 VT=DI NG=2
MO MO=SE P1 P3 NE=1 LY=FR PS=FI TA=FR AL=FI
EQ LY(1,1) LY(2,1) LY(3,1) LY(4,1)
VA 0.5 LY(1,1)
VA 1.0 PS(1,1)
OU WF ES ST ED RS SE TV
FP FO UN='SPELLM.DAT'
(16F3.0)
TI GIRDER DIF, FEMALES
DA NO=374 IY=4 VT=DI
MO MO=SE P1 P3 NE=1 LY=FR PS=FI TA=FR AL=FR
EQ LY(2,1,1) LY(1,1,1)
EQ LY(2,2,1) LY(1,2,1)
EQ LY(2,3,1) LY(1,3,1)
EQ LY(2,4,1) LY(1,4,1)
EQ TA(2,1) TA(1,1)
EQ TA(2,2) TA(1,2)
EQ TA(2,3) TA(1,3)
OU WF ES ST ED RS SE TV
FP FO UN='SPELLF.DAT'
(16F3.0)
```

After LISCOMP was run to obtain the parameter estimates summarized in Table 4.5, the following command file was used to set τ_4 equal for the reference and focal groups, and LISCOMP was run again to obtain the value of G^2 for the no-DIF model.

```
TI GIRDER CONSTRAINED EQUAL FOR BOTH SEXES, MALES
DA NO=285 IY=4 VT=DI NG=2
MO MO=SE P1 P3 NE=1 LY=FR PS=FI TA=FR AL=FI
EQ LY(1,1) LY(2,1) LY(3,1) LY(4,1)
VA 0.5 LY(1,1)
VA 1.0 PS(1,1)
OU WF ES ST ED RS SE TV
FP FO UN='SPELLM.DAT'
(16F3.0)
TI GIRDER CONSTRAINED EQUAL FOR BOTH SEXES, FEMALES
DA NO=374 IY=4 VT=DI
MO MO=SE P1 P3 NE=1 LY=FR PS=FI TA=FR AL=FR
EQ LY(2,1,1) LY(1,1,1)
EQ LY(2,2,1) LY(1,2,1)
EQ LY(2,3,1) LY(1,3,1)
EQ LY(2,4,1) LY(1,4,1)
EQ TA(2,1) TA(1,1)
EQ TA(2,2) TA(1,2)
EQ TA(2,3) TA(1,3)
EQ TA(2,4) TA(1,4)
OU WF ES ST ED RS SE TV
FP FO UN='SPELLF.DAT'
(16F3.0)
```

SPSS-X LOGLINEAR

The data are in a file called SPELLT.DAT, which is reproduced here. The binary response patterns (columns 5–8) are not read by SPSS-X; they are in the file only for clarity of presentation. Within each sex (males and females; coded 1 and 2 in column 3) the response patterns are numbered 1–16; these numbers are read as the SPSS-variable PATTERN and used (in conjunction with the SPECIAL CONTRAST matrix to define the IRT model. (See Thissen & Mooney [1989] for a description of this and alternative constructions of the contrast matrix.) The observed zero for females, for response pattern 0011, is

replaced with .0001 because SPSS-X LOGLINEAR requires that all cell entries
be non-zero; the very small value has no noticeable effect on the results.

11	0000	22
21	0001	10
31	1000	30
41	1001	27
51	0100	13
61	0101	14
71	0010	1
81	0011	1
91	1100	24
101	1101	54
111	1010	5
121	1011	8
131	0110	1
141	0111	8
151	1110	10
161	1111	57
12	0000	29
22	0001	7
32	1000	50
42	1001	30
52	0100	15
62	0101	4
72	0010	6
82	0011	.0001
92	1100	67
102	1101	63
112	1010	12
122	1011	10
132	0110	2
142	0111	6
152	1110	22
162	1111	51

What follows is the input file for SPSS-X LOGLINEAR (version 3.1) used to produce the estimates and G^2 statistics for the conditional Rasch model. As with MULTILOG and LISCOMP, the parameters of the models are estimated twice, but that is done in a single run: The two DESIGN statements each produce a complete analysis. The first DESIGN statement, including SEX BY PATTERN (3), fits the model with different values of b_4 for the two groups (males and females); the second DESIGN statement fits the model with all of the bs constrained equal for the two groups. For information on the meaning of the control lines and keywords, see the *SPSS-X User's Guide, 3rd Edition* (1988). For a description of the interpretation of loglinear parameters as the Rasch (1960) model, see Thissen and Mooney (1989).

```
TITLE 'Spelling girder-dif, 4-5-25 anchor, Polynomial'
FILE HANDLE SPELL/NAME='SPELL.DAT'
DATA LIST FILE=SPELL/PATTERN 1-2 SEX 3 COUNT 9-13
WEIGHT BY COUNT
LOGLINEAR PATTERN(1,16) BY SEX(1,2)/
 PRINT=DEFAULT ESTIM DESIGN/
 CONTRAST (PATTERN) =SPECIAL(16*1,
          0,0,0,0,1,1,0,0,1,1,0,0,1,1,1,1,
          0,0,0,0,0,0,1,1,0,0,1,1,1,1,1,1,
          0,1,0,1,0,1,0,1,0,1,0,1,0,1,0,1,
          0,1,1,2,1,2,1,2,2,3,2,3,2,3,3,4,
          0,1,1,4,1,4,1,4,4,9,4,9,4,9,9,16,
          0,1,1,8,1,8,1,8,8,27,8,27,8,27,27,64,
          0,1,1,16,1,16,1,16,16,81,16,81,16,81,81,256,
                          128*0)/
    DESIGN=PATTERN(1) PATTERN(2) PATTERN(3) PATTERN(4)
           PATTERN(5) PATTERN(6) PATTERN(7) SEX BY PATTERN(3)
           SEX BY PATTERN(4) SEX BY PATTERN(5) SEX BY PATTERN(6)
           SEX BY PATTERN(7)/
    DESIGN=PATTERN(1) PATTERN(2) PATTERN(3) PATTERN(4)
           PATTERN(5) PATTERN(6) PATTERN(7)
           SEX BY PATTERN(4) SEX BY PATTERN(5) SEX BY PATTERN(6)
           SEX BY PATTERN(7)
    FINISH
```

LOGIMO

LOGIMO uses the same data file used in the SPSS-X example just shown, except that the .0001 entry for pattern 0011 for the females is replaced with its actual value of zero. As is the case with MULTILOG and LISCOMP, the program is run twice to obtain the estimates and goodness-of-fit statistics for the model with and without DIF. The input command-line file for LOGIMO for the model including DIF for the fourth item is reproduced here. The response pattern frequency is read in F2.0 format from columns 12–13; then, sex (1=male; 2=female) is read in I1 format from column 3, and (finally) the response patterns themselves are read in 4I1 format from columns 5–8. LOGIMO works with numbered variables; in this case, sex is variable *1*, items 1–4 are variables *2–5*, and the total raw score is variable *6*. Thus, on the MODEL line, interactions between variables *1* and *6* (sex and raw score) and *1* and *5* (sex and item 4) are specified. For further explanation of the various command lines and keywords used here, see *LOGIMO I: Loglinear Item Response Theory Modeling* (Kelderman & Steen, 1988).

```
TITLE GIRDER-DIF/MALES-FEMALES RUN WITH DIF
WEIGHT 2
FORMAT (11X,F2.0,T3,I1,1X,4I1)
DATAFILE SPELLT.DAT
NINPVAR 5
NSCORVAR 1
SCORING [2..5] 6 [1] 1
MODEL 2 [1,6] [1,5]
FIT
PEARSON 1 [1..5] WHOLE
FINISH
```

To obtain the parameter estimates and goodness-of-fit statistics for the model specifying no DIF for item 4, the input command file is exactly as shown, except that the interaction term [1,5] is deleted from the MODEL line.

```
TITLE GIRDER-DIF/MALES-FEMALES RUN WITH NO DIF
WEIGHT 2
FORMAT (11X,F2.0,T3,I1,1X,4I1)
DATAFILE SPELLT.DAT
NINPVAR 5
NSCORVAR 1
SCORING [2..5] 6 [1] 1
MODEL 1 [1,6]
FIT
PEARSON 1 [1..5] WHOLE
FINISH
```

BIMAIN

BIMAIN uses the same data file used in the LOGIMO example just shown. The input command-line file for BIMAIN reproduced here reads the index number (1–16; columns 1–2) in the data file as "ID" numbers. Sex (1=male; 2=female) is read in I1 format from column 3, then the response pattern frequency is read in F3.0 format from columns 12–13. Finally, the response patterns themselves are read in 4A1 format from columns 5–8. For an explanation of the various command lines and keywords used here, see *BIMAIN: A Program for Item Pool Maintenance in the Presence of Item Parameter Drift* (Muraki et al., 1987); we note that most of the command lines and keywords are also those used in BILOG (Mislevy & Bock, 1986).

```
MALE VS FEMALE        BIAS MODEL
SPELLING, GIRDER ITEM 4, OTHER 3 ITEMS 1-3
>GLOBAL DFNAME='SPELLT.DAT',DFDISP=2,NIDW=2,NPARM=1,NWGHT=3,LOGISTIC;
>LENGTH NITEMS=4;
>INPUT NTOT=4,FORM=2,BIAS;
>TEST TNAME=SPELL,ITEMS=(1(1)4);
>FORM1 LENGTH=4,ITEMS=(1(1)4);
>FORM2 LENGTH=4,ITEMS=(1(1)4);
(2A1,I1,T12,F2.0,T5,4A1)
>CALIB ADJ=1,NQPT=10,CYCLES=30,NEWTON=10;
```

5 Different DIFs: Comment on the Papers Read by Neil Dorans and David Thissen

R. Darrell Bock
The University of Chicago

It is a pleasure to compliment the authors on their excellent reviews of the methodology for detecting and estimating differential item functioning (DIF). They give a clear account of the three major techniques for studying DIF—standardization, the Mantel–Haenszel statistic, and comparisons of item response functions (IRT). Although the papers divide along the lines of nonparametric versus parametric approaches to data analysis, the authors are entirely fair in their respective positions. And in the context of the Scholastic Aptitude Test, which Dorans is assuming, these positions are not all that far apart. For a test containing such a large number of items as the SAT, the standardization and IRT approaches are essentially equivalent.

Test scores based on large numbers of homogeneous items locate respondents on the proficiency dimension with sufficient accuracy that the observed regression of item score on test score is essentially an item response function. If the number of respondents is large, which Dorans also assumes, the only possible inconsistency between the standardization and IRT methodology would lie in the failure of the response function assumed in IRT to adequately describe the observed regression. The IRT procedures are of course more demanding in that they attempt to describe all of the item regressions in terms of the same family of response functions. But considerable experience with fitting such functions by modern methods—marginal maximum likelihood (MML) estimation, in particular—has shown that if the IRT model is sufficiently general, satisfactory fit is almost always obtained. The relationships that Dorans and Holland show in Fig. 3.1 could easily be fit by the upper limb of a logistic function. In most cases, the entire range of the item regression can be fit by the three-parameter logistic model typically required for more difficult multiple-choice items.

115

There are some exceptions, but they can be dealt with. As pointed out by Samejima (1979), an item will sometimes have a plausible distractor that picks up positive misinformation on the part of some examinees. These items are the familiar "trick questions" that lead examinees of intermediate proficiency to choose a deceptive incorrect alternative. This results in an item response function that is nonmonotonic, with the probability of correct response between chance levels in the middle to low range of proficiency. At even lower ranges of proficiency the examinees tend to mark alternatives randomly without understanding or even reading the item and thus exhibit the somewhat higher random-guessing probability. Only at higher levels do examinees see through the trick question and respond with the correct alternative.

Thissen and I have proposed a four-parameter logistic model that fits this type of item very well. The response function is the sum of two logistic components, one decreasing from the random guessing level in order to model the chance-correct responses. By including in the model a parameter for the distance between the locations of these two functions, the nonmonotonicity of the overall function is flexibly described.

The only other frequently seen failures of the logistic family of item response functions (including the 4-PL model) appear to be due to poor item writing that leads to spurious correct responses. An example of this situation is shown in Fig. 5.1, which exhibits poor fit to the 3-PL model because of an excess of correct responses among examinees of modest proficiency. These examinees get the right answer for the wrong reason: The item writer has inadvertently included the number *six* in the item stem and also in the correct alternative, namely B. Low-level examinees who do not understand the question are likely to respond to fortuitous associations between the stem and the alternatives. Still lower level examinees guess randomly without reading the item, thus producing an item response function that is monitonically increasing but exhibits two inflection points instead of one. Although the fault in this particular item is fairly obvious, I

Mary has three feet of candy cane that she wants to divide equally among six friends. How long will each piece be?

> A. $\frac{1}{2}$ inch
> B. 6 inches
> C. 1 foot
> D. 18 inches
> E. 2 feet

FIG. 5.1.   An item exhibiting poor fit to the 3-PL model. The inadvertent association between the six in the stem and the correct alternative leads to spurious correct responses.

am embarrassed to say that it slipped through item screening and was not identified until picked up in the IRT item analysis. Apart from adopting a multiple-alternative response model, the only cure for this source of poor fit is to rewrite the item.

The Mantel–Haenszel (MH) statistic as a measure of DIF benefits from the test having a large number of homogeneous items. For in that case, the scores of the examinees accurately assign them to score groups and the loglinear methods of IRT analysis under Rasch-model assumptions apply. Even if the items do not have uniform discriminating power as assumed, the accuracy of assignment improves as the number of items increases. As Holland and Thayer (1988) showed, the Mantel–Haenszel common log–odds ratio and the difference in IRT location parameters estimated by loglinear item analysis (where item slopes are assumed equal) are essentially equivalent.

The trouble with the MH statistic is that it shows only the difference in the intercepts of the response functions in the focal and reference groups. It gives no evidence that the functions may have different slopes, or different shapes. It does not show which part of the proficiency distribution is most seriously affected by DIF. Its chief merit is that it can be computed quickly enough to make it practical for screening large numbers of items in very large samples. The general IRT methods are too computationally intensive to be used for this purpose.

A better method for investigating DIF in large-scale applications can be elaborated from Fisher's arcsine transformation for binomial proportions (Fisher & Yates, 1963). This approach combines the salient features of the standardization and IRT methods, while providing a test of the difference of intercepts that is essentially identical to the MH chi-square in the null case, and at the same time offering a test of each coefficient. Basically, this *ARCDIF* procedure is a weighted regression of the difference between the arcsine transformed proportions of correct responses in the reference and focus score groups. I have used a cubic polynomial regression for this purpose: the intercept coefficient measures differences in the location of the response functions, the linear measures differences in slope, and the quadratic and cubic coefficients measure differences in shape. I provide step-wise tests of the successive coefficients based on partial chi-square statistics for each degree-of-freedom.

My procedure uses the version of the arcsine transform recommended in Bock and Jones (1968):

$$Y = 2 \left(\arcsin \sqrt{\frac{Np + .25}{N + .5}} \right) - \pi/2. \tag{1}$$

The great advantage of this version of the transform is the virtual absence of bias and the nearly uniform information over almost all of its range. Bock and Jones (1968) showed that even in samples as small as 20, this version is almost unbiased and has variance very close to $1/N$ out as far as $P = .05$ and $.95$. Neither the sample p-value nor the logit have these useful properties. Over the range where the zero bias and constant variance conditions are tenable, the weighted ARCDIF estimator of the polynomial regression coefficients is Gauss–Markoff (unbiased minimum variance) and the step-wise tests are uniformly most powerful.

For the i-th reference and focus groups, the weights for the regression analysis are

$$\frac{N_{ri}N_{fi}}{N_{ri} + N_{fi}}.$$ (2)

These weights are the same for all items and need only be calculated once for the entire test. Logistic regression does not have this property. Neither is it necessary to compute expected frequencies and variances for each group, as it is for the MH statistics. Thus, apart from the arcsine transformation itself, for which very fast standard routines are available, the ARCDIF analysis is actually faster than MH for long tests.

Table 5.1 shows the results of the ARCDIF and MH analysis of 14 selected items from SAT-Verbal. The data were kindly provided to me by Neil Dorans. The close agreement of the intercept and MH chi-squares are apparent. (The MH chi-square is computed without the correction for continuity.) The fact that the ARCDIF chi-square is smaller than the MH chi-square as it departs from expectation is due to the different scaling for the effect measure. The log ARCDIF intercept estimate is almost identical to the MH common log–odds ratio (see Fig. 5.2).

TABLE 5.1
Chi-square Statistics for the Arcsine and Mantel–Haenszel Tests of DIF:
Selected SAT-Verbal Items
(Reference Group, White; Focal Group, Black)

Item Number	Partial Chi-square Statistics (DF = 1)				MH Chi-square (DF = 1)
	Intercept	Linear	Quadratic	Cubic	
10	1124	24	16	5	1274
20	482	0	28	0	502
42	170	5	33	0	197
22	176	0	9	0	185
59	127	17	4	0	133
13	68	0	0	1	69
18	64	1	23	1	67
1	31	15	3	2	43
57	16	62	2	0	28
69	22	0	8	3	25
24	6	2	1	5	9
54	6	4	17	3	6
6	1	24	7	8	1
68	1	0	0	1	1

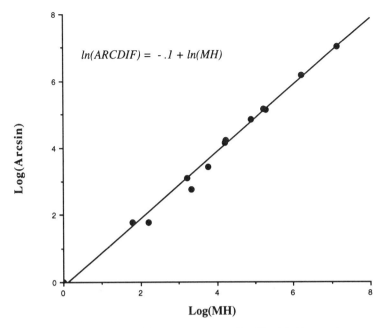

FIG. 5.2. Log (ARCDIF) intercept versus the Mantel–Haenszel common log–odds ratio for the SAT item in Table 5.1.

There is only one case (item 54) with some evidence of quadratic DIF in the absence of intercept and linear DIF, but there are two items (6 and 57) that show a strong linear DIF (difference in slopes or discriminating power) when the intercept difference is moderate. Fig. 5.3 shows the ARCDIF graph for item 57. The linear trend in the ARCDIF as a function of the test score is readily apparent. The figure illustrates the value of the arcsine difference as an effect-size measure in binomial data.

The problem with the raw difference in percentages, as used in the standardization method described in the Dorans and Holland chapter, is its failure to account for the p-values being more informative toward the extremes of the scale. This means that standardization is less likely to detect DIF as the p-values depart from 50%. The ARCDIF evaluates more fairly both the hard and easy items on the test, and it is more suitable for interpretation because its units are uniform with respect to detecting DIF.

Regrettably, all three of these techniques—ARCDIF, standardization, and MH—tend to break down when the number of items on the test is relatively small. The problem is, of course, that the test score does not then place the examinee accurately on the proficiency continuum. As a result, the true regression of item score on proficiency is poorly represented by the observed regression on test score. We are in the position of having errors in the independent variable, which, as we know, complicates the estimation of the regression func-

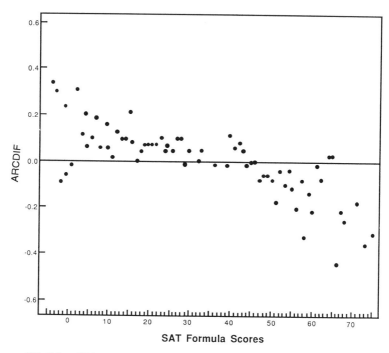

FIG. 5.3. ARCDIF analysis of SAT-Verbal item 57, which exhibits marked DIF in discriminating power.

tion. Similarly, in the Mantel–Haenszel calculations and loglinear analysis, the assignment of examinees to homogeneous proficiency groups is subject to error when proxied by the score groups. These errors of classification vitiate conventional loglinear analysis.

It is for the shorter tests that the IRT methods, implemented by marginal maximum likelihood (MML) estimation, have a definite advantage. MML estimation does not assume that the test score is equivalent to the examinee's proficiency. Instead, the examinee's pattern of correct and incorrect item responses merely conditions the probability that the examinee is at any particular point on the proficiency continuum. From these conditional probabilities, the latent distribution is estimated in terms of the numbers of examinees expected to be in the neighborhood of given points on the continuum. Among the number of examinees expected at these points, the proportion expected to respond correctly provides an estimate of the corresponding ordinate of the item response function. The assumed item response model is then fitted to these ordinates by the maximum likelihood (ML) or maximum a posteriori (MAP) methods.

This procedure is general for even small numbers of items; we have seen in Thissen's examples that it works straightforwardly with as few as four items. Moreover, it applies to any parametric response model, even the difficult-to-fit three-parameter logistic model, the more elaborate graded-category models (Samejima, 1969), and the multiple-alternative models analyzed by Thissen, Steinberg, and Wainer in chapter 4 of this volume. By fitting the parameters of, for example, the three-parameter logistic model in the groups in question, while restricting the guessing parameter and also possibly the slope parameter to a common value in both groups, we are able to express the DIF as the difference in the location (difficulty) parameters of the items for the two groups. The MML methods thus are suitable for DIF analyses of tests in the range of 10 to 20 items, where the ARCDIF, standardization, and Mantel–Haenszel procedures would be questionable. And the MML methods, of course, also apply to longer tests; in fact, they become more efficient computationally because the number of iterations required to determine the latent distribution is reduced as it becomes more similar to the observed score distribution. (This method of IRT DIF analysis is implemented in the BIMAIN program of Muraki, Mislevy, & Bock, 1987.)

If methods such as ARCDIF, which detect DIF in item-discriminating power come into wide use, the kind of examples of these effects shown in Thissen et al. (this volume) will have to be accounted for. They will not be as easy to explain as the differences in difficulty that the MH method detects, but perhaps they can also be attributed to poor judgment in writing the alternatives for multiple-choice items. In my experience, fine points in phrasing of alternatives that unsettle the more proficient examinees but are lost on the less proficient are a common source of poor discriminating power. The latter go for the nominally correct answer— whereas those at higher levels find none of the alternatives strictly correct and so may omit the item. If this occurs, we have a paradoxical situation in which an item is more discriminating in the group for which the ambiguity is not apparent, and less discriminating in the group for which it is a source of confusion. This could very well lead to DIF in discriminating power with relatively little DIF in item difficulty. As we gain experience in the study of differential item functioning, we should begin to understand how poor item-writing practices contribute to these effects and learn to avoid them.

But these kinds of effects may be relatively minor compared to the broad social factors that make different aspects of the item content more or less familiar to different groups within the population. One would expect such effects to show up as departures from unidimensionality in item factor analysis studies. Robert Mislevy and I found, for example, that the General Science test of the Armed Services Vocational Aptitude Battery (ASVAB) shows considerable DIF for sex affecting the Physical Science items and the Biological Science items (Bock & Mislevy, 1981). Generally, males are at an advantage in Physical Science content and females, in the Biological Science content. Later, Michele Zimowski and I found, using full-information item factor analysis, that items for the General Science test showed two factors clearly resolved along the same lines (Zimowski & Bock, 1987).

Similarly, Mislevy and I found some evidence for DIF between Hispanic and other groups with respect to Latinate or Germanic origin of words on the ASVAB Word Knowledge test (Bock & Mislevy, 1981). Presumably, those two types of words would show up as distinct factors in a factor analysis of data that included a substantial number of Hispanics in the sample. In the case of the General Science test, the obvious cure to this problem of DIF is to score the Biology and Physical Science items separately, thus changing DIF into differential impact for the two sexes. The two scores can then be used in various sorts of composites or predicting equations without any pejorative interpretation. Because educational tests must always distinguish these two content-matters, there would be ample precedent for scoring them separately.

In the case of the Latinate and the Germanic words, however, it would be hard to find a justification for scoring those domains separately. In that case, DIF could not be avoided but the item content could be balanced between the two historical groups of words to represent in some reasonable way the examinee's knowledge of English words in general. My experience in working with the ASVAB convinces me that DIF from these sorts of social and cultural effects will be found widely in cognitive tests when the item content is heterogeneous. They can be minimized by creating factored tests and reporting score profiles, but they will be difficult to remove from tests that are factorially complex and reported in a single score.

These observations suggest that the elimination of DIF should not be a routine procedure, but must be broadly informed by the social background from which it arises. Otherwise, the test that has been freed of DIF by item selection may end up showing an unintended and undesirable adverse impact on the very groups it was meant to protect.

6 Model-Based Standardized Measurement of an Item's Differential Impact

Howard Wainer
Educational Testing Service

Over the past decade there has been increasing concern about the fairness of test items to various identifiable subgroups in the test-taking population. One manifestation of this concern is the increase in research on differential item functioning (DIF). Although there had been a substantial number of procedures developed to uncover DIF (see Shepard, Camilli, & Williams, 1985, for a survey of some of these), most were very much engineering approaches that were seat-of-the-pants approximations of as-yet-undeveloped statistically rigorous procedures (i.e., Angoff & Ford's 1973 delta method; Camilli's chi-square method [given in Shepard, Camilli, & Averill, 1981]). Because of this lack of rigor some were just plain wrong (Scheuneman, 1979). Recently, we have seen the emergence of two kinds of statistically rigorous procedures for identifying DIF. A sampling from each of these is:

Empirically Based Procedures:

- *The Mantel–Haenszel statistic*—Holland and Thayer (1988).
- *Logistic regression methods*—Rogers and Swaminathan (1989).
- *Standardization procedures*—Dorans and Kulick (1986).

Model-Based Procedures:

- *General item response theory likelihood ratio* (general IRT-LR, can be accomplished using MULTILOG computer program)—Thissen, Steinberg, and Wainer (1988).

123

- *Limited-information IRT-LR* (can be accomplished using LISCOMP computer program)—Muthén and Lehman (1985).
- *Full-information IRT-D²* (can be accomplished using BIMAIN computer program)—Bock, Muraki, and Pfeiffenberger (1988).

This classification is somewhat arbitrary—the Mantel–Haenszel statistic has much in common with the Rasch approach espoused by Kelderman (1985) and by Thissen and Mooney (1989), which in turn is a loglinear-likelihood ratio (loglinear-LR) procedure; Rogers and Swaminathan's (1989) logistic regression approach is a generalization of the Mantel–Haenszel, but moves toward a more complex IRT model; standardization can be thought of as an empirical item characteristic curve (ICC) approach. Among the model-based procedures, all methods tend to fit a model that allows DIF and a less general one that does not; they then use a likelihood ratio (this ratio is sometimes called a Wald statistic or Mahalanobis D^2) to see whether the generalization yields a significant increase in the quality of fit. If not, no DIF.

Expressed in IRT vocabulary, DIF occurs when an ICC calculated for an item within the reference population is different from an ICC for that same item in some focal population. All of the procedures mentioned previously are primarily aimed at detecting DIF; there is a similar list for measuring it. Prominent among these are a set of measures that assess the amount of DIF by the area between the two ICCs (Linn, Levine, Hasting, & Wardrop, 1981; Rudner, 1977). In Figs. 6.1 and 6.2 are shown two representations of such measures. In Fig. 6.1 there is a lot of area (ergo a lot of DIF), in Fig. 6.2 much less area (less DIF).

At first blush this seems like a reasonable way to characterize DIF. A more careful look reveals that there are several problems with using area. First, it does not work for the three parameter logistic model (3-PL) (the most popular model for multiple-choice items), because a difference in the lower asymptote, regard-

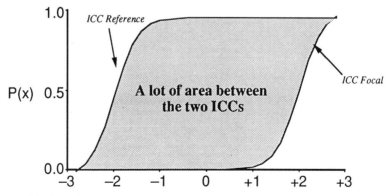

FIG. 6.1.   An example of two Item Characteristic Curves (ICCs) that are far apart.

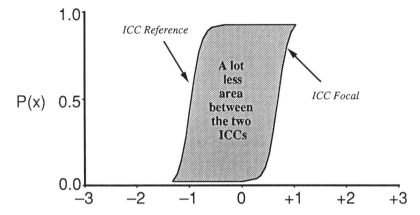

FIG. 6.2. An example of two ICCs that are somewhat closer together.

less of how small, yields an infinite area unless one institutes ad hoc restraints (i.e., area only for $|\theta| < 3$). Second, when the proficiency distributions are quite separate (a common occurrence in most DIF studies), what appears to be a large area may in fact affect very few people. (See Fig. 6.3, in which very few examinees in the focal group would get the item correct regardless of which ICC was appropriate.) On the other hand, an item with a much smaller area between the

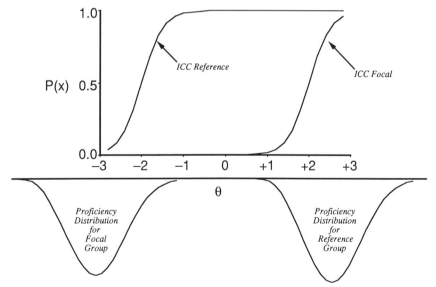

FIG. 6.3. An example showing two ICCs that are far apart but when their associated proficiency distributions are considered we can see that the difference in the ICCs affects almost no one.

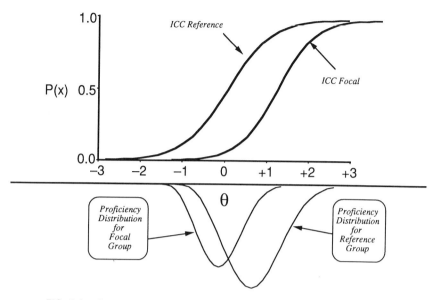

FIG. 6.4.   A contrast to Figure 6.3, showing two ICCs that appear near-
er to one another, but because of the location of the proficiency distributions this difference has a more profound effect.

curves may affect more people (see Fig. 6.4). Thus, one must somehow take into
account the proficiency distributions. But how?

In this chapter I describe a general approach toward characterizing the amount
of DIF and I develop four indices, each of which may prove useful with a
specified domain of problem. These indices are motivated and developed in the
next section. Following that, some statistical issues involving the estimation of
the proficiency distributions are explored, and in the section following some
suggestions regarding the assessment of the accuracy of the indices are made.
The last section recapitulates and muses.

FOUR MODEL-BASED INDICES
OF STANDARDIZED IMPACT

In this section I define an approach toward measuring the amount of DIF and
develop four model-based standardized indices of impact that grow naturally out
of this approach. The basic notion supposes that the impact of item i is the
difference between the probability of getting that item correct if one is a member
of the focal group versus what would have been the probability of a correct
response if one was a member of the reference group (i.e., suppose one went to
sleep *focal* and awoke *reference;* how much does the likelihood of getting the
item correct change?).

To answer this we need a little notation:

Define:

$P_F(x_i = 1|\theta)$ as the probability of getting item i correct for a member of the focal group, conditioned on having proficiency θ, and

$P_R(x_i = 1|\theta)$ as the probability of getting item i correct for a member of the reference group with the same proficiency.

Further, let us define proficiency distributions for each group as $G_F(\theta)$ and $G_R(\theta)$ respectively (whether these are the *estimated distributions* or the *distributions of the estimates* is an issue I discuss later).

Last, suppose there are N_F and N_R individuals in each group.

Now we can get on with the derivation of the indices of standardized impact.

If a person changes group membership overnight, the probability of getting the item correct changes. Thus, the amount of impact is

$$P_F(\theta) - P_R(\theta).$$

But, this must be weighted by the distribution of all of those affected, specifically, by $G_F(\theta)$. Thus, we define the standardized index of impact, $T(1)$, as

$$T(1) = \int_{-\infty}^{\infty} [P_F(\theta) - P_R(\theta)] \, dG_F(\theta). \tag{1}$$

Obviously, this is the average impact for each person in the focal group. Note that this is bounded regardless of the model used to generate the Ps. This index comes close to characterizing what we want. Indeed, for many purposes this may be just right.

Is this always the right thing to be looking at? The amount of an item's impact depends on the choice of the focal group. An item might be unjust to one focal group, but just fine for another. Thus, it might be important for purposes of comparison to have a measure of *total impact*, or $T(2) = N_F T(1)$, or

$$T(2) = N_F \int_{-\infty}^{\infty} [P_F(\theta) - P_R(\theta)] \, dG_F(\theta). \tag{2}$$

The concept of *total impact* may be a useful one in test construction. Consider that one constraint in test construction might be to choose a subset of items from a pool such that the total impact is minimized. N. J. Dorans (personal communication October 26, 1988) described a "melting pot" reference population, which is made up of all of the various focal groups. He suggested that one might then calculate the total impact (using an index like $T(2)$) for each group relative to the whole. The operational item pool might be the one of requisite size that minimizes total impact (summed over the entire examinee population).

The concept of total impact allows us to consider the situation in which one item has only a small amount of gender DIF but no Aztec DIF, whereas another item might have more Aztec DIF but no gender DIF. This method allows us to

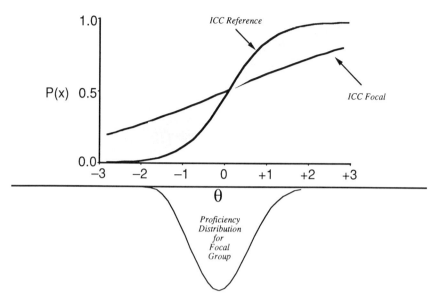

FIG. 6.5. An example of a situation in which the two ICCs differ in
slope and hence cross. This crossing in conjunction with the centrally
location of the proficiency distribution can allow the adverse impact of
high proficiency members of the focal group to be compensated for by
the positive impact for lower scoring members.

choose between them based on their total effect (gender groups are typically
much larger than the number of SAT-taking Aztecs).[1]

So far, we have considered the focal group as a unitary body, where an
injustice to some of its members can be compensated for by generosity to others.
This is the case when the ICCs for the focal and reference groups cross (as in Fig.
6.5). The amount of compensation depends on where the ICCs cross and the
relative location of the focal group's proficiency distribution. Do we want a
measure that allows such compensatory effects? Or would we rather view differential impact as undesirable regardless of its direction? Under many circumstances the indices $T(1)$ and $T(2)$ would be fine, but sometimes we might want to
get an unsigned index. One way to accomplish this is merely to use the average

---

[1]Another variation on this theme was suggested by Nambury Raju (personal communication,
August 16, 1989). He suggests that it might be more useful to have a measure of *proportional impact*
rather than *total impact*. To calculate this we need only replace "N_F with N_F/N, where N refers to the
size of the melting pot reference population." I am fond of this idea, but it remains for experience
with such indices in practical situations to inform us more fully of their worth.

absolute or squared standardized impact. Such indices are depicted as $T(3)$, average squared impact,

$$T(3) = \int_{-\infty}^{\infty} [P_F(\theta) - P_R(\theta)]^2 \, dG_F(\theta), \tag{3}$$

and $T(4)$, total squared impact:

$$T(4) = N_F \int_{-\infty}^{\infty} [P_F(\theta) - P_R(\theta)]^2 \, dG_F(\theta). \tag{4}$$

These indices, like their parallels $T(1)$ and $T(2)$, are bounded. Note the similarity between Equations (3) and (4) and the Cramér–von Mises statistic (Cramér, 1928; von Mises, 1931) proposed as an alternative to the chi-square goodness-of-fit statistic. In that instance the two ICCs are replaced by a hypothesized and an empirical CDF (cumulative density function). Its asymptotic properties were derived by Smirnov (1936) and it was subsequently generalized into a form very much like Equation (4), which is commonly called the Anderson–Darling statistic (Darling, 1957). Its mode of computation has been provided by Pearson and Hartley (1972).[2]

ESTIMATION OF THE STANDARDIZED INDICES OF IMPACT

The indices described in the previous section are straightforward and clear if we assume that we have the population values of the various components; the ICCs for the focal and reference groups, and the focal group's proficiency distribution. Of course, we never do. An important question, then, is how to estimate these quantities. Estimating the ICCs is an old and well-explored question, hence I will not go into it here. Instead, let me direct the interested reader to Wainer and Mislevy (1990) for a full description of such issues generally, and to Thissen et al. (1988, especially pp. 152–155) for specifics. Similarly, maximum likelihood methods for estimating the focal group's proficiency distribution, $G_F(\theta)$, have also been worked out (Mislevy, 1984). I want to take this opportunity to emphasize how these quantities ought to be estimated, and why, and then to sketch a computational strategy useful with existing software.

One approach is to do numerical integration over the empirical *distribution of the estimates of proficiency* ($\hat{\Theta}$). This is closely allied to what was proposed by

---

[2]The parallelism between Equations (3) and (4) and the Cramér–von Mises can be useful and important when the ICCs resemble cumulative density functions, that is when they are monotonic. It becomes less important if we are looking at trace-lines for distractors, which are decidedly non-monotonic.

Dorans and Kulick (1986). This is possible to do accurately if one has both large samples as well as long tests, but under commonly occurring circumstances "the distribution of the estimates of individual subjects' parameters may then depart radically from the distribution of the parameters themselves, thereby invalidating any analyses that would treat the estimates as if they were the parameters they represent" (Mislevy, 1984, p. 359). Thus, it is better to use the *estimated distribution of proficiency* obtained directly from the observed data rather than from derived parameters (Bock & Aitkin, 1981; Sörbom, 1974).

How can this be accomplished? A strategy, using standard IRT software, that was employed earlier (Thissen et al., 1988) to detect DIF, works here as well. Suppose we have a test of length n on which there is no detectable DIF. Let us call this the *anchor test*. We are interested in assessing the impact for another item. We will call this the *studied item*. Standard IRT programs that use marginal maximum likelihood estimation procedures (e.g., BILOG [Mislevy & Bock, 1983] or MULTILOG [Thissen, 1991]) will provide us with all the pieces we need to compute any of the four indices of impact. We do this by analyzing the test data as if there are $n + 2$ items. The anchor test is seen as being responded to by both the reference and the focal groups and contributes n items. The studied item is included twice; the first time (denoted as item $n + 1$) as if it were responded to only by the reference group, the second time (denoted as item $n + 2*$) as if only by the focal group. The program will then estimate item parameters for it for each of the two groups on the same scale. From these parameters we can generate estimates of $P_R(x_i = 1|\theta)$ and $P_F(x_i = 1|\theta)$. In addition, because the program has the anchor test, it will generate an estimate of the proficiency distribution for the focal group, $G_F(\theta)$. This distribution can be of two types. If you wish, it can estimate the best fitting Gaussian distribution, or it can provide an estimated empirical distribution (histogram). By specifying the number of histobars to be the same as the number of quadrature points, one can use the latter directly in the numerical integration required for the computation of the indices of impact. The latter approach is the one I would prefer initially, because if the data are skewed it will still give useful results. The Gaussian assumption is used quite broadly and, if justified, gives rock-steady results. This scheme is depicted schematically in Fig. 6.6.

MEASURING THE VARIABILITY OF THE INDICES OF IMPACT

What are the distributions of these indices? How much variability should we expect? These are difficult questions to answer because we are using model-based estimates of response probabilities that are of differential accuracy. Although the delta method and a lot of algebra may get us started in the right

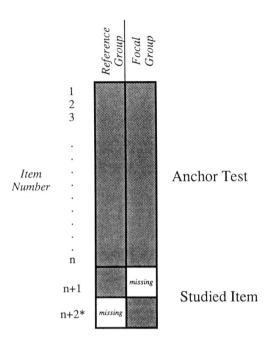

FIG. 6.6. A schematic representation of how the analysis measures the impact of a particular item.

direction, I believe a better answer is available through direct assessment. Let me propose an approximate method for doing so.

The variability of the various components might differ substantially. For example, in the situation depicted in Fig. 6.3, the variability of T is going to be driven by the uncertainty in the estimation of the ICC for the reference group. This may seem odd at first because, after all, isn't the reference group typically the largest? Yet if we study Fig. 6.3 we note that the data from the reference group establishes the top of their ICC, but the values of the ICC in the region of the focal group's proficiency are extrapolated. The value of the ICC for the focal group in the region of the focal group is well established (the upper end is more iffy). $G_F(\theta)$, because it is estimated from the entire anchor test, is relatively well estimated. Thus, if we can capture the variability in T caused by the variability in $P_R(x_i = 1|\theta)$, we will have gotten most of the way to an answer. This is not going to be the case in other situations (e.g., sex DIF), but let us use this case to illustrate a technique to measure the variability.

A straightforward way to obtain estimates of variability is to use a statistical methodology commonly called *multiple imputation* (Rubin, 1987). Simply described, it involves substituting a variety of plausible values for $P_R(x_i = 1|\theta)$, each of which will yield a different estimate of T. The variation observed in T as a consequence of these multiple imputations serves as an estimate of the sampling distribution of T. This method bears a similarity to the bootstrap (Efron, 1982), although it does offer some unique aspects. One of its attractive features is that it does not require special programming, but rather allows the use of existing software.

How do we choose alternative values of $P_R(x_i = 1|\theta)$? To answer this, consider the mapping of the ICC, usually plotted in a space of functions (P vs. θ), into the parameter space of the IRT model in use. Such a *duality diagram* (Ramsay, 1982) is depicted in Fig. 6.7. The version shown in Fig. 6.7 represents the ICC in a two-dimensional parameter space strictly for ease of presentation; the solution is the same for the three-parameter model. Note that each point in the parameter space maps into a curve in the function space. If we construct the 95% highest density region (Novick & Jackson, 1977) around the point in the parameter space that represents the estimated parameters for the reference group's ICC (a description of how to construct such a region within the framework of IRT is contained in Thissen & Wainer, 1983, 1990), we can sample from within this region for alternative imputed values of $P_R(x_i = 1|\theta)$. Each imputation allows us to compute a value for T. The variance of these Ts provides an estimate of the variability of T. Rubin (1987) suggested that as few as four imputations are usually enough to get a satisfactory estimate.

The procedure just outlined seems like a reasonable approximation based, as it is, on the greater variability of P_R; but of course in general one must impute values for both P_R and P_F at the same time. Thus, this initial discussion was more for didactic purposes than operational ones. Once we understand how to do this multiple imputation for just one of the ICCs, it becomes clearer how to do it for both at once. The extra computation gains us greater precision in the estimation of variability. Imputing from both, that is, drawing from an item's P_R and P_F posterior covariance matrix as if they were independent, is not only

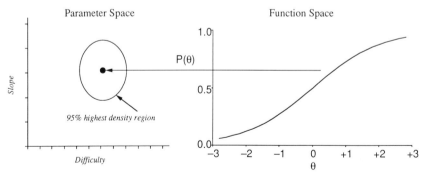

FIG. 6.7. A duality diagram that shows how an entire curve in the function space maps into a single point in the parameter space; and vice versa. Because of this inverse relationship the 95% highest density region surrounding the parameter representing the ICC can be mapped back into the function space yielding simultaneous confidence bounds around the observed curve.

easy, it "is reasonable, as their shared variance goes to zero as the length of the anchor test increases" (Robert Mislevy, personal communication, July 7, 1989).

A SPECIALIZATION, SOME POTENTIAL SHORTCUTS, AND SOME HAZARDS

So far, all discussion of the various indices of standardized impact have been in the absence of any specific IRT model. This was not done accidentally; I did not want to make these suggestions dependent upon choice of model. One might choose a specific model with the hope that many of the problems of estimation of the index and its associated variability would diminish. To briefly illustrate how this might work for one model, let us consider the three-parameter logistic model (3-PL) for index $T(1)$. Obviously, this can be decomposed into

$$T(1) = \int_{-\infty}^{\infty} P_F(\theta) \, dG_F(\theta) - \int_{-\infty}^{\infty} P_R(\theta) \, dG_F(\theta), \tag{5}$$

which, for ease of discussion we denote as

$$T(1) = A_1 - A_2 . \tag{6}$$

For the 3-PL, one obvious asymptotic approximation for A_1 can be written as

$$A_1 \cong c_F + (1 - c_F) \, \frac{e^{a_F(\theta_F - b_F)}}{1 + e^{a_F(\bar{\theta}_F - b_F)}}, \tag{7}$$

where $\overline{\theta_F}$ is the mean proficiency for the focal group. Similarly,

$$A_2 \cong c_R + (1 - c_R) \, \frac{e^{a_R(\theta_F - b_R)}}{1 + e^{a_R(\bar{\theta}_F - b_R)}} . \tag{8}$$

Using this approximation makes computation of $T(1)$ and $T(2)$ seem no more difficult than running test data through an IRT program (e.g., BILOG or MULTI-LOG). This would be a mistake.

This kind of approximation has been studied previously, by N. S. Raju (personal communication, August 30, 1989), for the one- and two-parameter logistic models, and so what appears here has just been a straightforward restatement of his work. Raju (1989) also used the delta method to derive asymptotic standard errors for this approximation. This method can be followed to provide estimates for the 3-PL as well. When this approximation is suitable, it appears to be easier than doing the numerical integration and multiple imputations that were described earlier as the estimation method of choice. The issue, of course, is "When is it suitable?" There are two circumstances when it is not:

1. *When the ICC is nonlinear*—The approximation depicted in Equations (7) and (8) strictly holds when the ICC referred to is linear, and deteriorates as the ICC over the region of $G(\theta)$ deviates from linearity. Thus, it appears to be more accurate in the situation depicted in Fig. 6.3 than for that shown in Fig. 6.4. The extent to which it is applicable in any particular situation requires more study. The more computationally intensive procedures previously discussed will work more generally. We would, of course, expand the approximation by, say, including a quadratic term from the Taylor expansion. This might increase the generality of the approximation, but it would further reduce the already meager savings in computation over doing the numerical integration and multiple imputation. The real advantage that the use of a simple approximation has (when it works) are the insights that it provides about the behavior of the index. (See Raju, 1988, for one example of how this can be used effectively.) But, if these insights are incorrect we are better off doing the integration.

2. *When we do not have the population values of the item parameters*—Equations (7) and (8) are asymptotic approximations, but we usually are dealing with situations very far indeed from having the population values of the item parameters. Estimates of these values often have large standard errors (Thissen & Wainer, 1982) and it is a snare and a delusion to believe the results obtained by inserting estimated parameter values into Equations (7) and (8). It is far better to deal with the function as a whole. Thus, we continue to recommend what might appear to be the overly conservative approach described in this section and the previous one.

FURTHER CONCLUSIONS AND DISCUSSIONS

In this chapter I have described a variety of ideas in an attempt to devise a statistically rigorous, practically workable, and generally explainable procedure to characterize the amount of DIF in an item. I have termed this concept *standardized impact* for two reasons. First, to match the terminology used by Dorans and Kulick (1986) in their observed-score approach, which this method closely parallels. And second, because what this chapter does (integrating with respect to the proficiency distribution of the focal group), is exactly what statisticians mean by standardization (Mosteller & Tukey, 1977, pp. 221–257). Despite these strong reasons, it is a cumbersome phrase and the more euphonious appellation *weighted impact* finished a close second.

The term *impact* came into use within this context as part of the Golden Rule agreement (Anrig, 1987, 1988; Holland, 1988). It was defined as the difference between the focal group and the reference group of the probability of getting the studied item correct. It has been widely criticized because it does not allow for the (commonly correct) possibility that the two groups may have different proficiency distributions. The index proposed here, albeit model-based, is a weighted impact measure that corrects this problem.

Although I have tried to be thorough in my presentation here, there still remain other issues to be explored. Many of them require the accumulation of experience with a measure like this within the context of an operational test. What is the average size of this statistic? Do we really want an unsigned statistic [$T(3)$ or $T(4)$]? Or, as I suspect, is it better to allow negative discrepancies at one end of the ICC to counterbalance positive ones at the other? Under what circumstances is average impact [$T(1)$ or $T(3)$] the right measure? When is total impact [$T(2)$ or $T(4)$] more useful? Is some other variation a better choice? What is the relationship of this measure to some of the other measures proposed? These and other questions remain, but for now I believe that we have accumulated enough to begin.

I am not unaware of the irony associated with both the topic and the approach espoused in this chapter. IRT is often touted as providing sample-independent estimates, and yet this chapter is concerned with measuring the amount of sample dependence. Also, in the study of DIF, IRT is often cited as "the theoretically preferred procedure, but it can only be used with large samples." This statement reflects ignorance of model-based measurement. In fact, the smaller the sample size the more we need to lean on a model for statistical stability. If we have large enough samples, the observed-score approach of Dorans and Kulick (1986) is fine. (See Bock's elaboration of this point in chapter 5.) It is only when samples are smallish (commonly found in the focal group in DIF studies) that the IRT approach is required. Following Spinoza, we must remember: *"Non redere, no lugere, neque detestari sed intelligere."* [not to laugh, not to weep, neither to detest but to understand].

ACKNOWLEDGEMENTS

Much of the work described here came from conversations over coffee that I have had with Nick Longford. In a fair world these indices ought to have the eponymous title of "Longford's Indices of Injustice"—an honor that Nick has too modestly declined. This is very much in line with what we would have predicted from knowledge of Stigler's Law of Eponymy. Nonetheless, I want to take this opportunity to record his role. In addition, this presentation has profited from my conversations with William Angoff, Henry Braun, Neil Dorans, Paul Holland, Charles Lewis, Robert Mislevy, Peter Pashley, Nambury Raju, and David Thissen. This work was partially supported by contract F41689-87-D-0012/5014 from the Air Force Human Resources Laboratory. I am grateful for this support as well as for the advice and wisdom of Malcolm Ree, who is responsible for our doing it. Despite all of this help, all errors in conception and execution are my own.

7

A Monte Carlo Study of Factors That Affect the Mantel–Haenszel and Standardization Measures of Differential Item Functioning

John R. Donoghue
Paul W. Holland
Dorothy T. Thayer
Educational Testing Service

The Mantel–Haenszel (MH) statistical procedure (Mantel & Haenszel, 1959) was proposed by Holland (1985) and Holland and Thayer (1988) as a tool for studying the differential functioning (DIF) of test items in different groups of examinees. The relation between the MH procedure and the other chi-square and item response theory (IRT) based procedures for studying DIF or "item bias" is discussed in Holland and Thayer (1988), Thissen, Steinberg, and Wainer (1988), and in chapters 3 and 4 of this volume. Currently, the MH statistical procedure is used at Educational Testing Service (ETS), first, to detect operational test items that exhibit substantial DIF for selected groups of examinees and, second, to eliminate such items from pretest item pools. In appropriate cases, items detected using the MH procedure are eliminated from scoring in operational tests. The standardization procedure, discussed in chapter 3, is closely related to the MH procedure and is also part of the information used at ETS to make decisions about items that exhibit DIF.

The purpose of this chapter is to investigate several factors that can influence the results of the MH and standardization procedures in DIF analyses in order to understand their implications for practice. Before describing the factors studied here, we give a brief summary of the MH and standardization procedures. For more details the reader is referred to chapter 3.

THE MANTEL–HAENSZEL AND THE STANDARDIZATION DIF PROCEDURES

The performance of two groups of examinees is compared in each DIF analysis. One group, the *focal group,* is of primary interest and the other, the *reference group,* is used as a basis of comparison. The test items are analyzed for DIF one at a time. The item under analysis at a given time is called the *studied item.* In addition, examinees are grouped into classes of comparable examinees on the basis of a *matching variable, M.* For most DIF applications the appropriate matching variable is a total test score—either the total score of a test (or appropriate subtest) in which the studied items is embedded or, if the studied item is being pretested, the total score on a separate operational test on the same subject as the studied item. These three quantities—performance on the studied item, membership in the focal or reference group, and the value of M for each examinee—define a $2 \times 2 \times K$ cross-classification of examinee data. This three-way classification forms the basis of both the MH and standardization procedures. One 2×2 layer of this $2 \times 2 \times K$ array is schematically represented here.

Performance
on the Studied Item

Group	Correct = 1	Incorrect = 0	Total
Reference	A_k	B_k	n_{Rk}
Focal	C_k	D_k	n_{Fk}
Total	m_{1k}	m_{0k}	T_k

In this notation, there are T_k examinees in the data, all with the same value of the matching variable, $M = k$. Of these, n_{Rk} are in the reference group and n_{Fk} are in the focal group. Of the n_{Rk} reference group members, A_k answered the studied item correctly and B_k did not. Similarly, of the n_{Fk} matched focal group members, C_k answered the studied item correctly and D_k did not. The MH measure of DIF is:

$$\text{MH D-DIF} = -2.35 \log_e(\hat{\alpha}_{MH}), \qquad (1)$$

where $\hat{\alpha}_{MH}$ is the Mantel–Haenszel (adjusted) odds-ratio estimator given by

$$\hat{\alpha}_{MH} = \frac{\sum_k A_k D_k / T_k}{\sum_k B_k C_k / T_k}. \qquad (2)$$

In Equation (1) the logarithm and the factor 2.35 are used to put MH D-DIF (delta-DIF) into the *delta scale* used at ETS to measure item difficulty. The negative sign in Equation (1) is included to make MH D-DIF *negative* when the item is more difficult for members of the focal group than it is for comparable members of the reference group. An estimated standard error for MH D-DIF is given in Holland and Thayer (1988), based on the work reported in Robins, Breslow, and Greenland (1986) and in Phillips and Holland (1987). It is

$$SE(\text{MH D-DIF}) = 2.35\sqrt{\text{Var}[\log_e(\hat{\alpha}_{MH})]}, \tag{3}$$

where $\text{Var}[\log_e(\hat{\alpha}_{MH})]$ is estimated by

$$\frac{\sum_k U_k V_k / T_k^2}{2\left(\sum_k A_k D_k / T_k\right)^2}, \tag{4}$$

where

$$
\begin{aligned}
U_k &= A_k D_k + \hat{\alpha}_{MH}(B_k C_k) \\
V_k &= (A_k + D_k) + \hat{\alpha}_{MH}(B_k + C_k).
\end{aligned} \tag{5}
$$

This expression for the standard error of MH D-DIF has been shown to be approximately valid in a variety of circumstances—Robins et al. (1986), Phillips and Holland (1987). In a later section we give additional evidence of its validity in the context of DIF studies.

The Mantel–Haenszel chi-square test of the null hypothesis of no difference between the performance of the focal group and of comparable members of the reference group on the studied item, described in chapter 3, is not part of the study reported here.

The standardization procedure used in this study is a special case of the more general procedure discussed in Dorans and Kulick (1986) and in chapter 3 of this volume. The standardization DIF measure is:

$$\text{STD P-DIF} = \hat{p}_F - \tilde{p}_R \tag{6}$$

where $\hat{p}_F$ is just the proportion in the focal group who get the studied item correct, and $\tilde{p}_R$ is an adjusted proportion correct on the item for the reference group. The adjustment makes use of the entries in the diagram as follows:

$$\tilde{p}_R = \sum_k \left(\frac{A_k}{n_{Rk}}\right) \frac{n_{Fk}}{n_F} \tag{7}$$

where $n_F = \sum_k n_{Fk}$ is the total number of examinees in the focal group. One interpretation of $\tilde{p}_R$ is that it is the proportion of reference group examinees who would have gotten the studied item right had the distribution of the matching variable in the reference group been the same as it is for the focal group.

The estimated standard error for STD P-DIF is given by the formula

$$SE(\text{STD P-DIF}) = \sqrt{\sigma_F^2 + \sigma_R^2}, \tag{8}$$

where

$$\sigma_F^2 = \frac{1}{n_F}\, \hat{p}_F (1 - \hat{p}_F), \qquad (9)$$

and

$$\sigma_R^2 = \frac{1}{n_F^2} \sum_k \frac{n_{Fk}^2\, A_k\, B_k}{n_{Rk}^3} \qquad (10)$$

ITEM RESPONSE THEORY DEFINITION OF DIF

Lord (1977, 1980) used item response theory (IRT) models to give a precise *definition* of DIF that is regarded by some (Shepard, Camilli, & Williams, 1984) as more fundamental than *measures* of DIF such as MH D-DIF and STD P-DIF. We have adopted that view in the present study and we use *IRT DIF* in this precise sense, which we now briefly review.

As usual, θ will denote a person's ability and the item response function (IRF), $P_j(\theta)$, will denote the probability of answering item j correctly for examinees with ability θ. The three-parameter logistic (3-PL) form for IRFs is:

$$P_j(\theta) = c_j + (1 - c_j)\,\{1 + \exp[-1.7a_j(\theta - b_j)]\}^{-1} \qquad (11)$$

The item parameters b_j, a_j and c_j are called *difficulty, discrimination*, and *guessing*, respectively. The factor 1.7 in the exponential in Equation (6) is included in order to make the logistic scale into an approximate probit scale (see Lord & Novick, 1968, p. 400).

If $P_{jR}(\theta)$ and $P_{jF}(\theta)$ denote the IRFs for item j in the reference and focal group, respectively, then Lord's definition of IRT DIF for item j is that $P_{jR}(\theta) \neq P_{jF}(\theta)$, that is, reference and focal examinees of the same ability θ have different probabilities of correctly answering the item. In our study, IRT DIF is modeled solely as a difference in the item difficulty parameter, that is, $b_{jR} \neq b_{jF}$, so that the amount of IRT DIF in our study is measured by the difference

$$B_j = b_{jF} - b_{jR}. \qquad (12)$$

It follows from Equation (11) that if the IRT DIF parameter, B_j, for item j is *positive* (i.e., that $b_{jF} > b_{jR}$) and the other item parameters, a_j and c_j, are the same for the reference and focal groups, then $P_{jF}(\theta) < P_{jR}(\theta)$ for any θ (i.e., the probability that a focal group member with ability θ correctly answers this item is lower than it is for any member of the reference group with the same ability, θ). Other kinds of IRT DIF can be modeled using the 3-PL IRF (Equation 11), but, in our opinion, differences in difficulty are the most important in practice, and are the only type studied here.

The question naturally arises as to what relationship should hold, if any, between DIF as measured by MH D-DIF and IRT DIF as described by $B_j = b_{jF} -$

b_{jR}. Holland and Thayer (1988) discussed this for the case of the Rasch model, which in Equation (11) corresponds to $c_j = 0$ for all items j (no guessing) and $a_j \equiv a$ for all items j (common discrimination parameter). Using their analysis, it can be shown that when (a) the Rasch model holds, (b) the matching variable, M, is a number-right score based on all the items *including* the studied item, and (c) none of the items contributing to the score for M, except possibly the studied item, have IRT DIF, then the underlying parameter, Δ, that MH D-DIF estimates is

$$\Delta = -4\,a\,B, \tag{13}$$

where a is the common discrimination parameter for all items in the analysis, and $B = b_F - b_R$ is the difference in the difficulty parameters for the studied item in the focal and reference groups, respectively. Thus, in this special circumstance MH D-DIF estimates a quantity that is exactly proportional to the IRT DIF parameter, $B = b_F - b_R$, for the studied item. This is good news, because it connects the DIF measure MH D-DIF directly to the IRT DIF parameter. As the amount of IRT DIF increases, so does MH D-DIF, if assumptions (a), (b), and (c) are met. In other words, under these assumptions the MH D-DIF *measure* of DIF and IRT *definition* of DIF are the same thing.

One purpose of this study is to investigate the effect of violations of these assumptions on the behavior of MH D-DIF and on the formula for SE(MH D-DIF) given by Equation (3). Unfortunately, there is no corresponding easy connection between the standardization procedure and IRT DIF. However, because MH D-DIF and STD P-DIF are usually highly correlated in real data, we expected that they would respond similarly to the various factors manipulated in this study.

Factors Varied in This Study

From Equation (13) we see that under assumptions (a), (b), and (c), MH D-DIF is only influenced by the common discrimination parameter, a, and the amount of IRT DIF in the studied item, B. In particular, MH D-DIF is not influenced by b_R, nor by the number of items, J, that contribute to the matching variable score. Even more importantly, MH D-DIF is not sensitive to differences in the distribution of the ability, θ, in the two groups, R and F. This last property makes MH D-DIF a measure of DIF in the studied item rather than a measure of the difference in the distribution of the ability between the reference and focal groups—the undesirable property that measures of "impact" possess and that DIF measures are designed to avoid.

Generally speaking, the factors that can influence MH D-DIF may be divided into two types: *differential item characteristics* between the reference and focal groups for the studied item, and *nuisance* factors. We are interested in being able to detect differential item characteristics using the MH and standardization procedures. The effect of nuisance factors is just that—a nuisance that must be lived with in real data. One purpose of this study is to give a quantitative assessment of the relative importance of these nuisance factors.

Differential Item Characteristics.   MH D-DIF is a measure of the average difference in difficulty between the reference and focal group and as such it should be sensitive to $B = b_F - b_R$. More generally, it should be sensitive to differential item characteristics that result in the item response function for one group being lower or higher than that of the other group for all θ values. However, it is not designed to be sensitive to differential item characteristics that result in the item response function of one group crossing that of the other group in the middle of the distribution of examinee ability—the so-called "cross-over" case.

Nuisance Factors.   Other factors that might influence MH D-DIF when assumptions (a), (b), and (c) are not met include: the reliability and dimensionality of the matching variable M, the distribution of item characteristics of the items in M, the amount of IRT DIF, B_j, in the items that make up M, the distribution of M in the reference and focal groups, the amount of grouping in the values of M, the deletion or not of items from M based on preliminary DIF or other analyses, and the sample sizes of the reference and focal groups. In addition, item characteristics of the studied item for the reference and focal groups may also influence MH D-DIF—for example, the overall difficulty and discrimination of the studied item.

This study examines the influence of some of these factors—one differential item characteristic, four nuisance factors, and a factor defined by the inclusion or exclusion of the studied item in M. The differential item characteristic factor is the amount of IRT DIF in the studied item, $B = b_F - b_R$, (two levels). The four nuisance factors are: (a) the number of items in M (four levels), (b) the shared discrimination parameter in the matching criterion items and the studied item (three levels), (c) the number of IRT DIF items in M (four levels), and (d) the average difficulty of the studied item in the reference group (three levels). We also decided to investigate the effect of including or excluding the studied item in the matching criterion because the proposal of Holland and Thayer (1988) to always include the studied item seems so counterintuitive. (However, see Lewis' discussion of this topic in chapter 15.) Holland and Thayer showed (1988, pp. 140–141) that under assumptions (a), (b), and (c), the exclusion of the studied item from the matching variable score causes MH D-DIF to be sensitive to differences in the distribution of ability in the reference and focal groups. In particular, their results imply that

$$\Delta = -4\,a\,B - H_{RF}, \tag{14}$$

where Δ, a, and B are as defined for Equation (13) and H_{RF} is a quantity that is zero only when the distribution of θ for R and F are identical. Furthermore, if the distribution of θ for the reference group is higher than (i.e., to the right of) the distribution of θ for the focal group, then H_{RF} is positive. When H_{RF} is positive, Δ will be negative even though there is no IRT DIF in the studied item ($B = 0$). This can result in the MH procedure detecting false positives at unacceptable rates. According to Zwick, the effect in Equation (14) holds quite generally. She showed (1990) that the undesirable sensitivity of Δ to reference–focal group differences in the θ distribution, illustrated by Equation (14), when M does not include the score on the studied item, will occur for any locally independent item response theory with monotone item characteristic curves under assumption (c) alone. For this reason, we take the position that including the studied item in M is the correct way to use the MH procedure in DIF analyses, but we varied this factor in our study to measure its relative importance.

The six factors are arranged in a six-way factorial design, and are described in more detail in the next section. The section after that summarizes the results of the simulation study and the final section contains discussion and conclusions.

DESIGN OF THE STUDY

This study used Monte Carlo methods to investigate the effects of several factors on the MH and standardization procedures for detecting DIF. Data were simulated for 2,000 reference group simulated examinees ("simulees") and 500 focal group simulees. The θ's for the 2,000 reference group simulees were drawn from the normal, $N(0,1)$, distribution and the θ's for the 500 focal group simulees were drawn from the $N(-1,1)$ distribution. This choice of θ distributions models a common situation with a relatively small focal group whose average scores are substantially below those of the larger reference group (for example, Black/White or Hispanic/White comparisons). Twelve data sets were generated and each of these was then analyzed in eight different modes, as described later.

All items in the study had 3-PL IRFs (Equation 11). For all items, $c_j \equiv .2$, a common choice for modeling 5-response multiple choice items. The discrimination parameters, a_j, in Equation (11) were all the same, that is, $a_j \equiv a$, for all items within a data set, but the value of a varied across the data sets, as described later. Each data set consisted of dichotomous item responses with no missing data or omitted responses.

The Six Factors in the Study

As mentioned in the previous section, six independent variables were manipulated in this study. The chief variable of interest was whether or not the studied item exhibited IRT DIF. Four nuisance factors were also varied, due to their high salience and known effect in previous DIF research. They are described later in this section. The sixth variable was the inclusion or exclusion of the studied item in the matching variable, as described in the previous section. The independent

TABLE 7.1
Factors Varied in the Study

Between Data Sets

A: *a* parameter (three levels; A = .3, 1.0, 1.5)
N: number of DIF criterion items in the matching variable (four levels; N = 0, 1, 2, 4).

Within Data Sets

B: amount of DIF in studied item (two levels; B = 0, B = .3)
D: difficulty of the studied item (three levels; D = b_R = −.5, 0, .5)

Mode of Analysis

I: inclusion or exclusion of the studied item in the matching variable (two levels; I = *in*, I = *out*)
J: number of criterion items in the matching variable (four levels; J = 4, 9, 19, 39)

---

variables are summarized in Table 7.1. Each of these factors is described in more detail later.

Two factors, A (the value of the common discrimination parameter; three values, *a* = .3, 1.0, 1.5), and N (the number of DIF items in the set of criterion items; four levels), were fully crossed to define 12 data sets. These are described as the *between data set* factors in Table 7.1. Each data set consisted of simulated responses to 39 *criterion items* and 600 *study items* (a total of 639 items) for all 2,000 reference group and 500 focal group simulees. The 39 criterion items had 3-PL IRFs given by Formula (11) for both the reference and focal group. In all 12 data sets, the b_j parameter values for the reference group were the 39 values given in Table 7.2. The b_j values for the reference group were equally spaced from −1.85 to 1.85 in steps of .10, with the sole exception of b_{20} = 0.

TABLE 7.2
The Difficulty Parameters (b_j) for the Criterion Items
for the Reference Group in All 12 Data Sets

Item	b_j	Item	b_j	Item	b_j	Item	b_j
1	−1.85	11	−.85	21	.05	31	1.05
2	−1.75	12	−.75	22	.15	32	1.15
3	−1.65	13	−.65	23	.25	33	1.25
4	−1.55	14	−.55	24	.35	34	1.35
5	−1.45	15	−.45	25	.45	35	1.45
6	−1.35	16	−.35	26	.55	36	1.55
7	−1.25	17	−.25	27	.65	37	1.65
8	−1.15	18	−.15	28	.75	38	1.75
9	−1.05	19	−.05	29	.85	39	1.85
10	−.95	20	0.00	30	.95		

DIF in the criterion items was varied in the following way: An item exhibiting DIF was modeled by setting $B_j = b_{jF} - b_{jR} = .3$ so that each DIF item was more difficult for the focal group. There were four numbers of DIF items in the criterion: no DIF items, one, two, or four DIF items. The b_j parameters for the criterion items for the focal group depended on the number of DIF items in the criterion and were as follows:

$$
\begin{array}{lll}
0 \text{ DIF items:} & b_{jF} = b_{jR} & j = 1, \ldots, 39 \\
1 \text{ DIF item:} & b_{jF} = b_{jR} & j \neq 11 \\
 & b_{11F} = b_{11R} + .3 = -.55 & \\
2 \text{ DIF items:} & b_{jF} = b_{jR} & j \neq 11, 17 \\
 & b_{11F} = b_{11R} + .3 = -.55 & \\
 & b_{17F} = b_{17R} + .3 = .05 & \\
4 \text{ DIF items:} & b_{jF} = b_{jR} & j \neq 11, 17, 23, 29 \\
 & b_{11F} = b_{11R} + .3 = -.55 & \\
 & b_{17F} = b_{17R} + .3 = .05 & \\
 & b_{23F} = b_{23R} + .3 = .55 & \\
 & b_{29F} = b_{29R} + .3 = 1.15 &
\end{array}
$$

These choices of DIF items in the set of criterion items cover the range from easy to difficult.

The 600 study items in a data set were divided into six blocks of 100 items each. Two factors, B (the DIF of the study items; two levels, DIF item or not), and D (the overall difficulty of the study items; three levels, $b_j = -.5, 0, .5$), were crossed within each data set to define the six blocks of study items. The 100 items in each block were replicates of each other in the sense that they all had the same reference group IRF and the same focal group IRF. The IRFs for the reference and focal group study items were the same if the block of study items did not exhibit DIF and they differed in their b-parameters when the block of study items did exhibit DIF (again, $B = b_F - b_R = .3$). Thus, the cross-classification of the study items systematically varied both the overall difficulty of the study items from easy to hard and varied two levels of DIF, $B = 0$ and $B = .3$.

The interpretation of the size of B takes some care. For example, if we use Equation (13) to interpret B in terms of the delta scale used at ETS, we note that the discrimination parameter a must be taken into account. The three levels of Δ that correspond to $a = .3, 1,$ and 1.5 and $B = .3$ are: $-.36, -1.2,$ and -1.8. Of these values, $-.36$ would not be regarded as a large value of Δ, -1.2 is a borderline value and -1.8 is a large value.

Two factors, I (inclusion or exclusion of the studied item in the matching variable; two levels, *in* or *out*), and J (the number of criterion items included in the matching variable; four levels, 4, 9, 19, or 39 items), were crossed to form the eight modes of analysis of each data set. When I = *out*, the matching variable was the number right score of the included criterion items. When I = *in*, the matching variable was the number right score of the studied item *and* the included criterion items.

We varied the number of (non-study) items in the matching variable from 4 to 39 in order to study the effect of matching variables of differing lengths. Matching variables based on 4 or 9 items seemed to use to be too unreliable for practical use, but we had no real evidence for this. In practice, matching variables based on 19 and 39 items often occur.

The non-study items included in the matching variable depend on the level of factor *J*. These choices of items are specified as follows:

Number of Criterion Items	*Items from Table 7.2*
4	11, 17, 23, 29
9	5, 9, 11, 17, 20, 23, 29, 31, 35
19	odd numbered items from 1–17, number 20, and odd numbered items from 23–39
39	all criterion items.

These combinations of items were selected to cover similar ranges of difficulty for each level of *J*.

Dependent Variables

There were four dependent variables in our study. Two were based on the MH measure of DIF. Two were based on the standardization method.

For a given data set and a given mode of analysis, 600 DIF analyses were performed. Each of the study items was analyzed individually. In each of the six blocks of study items we averaged the 100 MH D-DIF values, the 100 STD P-DIF values, the 100 estimated standard errors of MH D-DIF, and the 100 estimated standard errors of STD P-DIF. In addition, we computed the standard deviation of the 100 MH D-DIF values and of the 100 STD P-DIF values.

The dependent variables used in our study were:

1. *MHD* = the average of the 100 MH D-DIF values.
2. *MH-RATIO* = the ratio of the standard deviation of the 100 MH D-DIF values to the average of the standard error of the 100 MH D-DIF values.
3. *STD-P* = the average of the 100 STD P-DIF values.
4. *STD-RATIO* = the ratio of the standard deviation of the 100 STD P-DIF values to the average of the standard error of the 100 STD P-DIF values.

MHD and *STD-P* allowed us to study how the population DIF values measured by the MH and standardization procedures vary as functions of the factors in Table 7.1. *MH-RATIO* and *STD-RATIO* allowed us to study the influence of the factors in Table 7.1 on the accuracy of the standard error estimates for MH D-DIF and STD P-DIF.

RESULTS

As described in Table 7.1, for each of the dependent variables in our study the basic data form a six-way classification of dimension ($3 \times 4 \times 2 \times 3 \times 2 \times 4$), for a total of 576 possible data values. In order to simplify the presentation of this large mass of information, we used the analysis of variance (ANOVA) main-effect and interaction mean-squares to identify those aspects of the simulation results that reveal interesting trends and large differences among the conditions. We first discuss the effect of the six factors on MH D-DIF, then on STD P-DIF, and then turn to their effect on the accuracy of the formulas for SE(MH D-DIF) given in Equation (3) and SE(STD P-DIF) given in Equation (8).

Effects on MH D-DIF

In the analyses reported in this subsection, the dependent variable is the average, MHD, of each set of 100 MH D-DIF values. MHD is an estimate of the true value, Δ, that underlies each observed value of MH D-DIF, and, being an average of 100 replicates, MHD is 10 times more accurate as an estimate of Δ than each single MH D-DIF value is. Because the average standard error of MH D-DIF in these data is about .3, the standard error of each MHD value is about .03. Thus, in our study the noise level due to Monte Carlo simulation is about .03 for MHD. Table 7.3 gives the six-way ANOVA results. Four-way and higher interactions, when pooled, yield a σ_{error} that is at the noise level (.03), so that we chose to ignore all interactions beyond three-way.

The Overall Picture

An examination of the mean squares in Table 3 shows that three of the factors (I, B, and D) have much larger main effects than the other three. In addition, four of the two-way interaction mean-squares (IJ, AB, AD, and BD) are at least twice as large as the others and two of the three-way interaction mean-squares (AIJ and ABD) are at least twice as large as the others.

In view of these results, in Table 7.4 we present the means for each of the six factors and for the BD, ABD, and AIJ cross-classifications. Even though from a strict testing point of view there are several other interactions that are statistically significant at the usual levels, they correspond to differences in the means that are smaller than those given in Table 7.4, and for simplicity of presentation we ignore them.

TABLE 7.3
ANOVA Results for Average Value of MH D–DIF

Effects	Source	df	SS	MS
Main Effects	A	2	1.392	0.696
	N	3	1.836	0.612
	B*	1	34.156	34.156*
	D*	2	16.373	8.186*
	I*	1	68.381	68.381*
	J	3	2.730	0.910
Two-way Interactions	AN	6	1.000	0.167
	AB*	2	4.800	2.400*
	AD*	4	5.657	1.414*
	AI	2	0.612	0.306
	AJ	6	0.157	0.026
	NB	3	0.013	0.004
	ND	6	0.070	0.012
	NI	3	0.312	0.104
	NJ	9	0.454	0.050
	BD*	2	1.435	0.718*
	BI	1	0.184	0.184
	BJ	3	0.048	0.016
	DI	2	0.129	0.065
	DJ	6	1.042	0.174
	IJ*	3	11.918	3.973*
Three-way Interactions	ANB	6	.062	.010
	AND	12	.156	.013
	ANI	6	.123	.021
	ANJ	18	.960	.053
	ABD*	4	.589	.147*
	ABI	2	.007	.004
	ABJ	6	.022	.004
	ADI	4	.054	.014
	ADJ	12	.470	.039
	AIJ*	6	1.064	.177*
	NBD	6	.005	.001
	NBI	3	.000	.000
	NBJ	9	.002	.000
	NDI	6	.002	.000
	NDJ	18	.017	.001
	NIJ	9	.143	.016
	BDI	2	.004	.002
	BDJ	6	.003	.000
	BIJ	3	.003	.001
	DIJ	6	.097	.016
Total of all Four- and Higher-way Interactions		361	.304	.001

$$\hat{\sigma}_{error} = .029$$

*The largest one-, two- and three-way mean squares.

TABLE 7.4
Means of Average Value of MH D–DIF Classified by the Six Factors
Singly and Cross-Classifed by Those Factors with the Largest
Two- and Three-way Interactions

I: $\dfrac{in}{-.1} \dfrac{out}{-.8}$ B: $\dfrac{0}{-.2} \dfrac{.3}{-.7}$ D: $\dfrac{-.5}{-.7} \dfrac{0}{-.5} \dfrac{.5}{-.3}$

J: $\dfrac{4}{-.6} \dfrac{9}{-.5} \dfrac{19}{-.5} \dfrac{39}{-.4}$ A: $\dfrac{.3}{-.4} \dfrac{1}{-.5} \dfrac{1.5}{-.5}$

N: $\dfrac{0}{-.6} \dfrac{1}{-.5} \dfrac{2}{-.5} \dfrac{4}{-.4}$

	D			
B	−.5	0	.5	*Average*
0	−.4	−.2	−.1	−.2
.3	−1.0	−.7	−.5	−.7
Average	−.7	−.5	−.3	−.5

		J				
I	A	4	9	19	39	*Average*
	.3	−.1	−.1	−.2	−.1	−.1
in	1	−.0	−.2	−.3	−.3	−.2
	1.5	.1	−.1	−.2	−.2	−.1
Average		−.0	−.1	−.2	−.2	−.1
	.3	−.9	−.8	−.7	−.5	−.7
out	1	−1.3	−1.0	−.8	−.6	−.9
	1.5	−1.2	−.9	−.8	−.6	−.9
Average		−1.1	−.9	−.7	−.5	−.8

		D			
A	B	−.5	0	.5	*Average*
.3	0	−.3	−.3	−.3	−.3
	.3	−.6	−.5	−.5	−.5
Average		−.5	−.4	−.4	−.4
1	0	−.4	−.3	−.1	−.3
	.3	−1.1	−.8	−.5	−.8
Average		−.8	−.5	−.3	−.5
1.5	0	−.4	−.2	.1	−.2
	.3	−1.3	−.8	−.4	−.8
Average		−.8	−.5	−.2	−.5

149

The true population mean value, Δ, that underlies the MHD value in each simulation condition (specified by A, N, B, D, I, and J) may be denoted by

$$\Delta(a,n,b,d,i,j).$$

The ANOVA results in Table 7.3 indicate that, to a reasonable approximation, as a function of the levels of the six factors, Δ has the following general form:

$$\Delta(a,n,b,d,i,j) = \beta_{abd} + \gamma_{aij} + \delta_n. \tag{15}$$

Equation (15) will be used to organize our discussion of the results displayed in Table 7.4.

The largest main-effect mean-square (MS) in Table 7.3 is for factor I (including or excluding the studied item from the matching variable). Equation (15) shows that the effect of excluding the studied item from the matching criterion is given by

$$\Delta(a,n,b,d,in,j) - \Delta(a,n,b,d,out,j) = \gamma_{a(in)j} - \gamma_{a(out)j}. \tag{16}$$

Thus, when I $=$ in, the value of Δ is shifted by the amount $\gamma_{a(in)j} - \gamma_{a(out)j}$ from what Δ is when I $=$ out. The shift depends only on the factors A and J, and does not depend on the other factors, B, D, or N. This finding is similar to the results discussed by Holland and Thayer (1988, p. 143) for the Rasch model case.

The values in Equation (16) can be calculated from the corresponding differences in the AIJ table of means in Table 7.4 and are given in Table 7.5.

From Table 7.5 we see that when J $=$ 4 or 9, A has a large, increasing effect on the shift, $\gamma_{a(in)j} - \gamma_{a(out)j}$, but when J $\geq$ 19, A has little effect on the shift. The effect of J is that increasing J decreases the differences between including and excluding the studied item from the matching variable. These results are not surprising—the more items in the matching variable, the less the other factors should matter.

The second largest main effect mean-square in Table 7.3 is for factor B (0 $=$ no IRT DIF, .3 $=$ IRT DIF). Equation (15) shows that the effect of B on Δ is given by

$$\Delta(a, n, .3, d, i, j) - \Delta(a, n, 0, d, i, j) = \beta_{a(.3)d} - \beta_{a(0)d}, \tag{17}$$

so that the effect of IRT DIF on MHD is moderated by A and D, but not by M, I, or J. The values of $\beta_{a(.3)d} - \beta_{a(0)d}$ in Equation (17) are given in Table 7.6.

The effect of increasing A in Table 7.6 is to increase the difference between Δ in the IRT DIF and no IRT DIF cases, and the effect of increasing D is to decrease this difference. If we were to use Formula (13) to compute values of Δ for B $=$ .3, we would get values of $-.36$, -1.2 and -1.8 corresponding to a $=$ .3, 1.0 and 1.5, respectively. Note that the corresponding values in Table 7.6 are generally smaller than these. Furthermore, the values in Table 7.6 $decrease$ in absolute value as D, the difficulty of the studied item for the reference group, increases. This is due to our choice of a common non-zero guessing parameter

TABLE 7.5
Value of $\gamma_{a(in)j} - \gamma_{a(out)j}$

A	J			
	4	9	19	39
.3	.8	.7	.5	.4
1	1.2	.8	.5	.3
1.5	1.3	.9	.5	.3

for the studied item in our study, that is, $c_R = c_F = .2$. Indeed, factor D has the third largest main effect mean-square in Table 7.3. The effect of increasing the level of D is to lower the value of MH D-DIF both as a main effect and in its interaction with both B and A (see Table 7.4).

Factor A has a small main effect in this study but it interacts strongly with both the BD and IJ cross-classifications, as described in Tables 7.5 and 7.6.

Finally, factor N, the number of IRT DIF items in the matching variable, has a small main effect and very small interactions with the rest of the factors in the study. The effect of increasing N is to slightly decrease the value of Δ over the range of values included in this study. This decrease is what one would expect, because IRT DIF items in the matching variable ought to dilute the ability of the MH procedure to detect IRT DIF in the studied items. The fact that this is one of the smallest effects in our study suggests that the potential harm to DIF analysis of IRT DIF in the matching variable is not as significant a consideration as other factors—for example, including the studied item in the matching criterion, or the difficulty of the studied item when it has a common non-zero guessing parameter.

Perhaps the most important result of this overall look at our simulation results is that, of the nuisance factors varied in this study, factor I (inclusion or exclusion of the studied item in the matching variable score) has the largest effect on the

TABLE 7.6
Value of $\beta_{a(.3)d} - \beta_{a(.0)d}$

A	D		
	−.5	0	.5
.3	−.3	−.2	−.2
1	−.7	−.6	−.4
1.5	−.9	−.6	−.4

amount of DIF in the studied item. The effect of factor I is even larger than the effect of the amount of IRT DIF in the studied item, that is, factor B. This result immediately raises the issue of whether to include the studied item or to exclude it from the matching variable score is preferable in operational DIF analyses. In our opinion, the choice is clear-cut on theoretical grounds, as we discussed in the section on the item response theory definition of DIF. Excluding the studied item from the matching variable score will result in items that have no IRT DIF exhibiting non-zero DIF (i.e., false positives), and this phenomenon is an increasing function of the differences in the matching variable score distributions for the focal and reference groups.

Analyses That Always Include the Studied Item in the Matching Variable

We take the position that a proper application of the MH procedure to DIF studies must *include* the studied item in the matching criterion, for reasons already stated, and we do not consider the case of excluding the studied item from M further in this section.

We divided the data into those cases in which the studied item has no IRT DIF (i.e., the null hypothesis) and those cases in which it does have IRT DIF. These correspond to B = 0 and B = .3 in this study. We discuss each in turn.

TABLE 7.7
ANOVA for Average Value of MH D-DIF
in Which B = 0 and I = *in*

Source	df	SS	MS
A	2	1.187	.594
N	3	.910	.303
D	2	2.467	1.234
J	3	.790	.263
AN*	6	.430	.072*
AD*	4	.808	.202*
AJ	6	.193	.032
ND	6	.017	.002
NJ	9	.264	.029
DJ*	6	.460	.077*
Total of all Three-way interactions	60	.740	.012
Four-way	36	.0134	.0004
		$\hat{\sigma}_{error}$ = .019	

*Largest two-way mean squares.

When B = 0 (a Studied Item with No IRT DIF).   Table 7.7 gives the ANOVA for B = 0 and I = *in*. The biggest main effects are A and D and the largest two-way interactions are AD, DJ, and AN. The higher-order interactions, although sometimes statistically significant at the usual levels, are quite small and are ignored in our discussion. Table 7.8 gives the means for MHD when B = 0 and I = *in*, for the four factors A, N, D, and J, and for the AD, DJ, and AN cross-classifications.

The ideal result would be for none of the factors in the study to influence MHD when B = 0 and I = *in*—that is, the same result as in Equation (13). In fact, the averages in Table 7.8 *are* generally smaller in absolute value than the corresponding average values in Table 7.4, and this is what we expect. However, there are a few values in Table 7.8 that are a cause for concern. For example, when D = .5 (a difficult studied item) the average value of MHD is .3. This is increased to .5 when A = 1.5 (all items are very highly discriminating). When there are few criterion items in the matching variable (J = 4 and 9) there is also a greater sensitivity of MHD to the level of D. When J = 19 or more, the sensitivity of MHD to the difficulty level of the studied item is probably not of great importance. Finally, the effect of IRT DIF items in the matching variable is most acute when A = 1.5. For the more realistic case of A = 1, MHD hardly varies at all with the value of N, and then only when there are four IRT DIF items in the matching criterion. When A = 1, the average value of MHD for combinations of J ≥ 19 and N are given in Table 7.9.

We see from Table 7.9 that, in the realistic cases of J, the influence of IRT DIF in the matching variable is quite small under the null hypothesis.

When B = .3 (a Studied Item with IRT DIF).   Table 7.10 gives the ANOVA of MHD when B = .3 and I = *in*. The same main effect and two-way interactions that we saw in Table 7.7 dominate in Table 7.10. Table 7.11 gives the means for each of the factors and important two-way interactions when B = .3 and I = *in*.

As we expected, when the studied item has IRT DIF against the focal group, MHD is more negative than it is when the studied item has no IRT DIF. By far the most important effect is that for the difficulty of the studied item. The overall result is that Δ is a *decreasing* function of the difficulty of the studied item, factor D, when the studied item has IRT DIF. The reason for this is that in our simulation the reference and focal groups have the same non-zero guessing parameters, c. What this means in practice is that if the guessing parameter is the same for the reference and focal group, then the MH procedure is less likely to detect a given amount of IRT DIF in a hard item than in an easy item. Table 7.12a gives the means for MHD for the realistic situation when A = 1 and J ≥ 19. Even in this case, the effect of D on MHD is quite dramatic. This is in contradistinction to the very small effect N has on MHD in Table 7.12b.

TABLE 7.8
Means of Average Value of MH D-DIF Classified by A, N, D, and J
Singly and Cross-Classified by AD, DJ, and AN (For B = 0 and I = *in*)

$$D: \frac{-.5 \quad 0 \quad .5}{-.1 \quad .1 \quad .3} \qquad A: \frac{.3 \quad 1 \quad 1.5}{-.0 \quad .1 \quad .2}$$

$$N: \frac{0 \quad 1 \quad 2 \quad 4}{-.0 \quad .1 \quad .1 \quad .2} \qquad J: \frac{4 \quad 9 \quad 19 \quad 39}{.2 \quad .1 \quad .0 \quad .0}$$

	D			
A	−.5	0	.5	*Average*
.3	−.0	−.0	.0	−.0
1	−.1	.1	.3	.1
1.5	−.1	.2	.5	.2
Average	−.1	.1	.3	.1

	D			
J	−.5	0	.5	*Average*
4	−.1	.2	.5	.2
9	−.1	.1	.3	.1
−19	−.1	.0	.2	.0
−39	−.0	.0	.1	.0
Average	−.1	.1	.3	.1

	N				
A	0	1	2	4	*Average*
.3	−.1	−.0	.1	.0	−.0
1	.1	.1	.1	.2	.1
1.5	0	.2	.2	.4	.2
Average	−0	.1	.1	.2	.1

154

TABLE 7.9
Means for Average Value of MH D-DIF
for B = 0, I = *in*, A = 1 and Combinations
of J ≥ 19 and N

J	N			
	0	1	2	4
19	.1	−.0	.0	.1
39	.0	.1	.1	.0

Effects on *STD-P*

It is routinely found in DIF analyses that the values of MH D-DIF and of STD P-DIF are highly correlated across test items. Thus, it is not a surprise to find that the conclusions discussed in the previous section for MH D-DIF are virtually the same as those for STD P-DIF. Table 7.13 gives the ANOVA results for STD P-DIF that are analogous to those given in Table 7.3 for MH D-DIF. Again we see that the largest main effects are for factors I, B, and D; the largest two-way interactions are for IJ, AB, AD, and BD; and the largest three-way interactions are for ABD and AIJ. Table 7.14 gives the means for all the main effects and the above-mentioned two- and three-way effects. In comparing Tables 7.3 and 7.13,

TABLE 7.10
ANOVA for Average Value of MH D–DIF
in Which B = .3 and I = *in*

Source	df	SS	MS
A	2	1.615	.808
N	3	.832	.277
D	2	8.034	4.017
J	3	1.086	.362
AN*	6	.343	.057*
AD*	4	2.917	.729*
AJ	6	.294	.049
ND	6	.028	.004
NJ	9	.261	.029
DJ*	6	.418	.070*
Total of all Three-way interactions	60	.6785	.011
Four-way	36	.0154	.0004
			$\hat{\sigma}_{error}$ = .021

*Largest two-way mean squares.

TABLE 7.11
Means of Average Value of MH D-DIF Classified by A, N, D, and J
Singly and Cross-Classified by AD, DJ, and AN
(For B = .3 and I = *in*)

$$D: \frac{-.5}{-.7} \; \frac{0}{-.4} \; \frac{.5}{-.1} \qquad A: \frac{.3}{-.2} \; \frac{1}{-.5} \; \frac{1.5}{-.5}$$

$$N: \frac{0}{-.5} \; \frac{1}{-.4} \; \frac{2}{-.4} \; \frac{4}{-.3} \qquad J: \frac{4}{-.3} \; \frac{9}{-.4} \; \frac{19}{-.4} \; \frac{39}{-.4}$$

	D			
A	−.5	0	.5	*Average*
.3	−.3	−.2	−.2	−.2
1	−.8	−.5	−.2	−.5
1.5	−1.0	−.4	−.0	−.5
Average	−.7	−.4	−.1	−.4

	D			
J	−.5	0	.5	*Average*
4	−.7	−.2	.1	−.3
9	−.7	−.4	−.1	−.4
19	−.7	−.4	−.2	−.4
39	−.7	−.5	−.3	−.4
Average	−.7	−.4	−.1	−.4

	N				
A	0	1	2	4	*Average*
.3	−.3	−.3	−.1	−.2	−.2
1	−.6	−.5	−.4	−.4	−.5
1.5	−.6	−.5	−.5	−.2	−.5
Average	−.5	−.4	−.4	−.3	−.4

TABLE 7.12
a: Means of Average Value of MH D-DIF
for B = .3, I = *in*, A = 1 and Combinations
of J ≥ 19 and D

	D		
J	−.5	0	.5
19	−.9	−.5	−.3
39	−.8	−.6	−.3

b: Means for Average Value of MH D-DIF
for B = .3, I = *in*, A = 1 and Combinations
of J ≥ 19 and N

	N			
J	0	1	2	4
19	−.5	−.6	−.6	−.5
39	−.5	−.5	−.5	−.6

remember that MH D-DIF is typically about 10 times bigger than the corresponding STD P-DIF value. Hence the mean squares in Table 7.13 have been multiplied by 100 to make them more comparable in magnitude to those in Table 7.3.

The conclusions reached for MH D-DIF also hold for STD P-DIF. In particular, the importance of including the studied item's score in the matching variable is as important for STD P-DIF as it is for MH D-DIF. The values in Table 7.14 are multiplied by 10 to make them more comparable to the values in Table 7.4.

There is one small difference between MH D-DIF and STD P-DIF, which can be seen in a comparison of Tables 7.4 and 7.14. STD P-DIF changes *slightly* more slowly as a function of the factors in the study than does MH D-DIF. This means that STD P-DIF is slightly less sensitive to the nuisance factors in the study than is MH D-DIF. This is a desirable result, but unfortunately it is coupled with a slightly decreased sensitivity to IRT DIF (i.e., factor B) as well. What is desired in an improvement over the MH D-DIF measure is a decreased sensitivity to the nuisance factors coupled with an increased sensitivity to IRT DIF.

Effects on *SE(MH D-DIF)*

In this section we discuss the effect of all six factors in our study on the accuracy of the estimated standard error of MH D-DIF given in Equation (3). Our approach is to study the variation in the variable called *MH-RATIO*—the ratio of the standard deviation of the 100 replications of MH D-DIF in each of the six sets

TABLE 7.13
ANOVA Results for Average Value of STD P-DIF

Effects	Source	df	SS	MS × 100
Main Effects	A	2	.00690210	0.35
	N	3	.01002729	0.33
	B*	1	.20249250	20.24*
	D*	2	.11786383	5.89*
	I*	1	.57843630	57.84*
	J	3	.03583375	1.19*
Two-way Interactions	AB*	2	.01566305	0.78*
	AD*	4	.03779932	0.94*
	AI	2	.00080543	0.04
	AJ	6	.00290611	0.05
	NA	6	.00586114	0.10
	NB	3	.00007482	0.00
	ND	6	.00041355	0.01
	NI	3	.00131399	0.04
	NJ	9	.00202140	0.02
	BI	1	.00073622	0.07
	BJ	3	.00032094	0.01
	DB*	2	.01154336	0.58*
	DI	2	.00046890	0.02
	DJ	6	.00583799	0.10
	JI*	3	.09966381	3.32*
Three-way Interactions	NAD	12	.00107789	0.01
	NAB	6	.00047656	0.01
	NAJ	18	.00586727	0.03
	NAI	6	.00066155	0.01
	NDB	6	.00004906	0.00
	NDJ	18	.00007699	0.00
	NDI	6	.00001140	0.00
	NBJ	9	.00000317	0.00
	NBI	3	.00000048	0.00
	ADB*	4	.00422144	0.11*
	ADJ	12	.00278566	0.02
	ADI	4	.00047868	0.01
	ABJ	6	.00003320	0.00
	ABI	2	.00009471	0.00
	AJI*	6	.00495088	0.08*
	DBJ	6	.00002130	0.00
	DBI	2	.00005353	0.00
	DJI	6	.00014292	0.00
	BJI	3	.00029297	0.01
Total of all Four- and Higher-way Interactions		361	.00149992	0.00

$10\ \hat{\sigma}_{error} = .0204$

*The largest one-, two- and three-way mean squares.

158

TABLE 7.14
Means of 10 × Average Value of STD P-DIF Classified by the Six Factors Singly and Cross-Classifed by Those Factors with the Largest Two- and Three-way Interactions

$$I: \frac{in}{-.1} \quad \frac{out}{-.7} \qquad B: \frac{0}{-.2} \quad \frac{.3}{-.6} \qquad D: \frac{-.5}{-.6} \quad \frac{0}{-.4} \quad \frac{.5}{-.3}$$

$$J: \frac{4}{-.5} \quad \frac{9}{-.5} \quad \frac{19}{-.4} \quad \frac{39}{-.3} \qquad A: \frac{.3}{-.4} \quad \frac{1}{-.5} \quad \frac{1.5}{-.4}$$

$$N: \frac{0}{-.5} \quad \frac{1}{-.4} \quad \frac{2}{-.4} \quad \frac{4}{-.4}$$

		D		
B	−.5	0	.5	Average
0	−.4	−.2	−.1	−.2
.3	−.9	−.6	−.4	−.6
Average	−.6	−.4	−.3	−.4

		J				
I	A	4	9	19	39	Average
in	.3	−.1	−.1	−.2	−.2	−.1
	1	−.0	−.1	−.2	−.2	−.1
	1.5	.0	−.0	−.1	−.2	−.1
Average		−.0	−.1	−.2	−.2	−.1
out	.3	−.9	−.8	−.7	−.5	−.8
	1	−1.2	−.9	−.7	−.5	−.8
	1.5	−1.0	−.7	−.6	−.4	−.7
Average		−1.0	−.8	−.7	−.5	−.7

		D			
A	B	−.5	0	.5	Average
.3	0	−.4	−.3	−.3	−.3
	.3	−.6	−.5	−.5	−.6
Average		−.5	−.4	−.4	−.4
1	0	−.4	−.2	−.9	−.2
	.3	−1.0	−.7	−.4	−.7
Average		−.7	−.5	−.2	−.5
1.5	0	−.3	−.1	−.0	−.2
	.3	−1.0	−.7	−.4	−.6
Average		−.7	−.4	−.1	−.5

of study items to the average value of the corresponding 100 values of the standard error of MH D-DIF computed using Equation (3). The use of the average value of these 100 standard error values is justified because there was very little variation in them across the 100 replicates (the standard deviation of the 100 standard error estimates was less than .01 in all 576 cases). *MH-RATIO* will be bigger than 1.0 when the true standard error is larger than the one

TABLE 7.15
ANOVA Results for Ratio (observed standard deviation of MH D-DIF)/
(average value standard error of MH D-DIF)

Effects	Source	df	SS	MS
Main Effects	A	2	.0347	.0174
	N	3	.0078	.0026
	B	1	.0142	.0142
	D*	2	.6490	.3245*
	I*	1	.1483	.1483*
	J*	3	.2768	.0923*
Two-way Interactions	AN*	6	.2186	.0364*
	AB*	2	.3990	.1995*
	AD*	4	.0734	.0184*
	AI	2	.0031	.0016
	AJ	6	.0067	.0011
	NB	3	.0407	.0136
	ND*	6	.2062	.0344*
	NI	3	.0004	.0001
	NJ	9	.0022	.0002
	BD*	2	.4237	.2119*
	BI	1	.0000	.0000
	BJ	3	.0008	.0003
	DI	2	.0005	.0003
	DJ	6	.0037	.0006
	IJ*	3	.1088	.0363*
Largest Three-way Interactions	ANB	6	.1312	.0219
	AND	12	.2037	.0170
	ABD	4	.0566	.0142
	NBD	6	.1463	.0244
Remaining Three-way Interactions		116	.0289	.0002
				$\hat{\sigma} = .016$
Four- and Higher-way Interactions		361	.1987	.0006
				$\hat{\sigma}_{error} = .023$

*The largest one-, and two-way mean squares.

estimated by Equation (3) and will be less than 1.0 when the true standard error is less than the one given by Equation (3).

Table 7.15 gives the six-way ANOVA results when *MH-RATIO* is the dependent variable. The largest main effects are for factors D, J, and I, and the largest two-way interactions are BD, AB, AN, IJ, AD, and ND. The corresponding tables of means are given in Table 7.16. Although there are other significant interactions in Table 7.15, they correspond to smaller differences across the factor levels and are ignored here.

The overall mean of *MH-RATIO* in this study is .96, indicating that, overall, the standard error formula given in Equation (3) tends to overestimate the actual standard error of MH D-DIF by about 4%. The value of *MH-RATIO* varies from a low of .75 to a high of 1.22 over all 576 data values. Some of this variation is due to statistical noise and some is due to real differences among the factors. By concentrating on those factors and interactions in Table 7.15 with the largest mean squares, we can identify the most important trends.

MH-RATIO averages 1.01 for D = 0, but is smaller (.93 and .95) for the other two levels of D. Thus, Formula (3) is most accurate for middle-difficulty items. When the studied item is excluded from the matching criterion, *MH-RATIO* is more nearly unity (.98) than it is when the studied item is included (.94). When J increases, *MH-RATIO* tends toward unity, so that when there are at least 19 items in the matching variable score, Formula (3) is an accurate estimate of the standard error of MH D-DIF. Increasing A decreases *MH-RATIO,* so that Formula (3) is the least accurate for highly discriminating items. The main effects of both B and N on *MH-RATIO* are quite small.

The interactions in Table 7.16 are complicated, often involving nonmonotonic trends, and are not summarized easily. For the most part, these results support the use of Formula (3) for the standard error of MH D-DIF. They suggest that confidence intervals based on Formula (3) will tend to be too large by approximately 5%, which is quite satisfactory for much practical work.

Effects on *SE(STD P-DIF)*

Tables 7.17 and 7.18, for *STD-RATIO,* are parallel to Tables 7.15 and 7.16 for *MH-RATIO.* They give information about the accuracy of the standard error formula in Formulas (8)–(10) for STD P-DIF. The average value of *STD-RATIO* is .92, which indicates that, in this study at least, Formula (8) tends to overestimate the actual standard error of STD P-DIF by 8% or 9%. Thus, Formula (8) is slightly worse at estimating the standard error of STD P-DIF than Formula (3) is at estimating the standard error of MH D-DIF. This is not too surprising because of the large amount of work that went into the development of a useful standard error for the Mantel–Haenszel log–odds–ratio estimator, starting with Hauck (1979). In contrast, Formulas (8)–(10) are based on simple asymptotic approx-

TABLE 7.16
Means for Ratio (observed standard deviation of MH D-DIF)/
(average value of standard error of MH D-DIF) Classified by the Six Factors
Singly and Cross-Classified by Those Factors with the Largest Two-way Interactions

D: $\dfrac{-.5}{.93} \dfrac{0}{1.01} \dfrac{.5}{.95}$ I: $\dfrac{in}{.94} \dfrac{out}{.98}$

J: $\dfrac{4}{.93} \dfrac{9}{.96} \dfrac{19}{.97} \dfrac{39}{.99}$

A: $\dfrac{.3}{.97} \dfrac{1}{.97} \dfrac{1.5}{.95}$ B: $\dfrac{0}{.97} \dfrac{.3}{.96}$

N: $\dfrac{0}{.95} \dfrac{1}{.96} \dfrac{2}{.96} \dfrac{4}{.96}$

	D					A			
B	−.5	0	.5	Average	B	.3	1	1.5	Average
0	.90	1.05	.95	.97	0	1.01	.95	.94	.97
.3	.95	.97	.95	.96	.3	.92	.98	.96	.96
Average	.93	1.01	.95	.96	Average	.97	.97	.95	.96

	N						N				
A	0	1	2	4	Average	D	0	1	2	4	Average
.3	.97	.98	.93	.99	.97	−.5	.95	.93	.91	.92	.93
1	.95	.97	1.00	.94	.97	0	1.02	.99	1.01	1.01	1.01
1.5	.95	.93	.96	.97	.95	.5	.90	.96	.96	.96	.95
Average	.95	.96	.96	.96	.96	Average	.95	.96	.96	.96	.96

	J						A			
I	4	9	19	39	Average	D	.3	1	1.5	Average
in	.89	.94	.97	.98	.94	−.5	.94	.93	.91	.93
out	.97	.97	.98	.99	.98	0	1.02	1.00	1.00	1.01
Average	.93	.96	.97	.99	.96	.5	.93	.97	.94	.95
						Average	.97	.97	.95	.96

TABLE 7.17
ANOVA Results for Ratio (observed standard deviation of STD P-DIF)/(average value of standard error of STD P-DIF)

Effects	Source	df	SS	MS
Main Effects	A*	2	.3760	.1880*
	N	3	.0150	.0050
	B	1	.0022	.0022
	D*	2	.7297	.3649*
	I*	1	.9728	.9728*
	J*	3	.7056	.2352*
Two-way Interactions	AN*	6	.2669	.0445*
	AB*	2	.4344	.2172*
	AD*	4	.2289	.0572*
	AI	2	.0003	.0001
	AJ	6	.0029	.0005
	NB	3	.0358	.0119
	ND*	6	.1540	.0257*
	NI	3	.0007	.0002
	NJ	9	.0054	.0006
	BD*	2	.3858	.1929*
	BI	1	.0000	.0000
	BJ	3	.0009	.0003
	DI	2	.0092	.0046
	DJ	6	.0060	.0010
	IJ*	3	.4214	.1404*
Largest Three-way Interactions	ANB	6	.1005	.0167
	AND	12	.1786	.0149
	ABD	4	.0472	.0118
	NBD	6	.1461	.0243
Remaining Three-way Interactions		116	.0700	.0006
				$\hat{\sigma} = .025$
Four- and Higher-way Interactions		361	.1876	.0005
				$\hat{\sigma}_{\text{error}} = .023$

*The largest one-, and two-way mean squares.

imations that are suspect when the number of cases in each 2×2 table is small. Nonetheless, for the range of cases examined in this study, Formula (8) gives a standard error that is good enough for much practical work.

The trends in the main effects in Table 7.17 and in the means in Table 7.18 are very similar to those found for *MH-RATIO*. Formula (8) is more accurate when D = 0 than when D = ±.5. Excluding the studied item from the matching criterion increases the accuracy of Formula (8). Increasing J increases the accuracy of

TABLE 7.18
Means for Ratio (observed standard deviation of STD P-DIF)/(average value of standard error of STD P-DIF) Classified by the Six Factors Singly and Cross-Classified by Those Factors with the Largest Two-way Interactions

D: $\dfrac{-.5}{.87} \dfrac{0}{.96} \dfrac{.5}{.92}$ I: $\dfrac{in}{.88} \dfrac{out}{.96}$

J: $\dfrac{4}{.86} \dfrac{9}{.91} \dfrac{10}{.94} \dfrac{39}{.96}$

A: $\dfrac{.3}{.95} \dfrac{1}{.92} \dfrac{1.5}{.89}$ B: $\dfrac{0}{.92} \dfrac{.3}{.91}$

N: $\dfrac{0}{.91} \dfrac{1}{.92} \dfrac{2}{.92} \dfrac{4}{.92}$

	D						A			
B	−.5	0	.5	Average		B	.3	1	1.5	Average
0	.85	1.00	.92	.92		0	.99	.90	.87	.92
.3	.90	.92	.92	.91		.3	.91	.94	.90	.91
Average	.87	.96	.92	.92		Average	.95	.92	.89	.92

	N						N				
A	0	1	2	4	Average	D	0	1	2	4	Average
.3	.94	.98	.91	.97	.95	−.5	.89	.88	.85	.87	.87
1	.90	.93	.95	.89	.92	0	.96	.94	.96	.97	.96
1.5	.88	.86	.89	.91	.89	.5	.88	.94	.94	.93	.92
Average	.91	.92	.92	.92	.92	Average	.91	.92	.92	.92	.92

	J						A			
I	4	9	19	39	Average	D	.3	1	1.5	Average
in	.78	.87	.91	.94	.88	−.5	.92	.86	.83	.87
out	.95	.95	.96	.97	.96	0	1.01	.95	.92	.96
Average	.86	.91	.94	.96	.92	.5	.91	.94	.91	.92
						Average	.95	.92	.89	.92

Formula (8), but increasing A decreases this accuracy to 89% for A = 1.5. The effects of both B and N on *STD-RATIO* are negligible.

As in Table 7.14 for *MH-RATIO,* the interactions shown in Table 7.18 for *STD-RATIO* are complicated, often showing nonmonotonic trends, and are not easily summarized. They suggest that confidence intervals based on Formulas (8)–(10) will tend to be too large by 5% to 10%. This may be satisfactory for practical work, but it also suggests that improvements in the estimation of this standard error estimate may be desirable.

DISCUSSION

Although the number of factors varied in this study resulted in 576 different combinations of conditions, it nonetheless represents only a small foray into the possibilities that Monte Carlo studies of DIF procedures can take. Even so, we believe that it has yielded useful information and suggests some important areas for future work.

First of all, it shows that the inclusion of the studied item in the matching variable score has the important effect of reducing false positives in DIF analyses. Furthermore, it shows that excluding the studied item from the matching variable score has a non-negligible effect in situations of practical significance. We would summarize the current state of knowledge about including the studied item in the matching criterion as follows: When the Rasch model holds it is exactly the right thing to do and when the Rasch model does not hold it has the desirable effect of reducing the false positive rate, but not as well as it does in the case of the Rasch model. Interestingly, when the studied item is included in M, Formula (3) for the standard error of MH D-DIF is somewhat less accurate than when it is excluded from M. We recommend including the studied item in the matching variable score whenever the MH procedure is used in DIF analyses, even though the accuracy of the standard error estimate will suffer slightly from this.

The most important problem that this study has uncovered is the effect item difficulty has on the ability of both the MH and the standardization procedures to detect a given amount of IRT DIF when both the reference and focal group have the same non-zero guessing parameter, c. We suspect that most DIF analysis procedures that do not make explicit corrections of guessing parameters will have this same problem. Lord (1980) discussed a related problem with the delta plot technique and his suggestions for corrections for guessing in that case may be a good starting point for similar corrections for the MH procedure. This is certainly an important area for future research.

It is also clear from our study that short tests should not be used routinely to construct matching variables. Only when J = 19 or 39, in our study, were MH D-DIF and STD P-DIF not overly affected by the nuisance factors.

The relatively small influence of IRT DIF in the matching variable score that occurs in our study suggests that this problem is not as serious in practice as it is often proposed to be. Factor N, the number of IRT DIF items in M, had small main effects and interactions with the other factors. Surely further work in this area is in order along the lines of our study.

Finally, although the standard error formula for both MH D-DIF and STD P-DIF are good enough for much of current practice, the larger amount of overestimation of the standard error of STD P-DIF suggests that work on improving this estimate is worthwhile.

8 Comments on the Monte Carlo Study of Donoghue, Holland, and Thayer

J. O. Ramsay
McGill University

It is a pleasure to begin by congratulating the authors on an unusually successful Monte Carlo study. Indeed, the study is so well designed and executed that I am resolved to use it as a model for students and colleagues contemplating a similar approach to their problems.

Although one normally would be daunted by a six-factor analysis of variance (ANOVA), it turns out that not one of the factors should have been eliminated. Although the presence of a small number of biased criterion items proved relatively harmless (Factor N), it was essential to find out. We also are reassured by the success of the estimated variance of $\text{Log}(\hat{\alpha})$. These are two potential problems that probably can be much downgraded in importance as a result of the study.

The important problems areas are now well delineated. It seems clear that the studied item should not be dropped from the matching test (Factor I), and Charles Lewis clarified this point further. (See chapter 15, this volume) The big influence of the difficulty factor (D) is perhaps a little surprising, and an approach to further study of this problem is outlined later. It also seems obvious that having as few as 9 items in the matching test is a bad idea, and that as many as 20 or so is probably adequate, but this hardly seems surprising.

The study leaves me less satisfied with respect to either the effect of the bias in the studied item (Factor B) or the presence of biased items in the matching test. In both cases there needs to be an investigation covering a wider range of values than were included in this study. Nevertheless, the study points us in the right direction for further research.

It only remains to ask where one goes from here. I have two reactions as a comparative outsider in this area to this use of the Mantel–Haenszel (MH) statistic. Both relate to the adequacy of the statistic itself:

1. Where a constant is being estimated, should we be thinking in terms of a (smooth) function?
2. Where something is being added, or an expectation being taken, would there be an advantage to a weighted sum or integral?

But before looking more closely at these issues, let us review the strengths and weaknesses of MH D-DIF as they appear to me. On the plus side, we have:

1. The conceptual and computational simplicity of the statistic.
2. Its consistency.
3. Its stability in terms of both high asymptotic efficiency and robustness.
4. Its power for an interesting alternative hypothesis.
5. Its simple additive metric properties.
6. The fact that it is well understood in terms of its statistical properties and in terms of its usefulness in other areas of application.

In particular, MH derives its robustness from the principle that ratios of sums are much more stable than sums of ratios, even if it is the latter that is being estimated.

On the negative side, there is:

1. The heavy emphasis on the MH literature and in this application on confirmation and hypothesis testing as opposed to exploration and data diagnostics.
2. The plausibility of a constant α as a model for DIF.
3. The necessity of conditioning on the noisy and potentially biased estimate of θ provided by the score on a matching test.

The first and second "weaknesses" just mentioned possibly can be addressed by the following generalization of $\hat{\alpha}_{WM}$:

$$\hat{\alpha}_{WMH} = \frac{\sum_k w_k A_k D_k / T_k}{\sum_k w_k B_k C_k / T_k}, \tag{1}$$

where the weights w_k are required to add to any fixed constant such as unity. By a suitable choice of these weights, a number of interesting things appear to be possible.

Of particular interest is the situation where all the w_k's except those of a small range or "window" are zero. This permits a kernel smoothing estimate of a localized value of α, and by moving this window along the range of index values, we can arrive at a relatively smooth function $\hat{\alpha}(\theta)$ rather than a simple constant. The smoothness of this function and other characteristics are determined by the width and shape of the kernel. In the simplest case, we can use the rectangular or uniform kernel,

$$w_k(k_0) = \begin{bmatrix} 1, |w_k - w_{k_0}| \leq C \\ 0, \text{ otherwise} \end{bmatrix}. \tag{2}$$

It is known that this simplest kernel actually behaves rather well relative to more sophisticated kernels, at least if one is not too near the boundaries on θ or the upper or lower limit on index k_0 (Eubank, 1988; Hardle, 1990). Of course, if the actual value of α is a constant rather than a varying function, this procedure will lose relatively little, and I suspect even can be proven a consistent estimator of this constant.

When one has learned to fear a particular type of nonconstant departure from the null model $\alpha = 1$, one can tailor these weights to be maximally sensitive to this departure, just as one does in contrast detection in ANOVA situations. This may be one way to deal with the effects of varying item difficulty (Factor D).

To say that a study has generated great excitement about new research is high praise indeed, and I thank the authors as well as the organizers of the conference most sincerely for the opportunity to discuss this most interesting article.

9 Stability of the MH D-DIF Statistics Across Populations

Nicholas T. Longford
Paul W. Holland
Dorothy T. Thayer
Educational Testing Service

The Mantel–Haenszel differential item functioning (MH D-DIF) statistics play an important role in the assessment of the appropriateness of test forms intended for administration to examinees from populations that contain identifiable disjoint subpopulations, such as ethnic groups, men and women, or sociodemographically or geographically defined subpopulations. A typical DIF (*differential item functioning*) analysis deals with a test form administered to a set of examinees from two disjoint population groups, referred to as the *focal* and *reference* groups. The examinees rarely are obtained as a sample drawn from a population using a sampling design, but for the purposes of DIF analysis it is assumed that they provide an adequate representation of the population. Suppose for this population there is a unidimensional ability scale underlying the performance on the test form. Then in the cross-classification of the two population subgroups by the scores on this scale we have pairs of matched subgroups, that is, members of the two population subgroups with identical abilities. An item in the test form is said to have no DIF if the proportions of correct responses to the item are identical for each pair of matched subgroups. Of principal interest is detection of the items with substantial DIF for at least one pair of population subgroups.

In a realistic situation the ability scale is not available, and it is replaced by a proxy, such as the observed score on a test. This proxy is referred to as the *matching variable*. It is important to distinguish between two kinds of matching variables: internal and external. The former is derived from the same test form as the one subject to the DIF analysis, whereas the latter is obtained from an external source, such as a different test.

One of the most important settings in which the DIF analysis is applied is that of pretesting of new test forms. A number of obvious factors influencing the DIF of an item has been identified in the past, and prior to each pretest the items are screened carefully for these factors. However, items with high DIF still occur in most pretests, due to the imperfect knowledge of the causes for high DIF, and possibly due to various sources of bias in the analysis and due to sampling variation of the estimates. Inference about DIF based on the pretest examinees is used as a prediction for DIF in a future administration, which will take place at a different time, and possibly on a set of examinees with a different composition than that in the pretest. Aware of this fact, users of the DIF analyses have been concerned for some time about the dependence of DIF on the underlying population. We note that by a population we have to consider a class of individuals with specified attributes at a given time, because the attributes (such as grade, occupation, qualification, etc.) are time-dependent, and the class is subject to changes such as social context, maturation, and aging.

Similarly, we cannot consider items as time- and, more generally, context-independent entities. An item may become easier (more difficult) over time because of increased (reduced) awareness about its content. With the advent of computerized testing, the dependence of DIF on the mode of administration (pen and paper versus computer) is likely to become an important issue. The DIF properties of an item may depend on the context of the item within the test form; that is, if the item were inserted in a different test form, its DIF properties would be altered. It is well known that the item difficulties are subject to a similar phenomenon.

To further the understanding of DIF, researchers in educational testing conduct experiments in which items are altered in an attempt to inject bias against/in favor of a specific population group. Data from such experiments, usually involving a small number of items and only a moderate number of test takers, are difficult to analyze by the standard statistical methods because of the multiple sources of variation, and because of inherently small sizes of the estimated effects.

This brief review of research issues highlights the important factors relevant to DIF: composition of the examinees (population), matching variable, the items and their context within the test form, mode of administration, and experimental conditions. This chapter addresses the following issues:

1. Combining information from multiple administrations of a test form, and assessing population differences.
2. Incorporation of population variation in the prediction of DIF in a future administration, based on one pretest.
3. Analysis of DIF experiments and the dependence of DIF on the mode of administration.

Without applying some form of repeated measurements analysis, separate DIF analyses of data from administrations of the same test form are bound to be very inefficient. Assessment of administration differences can be carried out by comparing the MH D-DIF statistics across the administrations, but these statistics are usually subject to sampling variation that is of the same order of magnitude as, or even larger than, the estimated or expected differences. Therefore, such comparisons are likely to be uninformative.

We propose a random effects model that provides a decomposition of the variation of the MH D-DIF statistics into three components: the sampling variation, as estimated by the method of Phillips and Holland (1987), the within-administration, and the between-administration variation. The within-administration variation provides a measure of DIF in the test form, as applicable to the collection of the subjects (populations) in the administrations, whereas the between-administration variation is a measure of instability of DIF across the populations.

The data from a single administration contain no information about the between-administration variance, but this variance has an impact on the quality of prediction of the DIF in a future administration. A range of feasible values for the between-administration variance can be imputed in the analysis for a single administration. It turns out that the impact of the population variation is much smaller than the difference between the currently used methods and the methods based on the random effects model.

The random effects model can be extended easily to a regression model that takes account of explanatory variables (attributes) defined for items (constant across administrations, e.g., item type) or specific to the administration of items (variable from administration to administration, e.g., difficulty of the item in the administration).

The chapter is organized as follows. The second section contains a summary of the currently used DIF procedures and a discussion of their deficiencies. In the third section, the random effects model for DIF analysis of data from multiple administrations of a test form is described. The fourth section explores the impact of the between-administration variation on the inference from a single administration of a test form and in the fifth section the feasibility of adjustments to the MH D-DIF estimates due to specific population or item characteristics or attributes is studied. The sixth section and the Appendix contain the details of the computational procedures. In the seventh section we propose alternative DIF procedures based on the random effects model and discuss model diagnostic procedures. The main results and conclusions of the report are summarized in the final section.

CURRENTLY USED DIF PROCEDURES

In the procedures for DIF analysis currently used at the Educational Testing Service (ETS), tests of statistical hypotheses for zero DIF are carried out separately for each item in the test form, and for several pairs of focal and reference groups. See Holland and Thayer (1986) for details. The large number of tests in these procedures create the obvious problem of false positives. For example, among the 100 items of a test form that has been pretested on a typical number of examinees, several items may be flagged as false positives in the analysis for one of the pairs of focal and reference groups, Male/Female, White/Black, White/Hispanic, and/or White/Asian American. More than 400 statistical tests would have been carried out. The hypothesis adopted is that the vast majority of items in the test involve no DIF, abiding by the general item specifications and standards, and that the few aberrant items should be detected easily and unambiguously.

Because the MH D-DIF statistics for a test form, using an internal matching variable, are "self-norming," there is no natural hypothesis for the relationship of these statistics across two different administrations. The values of the MH D-DIF statistics in one administration may be uniformly more spread than those in the other administration, or the MH D-DIF statistics for the more difficult items may shift in a particular direction. No empirical evidence for such deterministic hypotheses has been found in the example discussed in the section entitled Random Effects Model for Multiple Administrations.

The current DIF procedures identify the items in the pretest, or more generally in the first administration, of a test form that have a large, and statistically significant, absolute value of the MH D-DIF statistic (Petersen, 1987) with respect to one of the pairs of focal and reference groups. The items are assigned into three categories, A, B and C, as indicated in Table 9.1.

Computation of MH D-DIF statistics is described in Phillips and Holland (1987) and we briefly summarize it as follows. Suppose the matching variable has possible values (observed scores) $j = 1, 2, \ldots, J$. For each item $i = 1, 2, \ldots, I$, and a focal and reference group we consider the common odds ratio, denoted by ψ_i, of the I 2×2 contingency tables.

	Correct	Incorrect	Total
Reference	A_{ij}	B_{ij}	n_{1ij}
Focal	C_{ij}	D_{ij}	n_{2ij}
Total	m_{1ij}	m_{2ij}	n_{ij}

$$(1)$$

where the rows contain the counts of examinees in the reference and focal groups, columns the counts of examinees with correct and incorrect response to item i, and each table refers to a specific value of the matching variable, j. The groups of examinees sharing the same score j are referred to as matched-score groups.

The natural estimator for ψ_i is

$$\hat{\psi}_i = R_i/S_i = \sum_j R_{ij} \Big/ \sum_j S_{ij} = \sum_j (A_{ij}D_{ij}/n_{ij}) \Big/ \sum_j (B_{ij}C_{ij}/n_{ij}) \qquad (2)$$

TABLE 9.1
Definition of the DIF Categories A, B, and C in the Currently Used Procedures
Based on the MH D-DIF Statistic, and the Action to Be Taken by Test Development

Category	Absolute Value and Significance of MH D-DIF	Action	
		During Test Assembly	Before Score Reporting
A	MH D-DIF not significantly different from 0 (.05 level) OR Absolute value less than 1	Select freely	No action required
B	MH D-DIF significantly different from 0 (.05 level) AND EITHER (1) Absolute value at least 1 but less than 1.5 OR (2) Absolute value at least 1 but not significantly greater than 1 (.05 level)	If there is a choice among otherwise equivalent items, select the item with the smallest absolute value of MH D-DIF.	No action required
C	Absolute value of MH D-DIF at least 1.5 and significantly greater than 1 (.05 level)	Select only if essential to meet specifications. Documentation and corroboration by reviewer required.	Documentation and corroboration by independent review panel required.

Note. Reproduced from Petersen (1987).

(Mantel & Haenszel, 1959), and Phillips and Holland (1987) derived a formula for the approximate asymptotic variance of the logarithm of the estimate of the odds ratio, $\log(\hat{\psi}_i)$,

$$S_i^2 = \widehat{\text{var}}\{\log(\hat{\psi}_i)\}$$
$$= \sum_j n_{ij}^{-2}(A_{ij}D_{ij} + \hat{\psi}_i B_{ij}C_{ij})[A_{ij} + D_{ij} + \hat{\psi}_i(B_{ij} + C_{ij})]/2R^2. \quad (3)$$

The MH D-DIF parameter is defined as the -2.35 multiple of the population log odds ratio $\log(\psi_i)$. This factor is used so that the MH D-DIF scale would correspond to the delta scale for item difficulty used at ETS. Throughout the report we denote its estimate by y_i,

$$y_i = -2.35 \log(\hat{\psi}_i), \quad (4)$$

and its estimated squared standard error by $s_i^2 (= 2.35^2 S_i^2)$. In the case of multiple administrations we use the notation y_{ik} and s_{ik}^2 for the MH D-DIF statistic and its squared standard error, respectively, for the item i in the administration k.

In a realistic situation the MH D-DIF estimates and the associated standard errors are computed from pretest data, and inference about aberrant items (large DIF) is based on the statistics $\{y_i, s_i^2\}$, $i = 1, 2, \ldots, I$. However, the inference refers to the future operation, in which a different population of test takers is involved (different year, examinees with different composition of background, changes in the society, curricula, etc.). Therefore, it is of considerable interest to know to what extent the MH D-DIF parameters are stable across (similar) populations. It has been observed in a variety of contexts that the difficulty of an item may vary substantially across populations; therefore the differences (or ratios) of difficulties, defined on a certain scale, also may vary from population to population. The specific case of interest is when a test form is administered on several occasions (say, each year). Then, differences in the DIF parameters may arise due to differing compositions of the focal and reference groups in the administration populations, the context of time, or other reasons. Differences in the within-administration DIF parameters can be demonstrated by comparing the variation in the estimated DIF statistics observed across administrations with the variation predicted by the estimates of sampling variation. The additional observed variation is ascribable to differences in populations.

Although there are guidelines for the minimum numbers of the examinees in the focal and reference groups, the administration size (the number of test takers in the focal group) can have a strong influence on the ABC categorization of the data, because statistical tests are used. More items tend to be categorized as B or C items when the sizes of both groups are substantial. If the size of the focal group is small (say, 100 to 250) the estimated MH D-DIF statistic for an item has to be very large for it to be significantly different from zero.

The procedures involving a large number of statistical tests reflect the optimistic view that most of the items contain no DIF, and the few aberrant items should be easy to identify. However, there is evidence that the true MH D-DIF parameters may be distributed continuously; for most items the MH D-DIF parameters (their estimates) are insubstantially different from zero. This evidence is supported by the examples presented in the next section.

RANDOM EFFECTS MODEL FOR MULTIPLE ADMINISTRATIONS

For the MH D-DIF statistics from a single administration, we consider the random effects model

$$y_i = \mu + \xi_i + \epsilon_i, \tag{5}$$

where $y_i = -2.35 \, log(\hat{\psi}_i)$, μ is an unknown constant (usually close to 0), and ξ_i and ϵ_i are random terms. We assume that $\epsilon_i \sim N(0, s_i^2)$, independently, where s_i^2 is the conditional variance of $log(\hat{\psi}_i)$ (conditional on ξ_i), as calculated by Equation 3, and $\xi_i \overset{i.i.d.}{\sim} N(0, \tau^2)$, where $\tau^2 \geq 0$ is unknown. We assume that the administration of the test involves a large number of examinees in both the reference and focal groups so that the estimate of each s_i^2 has negligible sampling variation, which we ignore henceforth.

The principal assumption is that each item involves a random deviation, ξ_i, from the average DIF μ. The DIF in a test form can be characterized by the variance (mean square) of these deviations, τ^2; $\tau^2 = 0$ corresponds to complete absence of DIF and a large value of τ^2 implies that either a large proportion of items have moderately large DIFs or a small number of items have very large DIFs.

The DIF analysis based on the random effects model in Equation 5 would consist of four steps. In the first step the MH D-DIF statistics $\{y_i\}$ and their standard errors $\{s_i\}$ are obtained by the same method of Phillips and Holland (1987) (as in the currently used DIF procedures). In the second step the "global" parameters μ and τ^2 are estimated. The third step consists of computation of the posterior distributions of the MH D-DIF *coefficients*, $\mu + \xi_i$. The mean of this posterior distribution, denoted by $\hat{\mu} + \hat{\xi}_i$, is a shrinkage estimator, and the amount of shrinkage depends on the size of the variances τ^2 and s_i^2. The more uncertainty about the MH D-DIF statistic, due to population variation, or due to small sample size of test takers, the more shrinkage toward the overall mean $\hat{\mu}$ is involved. The final step would involve a decision for each item whether to retain or replace it, based on the chances of reduction in the value of the within-administration variation τ^2. Computational details are postponed until the section Computational Procedures, and the proposed decision rule is elaborated in the section following that.

When the same test is administered on several (say, K) occasions it is of interest whether the underlying MH D-DIF coefficients are identical across the populations in which the administrations have taken place. In such a situation, the within-administration DIF analyses are unsatisfactory because they involve a large number of comparisons of estimates, each of which has a standard error of the magnitude at least as large as the expected differences.

The variation of each MH D-DIF coefficient across the administrations can be represented in the random effects model by another random term. We denote the MH D-DIF statistic for the item i in administration k by y_{ik}. If the populations have identical MH D-DIF parameters, then the model (Equation 5) is applicable for each administration:

$$y_{ik} = \mu + \xi_i + \epsilon_{ik}, \tag{6}$$

where $\epsilon_{ik} \sim N(0, s_{ik}^2)$, and the $K \times I$ ϵ's are mutually independent (s_{ik}^2 are the standard errors for y_{ik} based on within-administration analyses). For populations with nonidentical DIF, we consider population-specific random terms ξ_{ik} with the decomposition $\xi_{ik} = \xi_i + \alpha_{ik}$ into the average MH D-DIF coefficient across the superpopulation encompassing all the administrations, ξ_i, and the deviation of the population-specific MH D-DIF coefficient from the superpopulation mean, α_{ik}, so that Equation 6 becomes a special case ($\alpha_{ik} \equiv 0$) of the model

$$y_{ik} = \mu + \xi_i + \alpha_{ik} + \epsilon_{ik}. \tag{7}$$

We assume that $\alpha_{ik} \overset{\text{i.i.d.}}{\sim} N(0,\sigma^2)$. The variance σ^2 is a measure of variation in DIF across the administrations; large value of σ^2 corresponds to greatly inconsistent values of the MH D-DIF coefficients for each item across the populations.

Information about the superpopulation deviations ξ_i is important for review of the items and amendments of the test for future administrations. Pooling information across several administrations enables more generalizable inference. The conditional (posterior) expectations of ξ_i, given the data and model parameters, are suitable estimates for ξ_i:

$$\hat{\xi}_i = E[\xi_i \mid \{y_{ik}, s_{ik}^2\}_k; \mu, \tau^2, \sigma^2]. \tag{8}$$

In practice the parameters μ, σ^2, τ^2 are estimated, and in Equation 8 these parameters are replaced by their estimates. The conditional variances

$$\text{var}(\xi_i \mid \{y_{ik}, s_{ik}^2\}_k; \mu, \tau^2, \sigma^2]) \tag{9}$$

are also informative. Because the conditional distribution of ξ_i is normal, it is completely determined by the conditional mean (Equation 8) and variance (Equation 9). The conditional expectations (Equation 8) are used as estimates of the MH-D DIF coefficients for the superpopulation encompassing all the administrations. The conditional variance (Equation 9) provides a measure of uncertainty about this estimate. Similarly, the conditional expectations and variances for the deviations α_{ik} of the item DIFs of an administration from the superpopulation are useful for detailed analysis of population differences in DIF. The formulas for these estimates/residuals are given in the Appendix.

Example 1: Multiple Administrations of a Test Form.   A form of the College Board Biology Achievement Test was administered on three occasions between December 1983 and June 1986. In the first two administrations identical forms were used, but before the third administration 2 of the 95 items were reviewed and/or replaced. Also, between the second and third administrations the background questionnaire was altered slightly and so the categorization of the examinees into the minority groups may have been affected. The numbers of students in the administrations, crossed by the subpopulations, are given in Table 9.2. Note that the first two administrations contain only juniors and seniors, whereas sophomores form almost 75% of the examinees in the third administration.

We have focused on the DIF analyses comparing male and female students, and White versus Black, and White versus Asian-American students for which the counts of examinees are sufficient for a meaningful analysis. The (within-administration) MH D-DIF statistics $\{y_{ik}\}$ and their standard errors $\{s_{ik}\}$, $i = 1, 2, \ldots, 93$, $k = 1, 2, 3$, for these comparisons were obtained by the standard program used at ETS.

The estimates of the test form variance τ^2 and of the between-administration

TABLE 9.2
Counts of Examinees in the Administration of the Studied Form

	Male/Female	White	Black	Hisp.	Asn.Am.
Admin 1	3,241/4,198	5,452	269	123	533
Admin 2	1,461/1,677	1,992	94	67	471
Admin 3	7,840/9,144	9,526	281	166	801
Admin 3 Jrs. & Srs.	2,091/2,215	2,924	115	74	394

Note. For the third administration the counts are given separately for all students, and juniors and seniors only.

variance σ^2 for the various analyses are given in Table 9.3. Note that the between-administration variance is small compared to the test form variance (about 10 to 30 times), but it is significant for the male/female and White/Asian-American analyses (at the 5% level, using the *t*-ratio statistic). Because in the computational procedure the square roots of the variances (*standard deviations*) are estimated, standard errors are provided for these standard deviations rather than for the variances. The test form standard deviation τ is highly significant for all the analyses—the test form contains a significant amount of DIF, but our analyses so far do not pinpoint the specific items that "cause" it. It would be extremely difficult to assemble a test of substantial length (say, of 100 items) for which the hypothesis of $\tau^2 = 0$ would be accepted. Note that inclusion of the sophomores in the third administration does not result in increased between-

TABLE 9.3
Estimates of the Test-Form and Between-Administration Variances
and Standard Deviations

Ref./Focal Group	No Sophomores		With Sophomores	
	$\hat\tau^2$ $\hat\tau$ (st.err. for τ)	$\hat\sigma^2$ $\hat\sigma$ (st.err. for σ)	$\hat\tau^2$ $\hat\tau$ (st.err. for τ)	$\hat\sigma^2$ $\hat\sigma$ (st.err. for σ)
Male/Female	.4054 .6367 (.0483)	.0121 .1101 (.0189)	.3545 .5954 (.0452)	.0194 .1394 (.0142)
White/Black	.2718 .5214 (.0505)	.0206 .1435 (.0884)	.2700 .5196 (.0462)	.0085 .0921 (.0880)
White/Asn.Am.	.3576 .5980 (.0470)	.0113 .1061 (.0355)	.2950 .5432 (.0436)	.0334 .1827 (.0233)

administration variation for every DIF analysis, contrary to our expectations.

It is more convenient to work with the standard deviations τ and σ than with the corresponding variances τ^2 and σ^2 for two reasons. First, the standard deviations are on the same scale as the MH D-DIF statistics and coefficients. That facilitates their natural interpretation as the average deviations. Second, the standard errors for τ and σ are easier to interpret than the standard errors for the variances. If a symmetric confidence interval is constructed around the estimate of a variance it may contain negative values, but that contradicts with the prior information that variances are non-negative. However, even if a confidence interval for a standard deviation does contain negative values, say it is $(-c, d)$, where $0 < c \leq d$, then the corresponding (nonsymmetric) confidence interval for the variance is $(0, d^2)$, containing 0, but excluding any negative values.

The most important statistical test associated with the model in Equation 7 is that of no population variation, $\sigma^2 = 0$. An approximate t-test can be carried using the ratio of the estimate of the standard deviation $\hat{\sigma}$ and its standard error. A more formal method for hypothesis testing is based on the likelihood ratio test. It involves comparison of the values of -2 loglikelihood for the fit to the model in Equation 7 with estimated σ^2 with the fit to the model in Equation 7 with σ^2 constrained to zero. In Example 1, the likelihood ratio test statistic is in all DIF analyses very close to the square of the corresponding t-statistic.

The fitted variance for a MH D-DIF statistic y_{ik} is equal to the sum $\hat{\tau}^2 + \hat{\sigma}^2 + s_{ij}^2$, and so the influence of the between-administration variation can be summarized by the ratio

$$\rho = \sigma^2 / (\tau^2 + \sigma^2 + s^2) \qquad (10)$$

where s^2 is a typical (average) value of s_{ik}^2 in the data. Obviously, if the administration sizes are unequal, then this ratio depends on the administration to which we want to refer.

The random effects model in Equation 7 can be used for comparison of DIF on two (or a larger number of) modes of test administration, for example, administration by computer versus pencil and paper. Suppose the two modes of administration of the same test form are applied to the same population, for example, by pseudorandom assignment of examinees to the modes. Then the two modes represent the two pseudopopulations, and the between-administration variance σ^2 is a measure for differences in MH D-DIF between the two modes of administration. The variance τ^2 provides a measure of DIF in the test form, common to the two modes.

Example 2: Two Modes of Administration of a Test Form.   Each of two blocks of Mathematics items for 17-year-olds in the administration year 1985–1986 of the National Assessment of Educational Progress (NAEP) were administered in two modes: (a) printed material, and (b) tape-recorded items.

The mode (a) corresponds to the classical way of administering items, with the test takers budgeting their time spent on each of the items individually, inspecting the reading blocks for the items several times if necessary, "jumping" the order of the items, "not reaching" items, and so on. In the mode (b), the responses of the individuals are uniformly paced, and items are read out only once. Of interest is to what extent the MH D-DIF coefficients for the male/female comparisons differ between the two modes of administration. An internal matching variable (number of items correct) has been used.

The two blocks of items, with 35 items each, were administered to different samples of individuals. The first block was administered in the modes (a) and (b) to 2,211 and 1,934 individuals, respectively, and the second block to 2,233 and 1,934 individuals, respectively. The proportion of men and women within each block was approximately 50%/50%.

The first block of items had very small observed MH D-DIF statistics; only one item had the statistics for both modes of administration above 1 (1.37 and 1.61). The standard errors associated with these MH D-DIF statistics ranged between .22 and .40. The estimated variances and standard deviations in the random effects model in Equation 7 are:

$$\hat{\tau}^2 = .315, \qquad \hat{\tau} = .561 \quad (.077),$$
$$\hat{\sigma}^2 = .00554, \qquad \hat{\sigma} = .0744 \ (.129). \tag{11}$$

This decomposition of the variation in the MH D-DIF statistics attributes less than 2% of the total variance to the between-modes component. The estimated between-mode variance $\hat{\sigma}^2$ is both statistically not significant and, if taken at face value, substantively unimportant, because an average change in the "true" MH D-DIF parameters of less than .10 (ignoring the sign of the change) would have no profound effect on the decision about administering the block using the new mode with tape-recorded items.

The second block of items contains two items with very large negative MH D-DIF statistics; one item has MH D-DIF statistics -2.35 and -2.22, the other item, -1.98 and -2.01, for the respective modes of administration. The standard errors for the MH D-DIF statistics are between .21 and .40, with exception of one item (none of those mentioned earlier) which has standard errors .54 and .44. The estimated variances in the random effects model in Equation 7 are:

$$\hat{\tau}^2 = .466, \qquad \hat{\tau} = .682 \quad (.0935),$$
$$\hat{\sigma}^2 = .0460, \qquad \hat{\sigma} = .2145 \ (.069). \tag{12}$$

We see that the between-mode variation for this block of items is substantially larger than in the first block, and is no longer unimportant. Among the within-mode residuals, two items stand out for which the estimated increase in MH D-DIF parameters was about .4 and .5, respectively. The corresponding observed differences are about .9 and 1.2, respectively. These items have moderate MH D-DIF statistics in both modes of administration.

Examples 1 and 2 demonstrate that extreme caution has to be exercised in any

generalization of the results about population or mode of administration dependence of the MH D-DIF statistics. The examples provide an idea of the scale of
the within- and between-administration standard deviation.

ADJUSTMENT OF THE MH D-DIF
IN A SINGLE ADMINISTRATION

The precision of the estimates is obviously affected by the value of the between-
administration variance σ^2, but with data from only a single administration this
variance cannot be estimated. Regarding this variance equal to zero corresponds
to the most optimistic scenario in terms of inference for a future administration.
The larger the variance σ^2 the less precise the pretest-based DIF estimation
procedures are.

If the between-administration variance σ^2 were known we would consider the
special case of Equation 7:

$$y_i = \mu + \xi_i + \eta_i, \tag{13}$$

where $\eta_i = \alpha_i + \epsilon_i$, so that $\eta_i \sim N(0, s_i^2 + \sigma^2)$. The impact of the between-
administration variance σ^2 can be explored by imputing a range of realistic
values of σ^2 in the procedure for estimation of the within-administration variance
τ^2 and the mean μ (multiple imputation technique; Rubin, 1982). The estimates
of between-administration variances (σ^2) obtained from other forms of the same
test, or closely related tests, each of which has been administered on several
occasions can be used to set this range.

The computational algorithm for fitting the model in Equation 13 is described
in the sixth section and the Appendix. The estimates of the variance τ^2 satisfy the
identity $\hat{\tau}^2 + \sigma^2 = $ const. (so long as σ^2 is not set to a value higher than this
total); increased σ^2 is compensated by lower $\hat{\tau}^2$, so that for each observation the
fitted variance var(y_i) = $\hat{\tau}^2 + \sigma^2 + s_i^2$ is independent of the imputed value σ^2.
The conditional expectations of the MH D-DIF,

$$E(\mu + \xi_i \mid y, \mu, \tau^2, \sigma^2), \tag{14}$$

with the unknown parameters μ and τ^2 replaced by their estimates, provide
estimates for ξ_i. Equation A.21 implies that Equation 14 involves shrinkage with
weight $1 - \hat{\tau}^2/(\hat{\tau}^2 + \sigma^2 + s_i^2)$ toward the fitted mean $\hat{\mu}$. The fitted conditional
variance $\hat{\tau}^4/(\hat{\tau}^2 + \sigma^2 + s_i^2)$ is always smaller than $\hat{\tau}^2$. As σ^2 is increased the
estimates of the MH D-DIF coefficients are shrunk more toward their mean and
the conditional variances decrease. Note, however, that the conditional variance
for the case $\sigma^2 = 0$, $\hat{\tau}^4/(\hat{\tau}^2 + s_i^2)$, may be substantially different from the
estimated sampling variance of y_i, s_i^2.

Example 3: DIF Analysis for a Single Administration.   Suppose the data
from only the first of the three administrations of the Biology Achievement test

form, analyzed in Example 1, are available, and inference about DIF in this test form is to be based solely on the first administration (e.g., if it was the pretest). Comparison of this DIF analysis with the analysis carried out in Example 1 provides a form of imperfect cross-validation; it is imperfect because the data from the first administration are used in both analyses. For the imputed values of σ^2 we have chosen the values 0, .01, .02, and .03, based on the estimates of σ^2 obtained in Example 1. Table 9.4 gives the conditional expectations and conditional standard deviations of the DIF coefficients for the comparison Whites versus Asian Americans for imputed values $\sigma^2 = .0, .01, .02, .03$. The fitted sum of the variances $\tau^2 + \sigma^2$ is equal to .3595. To conserve space the estimates for only the items with extreme DIFs are displayed. We can see that increase in σ^2 results in lower conditional expectation and lower conditional standard deviation—on the whole inferences about the items are not unduly influenced by the imputed value of σ^2, and so its choice, within the range [.0, .03], is not critical. The most striking feature is the substantial inflation of the standard

TABLE 9.4
DIF Estimation Based on a Single Administration,
with Imputed Values of the Between Administration Variance

Item No.	Raw DIF y_{ij}	Conditional Expectation of DIF for Imputed Values of σ^2.			
		.0	.01	.02	.03
75	−1.97 (.24)	−1.62 (.56)	−1.58 (.54)	−1.53 (.52)	−1.49 (.51)
8	−1.74 (.28)	−1.36 (.54)	−1.32 (.53)	−1.28 (.51)	−1.24 (.50)
74	−1.61 (.21)	−1.36 (.57)	−1.32 (.55)	−1.29 (.53)	−1.25 (.52)
92	−1.42 (.30)	−1.07 (.54)	−1.04 (.53)	−1.01 (.51)	−.98 (.49)
60	−1.28 (.29)	−.96 (.54)	−.93 (.52)	−.91 (.51)	−.88 (.49)
64	.98 (.24)	.92 (.56)	.89 (.54)	.87 (.53)	.84 (.52)
68	1.24 (.22)	1.17 (.56)	1.14 (.55)	1.11 (.53)	1.08 (.52)
67	1.74 (.23)	1.59 (.61)	1.55 (.54)	1.50 (.53)	1.46 (.51)

Note. White/Asian-American DIF in the first administration.

184

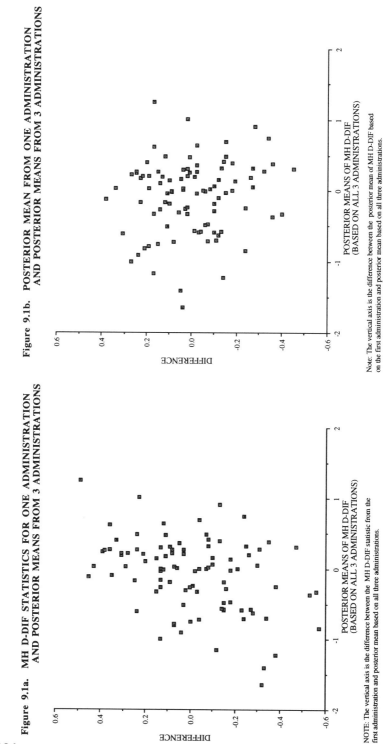

Figure 9.1a. MH D-DIF STATISTICS FOR ONE ADMINISTRATION AND POSTERIOR MEANS FROM 3 ADMINISTRATIONS

POSTERIOR MEANS OF MH D-DIF
(BASED ON ALL 3 ADMINISTRATIONS)

DIFFERENCE

NOTE: The vertical axis is the difference between the MH D-DIF statistic from the first administration and posterior mean based on all three administrations.

Figure 9.1b. POSTERIOR MEAN FROM ONE ADMINISTRATION AND POSTERIOR MEANS FROM 3 ADMINISTRATIONS

POSTERIOR MEANS OF MH D-DIF
(BASED ON ALL 3 ADMINISTRATIONS)

DIFFERENCE

Note: The vertical axis is the difference between the posterior mean of MH D-DIF based on the first administration and posterior mean based on all three administrations.

deviations of the DIF parameters—the traditional DIF analysis is far too optimistic about the information on DIF. This is caused by the within-administration variance τ^2 being substantially larger than the standard errors $s_i{}^2$. From the plots in Figs. 9.1a and 9.1b, we can compare the prediction properties of the posterior means of the MH D-DIF coefficients based on the first administration with the "raw" MH D-DIF statistics. In order to improve the resolution of the figures, we have plotted the differences of these estimates from the posterior means of the MH D-DIF coefficients based on all three administrations, which were obtained in Example 1. We see that the posterior means (Fig. 9.1b) are in closer agreement with the results of Example 1 than are the raw DIF statistics.

REGRESSION IN RANDOM EFFECTS MODELS—
DIF EXPERIMENTS

It has been observed in several DIF analyses that the MH D-DIF statistics are correlated with other item properties or attributes, such as item difficulty and item type. Such an association can be incorporated in the random effects model in Equation 7 by replacing the overall constant with a linear predictor,

$$y_{ik} = a + bx_{ik} + \xi_i + \alpha_{ik} + \epsilon_{ik}, \tag{15}$$

with an obvious extension to more than one regressor variable x. The (within-administration) item difficulties are a natural choice for x. Although the assumption underlying the model in Equation 15 is that the x_{ik} are measured accurately, for all practical purposes we ignore the sampling variation of the estimates of the item difficulties, because it is usually much smaller than the sampling variance of the estimated slope on difficulty, or the sampling variation associated with the MH D-DIF statistics.

The computational formulas for the model in Equation 15 set forth in the Appendix assume a linear predictor with an arbitrary number of regressor variables.

Example 4: Adjustment for Item Difficulty.   The random effects DIF analysis of the data reported in Example 1 (Biology Achievement Test) was repeated for the White/Asian-American and White/Black comparisons (sophomores included) with the within-administration delta-difficulties as a regressor. Note that in the second comparison the subpopulations involved differ substantially in abilities. The slope on the difficulty is positive (more difficult items involve higher DIF) and statistically significant in both analyses, but the variance estimates are reduced only by a small proportion. For the White/Asian-American analysis the prediction formula for DIF is

$$-1.637 + .131x ,$$
$$(.022) \tag{16}$$

where x is the item difficulty, with the fitted standard deviations $\hat{\tau}^2 = .491$, (reduced from .543) and $\hat{\sigma} = .164$ (reduced from .183).

For the White/Black analysis the prediction formula is

$$-1.115 + .091x ,$$
$$(.027) \tag{17}$$

with fitted standard deviations $\hat{\tau} = .483$ and $\hat{\sigma} = .078$.

In both White/Asian-American and White/Black analyses the standard errors for the standard deviations are similar to those in the analysis not applying adjustment for item difficulty (the difference is 10% or less).

The conditional expectations and conditional variances of the MH D-DIF coefficients, computed by the formulas given in the Appendix, can be used in a detailed item-level analysis. It turns out that this analysis is affected only minimally by the adjustment for item difficulty, even though the regression parameter on item difficulty is highly significant.

In summary, the item-difficulty is useful as a predictor of DIF but it reduces the within- and between-administration variances in DIF only by a small proportion.

Because DIF plays an important role in test construction at ETS, substantial resources are expended on studies/experiments that would further researchers' understanding and insight into DIF. Such studies are usually expensive and involve relatively small numbers of subjects (by the DIF "standards"); the small observed "treatment" differences usually are swamped by the large standard errors of the compared MH D-DIF statistics.

In designing a DIF experiment, the factors affecting the DIF should be considered: population, items, matching variable, and modes of administration. Usually one of these factors can be designated as the treatment, that is, under the control of the experimenter, such as the modes of administration in Example 2, and of primary interest is the assessment of the changes in DIF between the two (or more generally a small number of) levels of this factor. It is important to ensure that the effects of the other factors are not confounded with the treatment. In Example 2, this has been ensured by pseudorandom allocation of the modes of administration to the students, by using the same items, the same matching variable, the same instruction (apart from the necessary differences due to different modes of administration), and so on.

Data from such experiments can be analyzed efficiently using the random effects model in Equation 15 in which the levels of the treatment are used as regressor variables. Use of the model in Equation 15 is demonstrated in the following two examples.

Example 5: Items Favoring Men and Women.   A DIF experiment has been conducted using a test form of the Graduate Management Admission Test (GMAT) containing 25 Sentence Correction items, in which certain items have been changed with deliberate intention to inject DIF in favor of male or female examinees (e.g., by altering the proper nouns and pronouns in the reading passages). Two versions of the test form were constructed (denoted by A and B) and used in two administrations (October 1987 and March 1988), with 2,082 men and 1,463 women and 739 men and 496 women in the respective administrations.

Within each version the items were presented with the changes assumed to favor men or women or in their neutral version. The version A contains 3 items with alterations favoring men, 5 items favoring women, and 17 items with no alterations ("neutral" items). The version B contains 6 items favoring men, 5 items favoring women, and 14 items with no alterations. Thirteen items have been used in their neutral form in both versions, 6 items have been "switched" from favoring men to favoring women or vice versa, and 6 items have been switched from neutral to favoring men or women or vice versa. The design of the study is summarized in Table 9.5. The MH D-DIF statistics were obtained by the standard method for both versions within each administration, and we denote them by $\{y_{ik}\}$, $i = 1,2, \ldots , 25$ and $k = 1,2,3,4$, where $k = 1$ and $k = 2$ correspond to the first administration, and $k = 1$ and $k = 3$ to the version A.

Of principal interest in this study is the effect of these deliberate alterations in the test items. We define the covariate x as the indicator for these alterations:

$$x_{ik} = \begin{cases} -1 & \text{if item } i \text{ in version/admin. } k \text{ is in the female favoring form} \\ 0 & \text{if item } i \text{ in version/admin. } k \text{ is in the neutral form} \\ 1 & \text{if item } i \text{ in version/admin. } k \text{ is in the male favoring form,} \end{cases}$$

where $i = 1,2, \ldots , 25$, and $k = 1,2,3,4$. Note that $x_{i3} = x_{i1}$ and $x_{i4} = x_{i2}$ for all items i. Suppose that the change in an item from neutral to favoring men causes the MH D-DIF to decrease by a constant b, and the change from neutral to favoring women causes an increase by b. Then in the model in Equation 15, with x_{ik} as just defined, the hypothetical difference in DIF is represented by the parameter b. Note that in this study there are two factors with multiple levels: the two versions of the test and the two different administrations/populations. Having the two versions crossed with the two administrations enables us to disentangle the effect of the item manipulation and of the population instability.

The estimated regression formula for the four version/administrations is

$$.109 - .068x ,$$
$$(.045) \tag{18}$$

that is, the mean of the male favoring items is .041, of the neutral items .109, and of the items favoring women .177 (the average DIF does not equal 0 because an external matching variable, the operational test score, was used). The estimate of the regression parameter for x has the expected sign, but it is not statistically significant at the 5% level. The estimated difference between a male and a female

TABLE 9.5
Design of the Study Using a Test Form
with 25 Sentence Correction Items, Example 5

Items	Version A			Version B		
	M	F	N	M	F	N
1			X			X
2			X			X
3	X				X	
4	X				X	
5			X	X		
6	X					X
7			X		X	
8			X	X		
9		X		X		
10			X			X
11			X			X
12		X		X		
13			X			X
14		X		X		
15		X		X		
16		X				X
17			X		X	
18			X		X	
19			X			X
20			X			X
21			X			X
22			X			X
23			X			X
24			X			X
25			X			X

Note. M = favoring men; F = favoring women; N = neutral (no alterations). The X indicates the type of alteration of the items; for example, item 12 was altered in Version A to favor women and in Version B to favor men.

favoring version of an item of .136 implies that this manipulation has most likely only a limited effect on the DIF.

The estimated within-version/administration standard deviation is .494 with the standard error .075, and the estimate of the between-version/administration standard deviation is .000 (standard error .105); according to this estimate the populations are identical, and the differences between the two versions of the test form are captured adequately by constant differences due to item alterations.

Within-version analyses also were carried out, and they confirm that the between-administration variation is very small (the estimated standard deviations $\hat{\sigma}$ in the two analyses are .000 and .116, with standard errors around .11). Unlike the pooled data analysis these analyses do not provide any direct estimate of the effect due to alterations of items.

Example 6: Different Matching Variables.   The data for this example were obtained from a complex study of DIF in Reading Comprehension items in GMAT. We focus on the male/female DIF analysis. For the purposes of illustrating our methods we consider the data from two sections of test forms, containing 16 and 8 items respectively. Each section was administered on two occasions, as part of two different test forms, to 6,599 men and 4,271 women on the first and to 1,015 men and 732 women on the second occasion. Different matching variables were used for the two administrations, based on the operational score on reading comprehension (two sections) in the first administration, and on the total verbal score in the second administration.

The main purpose of this example is to highlight the dependence of DIF on the choice of the matching variable. Because different matching variables are used, we can expect administration-specific means of the MH D-DIF coefficients. These can be accounted for by using Equation 15 with an indicator variable:

$$x_{ik} = 0 \text{ for } k = 1$$
$$x_{ik} = 1 \text{ for } k = 2, \tag{19}$$

where i represents the items, and k the administrations.

The estimated regression formulas for the two test forms are:

$$-.812 + .517x \qquad .210 - .327x, \tag{20}$$
$$(.468) \qquad\qquad (.258)$$

and the estimates of the standard deviations are:

$$\hat{\tau} = .375 \qquad\qquad \hat{\tau} = .155$$
$$(.115) \qquad\qquad (.147)$$
$$\hat{\sigma} = .404 \qquad\qquad \hat{\sigma} = .430 \tag{21}$$
$$(.081) \qquad\qquad (.147)$$

In view of results in the other examples, the estimated between-population standard deviation $\hat{\sigma}$ is substantial. This reflects the differences in the matching variables used in the two administrations. Note that both test forms have very small within-administration DIF. Findings about the difference in the mean DIF between the two administrations are not replicated on the two test forms, although the standard errors are so large that both estimated between-administration differences are not statistically significant.

COMPUTATIONAL PROCEDURES

Estimation of the mean μ, or of the regression coefficients, and of the standard deviations σ and τ is carried out by a Fisher scoring algorithm. The algorithm uses the parametrization (μ, σ, τ), so as to avoid problems with negative estimated variances. Asymptotic standard errors for the regression parameters and for the standard deviations are obtained from the inverse of the estimated expected information matrix. Zero variances are a stationary point of the algorithm, and so the model with σ^2 or τ^2 constrained to 0 is fitted by setting the initial solution for the appropriate variance to zero. For each model fit the value of the loglikelihood is obtained, and so likelihood ratio tests are straightforward to carry out. Computational details are given in the Appendix. The iterative algorithm requires usually less than five iterations.

DECISIONS ABOUT ITEMS WITH LARGE DIF

The most important application of the DIF analysis is in pretesting of test forms. The currently used DIF procedures for reviewing pretest items, summarized in Table 9.1, do not incorporate information about population instability of DIF, and ignore the between-item information in the DIF statistics. Example 3 and Table 9.4 suggest that the latter has a profound effect in our DIF estimation procedures, whereas the influence of population instability is much smaller, though not ignorable.

In the framework based on Equation 13 with an imputed population variance σ^2, the MH D-DIF coefficients are estimated from their posterior distributions, $N(\hat{\mu} + \hat{\xi}_i, \widehat{\text{var}}[\hat{\xi}_i])$; for all purposes we can ignore the sampling variation of $\hat{\mu}$, which is always much smaller than $\widehat{\text{var}}(\hat{\xi}_i)$. Suppose we have to make a decision whether replacing the item i by a different item with the same specifications would reduce the DIF in the test form. In absence of any information about the DIF of the replacement item, a reasonable prior for the distribution of its DIF is $N(0, \hat{\tau}^2 + \sigma^2)$. A decision rule about replacement can be based on the comparison of the posterior distribution for the DIF of the item i with the prior distribution for the DIF of the replacement item. For example, we may want to make sure that the probability of improvement of the DIF in the test form is high, or equivalently, that the probability of increasing the DIF in the test form is low; that is,

$$\Pr\{|N(\hat{\mu} + \hat{\xi}_i, \widehat{\text{var}}[\hat{\xi}_i])| > |N(0, \hat{\tau}^2 + \sigma^2)|\} > \omega \ , \qquad (22)$$

($|a|$ stands for the absolute value of a) where $.5 < \omega < 1$ is a suitable tuning constant. More experience with fitting random effects models to data from a variety of testing programs is required to make a well-informed choice for ω. The precision of the estimate of the MH D-DIF coefficient for item i, $\widehat{\text{var}}(\hat{\xi}_i)$, plays an important role in the decision rule (22). The higher this estimated variance, keeping $\hat{\tau}$ and σ constant, the larger the absolute MH D-DIF estimate $\hat{\mu} + \hat{\xi}_i$ has to be for (22) to be satisfied. Note that the posterior variance $\widehat{\text{var}}(\hat{\xi}_i)$ is an increasing function of τ^2; therefore, for a fixed $\hat{\mu} + \hat{\xi}_i$ we are less likely to decide to replace an item in test forms with large DIF.

Note that the posterior variances of all the items tend to be very similar because the influence of the item-specific standard error s_i on the posterior variance usually is reduced greatly when τ and s_i are of comparable magnitude. Therefore, the Rule 22 is likely to be very similar to a rule according to which an item with outlying posterior mean of its MH D-DIF coefficient would be excluded.

Diagnostics should be an integral component of any statistical procedure. In the random effects model an important assumption that has to be checked is that of normality of the random effects. We distinguish two types of departure from normality: outliers, which also have a substantive interpretation (large DIF, or large difference of DIF between administrations), and skewness and kurtosis. In a practical situation we consider the posterior means of the random effects $\{\xi_i\}_i$, and (if applicable) of the administration deviations $\{\alpha_{ik}\}_{i,k}$, and regard them as "residuals." Normality of these residuals can be checked by the normal plots in which departure from normality is indicated by deviation of the plot of the ordered residuals from the straight line. We have produced and inspected these plots for all the models fitted and found that large residuals do occur, but the skewness and kurtosis of the residuals conform with those for the normal distribution. Therefore, these normal plots can be used informally in conjunction with the more formal Rule 22 to review or replace items in a test form.

CONCLUSIONS: MODEL CRITICISM

The root of inefficiency of the established MH D-DIF procedures is in the large number of estimated parameters, most of which can be regarded as nuisance parameters. The procedure based on the random effects models proposed in this chapter is much more efficient and it can incorporate available information about population dependence of DIF. The within-administration standard deviation τ provides a suitable summary of DIF in a test form, preferable to the MH D-DIF statistics for the individual items, each of which is subject to substantial sampling variation. Another rationale for having a measure of DIF defined for test forms is that DIF is closely tied to the context in which the items appear in the test form, and so it is more appropriate to consider DIF as an attribute of a test form, or part of the test, than as separate attributes of each item constituting the test form. Nevertheless, (shrunken) estimates of the MH D-DIF coefficients for the items are available in our procedure, and they can be used for review of pretested items. The random effects models easily can incorporate regressor variables, thus relating DIF to other characteristics or attributes of items. Two examples of analysis of DIF studies (experiments) using our method were given.

It should be appreciated that the random effects models used in this chapter are a simplified representation for the MH D-DIF statistics. First, we ignore the sampling variation of the estimate of the standard errors s_{ik} from the within-administration analyses, as well as in some instances the sampling variation of the regressor variable, and second, we assume that the random terms ϵ_{ik} are mutually independent, even though the within-administration MH D-DIF statistics y_{ik} have a complex correlation structure that is difficult to describe and incorporate in our analysis.

APPENDIX

THE FISHER SCORING ALGORITHM FOR ESTIMATION IN RANDOM EFFECTS DIF MODELS

Suppose there are J administrations of the test form with I items, $\{y_{ij}\}$ and $\{s_{ij}{}^2\}$ are the MH D-DIF estimates and their estimated squared standard errors, respectively, $j = 1, \ldots, J, i = 1, \ldots, I$. The loglikelihood associated with this set of observations/statistics is

$$\log\lambda = -\tfrac{1}{2}(\log \det V + e^T V^{-1} e), \tag{A.1}$$

where $e = y - X\beta$ is the vector ($IJ \times 1$) of residuals (y the vector of raw DIF statistics and $X\beta$ the vector of linear predictors), and V the variance matrix associated with y. For Equation 7, which contains no regressors, we have $X = 1$ (vector of 1's) and $\beta = \mu$. The item difficulty, and/or any other regressor variable, can be incorporated in the regression design; then columns of X represent the values of these regressor variables, and the vector β contains the corresponding regression coefficients.

Suppose the components of the vector y (and of the other relevant vectors and matrix V) are in the order of the items, with the statistics for the J administrations forming a set of contiguous records. The matrix V is block-diagonal, with the blocks corresponding to the items, $V = \text{diag}_i(V_i)$, with

$$V_i = D_i + \tau^2 1_J 1_J^T \tag{A.2}$$

where $D_i = \text{diag}_j(s_{ij}{}^2 + \sigma_i{}^2)$ are diagonal matrices of size $J \times J$ and 1_J is $J \times 1$ vector of 1's. It is easy to show that

$$V_i^{-1} = D_i^{-1} - D_i^{-1} 1_J 1_J^T D_i^{-1} \cdot \tau^2 / C_i, \tag{A.3}$$

where $C_i = 1 + \tau^2 \omega_i = 1 + \tau^2 1_J^T D_i^{-1} 1_j = 1 + \tau^2 \sum_j (s_{ij}{}^2 + \sigma^2)^{-1}$. Hence

$$e^T V^{-1} e = \sum_i e_i^T V_i^{-1} e_i = e^T D^{-1} e - \sum_i (e_i^T D_i^{-1} 1_J)^2 \cdot \tau^2 / C_i, \tag{A.4}$$

where e_i is the segment of the vector e corresponding to the item i, and $D = \text{diag}_i(D_i)$.

Furthermore,

$$\log \det V_i = \sum_j \log(s_{ij}^2 + \sigma^2) + \log C_i, \tag{A.5}$$

and so evaluation of the loglikelihood (Equation A.1) is straightforward, without inversion of any matrices.

The formulas for the first partial derivatives and for the expectations of the second partial derivatives are obtained by formal differentiation. We have

$$\begin{aligned} d\log\lambda/d\beta &= X^T V^{-1} e, \\ d^2\log\lambda/(d\beta)^2 &= X^T V^{-1} X, \end{aligned} \tag{A.6}$$

which can be evaluated using Equation A.3, as in Equation A.4, but for the case of no regressor variables we have

$$d\log\lambda/d\mu = 1^T V^{-1} e = \sum_i e_i^T D_i^{-1} 1_J / C_i,$$

$$d^2\log\lambda/(d\mu)^2 = 1^T V^{-1} 1 = \sum_i \omega_i / C_i. \tag{A.7}$$

It is easy to show that $E\{d^2\log\lambda/(d\beta d\tau^2)\} = E\{d^2\log\lambda/(d\beta d\sigma^2)\} = 0$. The derivatives involving variance components are

$$d^2\log\lambda/(d\tau^2) = -\tfrac{1}{2}\operatorname{tr}(1^T V^{-1} 1) + \tfrac{1}{2}\sum_i (e_i^T V_i^{-1} 1_J)^2$$

$$= -\tfrac{1}{2}\sum_i \omega_i / C_i + \tfrac{1}{2}\sum_i (e_i^T D_i^{-1} 1_J / C_i)^2,$$

$$d^2\log\lambda/d\sigma^2) = -\tfrac{1}{2}\operatorname{tr}(V^{-1}) + \tfrac{1}{2}(e^T V^{-2} e)$$

$$= \tfrac{1}{2}\sum_j \{\omega_i - 1_J^T D_i^{-2} 1_J \, \tau^2 / C_i - e_i^T D_i^{-2} e_i + 2 \cdot e_i^T D_i^{-2} 1_J$$

$$\cdot e_i^T D_i^{-1} 1_J \cdot \tau^2 / C_i - (e_i^T D_i^{-1} 1_J)^2 1_J^T D_i^{-2} 1_J \cdot \tau^2 / C_i\},$$

$$E\{d^2\log\lambda/(d\tau^2)^2\} = -\tfrac{1}{2}\sum_i (1_J^T V_i^{-1} 1_J)^2 = -\tfrac{1}{2}\sum_i \omega_i^2 / C_i^2,$$

$$E\{d^2\log\lambda/(d\sigma^2)^2\} = -\tfrac{1}{2}\operatorname{tr}(V^{-2}) = -\tfrac{1}{2}\sum_i \{1_J^T D_i^{-2} 1_J - 2 \cdot 1_J^T D_i^{-3} 1_J \tau^2 / C_i$$

$$+ (1_J^T D_i^{-2} 1_J \tau^2 / C_i)^2\}$$

and

$$E\{d^2\log\lambda/(d\sigma^2 d\tau^2)\} = -\tfrac{1}{2} 1^T V^{-2} 1 = -\tfrac{1}{2} \sum_i 1_j^T D_i^{-2} 1_J/C_i^2 \quad (A.8)$$

The Fisher scoring procedure for maximizing Equation A.1 involves iterations, and the first iteration requires initial values for the estimated parameters. The following set of initial values is suitable:

$$\hat{\beta}_0 = (X^T X)^{-1} X^T y \qquad (\hat{\mu}_0 = y)$$

$$\hat{\tau}_0^2 = \sum_i (y_{i\cdot} - y_{\cdot\cdot})^2/I$$

$$\hat{\sigma}_0^2 = \sum_i \sum_j (y_{ij} - y_{i\cdot})^2/IJ - s_{\cdot}^2/2 \qquad (A.9)$$

where $y_{\cdot\cdot}$, $y_{1\cdot}$, and $s_{\cdot}^2$ are the sample mean for y, the within item mean $\sum_j y_{ij}/J$, and the sample mean for s_{ij}^2, respectively.

An iteration of the procedure consists of calculation of the corrections for the estimated parameters:

$$\hat{\beta}_{new} = \hat{\beta}_{old} + (X^T V^{-1} X)^{-1}(X^T V^{-1} e) = (X^T V^{-1} y) \quad (A.10a)$$

and

$$\begin{pmatrix} \hat{\tau}_{new}^2 \\ \hat{\sigma}_{new}^2 \end{pmatrix} = \begin{pmatrix} \hat{\tau}_{old}^2 \\ \hat{\sigma}_{old}^2 \end{pmatrix} + H^{-1}h, \qquad (A.10b)$$

where

$$H = - \begin{pmatrix} E\{d^2\log\lambda/(d\tau^2)^2\} & E\{d^2\log\lambda/(d\tau^2 d\sigma^2)\} \\ E\{d^2\log\lambda/(d\tau^2 d\sigma^2)\} & E\{d^2\log\lambda/(d\sigma^2)^2\} \end{pmatrix} \quad (A.11a)$$

and

$$h^T = (d\log\lambda/d\tau^2 \quad d\log\lambda/d\sigma^2) \qquad (A.11b)$$

It is advantageous to estimate the square roots of the variances, τ and σ. The corresponding expressions for the Fisher scoring algorithm are obtained using the chain rule,

$$\begin{pmatrix} \hat{\tau}_{new} \\ \hat{\sigma}_{new} \end{pmatrix} = \begin{pmatrix} \hat{\tau}_{old} \\ \hat{\sigma}_{old} \end{pmatrix} + H^{*-1}h^{*}, \qquad (A.12)$$

where the elements of H^* and h^* are

$$H_{11}^* = 4H_{11}\hat{\tau}^2 - 2h_1,$$
$$H_{22}^* = 4H_{11}\hat{\sigma}^2 - 2h_2,$$
$$H_{12}^* = 4H_{12}\sigma\tau,$$

$$h_1^* = 2h_1\tau,$$
$$h_2^* = 2h_2\sigma, \qquad (A.13)$$

A suitable criterion for convergence is that the changes in both the loglikelihood and each of the estimated parameters are smaller than 10^{-3}. Using this criterion, 3 to 6 iterations were required for the analysis reported in this chapter.

The conditional expectations for the superpopulation DIF coefficients are given by the formula

$$\hat{\xi}_i = E[\xi_i|\mu, \tau^2, \sigma^2; y, \{s_{ij}\}] = \tau^2 e_i^T V_i^{-1} 1_J = \tau^2 e_i^T D_i^{-1} 1_J / D_i \quad (A.14a)$$

with conditional variance τ^2/C_i. The conditional expectations for the administration deviations are

$$\hat{\alpha}_{ij} = \sigma^2 \{V_i^{-1} e_i\}_j \qquad (A.14b)$$

with conditional variance $\sigma^2 - \sigma^4 \{V_i^{-1}\}_{jj}$.

Note that $\tau^2 = 0$ and $\sigma^2 = 0$ are fixed points of the procedure. Therefore, submodels with variances constrained to zero can be fitted by setting the initial solution for the variance to zero, instead of Equation A.9. This is useful for likelihood ratio testing of the hypothesis of no between-population variation ($\sigma^2 = 0$). The difference in the values of the -2 loglikelihood for the models with σ^2 constrained to 0 and σ^2 estimated has the χ_1^2 distribution under the hypothesis of $\sigma^2 = 0$.

The computations required for an iteration of the Fisher scoring algorithm can be organized efficiently in the following steps:

1. Item-by-administration calculations:
   $\omega_i = 1_J^T D_i^{-1} 1_J$, $C_i = 1 + \tau^2 \omega_i$, $e_i^T D_i^{-1} 1_J$, $e_i^T D_i^{-2} 1_J$, $e_i^T D_i^{-3} 1_J$
2. Item-wise calculations:
   loglikelihood (A.3), using (A.4) and (A.5), the Jacobian and Hessian (A.13) with (A.8), and (A.6) or (A.7).
3. Corrections (A.10a) and (A.12) and check for convergence.

For estimation of MH D-DIF variance in a single administration with imputed between-administration variance σ^2 we assume the model

$$y_i = X\beta + \xi_i + \mu_i, \quad i = 1, \ldots, I \qquad (A.15)$$

where y_i is the MH-D DIF statistic for item i, $\xi_i \overset{\text{i.i.d.}}{\sim} N(0, \tau^2)$ and μ_i is the composite of the population deviation and the sampling error, $\mu_i \sim N(0, s_i^2 + \sigma^2)$. The parameters β and τ^2 are to be estimated and a value for σ^2 is imputed.

The variance matrix V for the vector of MH-D DIF statistics $y = (y_i, \ldots, y_I)$ is diagonal, $V = \text{diag}_i(V_i)$, with

$$v_i = \tau^2 + \sigma^2 + s_i^2, \qquad (A.16)$$

and so the generalized least squares estimate for β is

$$\hat{\beta} = (X^T V^{-1} X)^{-1} (X^T V^{-1} y), \tag{A.17}$$

or for the case of no regressor variables

$$\hat{\mu} = \sum_i y_i v_i^{-1} \Big/ \sum_i v_i^{-1}, \tag{A.18}$$

which depends on the value of τ^2. Therefore an iterative procedure has to be employed, with the correction formula

$$\hat{\tau}^2_{\text{new}} = \hat{\tau}^2_{\text{old}} + \left\{ -\sum_i v_i^{-1} + \sum_i [(y_i - \mu_i)/v_i]^2 \right\} \Big/ \sum_i v_i^{-2}, \tag{A.19}$$

where μ_i is the linear predictor for item i, $\mu_i = (X\beta)_i$.

A suitable initial solution, such as

$$\hat{\tau}^2_0 = \left(I^{-1} \sum_i y_i^2 - \sigma^2 - y_i^2 \right)/1.5 \tag{A.20}$$

can be used. The conditional expectation for the MH-D DIF coefficient ξ_i is given by

$$\tau^2 v_i^{-1}(y_i - \mu_i), \tag{A.21}$$

with conditional variance $\tau^4 v_i^{-1}$.

10 An Item Response Theory Model for Test Bias and Differential Test Functioning

Robin T. Shealy
William F. Stout
University of Illinois at Urbana-Champaign

The purpose of this chapter is to present an item response theory (IRT) conceptualization of differential test functioning (DTF) and of test bias for standardized ability tests. That is, the influence of differential item functioning (DIF) and item bias will each be considered at the test score level.

Suppose, as is required for a DIF analysis, that by some criterion the examinee population has been partitioned into matched subgroups. Then an item displays DIF if within one or more of the matched subgroups, the item favors examinees of one category over another. Further, if the matching criterion is judged to be construct-valid in the sense that it is matching examinees on the basis of the latent trait (target ability) the test is designed to measure without contamination from other unintended to be measured abilities then the DIF item is said to be biased. That is, the distinction between DIF and item bias lies in the extent to which a convincing construct validity argument has been given for the matching criterion. Thus, it is clear that most analyses of test data will be DIF analyses rather than item bias analyses. Further, in the absence of any construct validity argument, the analysis certainly cannot be scientifically viewed as a bias analysis.

In order to avoid repeated dual references to bias and differential functioning we will usually only refer to "bias," with the understanding that a companion statement about DIF or DTF can also be made. Whether a bias statement or its companion DIF/DTF statement is more appropriate or accurate in a particular ability test setting depends on the degree to which the user or researcher has embraced a construct validity argument. It is essential to realize that the multidimensional IRT modeling approach presented herein, even though couched in bias language, is equally relevant to the differential functioning (DIF, DTF) paradigm.

197

By *test bias,* we mean a formalization of the intuitive idea that a test is less valid for one group of examinees than for another group in its attempt to assess examinee differences in a prescribed latent trait, such as mathematics ability. It can be seen that test bias is the result of individually biased items acting in concert through a test-scoring method, such as number correct, to produce a biased test. In another article of ours, this new conceptualization of test bias is used to undergird a new statistical test (SIBTEST) for psychological test bias (Shealy & Stout, in press). SIBTEST can be used to detect DIF, DTF, item bias, or test bias. Also, a large-scale simulation study was conducted of the performance properties of this statistical procedure, in particular as compared with the Holland and Thayer (1988) modification of the Mantel–Haenszel test. SIBTEST software with accompanying manual can be obtained from Stout.

We mention three distinct features of the conceptualization of bias presented herein. First, it provides a mechanism for explaining how several individually biased items can combine through a test score to exhibit a coherent and major biasing influence at the test level. In particular, this can be true even if each individual item displays only a minor amount of item bias. For example, "word problems" on a "mathematics test" that are too dependent on sophisticated written English comprehension could combine to produce pervasive test bias against English-as-a-second-language examinees. A second feature, possible because of our multidimensional modeling approach, is that the underlying mechanism that produces bias is addressed. This mechanism lies in the distinction made between the ability the test is intended to measure, called the *target ability,* and other abilities influencing test performance that the test does not intend to measure, called *nuisance determinants.* Test bias occurs because of the presence of nuisance determinants possessed in differing amounts by different examinee groups. Through the presence of these nuisance determinants, bias then is expressed in one or more items. A third feature, also possible because of our multidimensional modeling approach, is that a careful distinction is made between genuine test bias and nonbias differences in examinee group performance that are caused by examinee group differences in target ability distributions. It is important that the latter not be labeled mistakenly as test bias.

The novelty of our approach to bias lies not so much with its recognition of the role of nuisance determinants in the expression of test bias, but rather in the explicit multidimensional IRT modeling of bias, which in turn promises a clear and thorough understanding of bias.

AN INFORMAL DESCRIPTION OF TEST BIAS

We begin with an informal definition of test bias: Test bias occurs if the test under consideration is measuring a quantity in addition to the one the test was designed to measure, a quantity that both groups do not possess equally.

It is important to note that this notion of test bias grows out of the traditional non-IRT notion of test bias based on differential predictive validity. Articles by Stanley and Porter (1967), Temp (1971), and in particular Cleary (1968) exemplify this classical predictive view of bias. These studies used standardized tests to predict performance on a particular task; if the predictive link from test to task was different for the two studied groups, then test bias was suspected. Cleary, in a seminal article on test bias, studied bias in the prediction of college success of Black and White students in integrated colleges, using SAT verbal and math scores. Her intent was to determine if the expected first-year grade point average (GPA) for Whites was different from that for Blacks, after the two groups had been *matched* on SAT score; hence, the linear regression of first-year GPA on SAT verbal (or math) score was separately fit for both groups and compared. If the expected criterion (GPA) for those examinees attaining a particular test score (e.g., SAT combined score) were different across group, the test score was considered a biased predictor of performance and test bias was deemed to be present. The purpose of the Cleary study was predictive; the regressions of criterion on test score therein were compared across group to see if the test score equitably predicts the performance measured by the criterion.

Our focus shifts hereafter to regressing test score on criterion. The purpose of the reversed regression is to corroborate that the prediction of a criterion by a test is equitable across group, thereby exposing the conceptual underpinning for IRT modeling of test bias—in particular our modeling of test bias. The regressions of test score on criterion are compared to answer the following question: Are the average test scores for both groups the same after the groups have been matched on criterion performance?

This shift to a corroborative point of view brings us again to the informal definition provided earlier. The difference across group in the regressions of test score on criterion (other than that caused by statistical error) is due to an undesirable causative factor other than the criterion; that is, at least some of the test questions must be measuring something in addition to what the criterion measures. Furthermore, this difference is due only to the undesirable factor, because the criterion has been held equal in the two groups.

If in addition to the reversal of the regression variables just described, the criterion now is chosen as internal to the test instead of external to it, the concept of the internal assessment of bias results. This internal criterion becomes the "yardstick" by which the test is judged biased or not; it is a portion of the test itself. The implicit assumption is that the yardstick portion of the test consists of items known to measure only what they are supposed to be measuring. Without this assumption only a DIF/DTF analysis is possible.

An example adapted from Shepard (1982) clearly illustrates this internally assessed bias: A verbal analogies test is used to compare reasoning abilities of German and Italian immigrants to the United States, the two populations matched on English fluency. However, 20% of the test items are based on words with Latin origins, whereas the remainder have linguistic structure equally familiar to both groups. Here, the items with Latin origin words are possibly biased. A reasonable internal criterion with which to assess this bias would be a score based on the responses to the linguistically neutral items, for it is assumed that these items are validly measuring what the test is intended to measure.

The internal assessment viewpoint of test bias can be clarified by noting two distinctions between it and the classical test theory-based differential regression conceptualization of Cleary (1968) and others:

1. The yardstick (criterion), which was a measurement of task performance (e.g., first-year GPA in the Cleary study), is now a score internal to the test (e.g., score on the linguistically neutral items in the Shepard (1982) example). This internal criterion is most often an aggregate measure of a portion of the test item responses (typically number right).

2. The differential regression approach used regressions of the external criterion on test score in a predictive context. In internally assessed bias studies, the responses of one or more items suspected of bias are regressed on the internal criterion as a corroborative statistical test that these "suspect" items are measuring the same thing that the internal criterion is measuring.

This brings us to an essential question: What is the internal criterion measuring? It is measuring a theoretically postulated psychometric construct that is intended to be generalizable to a variety of possible future tasks; that is, a latent ability of an IRT model. Thus IRT modeling of bias becomes appropriate. An example illustrates: The SAT math test is designed to measure a construct, "mathematical aptitude," which is intended to help predict an examinee's future success in a set of quantitatively oriented college courses that require a component of such ability. Rather than assessing the SAT test against the corresponding set of criterion measures of performance in these courses, we wish to assess the test against the construct itself; to do so we turn to the test itself to verify that the proper measurement of mathematical ability is being done. The internal criterion measures this ability construct, and internal test bias is defined with respect to this construct.

The generalizability of performance measurements on a variety of tasks to a single construct, as described earlier, provides one motivation to shift to internally assessed bias studies. An additional motivation is the practice in recent years of creating *item pools,* large numbers of items that are to be used in forming multiple versions of a standardized test (see, e.g., Hambleton & Swaminathan, 1985, chapter 12). A newly constructed set of items intended for inclusion in the item pool can be tested for bias, relative to the ability construct that the pool supposedly is measuring, by employing internal bias detection techniques.

Internally assessed bias studies with a variety of test populations have been done: Cotter and Berk (1981) attempted to detect bias in the Wechsler Intelligence Scale for Children–Revised (WISC–R) test with White and minority children. Dorans and Kulick (1983b), in a series of studies done at Educational Testing Service (ETS), studied the possible effect of differential mastery of written English between native-born Americans and English-as-a-second-language Asian-American students on scores of selected items on a mathematics "word problem" test.

Item bias studies such as the ones just described usually focus on a single item at a time; if several items in these studies simultaneously are found to be biased, it is a result of statistical bias procedures conducted for each item separately, which raises delicate questions about simultaneous statistical inference. Moreover, in a modeling sense, no causative reasons for the observed simultaneous bias are explored by item bias studies. This article studies a form of test bias relative to an internal criterion; this kind of test bias considers the set of test items acting as a unit (via a common causal mechanism) and combining through a test scoring method. The precise formulation of test bias and a contrast of it to item bias is presented in the section entitled Test Bias in the IRT Model.

We now consider the question of test bias relative to an internal criterion more carefully. Consider a situation where a single verbal analogy item is embedded in two different tests, tests M and V say. Test V is composed of verbal analogy items, as intended, and Test M consists of mathematics calculation items, as intended, except for the single embedded item. Assume that each item in Test V does not contain any culture-dependent material that may favor one group. The embedded verbal item is not biased in Test V, but the potential for bias of this item is large in Test M, because the item measures something other than the intended-to-be-measured mathematical calculation skill. This illustrates a key component of test bias, aptly stated by Mellenbergh (1983): "An item can be biased in one set of items, whereas it is unbiased in another set" (p. 294). Shepard (1982) also pointed out this relativity feature: ". . . if a test of spatial reasoning inadvertently included several vocabulary items, they would be biased indicators of the [ability being measured]" and ". . . in a test composed equally of two types of items reflecting . . . two different [ability] constructs, it will be a dead heat to decide statistically which set defines the test [ability] and which set becomes a biased measure of it" (p. 24).

Implicit in the previous discussion is the assumption that a portion of the test defines the internal criterion by which the remainder is measured for the presence of bias. A collection of items defining the internal criterion is called a *valid subtest*. An informal definition of a valid subtest now can be given: A subtest is valid with respect to a specified "target" ability if the subtest score is judged to be measuring only the intended target test ability; that is, it stands as a "proxy" of the ability one intends to measure. More precisely, if all of the items of the subtest measure only the intended ability then the subtest is said to be valid.

There is a point about this definition that needs mentioning. Primarily, the existence and identification of a valid subtest is an empirical decision based on expert opinion or data at least in part external to the data set in question. Subtest validity cannot be established based on the test data set alone nor can it be deduced theoretically. The "burden of proof" is an empirical one and lies with the test constructor. It is, of course, a construct-validity issue. If all the items of a test depend on a second determinant (e.g., if the responses to all items depend on familiarity with standardized tests), then a valid subtest will not exist. Note that this is true even if the two groups are not penalized differentially by this dependence of test items on familiarity with standardized tests. Thus, the actual presence of test bias is logically independent of the existence of a valid subtest to be used for the assessment of test bias.

In our framework, it must be assumed that there is a valid subtest if we are to detect test bias internally; otherwise, it is intrinsically nondetectable internally. Of course, any subtest can be labeled as the valid subtest, in which case a DIF/DTF analysis with the subtest used as an examinee matching criterion becomes possible. The responses to the valid subtest are used to tackle the central problem in the identification of test bias: the need to distinguish between group differences attributable to the ability construct intended to be measured and that due to unwanted ability determinants. Because the valid subtest is assumed to measure only the desired ability, then no measures external to the test are required to assess that ability, although to improve accuracy it may be beneficial also to use external data, especially if the valid subtest is short or if the assumption of its validity is at all suspect. Matching examinees using a valid subtest score controls for group differences in the intended-to-be-measured ability and isolates differences due to the unwanted determinants. A more rigorous formulation of "valid subtest" is set out in the section, Test Bias in the IRT Model.

In these discussions of test bias relative to an internal criterion, multidimensionality implicitly has been invoked; it is impossible to carefully discuss test bias without invoking it. The informal definition of test bias stated earlier employs multidimensionality: There is mention of the quantity the "test was designed to measure" and one "in addition to" this quantity. Lord (1980) recognized this in his discussion of item bias: "if many of the items [in a test] are found to be seriously biased, it appears that the items are not strictly unidimensional" (p. 220).

Bias in one or more items typically has been attributed to special knowledge, unintended to be measured, that is more accessible to one of the test-taking groups. Ironson, Homan, Willis, and Signer (1984) performed a bias study that involved planting within a mathematics test mathematics word problems that required an extremely high reading level to solve them. They stated their conclusion that ". . . bias is sometimes thought of as a kind of multidimensionality involving measurement of a primary dimension and a second confounding dimension." Our viewpoint here is that bias is always the result of multidimensionality.

The "primary dimension" is referred to in this chapter as *target ability*, because this is the ability the test intends to measure. The "confounding dimension" is referred to as a *nuisance determinant*. In the Shepard (1982) verbal analogies example cited previously, the target ability is reasoning ability, which 80% of the items solely measure, whereas the nuisance determinant is familiarity with Latin linguistic roots.

The full formulation of test bias is set out in the Test Bias in the IRT Model section—it involves certain subtleties not discussed here. The group differences in ability level of a latent nuisance determinant provide a common causative mechanism for bias in any collection of items on a test contaminated with such a determinant. This is the single most important conceptual difference between the test bias model developed in this chapter and previous item bias work: the existence of a postulated common latent cause for the manifestation of bias across a group of test items.

THE IRT MODEL FOR TEST RESPONSES

Herein we present the nonparametric multidimensional IRT model underlying our modeling of test bias. Consider a group of G of examinees; the sample of examinees to take a test is considered to be drawn at random from this population. For the reader less interested in mathematical details, skimming this section is recommended. A test is simply a collection of items; a *test response* of length N is the corresponding set of responses, for a randomly chosen examinee from G, denoted by

$$\mathbf{U} = (U_1, \ldots, U_N) \tag{1}$$

where the U_i are random variables taking on

$$U_i = \begin{cases} 0 & \text{if response to item } i \text{ is incorrect;} \\ 1 & \text{if response is correct.} \end{cases}$$

The IRT model is composed of two components that generate $\mathbf{U}$: (a) a d-dimensional examinee ability parameter, and (b) a set of item response functions (IRFs), one for each item, which determine the probability of correct response for the items. The IRT model usually is conceived as a unidimensional ($d = 1$) model; here, a multidimensional ($d > 1$) model is presumed.

Let us now further set notation. The ability vector is

$$\boldsymbol{\theta} = (\theta^1, \ldots, \theta^d) \tag{2}$$

for an arbitrary examinee from G. A distribution of $\boldsymbol{\theta}$ over G is induced by choosing examinees at random from G; the multivariate random variable is designated

$$\boldsymbol{\Theta} = (\Theta^1, \ldots, \Theta^d). \tag{3}$$

Examinee independence is assumed; that is, J examinees from G have ability parameters

$$\{\Theta(j) : j = 1, \ldots , J\} \quad (4)$$

independent and identically distributed (iid) in j. Item i's IRF, which is interpreted as the probability that an examinee with ability θ will answer item i correctly, is denoted:

$$P_i(\theta) = P[U_i = 1 | \Theta = \theta] \equiv P[U_i = 1 | \theta]. \quad (5)$$

Our interpretation of $P_i(\theta)$ is the sampling one: Among all examinees having ability θ, the expected proportion of them getting item i correct is $P_i(\theta)$.

The basic philosophy of the IRT model is that a latent distribution of abilities in a Group G drives the manifest distribution of item responses. The fundamental identity relating the responses $\mathbf{U}$ to the examinee group ability variable Θ is

$$P[\mathbf{U} = \mathbf{u}] = \int_\theta P[\mathbf{U} = \mathbf{u} | \Theta = \theta] dF(\theta),$$

$$\text{for all } \mathbf{u} = (u_1, \ldots , u_N), \quad (\text{each } u_i = 0 \text{ or } 1), \quad (6)$$

where $F(\cdot)$ is the cumulative distribution function (cdf) of Θ. There are two fundamental assumptions on the conditional test response probability $P[\mathbf{U} = \mathbf{u} | \theta] \equiv P[\mathbf{U} = \mathbf{u} | \Theta = \theta]$ usually assumed in IRT modeling. To introduce these, recall two standard definitions about ordering in d-dimensional Euclidean space: (a) Let $\mathbf{z}$ and $\mathbf{z}'$ be vectors. Then $\mathbf{z} < \mathbf{z}'$ if $z_i \leq z_i'$ for $i = 1, \ldots d$ and for at least one i, $z_i < z_i'$. (b) Let $\mathbf{z}$ and $\mathbf{z}'$ be vectors. The real valued function $f(\mathbf{z})$ is strictly monotone if for any $\mathbf{z} < \mathbf{z}'$, $f(\mathbf{z}) < f(\mathbf{z}')$.

The fundamental IRT assumptions are:

Assumption 1: Local independence in θ: for every θ,

$$P[\mathbf{U} = \mathbf{u} | \theta] = \prod_{i=1}^{N} P[U_i = u_i | \theta] \quad \text{for all } u_i = 0 \text{ or } 1; i = 1, \ldots , N. \quad (7)$$

Assumption 2: Strict monotonicity of IRFs: The item IRFs $\{P_i(\theta) : i = 1, \ldots , N\}$ are strictly monotone in θ. That is, for any i, $P_i(\theta') > P_i(\theta)$ if $\theta' > \theta$ in the sense of (a) stated previously.

It is convenient to combine Equation 6 and Assumption 1 in the following manner:

$$P[\mathbf{U} = \mathbf{u}] = \int_\theta \prod_{i=1}^{N} P_i(\theta)^{u_i} (1 - P_i(\theta))^{1-u_i} dF(\theta) \quad (8)$$

for all $\mathbf{u}$.

The notion of the dimensionality d of $\mathbf{U}$ can be formalized mathematically, but for the purposes of this article it is unnecessary to do so.

Definition 1.   Let $\mathbf{U}$ be a test response as in Equation 1. An IRT representation of $\mathbf{U}$ is the structure

$$\{d,\mathbf{\Theta},F(\mathbf{\theta}),\{P_i(\mathbf{\theta}): \quad i = 1, \ldots ,N\}\} \tag{9}$$

where Equation 6, Assumption 1, and Assumption 2 hold.

In this chapter we often want to consider a test item's operating characteristic with respect to a specific single component of $\mathbf{\theta}$ (say θ^1). This is accomplished by "marginalizing out" the remaining components in the $\mathbf{\theta}$-vector from the item's IRF, resulting in the *marginal item response function* (marginal IRF). Conceptually, this IRF is a unidimensional reduction of the original one and can be considered as a unidimensional IRF for the unidimensional ability θ_1. The following definition is due to Stout (1990).

Definition 2.   Let $P(\mathbf{\theta})$ be an IRF. The marginal IRF $T(\theta^1)$ of $P(\mathbf{\theta})$ with respect to Θ^1 is defined by

$$T(\theta^1) = E[P(\mathbf{\Theta})|\Theta^1 = \theta^1]. \tag{10}$$

The marginal IRF is essential in the discussion of modeling test bias in the fourth section of this chapter, where a single component θ^1 of $\mathbf{\theta}$ designated as the *target ability* is considered. Because target ability is the ability the test designer desires to measure using the items, the marginal IRF with respect to this ability is a useful concept.

In order for $T(\theta^1)$ to be an IRF it must be strictly monotone; this does not follow for the marginal IRFs of a test from the assumptions of our IRT representation in Expression 9. However, very mild regularity conditions suffice to produce strict monotonicity, as has been shown by Stout (1990). To this end, we need the concept of stochastic ordering.

Definition 3.   Let $\mathbf{Z}$ be a random vector with distribution indexed by a parameter γ. $\mathbf{Z}$ is strictly stochastically increasing in γ if for every $\mathbf{z}$ in the range of $\mathbf{Z}$

$$P[\mathbf{Z} > \mathbf{z};\gamma] < P[\mathbf{Z} > \mathbf{z};\gamma'] \ if \ \gamma < \gamma'. \tag{11}$$

Strict monotonicity of the marginal IRF with respect to θ^1 follows under the reasonable assumption of stochastic order in Θ^1:

Theorem 1: (See Stout, 1990). If $\mathbf{\Theta}|\Theta^1 = \theta^1$ is strictly stochastically increasing in θ^1 in the sense of Definition 3 and the IRF $P(\mathbf{\theta})$ is strictly monotone in $(\theta^2, \ldots ,\theta^d)$ then the marginal IRF $T(\theta^1)$ of $P(\mathbf{\theta})$ with respect to Θ^1 is strictly monotonic.

Remark: Note in Theorem 1 that $P(\boldsymbol{\theta})$ is not assumed to be strictly monotone in θ^1, the first component of $\boldsymbol{\theta} \equiv (\theta^1, \theta^2, \ldots, \theta^d)$.

A note on IRT model assumptions should be emphasized here. IRT models are commonly parameterized; that is, the IRFs and ability distribution are members of parametric families. Typical assumptions are that $\boldsymbol{\Theta}$ is unidimensional with a standard normal distribution and that a two or three parameter normal ogive model or a one, two, or three parameter logistic model is assumed for the IRFs. In this article, we assume only that the IRFs $\{P_i(\boldsymbol{\theta})\}$ are continuous, with $\boldsymbol{\theta}$ usually multidimensional.

TEST BIAS IN THE IRT MODEL

In this section our multidimensional IRT based notion of test bias using the IRT model of the previous section is developed. The first subsection provides a brief presentation on IRT *item bias* as currently usually defined in the psychometric literature. The subsection that follows sets up the multidimensional IRT framework for test bias modeling; target ability and nuisance determinants are defined. In the next subsection we develop test bias in terms of its components: *potential* for bias, *expressed* bias, and the combining of expressed item biases through a test scoring method. The following subsection considers item bias cancellation when the nuisance determinants are multidimensional. The final subsection formally considers the notion of a valid subtest. The less mathematically oriented reader is advised to concentrate on the statements of definitions, assumptions, and theorems and on the accompanying discussions.

Existing Unidimensional Formulation of IRT Item Bias

In this subsection the unidimensionality based concept of IRT-modeled item bias or DIF currently in widespread use is presented as a backdrop for the development of multiple-item test bias, which is treated in the two subsections following this one. An item is biased, according to Hambleton and Swaminathan (1985), if its (necessarily unidimensional) item response functions across groups are not identical. A formal definition is given next.

Definition 4. Item bias. Let two groups of examinees be indexed by $g = 1,2$. For each g, denote

$$\mathbf{U}_g = (U_{1g}, \ldots U_{Ng}) \tag{12}$$

to be the test response from an N-item test for a randomly chosen examinee from Group g. Let $\boldsymbol{\Theta}_g$ refer to a unidimensional ability restricted to group g. Assume that a *unidimensional* IRT model fits each group, with a combined IRT representation for $\{\mathbf{U}_g; g = 1,2\}$ (recall Definition 1):

$$\{d = 1, \Theta_g, F_g(\theta), \{P_j(\theta): \quad j = 1, \ldots, i - 1, i + 1$$
$$, \ldots, N; P_{ig}(\theta)\}, g = 1, 2\}, \quad (13)$$

where $F_g(\theta)$ denotes the cdf of Θ_g. (Note, as the subscript notation indicates, that all items except the ith item have group invariant IRFs whereas item i has an IRF that possibly differs for the two groups.)

(a) Item bias occurs in item i at θ if the group specific probabilities of correct response at θ are different; that is, the group IRFs are different at θ:

$$P_{i1}(\theta) \equiv P[U_{i1} = 1 \mid \Theta_1 = \theta] \neq P[U_{i2} = 1 \mid \Theta_2 = \theta] \equiv P_{i2}(\theta). \quad (14)$$

(b) Item bias occurs in item i if there exists some value θ for which item bias occurs at θ.

It is important to observe that the bias of item i is defined relative to the other $N - 1$ items, which are assumed invariant and hence "unbiased" with respect to the two groups.

Item bias models traditionally have been parametric. Wright, Mead, and Draba (1976) and Holland and Thayer (1988) considered a biased item generated by Rasch IRFs with the IRF difficulties (b's) different for the two groups. The more general 2PL and 3PL models, with different discriminations (a's) and guessing parameters (c's) across group, have been studied by Hulin, Drasgow, and Komocar (1982); Linn, Levine, Hastings, and Wardrop (1981); and Thissen, Steinberg, and Wainer (1988), among many others.

Item bias and DIF each address differential performance across group for a single item at a time. If several items display bias relative to the remaining assumed group invariant items according to Definition 4 (modified to allow several IRFs to possibly differ across group), there are no components in Definition 4 that provide the facility to explain simultaneous item biasing due to a single underlying reason. This provides the motivation for a multidimensional IRT framework that explains such pervasiveness of item bias.

The Required Multidimensional IRT Framework

In our treatment, test bias is modeled using the nonparametric multidimensional IRT framework described in the previous section. The multidimensionality of the underlying latent abilities for the two groups provides the environment from which bias expresses itself in one or more items. A crucial component in this test bias model is the modeling of a *pervasive* nuisance determinant, which contaminates a significant portion of the test items. This modeling viewpoint is an attempt to retain the view that bias originates at the test question level yet to allow for the possibility of bias expressed through a test score as in the classical differential regression approach discussed earlier in the section entitled An Informal Description of Test Bias.

The setup of the multidimensional IRT model for a test administration to two groups is as follows. The IRT representation in Expression 9 is assumed to hold for the combined two-group population of examinees. This representation induces a separate IRT representation of the form of Equation 9 for each of the two groups:

$$\{d, \Theta_g, F_g(\mathbf{\theta}), \{P_{ig}(\mathbf{\theta}): \quad i = 1, \ldots N\}\}, g = 1, 2, \tag{15}$$

where Group g latent ability Θ_g here denotes Θ restricted to Group g, $F_g(\mathbf{\theta})$ denotes the distribution function of Θ_g, and $P_{ig}(\mathbf{\theta})$ denotes the ith IRF for a randomly selected examinee from the subpopulation of Group g examinees of ability $\mathbf{\theta}$. Note that the distribution of Θ_1 in general will be different from that of Θ_2. It is convenient to denote the combined two group IRT representation by

$$\{d, \Theta_g, F_g(\mathbf{\theta}), \{P_{ig}(\mathbf{\theta}): \quad i = 1, \ldots N\}: \quad g = 1, 2\}. \tag{16}$$

The IRT representation (Equation 16) is assumed throughout the remainder of this section (with Equation 6 and Assumptions 1 and 2 assumed to hold within each group of course). Implicit in Expression 16 is the assumption that the test measures the same psychometrically defined ability construct $\mathbf{\theta}$ in both groups.

Two basic assumptions additional to Assumptions 1 and 2 about the IRT representation given by Expression 16 are necessary: (a) common multidimensional IRFs for each of the two groups in the representation given by Expression 16 (i.e., IRF invariance across group), and (b) the capability of the test to measure (possibly with contamination) the intended-to-be-measured ability (target ability):

Assumption 3: In the assumed IRT representation given by Expression 16, assume IRF group invariance, that is

$$P_{i1}(\mathbf{\theta}) = P_{i2}(\mathbf{\theta}) \equiv P_i(\mathbf{\theta}) \tag{17}$$

for all $\mathbf{\theta}$.

This first additional assumption states that the usual IRT item parameter invariance assumed in unidimensional IRT modeling is assumed to hold for our multidimensional IRT model, where $\mathbf{\theta}$ includes all the abilities influencing test performance (hence the assumption of IRF group invariance is appropriate in this context). Such invariance does not necessarily hold for any subset of the components of $\mathbf{\theta}$, in particular not for the target ability alone. Indeed if invariance with respect to target ability held for all items, it is intuitively clear there could be no bias. For example, in the usual definition of item bias (Definition 4) invariance is not assumed for the biased item. Equation 17 is assumed throughout the rest of the chapter.

We now define target ability.

Definition 5. Target ability is the unidimensional latent ability the test intends to measure. The target ability component is denoted by θ, and the target ability random variable for Group g is denoted Θ_g.

Remark: The univariate target ability Θ_g is not to be confused with the multivariate complete latent ability $\mathbf{\Theta}_g$ as defined in Equation 16.

If a discussion of test bias is appropriate in a test administration, then it must be the case that the test is designed so that it is in fact measuring θ, as well as possibly some nuisance components inadvertently. We thus informally make the second additional assumption that all items of the test in fact do measure target ability θ and possibly nuisance components $\mathbf{\eta}$ as well. That is, all IRFs $P_i(\theta,\mathbf{\eta})$ are assumed strictly increasing in θ throughout the article. In Shealy (1989), this assumption is formalized and it then is proved that the existence of a representation (Equation 16) in turn implies the existence of an analogous representation in terms of $(\theta,\mathbf{\eta})$; that is in terms of target ability and nuisance components. Here we bypass presentation of this formalism and instead assume an IRT representation of the form given by Expression 16 with

$$\mathbf{\Theta}_g \equiv (\Theta_g, \mathbf{H}_g) \tag{18}$$

where Θ_g denotes target ability and $\mathbf{H}_g$ denotes nuisance ability for a randomly chosen group g examinee. That is, the two-group IRT representation

$$\{d, (\Theta_g, \mathbf{H}_g), F_g(\theta,\mathbf{\eta}), \{P_i(\theta,\mathbf{\eta}): \quad i = 1, \ldots, N\}: \quad g = 1,2\} \tag{19}$$

where the P_i's are the group invariant IRFs guaranteed to exist by Assumption 3, is assumed throughout the remainder of the chapter.

A Multidimensional Formulation of Test Bias

Item bias postulates that examinees scaled on a univariate latent θ (as in Definition 4) display differing item response probability across group for the biased item. We take the postulated ability θ to be the target ability to create a multivariate IRT-based definition of test bias.

As in item bias studies, test bias of this sort is an entity studied at the "microlevel" of each fixed value of θ; so one may speak of "test bias at θ." Test bias at the "macrolevel" may be defined to exist if it exists at one or more single θ-values; important aspects of this micro/macro duality are considered in the section Test Bias as a Function of Target Ability. The following formulation of test bias is composed of three components: (a) The potential for bias, if it exists, resides within the multidimensional target/nuisance ability distributions in two groups; (b) potential for bias is expressed in items whose responses depend on one or more nuisance determinants, and (c) the scoring method of the test, to be viewed as an estimate of target ability, transmits expressed item biases into test bias.

Potential for Test Bias

Before the concept of potential for test bias can be developed, it is necessary to introduce conditions postulating stochastic ordering of ability distributions.

Consider a nuisance ability H_g, assumed unidimensional for simplicity of explication, for two groups g, $g = 1,2$. Either the distribution is the same for both groups or, by definition, there exists some η for which

$$P[H_1 > \eta] \neq P[H_2 > \eta]. \tag{20}$$

Say that, as psychometricians, we believe that Group 2 has "more" of this ability. Likely the most natural way to mathematize this belief is to assume stochastic ordering, that is to assume

$$P[H_2 > \eta] > P[H_1 > \eta] \tag{21}$$

for *all* η. For H_1 and H_2 that possess densities, the graphical intuition is given in Fig. 10.1. For example, as Fig. 10.1 suggests, the densities might be identical except for translation. Of course, if two groups differ in ability distribution, it does not follow logically that one or the other group has more ability. For example, a situation where the variances of H_1 and H_2 are not equal might produce

$$P[H_1 > \eta] < P[H_2 > \eta] \text{ for } \eta > 0 \tag{22}$$

and

$$P[H_1 < \eta] < P[H_2 < \eta] \text{ for } \eta < 0. \tag{23}$$

In particular, H_1 and H_2 might be symmetrically distributed about 0 with H_2 having the larger variance, as displayed in Fig. 10.2. Nonetheless, for many psychometric applications, it seems plausible to assume stochastic ordering whenever ability distributions are not equal, as we do throughout the remainder of the chapter.

The potential for test bias is modeled via one or more nuisance determinants that simultaneously cause bias in a collection of items. In particular, this cause is rooted in the conditional distributions of $\mathbf{H}_g \mid \Theta_g = \theta$ (note that $\mathbf{H}_g$ can be multidimensional here). For a fixed θ, we assume stochastic ordering for the distributions of $\mathbf{H}_g \mid \Theta_g = \theta$ ($g = 1,2$) when they are not equal:

Assumption 4. Let $(\Theta_g, \mathbf{H}_g)$ be as in Equation 19 and fix a target ability value θ. If the conditional distributions $\mathbf{H}_1 \mid \Theta_1 = \theta$ and $\mathbf{H}_2 \mid \Theta_2 = \theta$ are different, then the assumption is that either

$$(\mathbf{H}_1 \mid \Theta_1 = \theta) < (\mathbf{H}_2 \mid \Theta_2 = \theta) \text{ or } (\mathbf{H}_1 \mid \Theta_2 = \theta) > (\mathbf{H}_2 \mid \Theta_2 = \theta) \tag{24}$$

stochastically; that is, either

$$P[\mathbf{H}_1 > \boldsymbol{\eta} \mid \Theta_1 = \theta] < P[\mathbf{H}_2 > \boldsymbol{\eta} \mid \Theta_2 = \theta] \tag{25}$$

for all $\boldsymbol{\eta}$ or

$$P[\mathbf{H}_1 > \boldsymbol{\eta} \mid \Theta_1 = \theta] > P[\mathbf{H}_2 > \boldsymbol{\eta} \mid \Theta_2 = \theta] \tag{26}$$

for all $\boldsymbol{\eta}$.

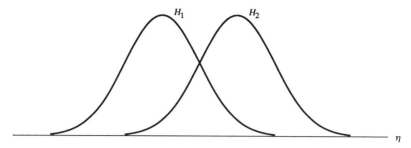

FIG. 10.1. H_1 stochastically smaller than H_2.

For example, let θ be mathematical ability and $\mathbf{\eta} \equiv \eta$ be verbal ability. Then Equation 25 says among all examinees of mathematical ability θ that, stochastically, Group 2 examinees are verbally superior to Group 1 examinees.

With the aforementioned preparation, potential for test bias can be defined.

Definition 6. Let two groups have ability distributions $(\Theta_1, \mathbf{H}_1)$ and $(\Theta_2, \mathbf{H}_2)$. Potential for test bias exists with respect to nuisance determinant $\mathbf{\eta}$ at target ability level θ if either Equation 25 or 26 holds. If Equation 25 holds, a potential disadvantage exists against Group 1 at target ability θ.

Definition 6 implies that a potential disadvantage can exist only if there is a nuisance determinant as a component of the latent ability vector.

Expression of Test Bias Potential

In order for test bias to occur, its potential must be expressed in one or more items. The concept of expressed bias, detailed in Definition 8, is similar to the item bias concept of Definition 4. It is stated in terms of the marginal IRFs with respect to target ability.

Definition 7. Refer to Expression 19. The marginal IRF

$$T_{ig}(\theta) = E[P_i(\Theta_g, \mathbf{H}_g) | \Theta_g = \theta]$$
$$= P[U_i = 1 \mid \Theta_g = \theta] \qquad i = 1, \ldots, N$$

is called the target marginal IRF for item i, Group g.

We now can define expressed bias in item i at target ability θ.

Definition 8. Let $\{T_{ig}(\theta):i = 1, \ldots, N\}$ be Group g's target marginal IRFs for a test with IRT representation in Expression 19.
(a) Expressed bias in item i exists at target ability θ if item i's target marginal IRF for Group 1 is not equal to the corresponding target marginal IRF for Group 2 at θ:

$$T_{i1}(\theta) \neq T_{i2}(\theta).$$

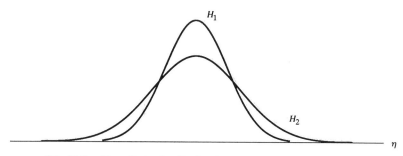

FIG. 10.2. $H_1 \neq H_2$ in distribution but not stochastically ordered.

(b) Expressed bias in item i exists if there is some value θ for which expressed bias for item i exists at θ. Item i is biased against Group 1 at θ if $T_{i1}(\theta) < T_{i2}(\theta)$.

Definition 8 (our multidimensional IRT expressed item bias definition) is equivalent to Definition 4 (the usual IRT item bias definition) if (a) the IRT models represented by Expressions 13 and 19 are both IRT representations of $\{U_g: g = 1,2\}$, (b) the ability θ of Expression 13 is the target ability θ of Definition 5, and (c) the group-dependent IRF $P_{ig}(\cdot)$ from Expression 13 is taken to be the target marginal IRF $T_{ig}(\cdot)$ from Definition 7. Henceforth in the chapter, item bias will refer specifically to the expressed item bias of Definition 8.

The link between potential for bias and expressed bias for an item is the heart of test bias. The following theorem is fundamental in establishing this link:

Theorem 2: Assume IRT representation Expression 19 and fix the number θ. If $P_i(\theta,\eta)$ is strictly increasing in η and a potential disadvantage exists against Group 1 at θ then item i is biased against Group 1 in the sense of Definition 8.

Proof: The result is an immediate corollary of Theorem 1.

Remark: In a sense, Theorem 2 formalizes the obvious; dependence of an item on nuisance determinants with respect to which one group is disadvantaged causes expressed item bias.

Transmission of Expressed Item Biases into Test Bias

Until now the discussion has focused on a single item; we see next that a test can consist of many items simultaneously biased by the same nuisance determinant. In this case, items can cohere and act through the prescribed test score to produce substantial bias against a particular group even if individual items display undetectably small amounts of item bias. That is, bias or DIF amplification can occur.

This is the final component of our formulation of test bias mentioned at the beginning of this section. We consider the large class of test scores of the form

$$h(\mathbf{U}) \tag{27}$$

where $h(\mathbf{u})$ is real valued with domain all $\mathbf{u} \equiv (u_1, \ldots, u_N)$ such that $u_i = 0$ or 1 for $i = 1, \ldots, N$ and $h(\mathbf{u})$ is coordinatewise nondecreasing in $\mathbf{u}$. This class contains many of the standard scoring procedures for many standard models; for example, number correct, linear formula scoring of the form $\Sigma_{i=1}^{N} a_i U_i$, with $a_i \geq 0$, maximum likelihood estimation of ability for certain logistic models with item parameters assumed known, and so on. One is surely willing to restrict attention to test scores of the form of Expression 27 if the test's IRFs are known to be increasing. Following Rosenbaum (1985), test scores of the form of Expression 27 are called *nondecreasing item summaries*.

Test bias is defined with respect to a specific test scoring method $h(\mathbf{u})$.

Definition 9.   A test $\mathbf{U}$ with target ability Θ and test score $h(\mathbf{U})$ displays test bias against Group 1 at θ if

$$E[h(\mathbf{U}_1)|\Theta_1 = \theta] < E[h(\mathbf{U}_2)|\Theta_2 = \theta], \tag{28}$$

where $\mathbf{U}_g$ is defined in Equation 12. If

$$E[h(\mathbf{U}_1)|\Theta_1 = \theta] = E[h(\mathbf{U}_2)|\Theta_2 = \theta] \tag{29}$$

then no test bias exists at θ.

The psychometric interpretation of Definition 9 is as follows. The left side of Equation 29 is the expected test score for a randomly chosen Group 1 examinee with target ability θ whereas the right-hand side is the same for a randomly chosen Group 2 examinee with target ability θ. In order to assess the appropriateness of Definition 9, consider a large number of Group 1 and a large number of Group 2 examinees taking the test, all of target ability θ. Then Equation 29 says that the average score of these Group 1 examinees will be approximately the same as that of the Group 2 examinees. Thus, on average, neither group is favored in the attempt to estimate target ability using $h(\mathbf{U}_g)$.

A Fundamental Relationship

We now elucidate how the three conceptual components of our formulation interact to produce test bias. For ease of interpretation we restrict ourselves to the case of a unidimensional η; however, the following results hold if a vector-valued nuisance determinant $\boldsymbol{\eta}$ is assumed.

The basic test bias result is given in Theorem 3, namely the precise mechanism by which potential for bias is transmitted into test bias. First a variation of a well-known lemma is needed, which for convenience is specialized to the present setting:

Lemma 1: Let $f(\eta)$ be strictly increasing in η and let stochastic ordering in the sense of Equation 25 hold for each fixed θ. Then for each fixed θ

$$E[f(H_1)|\Theta_1 = \theta] < E[f(H_2)|\Theta_2 = \theta].$$

Proof: Fix θ and let $F_g(\eta)$ denote the cdf of $f(H_g)|\Theta_g = \theta$. Assume, for simplicity of argument and without loss of generality, that $F_g(0) = 0$ for $g = 1,2$. Then

$$E[f(H_g)|\Theta_g = \theta] = \int_0^\infty x dF_g(x).$$

Integration by parts yields

$$\int_0^\infty x dF_g(x) = \int_0^\infty (1 - F_g(x)) dx. \tag{30}$$

But Equation 25 and $f(\eta)$ strictly increasing implies that

$$F_1(x) > F_2(x) \text{ for all } x > 0. \tag{31}$$

Using Equation 30 and noting that

$$\int_0^\infty (1 - F_1(x)) dx < \int_0^\infty (1 - F_2(x)) dx, \tag{32}$$

the desired result follows.

The theory of associated random variables is helpful in establishing the basic test bias result. As defined by Esary, Proschan, and Walkup (1967), a random vector $\mathbf{X}$ is associated if, and only if, for all nondecreasing $f(\mathbf{x}), g(\mathbf{x})$, it follows that

$$cov(f(\mathbf{X}), g(\mathbf{X})) \geq 0. \tag{33}$$

The main result of Esary et al. (1967) that we wish to use is that a vector of independent random variables is associated. The basic result now can be stated and proved.

Theorem 3: Assume the IRT representation of Expression 19 with $\boldsymbol{\eta} \equiv \eta$ being unidimensional. Fix the number θ and assume the test scoring method of the form Expression 27. Suppose for some i that $h(\mathbf{u})$ is strictly increasing as $u_i = 0$ increases to $u_i = 1$ and that $P_i(\theta, \eta)$ is strictly increasing in η. Assume potential for bias at θ against Group 1, that is, that Equation 25 holds. Then test bias at θ against Group 1 holds.

Proof: It suffices to prove Equation 28. By IRF invariance with respect to (θ, η), it follows for all η and the fixed θ that

$$E[h(\mathbf{U}_1)|\Theta_1 = \theta, H_1 = \eta] = E[h(\mathbf{U}_2)|\Theta_2 = \theta, H_2 = \eta] \qquad (34)$$

Conditioning on $\Theta_g = \theta$, $H_g = \eta$ will be denoted by θ, η. Let

$$f(\eta) \equiv E[h(\mathbf{U}_g)|\theta,\eta],$$

Note that $f(\eta)$ does not depend on g by Equation 34, hence let $\mathbf{U} \equiv \mathbf{U}_1$ throughout the remainder of the proof. We first show that $f(\eta)$ is strictly increasing in η. Fix $\eta' > \eta$. Then, by local independence

$$q(\mathbf{u}) \equiv \frac{P[\mathbf{U} = \mathbf{u}|\theta,\eta']}{P[\mathbf{U} = \mathbf{u}|\theta,\eta]} = \frac{\displaystyle\prod_{i=1}^{N} P_i(\theta,\eta')^{u_i}(1 - P_i(\theta,\eta'))^{1-u_i}}{\displaystyle\prod_{i=1}^{N} P_i(\theta,\eta)^{u_i}(1 - P_i(\theta,\eta))^{1-u_i}} \qquad (35)$$

Thus, $q(\mathbf{u})$ is strictly increasing as $u_i = 0$ increases to $u_i = 1$ because $P_i(\theta,\eta')/P_i(\theta,\eta) > 1$. Now

$$E(h(\mathbf{U})|\theta,\eta') - E(h(\mathbf{U})|\theta,\eta) = \sum_{\mathbf{u}} h(\mathbf{u})(P[\mathbf{U} = \mathbf{u}|\theta,\eta'] - P[\mathbf{U} = \mathbf{u}|\theta,\eta])$$

$$= \sum_{\mathbf{u}} h(\mathbf{u})[q(\mathbf{u}) - 1]P[\mathbf{U} = \mathbf{u}|\theta,\eta]$$

$$= \text{cov}(h(\mathbf{U}),q(\mathbf{U}) - 1|\theta,\eta). \qquad (36)$$

Partition

$$\mathbf{U} = (\mathbf{U}\backslash U_i, U_i) \equiv (\mathbf{U}', U_i)$$

where

$$\mathbf{U}' \equiv \mathbf{U}\backslash U_i \equiv (U_1, \ldots, U_{i-1}, U_{i+1}, \ldots, U_N). $$

Let E_W and cov_W denote expectation and covariance over the distribution of W, respectively. By a basic identity for covariance, stated here conditional on (θ,η),

$$cov(h(\mathbf{U}),q(\mathbf{U}) - 1|\theta,\eta) = E_{\mathbf{U}'}\{cov_{U_i}[h(\mathbf{U}),q(\mathbf{U}) - 1|\theta,\eta]|\theta,\eta\} \\ + cov_{\mathbf{U}'}\{E_{U_i}(h(\mathbf{U})|\theta,\eta),E_{U_i}(q(\mathbf{U}) - 1|\theta,\eta)|\theta,\eta\}. \qquad (37)$$

Both $h(\mathbf{u})$ and $q(\mathbf{u}) - 1$ are strictly increasing as $u_i = 0$ increases to $u_i = 1$. Thus, for all possible values of $\mathbf{U}'$,

$$cov_{U_i}[h(\mathbf{U}),q(\mathbf{U}) - 1|\theta,\eta] > 0. \qquad (38)$$

Thus, the first term on the right-hand side of Equation 37 is strictly positive. Because of the association of independent random variables and the fact that $\mathbf{U}'$ given θ, η has independent components, it follows that the second term on the right-hand side of Equation 37 is nonnegative, using also the fact that

$$E_{U_i}(h(\mathbf{U})|\theta,\eta) \text{ and } E_{U_i}(q(\mathbf{U}) - 1|\theta,\eta) \qquad (39)$$

are nondecreasing in $\mathbf{U}'$. Thus,

$$cov(h(\mathbf{U}), q(\mathbf{U}) - 1|\theta,\eta) > 0. \qquad (40)$$

But, recalling Equation 36,

$$E(h(\mathbf{U})|\theta,\eta') - E(h(\mathbf{U})|\theta,\eta) > 0; \qquad (41)$$

that is, $f(\eta)$ is strictly increasing in η, as claimed. Then, applying Lemma 1 and Equation 25 to $f(\eta)$, it follows that Equation 28 holds, as required.

Remarks:

1. It is important to reemphasize that Theorem 3 holds if a vector valued nuisance parameter $\boldsymbol{\eta}$ is assumed, provided Equation 25, the potential for bias at θ, holds for $\boldsymbol{\eta}$. That is, the nuisance determinants $\eta_1, \ldots, \eta_{d-1}$ must each create bias in the same direction, say against Group 1.

2. Stripped of its test bias context and stated as a general theorem about IRT models, a minor variant of Theorem 3 with $<$ replaced by $\leq$ at appropriate places is due to Rosenbaum (1985). For our purposes, strict inequality is needed. The proof of Rosenbaum's result is similar to our proof.

3. It is important to note that Theorem 3 displays the mechanism by which several biased items can cause an amplification of bias at the test scoring level. It is conceivable that small amounts of bias at the item level could be amplified into a large amount of bias at the test score level.

A final interesting relationship to note is that the presence of test bias implies the potential for test bias:

Theorem 4: Suppose that test bias against Group 1 holds at θ in the sense of Equation 28. Then the potential for bias against Group 1 at θ exists in the sense that Equation 25 holds.

Proof: Recall Equation 34, replacing η by $\boldsymbol{\eta}$ there. Thus for $g = 1,2$, it holds that

$$E[h(\mathbf{U}_g)|\Theta_g = \theta] = \int E[h(\mathbf{U}_1)|\Theta_1 = \theta, \mathbf{H}_1 = \boldsymbol{\eta}]dF_g(\boldsymbol{\eta}|\theta) \qquad (42)$$

where $F_g(\boldsymbol{\eta}|\theta)$ is the cdf of $\mathbf{H}_g|\Theta_g = \theta$. Suppose Equation 28. Thus, using Equation 42 for $g = 1,2$ it follows

$$\int E[h(\mathbf{U}_1)|\Theta_1 = \theta, \mathbf{H}_1 = \boldsymbol{\eta}]dF_1(\boldsymbol{\eta}|\theta) < \int E[h(\mathbf{U}_1)|\Theta_1 = \theta,$$

$$\mathbf{H}_1 = \boldsymbol{\eta}]dF_2(\boldsymbol{\eta}|\theta). \tag{43}$$

But this implies that the distributions of $\mathbf{H}_1|\Theta_1 = \theta$ and $\mathbf{H}_2|\Theta_2 = \theta$ are different. Thus, invoking Assumption 4, it follows that Equation 25 holds.

Item Bias Cancellation

As discussed earlier, and epitomized by the assumptions of Theorem 3, holding for multiple items simultaneously, items can combine to amplify bias at the test level. In contrast, items displaying bias also can tend to cancel each other out, thus producing little or no bias at the test level. This becomes possible only when the nuisance determinant $\boldsymbol{\eta}$ is multidimensional with some of its components displaying potential for bias against Group 1 and others displaying potential for bias against Group 2. The amount of expressed test bias will be a result of the amount of cancellation at the test level and will be dependent on the particular test score $h(\mathbf{u})$ used. The theme of cancellation has been presented by Humphreys (1986) and Roznowski (1987) in the non-IRT classical predictive validity context.

The following example illustrates how cancellation can function to produce negligible test bias:

Example 1: A test of length N (N an even number for convenience) intended to measure mathematics skills has IRT representation

$$\{d = 3,(\Theta_g,H_{1g},H_{2g}),F_g(\theta,\eta_1,\eta_2),\{P_i(\theta,\eta_1,\eta_2): \quad i = 1, \ldots ,N\},$$
$$g = 1,2\} \tag{44}$$

where θ = mathematics skills, η_1 = physics knowledge, and η_2 = reading knowledge. Let S_1 be a subtest with IRFs

$$\left\{ P_i(\theta,\eta_1):i = 1, \ldots , \frac{N}{2} \right\} \tag{45}$$

(subtest containing problems with a mathematical physics flavor) strictly increasing in η_1 for every θ and S_2 be a subtest with IRFs

$$\left\{ P_i(\theta,\eta_2):i = \frac{N}{2} + 1, \ldots , N \right\} \tag{46}$$

(subtest containing mathematical "word problems") strictly increasing in η_2 for every θ. Suppose that the ith physics IRF is identical to the ith word problem IRF, which is the $(N/2 + i)$th item.

Now, condition on a particular mathematics ability θ, and assume for examinees of ability θ that Group 2 has greater knowledge of physics and Group 1 has greater reading skill. So $H_{12}|\theta > H_{11}|\theta$ stochastically and $H_{21}|\theta > H_{22}|\theta$ stochastically for each choice of θ. Say that this holds for each choice of θ. Furthermore suppose that as distributions, $H_{12}|\theta = H_{21}|\theta$ and $H_{11}|\theta = H_{22}|\theta$ for all θ. Then by Theorem 3, if subtest S_1 were the entire test, it would exhibit test bias against Group 1 at θ for every θ. By contrast if S_2 were the entire test, it would exhibit test bias against Group 2 at θ for every θ. But, for a large class of test scores— those giving approximately equal weight to the S_1 items and to the S_2 items— almost total cancellation of the item biases could occur thus producing an unbiased test. That is, for such a test scoring method $h(\mathbf{u})$,

$$E[h(\mathbf{U}_1)|\Theta_1 = \theta] \doteq E[h(\mathbf{U}_2)|\Theta_2 = \theta] \tag{47}$$

for every θ. Indeed, if $h(\mathbf{u})$ is number correct, then exact equality and hence total cancellation results.

Remark: Note that the concept of test bias compares groups, not individuals. For a particular examinee, a test might be biased against her, even though the test is not biased against Group 1 of which she is a member. This important aspect of bias is an unfortunate consequence of the multidimensional nature of items in most tests. Moreover, it is also a consequence of the unfortunate (and perhaps economically unavoidable) fact that only statistical (i.e., group-level) bias analysis is done, as opposed to individual case-by-case analysis. The previously discussed phenomenon of cancellation possibly could alleviate the impact at the individual examinee level (as well, as just discussed, as at group level).

It is worthwhile to develop item bias cancellation in a formal manner.

Definition 10.   Item bias cancellation at θ is said to occur if the test consists both of items biased against Group 1 at θ and items biased against Group 2 at θ.

Remark: It is theoretically possible that cancellation could occur within an item if the item depends on at least two nuisance dimensions, as contrasted with the between-item cancellation of Definition 10. This source of cancellation, which seems less likely to occur in practice, is not considered in this article.

Intuitively, the presence of expressed item bias and no cancellation implies test bias. This is the content of Theorem 5.

Theorem 5: Assume that at least one item displays expressed item bias at θ in the sense of Definition 8, and assume that no item bias cancellation occurs at θ. Then test bias occurs at θ in all nondecreasing item summary test scores $h(\mathbf{u})$ (see Equation 27) provided $h(\mathbf{u})$ is strictly increasing in at least one coordinate corresponding to one of the biased items.

Proof: At the item level, each item is either biased only against one group (Group 1, say) or displays no expressed bias by the assumption of no cancellation. Thus, for all i,

$$P[U_{i1} = 1 | \Theta_1 = \theta] \leq P[U_{i2} = 1 | \Theta_2 = \theta] \tag{48}$$

with strict inequality for at least one i. Now, by item invariance, for all i,

$$P[U_{i1} = 1 | \Theta_1 = \theta, \mathbf{H}_1 = \boldsymbol{\eta}] = P[U_{i2} = 1 | \Theta_2 = \theta, \mathbf{H}_2 = \boldsymbol{\eta}] \equiv$$
$$P_i(\theta, \boldsymbol{\eta}). \tag{49}$$

Recall Assumption 4. Note that, denoting the cdf of $(\mathbf{H}_g | \Theta_g = \theta)$ by $F_g(\boldsymbol{\eta}|\theta)$,

$$P[U_{ig} = 1 | \Theta_1 = \theta] = \int P_i(\theta, \boldsymbol{\eta}) dF_g(\boldsymbol{\eta}|\theta) \tag{50}$$

where the integrand does not depend on g. It follows from Assumption 4 that strict inequality in Equation 48 for some i implies that $(\mathbf{H}_1 | \Theta_1 = \theta) < (\mathbf{H}_2 | \Theta_2 = \theta)$ stochastically. Thus, using the monotone condition for $h(\mathbf{u})$ the conclusion follows from Theorem 3, noting the remark following the proof of Theorem 3 concerning multiple nuisance determinants.

It is interesting to note, as Theorem 6 now states, that when there is no item bias cancellation that test bias for number correct is equivalent to test bias for all nondecreasing item summary test scores with strict increase for every coordinate of $\mathbf{u}$:

Theorem 6: (a) If test bias at θ occurs for the test score number correct ($\Sigma_{i=1}^n u_i$) and there is no item bias cancellation at θ, then test bias occurs at θ for every nondecreasing item summary test score $h(\mathbf{u})$ for which $h(\mathbf{u})$ is strictly increasing in every coordinate of $\mathbf{u}$. (b) If test bias at θ holds for some nondecreasing item summary test score $h(\mathbf{u})$ and there is no item bias cancellation at θ, then test bias at θ hold for $h(\mathbf{u}) = \Sigma_{i=1}^n u_i$.
Proof: Note that

$$E\left[\sum_{i=1}^N U_{ig} \Big| \Theta_g = \theta \right] = \sum_{i=1}^n \int P_i(\theta, \boldsymbol{\eta}) dF_g(\boldsymbol{\eta}|\boldsymbol{\theta}). \tag{51}$$

Then, obvious and minor modifications in the proof of Theorem 5 suffice to prove both (a) and (b). Details are omitted.

Intuitively, no test bias and no cancellation implies that none of the items display bias. This is the content of Theorem 7.

Theorem 7: Assume that no test bias exists at θ with respect to score $h(\mathbf{u})$. Assume no item bias cancellation at θ in the sense of Definition 10. In addition, assume that there exists at least one i such that both $P_i(\theta,\mathbf{\eta})$ is strictly increasing in $\mathbf{\eta}$ and $h(\mathbf{u})$ is strictly increasing as $u_i = 0$ increases to $u_i = 1$. Then there is no potential for test bias and (hence) none of the items display item bias.

Proof: By assumption of no test bias at θ,

$$E[h(\mathbf{U}_1)|\Theta_1 = \theta] = E[h(\mathbf{U}_2)|\Theta_2 = \theta]. \tag{52}$$

By the strict increasing assumption for $P_i(\theta,\mathbf{\eta})$ and $h(\mathbf{u})$, it follows that $E[h(\mathbf{U}_g)|\theta,\mathbf{\eta}]$ is strictly increasing in $\mathbf{\eta}$. Recall Equation 42. If either Equation 25 or Equation 26 were to hold, it would thus be impossible for Equation 52 to hold. Thus by regularity Assumption 4, it follows that $(\mathbf{H}_1|\Theta_1 = \theta) = (\mathbf{H}_2|\Theta_2 = \theta)$ stochastically; that is, there is no potential for test bias. Referring to Theorem 2, we see that none of the items display item bias.

Remarks:

1. Assuming a scoring method really dependent on all items and that at least one of the items actually depends on $\mathbf{\eta}$, Theorem 7 implies that if there is potential for bias, then either test bias results or item bias cancellation results (and possibly both result simultaneously).

2. Theorems 3 and 7 can be interpreted together as stating a set of conditions under which the potential for test bias is equivalent to test bias.

3. For an interesting study of item bias amplification and cancellation based upon SIBTEST analyses of real and simulated data, see Nandakumar (in press).

Valid Subtest

Recall the informal definition of a valid subtest from the section An Informal Description of Test Bias. As mentioned therein, the reason for requiring a valid subtest to exist is that it is statistically impossible to detect test bias using only data from an ability test unless there exists an internal criterion measuring only the target ability; that is, a valid subtest. Here we formally define the validity of a subtest. Let θ denote the target ability. Recall also from that section that all IRFs are assumed strictly increasing in θ.

Definition 11. Let $\mathbf{U}$ be a test response with IRT representation given by Expression 9, let $\mathbf{\theta} = (\theta,\mathbf{\eta})$, and let S be a subset of the items $1, \ldots, N$. S is a valid subtest if the IRFs of all items in S depend only on θ; i.e., $P_i(\theta,\mathbf{\eta}) = P_i(\theta)$ for each i in S.

Remarks:

1. From a practical viewpoint one wants S to consist of as many of the items of the test as possible; the statistical power of detecting test bias or DTF increases as the proportion of valid items does.

2. Consider a specified nondecreasing item summary scoring method $h(\mathbf{u})$ for a test response $\mathbf{U}$ (recall Expression 27). Suitably restrict this scoring method to a subtest response $\mathbf{U}'$, denoting it by $h'(\mathbf{u}')$. For example, if $h(\mathbf{u}) = \Sigma_{i=1}^{N} u_i/N$, then $h'(\mathbf{u}') = \Sigma' u_i/N'$ is the obvious "restriction," where N' is the cardinality of $\mathbf{U}'$ and Σ' denotes summation over the components of $\mathbf{U}'$. A plausible alternative definition of subtest validity consistent with this chapter's emphasis on the expression of bias at the test level expressed through the test score would be to require of $h'(\mathbf{u}')$ that for all θ, given

$$E[h'(\mathbf{U}')|(\Theta,\mathbf{H}) = (\theta,\boldsymbol{\eta})] \tag{53}$$

depends only on θ and not on $\boldsymbol{\eta}$. This assertion is equivalent to asserting for all $(\theta,\boldsymbol{\eta})$ that

$$E[h'(\mathbf{U}')|(\Theta,\mathbf{H}) = (\theta,\boldsymbol{\eta})] = E[h'(\mathbf{U}')|\Theta = \theta]. \tag{54}$$

Equation 54 is appealing as a possible definition of subtest validity because it functions in an aggregate way at the test level based on the specified test scoring method restricted to the subtest. Evoking the usual empirical interpretation of expectation, Equation 54 says that repeated sampling of examinees from ability groups, both with the same value of θ but with any choice of two different values of $\boldsymbol{\eta}$, produces on average approximately the same value of $h'(\mathbf{U}')$, as one would wish a "valid subtest" to do.

Fortunately, however, this alternate and appealing definition is actually *equivalent* to our Definition 11, under the natural and mild regularity condition that $h'(\mathbf{u}')$ be strictly increasing as $u_i = 0$ is increased to $u_i = 1$ for each component u_i of $\mathbf{u}'$; that is that $h'(\mathbf{u}')$ really must depend on each of the valid subtest item responses. This assertion follows from a modification of the proof of Theorem 3. Thus our definition of subtest validity can be thought of as operating either at the item level (Definition 11) or at the test level (Equation 54).

3. Assume a two-group representation (Expression 16). It is perhaps interesting to note it is possible for all θ that

$$E[h'(\mathbf{U}'_1)|\Theta_1 = \theta] = E[h'(\mathbf{U}'_2)|\Theta_2 = \theta] \tag{55}$$

and yet subtest validity not hold. Note here that Equation 54, equivalent to subtest validity, implies Equation 55; however, Equation 55 should not be used as a definition of subtest validity. As an extreme example demonstrating this claim, each item of S could be measuring $\boldsymbol{\eta}$ alone with $\mathbf{H}_g$ independent of Θ_g for

$g = 1$ and $g = 2$ and $\mathbf{H}_g$ having the same distribution for $g = 1,2$. Subtest validity obviously does not hold here because the supposed-to-be valid items may be heavily influenced by $\mathbf{\eta}$; however,

$$
\begin{aligned}
E[h'(\mathbf{U'}_1)|\Theta_1 = \theta] &= E[E\{h'(\mathbf{U'}_1)|\Theta_1 = \theta,\mathbf{H}_1\}|\Theta_1 = \theta] \\
&= E[E\{h'(\mathbf{U'}_1)|\mathbf{H}_1\}|\Theta_1 = \theta] \\
&= Eh'(\mathbf{U'}_1) \\
&= Eh'(\mathbf{U'}_2) = \ldots \\
&= E[h'(\mathbf{U'}_2)|\Theta_2 = \theta];
\end{aligned}
\tag{56}
$$

so Equation 55 does hold here. The point we have just shown is that the absence of test bias for the subtest (i.e., that Equation 55 holds) does not imply subtest invalidity (i.e., that Equation 54 fails). Related to this fact, note that test validity for the entire test in the sense that Equation 54 holds for all $(\theta,\mathbf{\eta})$ for some scoring method $h(\mathbf{u})$ that is increasing in every component u_i of $\mathbf{u}$ does imply for every θ that no test bias exists. This follows trivially from the fact that test validity for the entire test means that every item depends only on θ.

TEST BIAS: THE LONG TEST CASE

The theory of test bias presented in the last section shows that if there is at least one nuisance dimension then test bias may be present. It is well known that purely unidimensional tests are rare among typical aptitude and achievement tests (see, e.g., Ansley & Forsyth, 1985; Humphreys, 1984; Reckase, Carlson, Ackerman, & Spray, 1986; and Yen, 1984). The position is summarized well in Humphreys: "The related problems of dimensionality and bias of items are being approached in an arbitrary and oversimplified fashion. It should be obvious that unidimensionality can only be approximated. . . . The large amount of unique variance in items is not random error, although it can be called error from the point of view of the attribute that one is attempting to measure. . . . We start with the assumption that responses to items have many causes or determinants" (p. 3).

How does the empirical reality of multiple determinants on a test interact with our multidimensional model of test bias? There are two cases to consider: Either the test is "long" or it is "short." By long it is meant that the number of items is large enough that asymptotic probabilistic arguments provide a useful approximation to the actual test-operating characteristics. For example, for many purposes a test of 40 items can be classified as long.

In the case of a short test, several of the results in the previous section are important: First, even if nuisance determinants are present in the items and influence examinee performance, the potential for bias against a group must exist in order for test bias to be possible. Second, if the amount of expressed bias at the item level is sufficiently small, then the amount of bias possible at the test level is bounded above. However, if little or no cancellation occurs, small amounts of bias at the item level can produce a substantial amount of test bias. Indeed, one can imagine a detrimental amount of test bias, but with statistical testing for individual item bias being unable to detect any bias at the item level. Third, the amount of test bias is dependent on the scoring method, the scoring method being the link between item and test bias. It is possible that some scoring methods might be more robust against the detrimental influence of item bias than others. Fourth, recalling Example 1 and the material on item bias cancellation, it is quite possible to minimize, with the help of an aptly chosen scoring method, the amount of test bias by having different biasing influences canceling each other out. For example, (again recall Example 1) if approximately equal numbers of items express approximately equal amounts of bias, respectively against and in favor of Group 1, then provided the scoring method gives approximately equal weight to the two classes of items, little or no test bias should occur. Intuitively, it seems likely that having many minor dimensions in addition to θ might increase the propensity for cancellation and actually result in less test bias. However, in spite of certain encouraging aspects of the previous remarks, it is surely the fact, because of the intrinsic multidimensional nature of ability tests, that serious amounts of test bias are likely when tests are short.

We now turn the discussion to the development of a long test scenario. In the study of test bias in a long test, the theory of essential unidimensionality of a test, as developed by Stout (1987, 1990) and refined by Junker (1989a, 1989b) turns out to be useful. First, we summarize the relevant concepts of this theory.

A long test response $\mathbf{U}_N$ is conceptualized as being the initial observed segment of a potentially observable infinite item pool $\{U_i, i \geq 1\}$. It is assumed that whatever process has been used to construct the first N items of the pool (i.e., the observed test $\mathbf{U}_N$) could have been continued in the same manner to produce $\{U_i, i \geq 1\}$. With this understanding, in order to do asymptotic statistical theory and for foundational purposes, we study $\{U_i, i \geq 1\}$ instead of $\mathbf{U}_N = \{U_i, 1 \leq i \leq N\}$, conceptualizing the item pool $\{U_i, i \geq 1\}$ as the "test." Note that letting $\mathbf{U}_{N+1} = (\mathbf{U}_N, U_{N+1})$ defines a sequence $\{\mathbf{U}_N, N \geq 1\}$ of finite length tests constructed from the initial segments of the item pool $\{U_i, i \geq 1\}$. $\{U_i, i \geq 1\}$ is defined to be essentially unidimensional ($d_E = 1$) if it has an IRT representation with monotone IRFs but instead of requiring local independence (Assumption 1), the weaker assumption is required that

$$\frac{\displaystyle\sum_{1 \leq i < j \leq N} \left| \operatorname{cov}(U_i, U_j | \Theta = \theta) \right|}{\dbinom{N}{2}} \to 0 \qquad (57)$$

as $N \to \infty$ for every θ. (The requirement of monotonicity can be weakened somewhat when modeling items where nonmonotonicity is suspected, but we omit discussion here [see Stout, 1990, Junker, 1989a]). When $d_E = 1$, it is shown that the latent ability is unique in the sense that any other $d_E = 1$ IRT representation has for its dominant latent ability a *monotone rescaling* of θ. (E.g., a mathematics test cannot be a test of geography for the reason that there exists no such rescaling.)

We now must specify a class of scoring methods for the sequence of long tests $\{U_N, N \geq 1\}$. It is convenient to consider a large class of scoring methods, but less extensive than the nondecreasing item summaries of Expression 27. Recall from mathematical analysis that a collection of functions $\{k_N(x)\}$ is *equicontinuous* if for every $\epsilon > 0$ there exists $\delta > 0$ such that

$$\left| k_N(x) - k_N(y) \right| < \epsilon \tag{58}$$

for all N and all x, y for which $|x - y| < \delta$. Note that the assumed continuity is uniform both in the argument and in the choice of function.

Definition 12. $\{k_N(\Sigma_{i=1}^N a_{Ni} U_i)\}$ is called an equicontinuous balanced scoring method provided
(a) $k_N(x)$ is defined on $[0,1]$, is nondecreasing, and satisfies

$$-\infty < \inf_N k_N(0) \leq \sup_N k_N(0) < \inf_N k_N(1) \leq \sup_N k_N(1) < \infty. \tag{59}$$

(b) $\{k_N(x)\}$ is equicontinuous, and
(c) $\{a_{Ni} : 1 \leq i \leq N, N \geq 1\}$ satisfies $0 \leq a_{Ni} \leq C/N$ for some $C > 0$ and for all i, N and $\Sigma_{i=1}^N a_{Ni} = 1$ for all N.
Remarks:
1. Equation 59 and (c) of Definition 12 merely guarantee that the "empirical" scale established by $k_N(\Sigma_{i=1}^N a_{Ni} U_i)$ does not shrink to 0 or stretch to ∞ as N varies. For example, if $k_N(1) - k_N(0) \to 0$ as $N \to \infty$, then $k_N(\Sigma_{i=1}^N a_{Ni} U_i)$ for large N is uninteresting.

2. The $a_{Ni} \leq C/N$ guarantees as N gets large that no single item dominates the score: that is, the scoring is "balanced."

3. A remark on notation is appropriate. An arbitrary scoring method $h_N(U_N)$ assigns a score to each test response U_N and hence $h_N(\cdot)$ is a function with an N-dimensional domain (such a score occurs in Expression 27). By contrast, an equicontinuous balanced scoring method $k_N(\Sigma_{i=1}^N a_{Ni} U_i)$ assigns a score to each linear combination $\Sigma_{i=1}^N a_{Ni} U_i$ for each N and hence $k_N(\cdot)$ is a function with a unidimensional domain.

A fundamental result of long test theory is that if a test $\{U_i, i \geq 1\}$ is essentially unidimensional, consistent estimation of θ is possible in the sense that for any equicontinuous balanced scoring method, given $\Theta_g = \theta$,

$$k_N \left(\sum_{i=1}^{N} a_{Ni} U_{ig} \right) - k_N \left(\sum_{i=1}^{N} a_{Ni} T_i(\theta) \right) \to 0 \tag{60}$$

in probability as $N \to \infty$ for $g = 1,2$ (established by a minor modification of the proof of Theorem 3.2 in Stout, 1990). That is, θ is estimated with total accuracy in the limit, using the latent scale

$$k_N \left(\sum_{i=1}^{N} a_{Ni} T_i(\theta) \right). \tag{61}$$

Here $T_i(\theta)$ denotes the marginal item response function defined by $T_i(\theta) = E[P_i(\Theta)|\Theta = \theta]$ (recalling Equation 10, with $\theta = (\theta_i, \eta)$ as in previous sections). Expectation is over both groups here; that is, Θ is the target ability of a randomly chosen examinee from the pooled group resulting from combining the two groups. An important special case is that when $d_E = 1$, given $\Theta_g = \theta$,

$$\sum_{i=1}^{N} U_{ig}/N - \sum_{i=1}^{N} T_i(\theta)/N \to 0 \tag{62}$$

in probability as $N \to \infty$, for $g = 1,2$. (Here $a_{Ni} = 1/N$ for $i \le N$ and $k_N(x) = x$.)

Armed with the aforementioned concepts, a long-test definition of test bias is now given. The intuitive idea is that if the test-scoring method being used measures target ability equally well in both groups as measured by its convergence in probability behavior as $N \to \infty$, then no test bias exists. Let

$$\mathbf{U}_g = (U_{1g}, \ldots U_{Ng}, U_{N+1,g}, \ldots) \tag{63}$$

denote the infinite item pool for Group g and let

$$\mathbf{U}_{Ng} = (U_{1g}, \ldots, U_{Ng}) \tag{64}$$

denote the finite observed segment of the item pool for g. To study long-test test bias, we make the assumption that $\mathbf{U}_g$ has a two-group representation of the form Expression 16 with Equation 6, Assumptions 1 and 2 holding within each group, and with Assumption 3 holding. It then follows from the ordinary weak law of large numbers in probability theory for any equicontinuous balanced test scoring method that, given $\Theta_1 = \theta$ and $\Theta_2 = \theta$,

$$k_N \left(\sum_{i=1}^{N} a_{Ni} U_{i1} \right) - k_N \left(\sum_{i=1}^{N} a_{Ni} P_i(\theta) \right) \to 0$$

and

$$k_N \left(\sum_{i=1}^{N} a_{Ni} U_{i2} \right) - k_N \left(\sum_{i=1}^{N} a_{Ni} P_i(\theta) \right) \to 0 \tag{65}$$

in probability as $N \rightarrow \infty$. Here $\boldsymbol{\theta} = (\theta, \boldsymbol{\eta})$ where θ is the target ability and $\boldsymbol{\eta}$ is the nuisance determinant. Of course, in order to be able to assume local independence for the representation given by Expression 16 and have good model fit, the dimension d of $\boldsymbol{\eta}$ may need to be quite large. It is easy to show that Equation 65 also holds for an d_E essential dimensional representation of the form given by Expression 16, with d_E possibly much smaller than d.

Because $k_N(\Sigma_{i=1}^{N} a_{Ni} U_{i1})$ and $k_N(\Sigma_{i=1}^{N} a_{Ni} U_{i2})$ have the same limit behavior in probability—hence $(\theta, \boldsymbol{\eta})$ is measured equally well asymptotically in both groups—Equation 65 seems to suggest that no test bias in a long-test sense is possible. However, Equation 65 is not the same as group-equivalent measurement of target ability θ alone. As in the finite test length case of the previous section, the source of bias is that the conditional distributions of $(\mathbf{H}_1 | \Theta_1 = \theta)$ and $(\mathbf{H}_2 | \Theta_2 = \theta)$ differ, thereby leading to superior limiting test scores used in the measurement of θ for one group versus another given $\Theta_1 = \theta$, $\Theta_2 = \theta$. An example should clarify this claim.

Example 2: Consider examinee subpopulations from the two groups defined by $\Theta_1 = \theta$ and $\Theta_2 = \theta$, respectively; that is, both subpopulations have the same target ability. Suppose that there is a single nuisance determinant and that

$$P[H_1 = 1 | \Theta_1 = \theta] = \tfrac{1}{4} \quad P[H_2 = 1 | \Theta_2 = \theta] = \tfrac{3}{4}$$
$$P[H_1 = 0 | \Theta_1 = \theta] = \tfrac{3}{4} \quad P[H_2 = 0 | \Theta_2 = \theta] = \tfrac{1}{4} \tag{66}$$

Clearly this is a case of potential for bias against Group 1 at θ. Suppose $k_N(x) = x$ for all N and $a_{Ni} = 1/N$ for $i \leq N$ and all N:

$$k_N \left(\sum a_{Ni} u_i \right) = \sum_{i=1}^{N} u_i / N. \tag{67}$$

Suppose local independence with respect to (θ, η) with

$$P_i(\theta, 1) = \tfrac{2}{3}, \, P_i(\theta, 0) = \tfrac{1}{3} \tag{68}$$

for all i. Then, Equation 65 specializes to

$$\frac{\sum_{i=1}^{N} U_{i1}}{N} \rightarrow \tfrac{2}{3}, \quad \frac{\sum_{i=1}^{N} U_{i2}}{N} \rightarrow \tfrac{2}{3} \tag{69}$$

given $\Theta_1 = \theta$, $H_1 = 1$ and $\Theta_2 = \theta$, $H_2 = 1$, respectively, in probability as $N \rightarrow \infty$. Also

$$\frac{\sum\limits_{i=1}^{N} U_{i1}}{N} \rightarrow \tfrac{1}{3}, \qquad \frac{\sum\limits_{i=1}^{N} U_{i2}}{N} \rightarrow \tfrac{1}{3} \qquad (70)$$

given $\Theta_1 = \theta$, $H_1 = 0$ and $\Theta_2 = \theta$, $H_2 = 0$, respectively, in probability as $N \rightarrow \infty$. But, conditioning on the intended to be measured abiliites $\Theta_1 = \theta$ and $\Theta_2 = \theta$, it follows using Equations 66 that

$$\frac{\sum\limits_{i=1}^{N} U_{i1}}{N} \rightarrow \tfrac{2}{3} \text{ with probability } \tfrac{1}{4} \text{ and}$$

$$\frac{\sum\limits_{i=1}^{N} U_{i2}}{N} \rightarrow \tfrac{1}{3} \text{ with probability } \tfrac{3}{4} \qquad (71)$$

as $N \rightarrow \infty$, as contrasted with

$$\frac{\sum\limits_{i=1}^{N} U_{i2}}{N} \rightarrow \tfrac{2}{3} \text{ with probability } \tfrac{3}{4} \text{ and}$$

$$\frac{\sum\limits_{i=1}^{N} U_{i1}}{N} \rightarrow \tfrac{1}{3} \text{ with probability } \tfrac{1}{4} \qquad (72)$$

as $N \rightarrow \infty$. Clearly Group 2 is favored among examinees of target ability θ. It may be interesting to note that

$$E\left[\frac{\sum\limits_{i=1}^{N} U_{i1}}{N} \,\middle|\, \Theta_1 = \theta \right] = \tfrac{3}{4} \cdot \tfrac{1}{3} + \tfrac{1}{4} \cdot \tfrac{2}{3} = \tfrac{5}{12} \qquad (73)$$

for all N, whereas

$$E\left[\frac{\sum\limits_{i=1}^{N} U_{i2}}{N} \,\middle|\, \Theta_2 = \theta \right] = \tfrac{1}{4} \cdot \tfrac{1}{3} + \tfrac{3}{4} \cdot \tfrac{2}{3} = \tfrac{7}{12}. \qquad (74)$$

Thus, in a trivial manner not dependent on N,

$$\underset{N\to\infty}{\text{Lim}}\left\{E\left[\frac{\sum\limits_{i=1}^{N}U_{i1}}{N}\,\Big|\,\Theta_1=\theta\right]-E\left[\frac{\sum\limits_{i=1}^{N}U_{i2}}{N}\,\Big|\,\Theta_2=\theta\right]\right\}$$

$$=-\tfrac{1}{6}<0. \tag{75}$$

We use the idea embodied in Equation 75 to define large-sample test bias.

Definition 13.   Let θ denote target ability.

1. There is no long-test test bias at θ with respect to an equicontinuous balanced scoring method

$$k_N\left(\sum_{i=1}^{N}a_{Ni}U_i\right) \tag{76}$$

   provided

$$E\left[k_N\left(\sum_{i=1}^{N}a_{Ni}U_{i1}\right)\Big|\,\Theta_1=\theta\right]$$

$$-E\left[k_N\left(\sum_{i=1}^{N}a_{Ni}U_{i2}\right)\Big|\,\Theta_2=\theta\right]\to 0 \tag{77}$$

   as $N\to\infty$.
2. If for every θ, there is no long-test test bias at θ, then there is no long-test test bias.
3. If at θ

$$E\left[k_N\left(\sum_{i=1}^{N}a_{Ni}U_{i1}\right)\Big|\,\Theta_1=\theta\right]$$

$$-E\left[k_N\left(\sum_{i=1}^{N}a_{Ni}U_{i2}\right)\Big|\,\Theta_2=\theta\right]\le C<0 \tag{78}$$

   for all sufficiently large N and some C, then long-test test bias exists at θ against Group 1.

We first show if there is no long-test test bias in the empirical sense that among examinees with the same target ability θ neither group is favored in their stochastic test score behavior as $N \to \infty$, the long-test test bias in the sense of Definition 13 holds.

Theorem 8: Suppose, given $\Theta_1 = \theta$ and $\Theta_2 = \theta$ that for an equicontinuous balanced scoring method,

$$k_N \left(\sum_{i=1}^{N} a_{Ni} U_{i1} \right) - c_{N1}(\theta) \to 0 \quad \text{and}$$

$$k_N \left(\sum_{i=1}^{N} a_{Ni} U_{i2} \right) - c_{N2}(\theta) \to 0 \tag{79}$$

in probability for some $c_{N1}(\theta), c_{N2}(\theta)$, as $N \to \infty$. Then Equation 77 holds; that is, there is no long-test test bias at θ for the given scoring method. Moreover, $c_{N1}(\theta), c_{N2}(\theta) \to 0$ as $N \to \infty$.

Remark: Note that it is not required that the centering functions $c_{Ng}(\theta)$ have to be the same for $g = 1,2$. What is required is the existence of a centering function dependent on θ alone and not $\boldsymbol{\eta}$ for each g, as contrasted with Equation 65 or Equations 69–70. Of course, the case where the centering functions are the same is of special interest and is the main motivation for the theorem, as the remark immediately prior to the statement of the theorem indicates.

Proof: By Equation 59, $|k_N(x)| \leq C$ for some $C > 0$. Thus $|c_{Ng}(\theta)| \leq C + D$ for some $D > 0$. By the Lebesgue dominated convergence theorem (see Serfling, 1980, p. 11), using Equation 79

$$E \left[\sum_{i=1}^{N} a_{Ni} U_{ig} - c_{Ng}(\theta) | \Theta_g = \theta \right] \to 0 \tag{80}$$

as $N \to \infty$, for $g = 1,2$. Now, trivially, the conclusion Equation 79 holds given $\Theta_1 = \theta$, $\mathbf{H}_1 = \boldsymbol{\eta}$ and $\Theta_2 = \theta$, $\mathbf{H}_2 = \boldsymbol{\eta}$ for all $\boldsymbol{\eta}$. Thus, subtracting the two results in Equation 79,

$$c_{N1}(\theta) - c_{N2}(\theta) \to 0 \tag{81}$$

as $N \to \infty$. Let $c_N(\theta) \equiv c_{N1}(\theta)$. It then follows from Equation 80 that

$$E \left[\sum_{i=1}^{N} a_{Ni} U_{ig} - c_N(\theta) | \Theta_g = \theta \right] \to 0 \tag{82}$$

as $N \to \infty$ for $g = 1,2$. Subtracting these two limits yields

$$E\left[\sum_{i=1}^{N} a_{Ni}U_{i1}|\Theta_1 = \theta\right] - E\left[\sum_{i=1}^{N} a_{Ni}U_{i2}|\Theta_2 = \theta\right] \to 0 \qquad (83)$$

as $N \to \infty$, i.e., no long-test test bias exists at θ.

Remark: We claim that Equation 79 (and hence the similar condition Equation 60) is inappropriately strong to use as a definition of lack of long-test bias. To see this, modify Example 2 by assuming

$$P[H_g = 0|\Theta_g = \theta] = \tfrac{3}{4}, P[H_g = 1|\Theta_g = \theta] = \tfrac{1}{4}, \qquad (84)$$

for $g = 1,2$. Hence no potential for bias exists. However note that, given $\Theta_1 = \theta$ and $\Theta_2 = \theta$

$$\frac{\sum_{i=1}^{N} U_{Ng}}{N} - \tfrac{2}{3} \to 0 \text{ with probability } \tfrac{1}{4} \qquad (85)$$

and

$$\sum_{i=1}^{N} U_{Ng} - \tfrac{1}{3} \to 0 \text{ with probability } \tfrac{3}{4} \qquad (86)$$

for both $g = 1$ and $g = 2$. Thus Equation 79 is precluded and thus long-test bias would be said to exist (even though no potential for bias exists) if Equation 79 was made the basis for deciding on the existence of long-test test bias. Note that the aforementioned convergence in probability behavior is identical for both groups. Intuitively, in this example the estimation of θ by $\Sigma_{i=1}^{N} U_{Ng}/N$ as $N \to \infty$ is equally bad for both groups in the sense that convergence in probability at θ fails to occur in exactly the same manner in both groups. Thus one would not wish to claim that test bias is occurring.

The following theorem states that essential unidimensionality is a sufficient condition for ensuring that no long-test test bias exists:

Theorem 9: Suppose $d_E = 1$ for target ability θ in the combined population consisting of Group 1 and Group 2 examinees. Then, with respect to all equicontinuous balanced scoring methods, no long-test test bias exists.

Proof: Let $\{k_N(\Sigma_{i=1}^{N} a_{Ni}U_i)\}$ be an arbitrary equicontinuous balanced scoring method. We need to prove Equation 77 for every θ. Fix θ. By work of Stout (1990), $d_E = 1$ implies Equation 60 for $g = 1,2$; that is, Equation 79 holds with $c_{Ng}(\theta) = k_N(\Sigma a_{Ni}T_i(\theta))$. Thus, by Theorem 8, the desired result holds.

By contrast, if the potential for bias exists at θ, then it follows that there exist balanced scoring methods for which long-test test bias at θ does exist.

Theorem 10: Assume that IRFs are differentiable in η. Let θ denote target ability, η denote the nuisance determinant and assume potential for bias against Group 1 at θ. Assume there exists a balanced scoring method $\{a_{Ni}\}$ (i.e., $k_N(x) = x$ in Definition 12) such that at θ,

$$\frac{d}{d\eta} \sum_{i=1}^{N} a_{Ni} P_i(\theta, \eta) > \epsilon_\eta > 0 \qquad (87)$$

for all η and all N. Then long-test test bias exists at θ against Group 1.

Proof: For $\boldsymbol{\theta} = (\theta, \eta)$, Equation 65 holds given $\Theta_1 = \theta$, $H_1 = \eta$; $\Theta_2 = \theta$, $H_2 = \eta$. Now, letting $F_g(\eta | \theta)$ denote the cdf of $H_g | \Theta_g = \theta$ and using Equation 87 and integration by parts

$$E\left[\sum_{i=1}^{N} a_{Ni} U_{i1} \bigg| \Theta_1 = \theta \right] - E\left[\sum_{i=1}^{N} a_{Ni} U_{i2} \bigg| \Theta_2 = \theta \right]$$

$$= \int_{-\infty}^{\infty} \left\{ \sum_{i=1}^{N} a_{Ni} P_i(\theta, \eta) \right\} d[F_1(\eta | \theta) - F_2(\eta | \theta)]$$

$$= - \int_{-\infty}^{\infty} \left\{ \frac{d}{d\eta} \sum_{i=1}^{N} a_{Ni} P_i(\theta, \eta) \right\} [F_1(\eta | \theta) - F_2(\eta | \theta)] d\eta$$

$$\leq \int_{-\infty}^{\infty} \epsilon_\eta [F_1(\eta | \theta) - F_2(\eta | \theta)] d\eta$$

$$\leq -c(\theta), \qquad (88)$$

where $c(\theta) > 0$ by the assumption of potential for bias against Group 1. Because this holds for all N, the result is proved by Definition 13.

How is the finite test length definition of test bias (Definition 9) related to the long-test test bias definition (Definition 13)? The answer is that lack of finite length test bias for all finite length tests $\mathbf{U}_N$ from the item pool $\{U_i, i \geq 1\}$ implies lack of long-test test bias for all equicontinuous balanced test scores.

Theorem 11: Assume an IRT representation for $\{U_i, i \geq 1\}$ of the form given by Expression 16 for $\boldsymbol{\theta} = (\theta, \boldsymbol{\eta})$. Let $\{k_N(\Sigma_{i=1}^{N} a_{Ni} U_i)\}$ be an equicontinuous balanced scoring method. Assume no finite length test bias exists; that is, Equation 29 holds for all N. Assume regularity Assumption 4. Then there is no long-test test bias; that is, Equation 77 holds.

Proof: Trivial from examination of Equations 29 and 77.

Remark: Of course, long-test test bias can fail to hold with finite length test bias holding. Nonetheless, it seems an appropriate way to describe biasedness of a test when the test is long.

From the long-test perspective, the need to produce a long-test definition of a valid subtest needs to be addressed. Previously in the short-test case, our definition of a valid subtest S with response $\mathbf{U}$ was stated to be equivalent to Equation 54 holding for all $(\theta, \mathbf{\eta})$. Just as the short-test version of no test bias (Equation 29) is modified for the long-test version of no test bias (Equation 77), a similar modification of Equation 54 yields an appropriate definition of a valid subtest. We consider only equicontinuous balanced scoring methods for subtests $\mathbf{U'}_N$ of $\mathbf{U}_N$. That is, we consider scoring $k'_N(\Sigma' a_{Ni} U_i)$ where Definition 12 holds, for each $k'_N(\Sigma' a_{Ni} U_i)$ where Σ' denotes summation over the indices of the components of $\mathbf{U'}_N$.

Definition 14. Let the item pool $\{U_i, i \geq 1\}$ have IRT representation given by Expression 9 with the usual accompanying assumptions. Let $\mathbf{U'}_N \subset \mathbf{U}_N$ denote a subtest of $\mathbf{U}_N$ for each N. Denoting the cardinality of a set A as card (A), assume

$$\mathbf{U'}_N \subset \mathbf{U'}_{N+1}, \quad \frac{\text{card } \mathbf{U'}_N}{N} \geq C > 0 \tag{89}$$

for some C and for all $N \geq N_0$ for some fixed N_0 (N_0 will be small in all applications). Then $\{\mathbf{U'}_N, N \geq 1\}$ is said to be a collection of valid subtests with respect to a specified equicontinuous balanced scoring method $\{k'_N(\Sigma' a_{Ni} U_i)\}$ provided there exists a function $c_N(\theta)$ such that for all $\theta, \mathbf{\eta}$,

$$E\left[k'_N\left(\sum{}' a_{Ni} U_i\right) \middle| (\Theta, \mathbf{H}) = (\theta, \mathbf{\eta}) \right] - c_N(\theta) \to 0 \tag{90}$$

as $N \to \infty$.

Remark: Recall that short-test bias validity, that is, Equation 54 holds for all $(\theta, \mathbf{\eta})$, for scoring method $k'_N(\Sigma' a_{Ni} U_i)$ say, simply means that for θ

$$m(\theta, \mathbf{\eta}) \equiv E\left[k'_N\left(\sum{}' a_{Ni} U_i\right) \middle| (\Theta, \mathbf{H}) = (\theta, \mathbf{\eta}) \right] \tag{91}$$

depends only on θ and not on $\mathbf{\eta}$. By contrast the long-test subtest validity just defined by Equation 90 weakens this to asserting that $m(\theta, \mathbf{\eta})$ for all θ is asymptotically not dependent on $\mathbf{\eta}$ as $N \to \infty$. That is, intuitively, for large fixed N, $m(\theta, \mathbf{\eta})$ for all θ is approximately constant as $\mathbf{\eta}$ varies.

As with long-test test bias, the theory of essential unidimensionality is useful in studying long-test subtest validity:

Theorem 12: Assume $d_E = 1$ with latent ability θ being target ability for subtests $\{U'_N, N \geq 1\}$ satisfying Equation 89. Then Equation 90 holds for all equicontinuous balanced scoring methods; that is, subtest validity holds for all equicontinuous balanced scoring methods.

Proof: It follows from a minor modification of the proof of Theorem 3.2 in Stout (1990) that for all $(\theta, \boldsymbol{\eta})$

$$k'_N \left(\sum{}' a_{Ni} U_i \right) - c_N(\theta) \to 0 \qquad (92)$$

in probability as $N \to \infty$. But $|k'_N(\sum' a_{Ni} U_i)| \leq C$ for some constant $C < \infty$. It is a standard result from the theory of convergence in probability that convergence in probability and the boundedness just stated together imply convergence in expectation. That is, for all $(\theta, \boldsymbol{\eta})$,

$$E\left[k'_N \left(\sum{}' a_{Ni} U_i \right) \middle| (\boldsymbol{\Theta}, \mathbf{H}) = (\theta, \boldsymbol{\eta}) \right] - c_N(\theta) \to 0 \qquad (93)$$

as $N \to \infty$. That is, Equation 90 holds.

Stout (1987) developed a statistical test for essential unidimensionality. Clearly this could be applied to a subtest to assess whether it can be used as a valid subtest in the case of a long test.

TEST BIAS AS A FUNCTION OF TARGET ABILITY

The previous sections focus on test bias for fixed values of target ability θ. In these sections it was argued that test bias (item bias also) is a phenomenon that expresses itself at each θ. In particular, it is the comparison of the distributions of $(\mathbf{H}_1 | \boldsymbol{\Theta}_1 = \theta)$ and $(\mathbf{H}_2 | \boldsymbol{\Theta}_2 = \theta)$ that dictates whether test bias is possible at θ and if such bias is possible, in which direction (biased in favor of or biased against Group 1) it occurs. Mathematically, without further assumptions, one cannot infer what the character of the bias at $\theta' \neq \theta$ is from the character of the bias at θ. This section develops the concept of considering test bias aggregated over target ability. We return to the convention of suppressing N in the notation when appropriate; for example, $\mathbf{U} \equiv \mathbf{U}_N$.

Definition 15.   Let $h(\mathbf{U})$ be a test scoring method and $\mathbf{U}$ be a test response as in Equation 1. The expected test bias at θ against Group 1 using test-scoring method $h(\mathbf{U})$ is given by

$$B(\theta) \equiv E[h(\mathbf{U}_2)|\Theta_2 = \theta] - E[h(\mathbf{U}_1)|\Theta_1 = \theta]. \tag{94}$$

Remarks:

1. Note that $B(\theta) > 0$ indicates test bias against Group 1 at θ.
2. Several special cases are of interest. If $h(\mathbf{u}) = \Sigma_{i=1}^{N} u_i/N$, then $B(\theta)$ is the difference of (marginal) test characteristic curves (average of marginal IRFs):

$$B(\theta) = \frac{\sum_{i=1}^{N} T_{i2}(\theta)}{N} - \frac{\sum_{i=1}^{N} T_{i1}(\theta)}{N}. \tag{95}$$

If $h(\mathbf{u}) = u_i$, then

$$B(\theta) = T_{i2}(\theta) - T_{i1}(\theta),$$

the amount of item i bias against Group 1 at θ.

Probably the most common pattern in the potential for bias as a function of θ is unidirectional potential for bias.

Definition 16. If potential for bias exists against the same group at every θ then unidirectional potential for bias is said to exist against the group.

Another less common, but still important pattern in the potential for bias as a function of θ is that the "direction" of the potential for bias changes from one end of the θ-continuum to the other.

Definition 17. Suppose for some fixed θ_0 that the potential for bias against one group exists for all $\theta < \theta_0$ and the potential for bias exists against the other group for all $\theta > \theta_0$. Then bidirectional potential for bias is said to exist.

The verbal analogies example in the section An Informal Description of Test Bias is an obvious practical example of unidirectional potential for bias. For, it seems likely that the potential for test bias against German immigrants will hold regardless of the level of verbal analogies ability being conditioned on.

As an example of bidirectional potential for bias, suppose Θ_1 and Θ_2 are both uniformly distributed on the interval $[-1,1]$. Suppose that in Group 1, Θ_1 and H_1 are statistically independent with H_1 uniformly distributed on $[-1,1]$. Suppose in Group 2 that $(H_2|\Theta_2 = \theta)$ has a uniform distribution on the interval with end points 0 and 2θ. That is, perhaps because of cultural differences, in Group 2 it follows that Θ and H_2 are highly positively correlated while Θ and H_1 are uncorrelated in Group 1. Elementary computation show that if $-1 < \theta < 0$,

Equation 26 holds, yet if $0 < \theta < 1$, Equation 25 holds. That is, potential for bias against Group 2 holds for $\theta < 0$ and potential for bias against Group 1 hold if $\theta > 0$; in other words, bidirectional potential for bias holds.

Test bias (and item bias) can be unidirectional or bidirectional.

Definition 18. If test bias (either in the ordinary sense of Definition 9 or in the long-test sense of Definition 13) exists against the same group at every θ, then unidirectional test bias against that group is said to hold.

Definition 19. If for some θ_0 test bias in the sense of Definition 9 holds against one group for all $\theta < \theta_0$ and against the other group for all $\theta > \theta_0$ then bidirectional test bias is said to occur.

A long-test version of Definition 19 is easy to give but is omitted for simplicity. The following results relate unidirectional potential for bias to unidirectional test bias:

Theorem 13: Suppose test bias exists against Group 1 at some θ in the sense of Definition 9, and suppose unidirectional potential for bias. Assume a test scoring method of the form Expression 27. Suppose for every θ' that there is some i (possibly dependent on θ') for which $h(\mathbf{u})$ is strictly increasing as $u_i = 0$ increases to $u_i = 1$ and for which $P_i(\theta',\boldsymbol{\eta})$ is strictly increasing in $\boldsymbol{\eta}$. Then unidirectional test bias against Group 1 holds.

Proof: By Theorem 4, the potential for bias against Group 1 at θ holds. By assumption of unidirectional potential for bias, the potential for bias against Group 1 thus holds for all θ'. Apply Theorem 3 together with the Remark 1 following it.

Theorem 14: Assume IRFs are differentiable in η. Suppose long-test test bias exists against Group 1 at some θ in the sense of Definition 13 for a balanced scoring method $\{a_{Ni}\}$ and suppose unidirectional potential for test bias. Assume for every θ'

$$\frac{d}{d\eta} \sum_{i=1}^{N} a_{Ni} P_i(\theta',\eta) > \epsilon_\eta > 0$$

for all η (without loss of generality unidimensional assumed here). The unidirectional (long-test) test bias against Group 1 holds in the sense of Definition 18.

Proof: Same as that of Theorem 13 except Theorem 10 is used in place of Theorem 3.

In order to study bidirectional test bias, attention is restricted to balanced scoring methods. For an arbitrary balanced scoring method $\sum_{i=1}^{N} a_{Ni} U_i$, letting

$$F_g(\eta|\theta) \equiv P[H_g \leq \eta|\Theta_g = \theta] \tag{96}$$

and assuming differentiability of IRFs and a unidimensional nuisance determinant, the following formula for $B(\theta)$ of Equation 94 obtained by integration by parts is useful

$$B(\theta) = \int_{-\infty}^{\infty} \left\{ \sum_{i=1}^{N} a_{Ni} \frac{d}{d\eta} P_i(\theta,\eta) \right\} [F_1(\eta|\theta) - F_2(\eta|\theta)] \, d\eta. \tag{97}$$

Theorem 15: Assume a balanced scoring method (Definition 12(c)) with differentiable IRFs. Assume a unidimensional nuisance trait η. Assume for each θ, there exists some i (possibly varying with θ) for which

$$a_{Ni} > 0, \quad \frac{d}{d\eta} P_i(\theta,\eta) > 0 \text{ for all } \eta > 0. \tag{98}$$

Then bidirectional potential for test bias holds if and only if bidirectional test bias holds.

Proof: By Assumption 4, for fixed θ either

$$F_1(\eta|\theta) - F_2(\eta|\theta) > 0 \text{ for all } \eta \tag{99}$$

or

$$F_1(\eta|\theta) - F_2(\eta|\theta) < 0 \text{ for all } \eta. \tag{100}$$

Thus, using Equations 97 and 98 and the strict monotonicity of every $P_i(\theta,\eta)$ in η, $B(\theta) > 0$ or $B(\theta) < 0$ accordingly as Equation 99 or 100 holds. Potential for bias at θ means that either Equation 99 or Equation 100 holds at θ. The desired result follows.

Assume number correct scoring, which implies Equation 95 and hence that test bias is controlled by the (marginal) item response functions with respect to target ability. Graphically, bidirectional test bias under this scoring method is shown in Fig. 10.3. Note the effect is that the test displays higher discrimination for Group 2 than for Group 1. That is, bidirectional test bias is expressed as differing test discriminations for the two groups. By contrast, under Equation 95, unidirectional test bias is shown in Fig. 10.4. Unidirectional test bias is not linked to differing test discriminations across group. Indeed, the two-test characteristic curves shown in Fig. 10.4 even can be translates of one another; for example, for some $c > 0$ for given $T_{i2}(\theta) \equiv T_i(\theta)$

$$\sum_{i=1}^{N} T_{i1}(\theta)/N = \sum_{i=1}^{N} T_i(\theta + c)/N \tag{101}$$

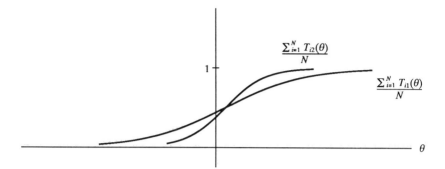

FIG. 10.3.   Bidirectional test bias.

for all θ. That is, items could be uniformly more difficult for Group 2 examinees at every θ.

Fix an item and consider its marginal IRFs with respect to target ability as group varies. There is a debate about whether from the cognitive perspective, differing discriminations across group is more the essence of bias than differing difficulties across group. Also, some practitioners claim that bidirectional test bias can be important in practice whereas others discount its importance. It is hoped that this section helps illuminate these issues.

DISCUSSION AND SUMMARY OF RESULTS

The central position of this chapter is that bias and DIF should each be conceptualized, studied, and measured at the test level rather than at the item level. A multidimensional but nonparametric IRT model of test bias is presented and a number of important properties derived. Our theory of test bias includes the often-used unidimensional IRT bias and DIF approaches as a special case.

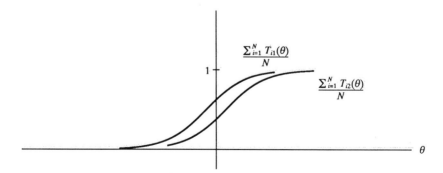

FIG. 10.4.   Unidirectional test bias.

The model hypothesizes a target ability intended to be measured by the test as well as other dimensions called nuisance determinants, not intended to be measured. Informally, test bias occurs when the test under consideration is measuring nuisance determinants in addition to the target ability, and moreover the two groups do not possess equal amounts of the nuisance determinants. Our view, an outgrowth of the classical predictive validity viewpoint of bias, is that bias is really something expressed at the test level via the particular test score in use and that bias rests in the across-group differences in the relationship between test scores and criterion. For us, the criterion is internal to the test and is expressed by a valid subtest. If by a construct validity argument it is known to consist of items measuring only target ability then test bias can be detected. Otherwise it is only differential test functioning (DTF) that can be detected.

In the IRT Model for Test Responses section, the multidimensional non-parametric IRT model is presented. The notion of the marginal IRF with respect to target ability is introduced.

In the Test Bias in the IRT Model section and its subsections, test bias is defined carefully using the IRT model introduced in the previous section. Test bias originates with the potential for test bias at a particular value of θ of target ability existing against a group in the sense of Definition 6. This potential for bias against Group 1 gets expressed at the item level if any of the marginal group IRFs satisfy $T_{i1}(\theta) < T_{i2}(\theta)$. The potential for test bias and a strictly increasing IRF in η implies expressed item bias (Theorem 2).

One main focus of this article is on biased DIF items acting in concert to produce test bias or DTF. Three components combine to produce test bias: (a) potential for bias, (b) dependence of the IRFs on η, and (c) the test-scoring method, which transmits simultaneous expressed item bias into test bias. Test bias is defined formally in Equation 28. It is shown that test bias at θ implies the potential for bias at θ (Theorem 4). The central result of the Test Bias section (Theorem 3) shows that potential for bias at θ translates into test bias at θ provided the scoring method depends on at least one item that has a strictly increasing IRF in η at θ.

The important topic of item bias cancellation is taken up next. Example 1 illustrates how cancellation actually can decrease the amount of item bias that gets expressed at the test level. That is, the potential for bias need not be transmitted strongly to the test level because in fact considerable cancellation can occur as the result of multidimensional nuisance determinants. By contrast, small and perhaps undetectable amounts of bias at the item level can be translated into a substantial amount of bias expressed at the test level when no cancellation occurs. Next, we formalize the notion of a valid subtest, which must exist for test bias (as opposed to DTF) to be detected. Shealy and Stout (in press) have presented a statistical test of test bias, making the question of whether test bias does exist for a particular data set an answerable one.

The Test Bias: The Long Test Case section presents a long-test viewpoint of test bias, making heavy use of Stout's (1990) theory of essential unidimensionality. Test bias holding for long tests is defined. It is shown that if an equicontinuous balanced test score (a large class of reasonable-to-use test scores are such) displays appropriate convergence in probability behavior separately in each examinee group, then there can be no long-test test bias. Essential unidimensionality ($d_E = 1$) of a test with target ability as its dominant latent trait is shown to exclude long-test test bias. Because one can test statistically for essential unidimensionality (Stout, 1987), this is a potentially very useful result. Theorem 10 is important as the long-test analogue to Theorem 3. It links potential for bias and scoring method to the existence of long-test test bias.

A long-test viewpoint of subtest validity is also present in this section. Informally stated, the main result is that $d_E = 1$ for a subtest with the latent trait being target ability implies subtest validity for all equicontinuous balanced scoring methods.

Finally, the Test Bias as a Function of Target Ability section considers test bias aggregated over target ability. The important concepts of unidirectional and bidirectional test bias are introduced. The relationship between differing discriminations across group and bidirectional test bias is explicated.

It is hoped that the theory of test validity we have presented proves useful to theoreticians and practitioners alike. The interested reader is also referred to Shealy & Stout (in press) for a detailed description of SIBTEST, the statistical procedure for the detection of bias or DIF at the item or test level that is based upon the theory of this article.

ACKNOWLEDGMENT

The authors found discussions with Terry Ackerman, Paul Holland, Lloyd Humphreys, Kumar Joagdev, Brian Junker, Ratna Nandakumar, and Mark Reckase extremely useful in conducting the research reported in this article. This research was supported by Office of Naval Research Grant No. 00014-90-J-1940 and National Science Foundation Grant NSF-DMS-91-01436. It is collaborative in every respect and the order of authorship is alphabetical.

11

A Model for Missing Information About the Group Membership of Examinees in DIF Studies

Nancy L. Allen
Paul W. Holland
Educational Testing Service

In differential item functioning (DIF) studies, examinees are classified into a reference group (r), or a focal group (f), or are ignored as members of other groups (o), based on their responses to a group identification question. Some examinees fail to answer this question and so introduce missing data that can affect the inferences that are based on DIF measures. Because DIF often is concerned with a comparison of an item's performance for a relatively small subpopulation (the focal group) versus its performance for a much larger subgroup (the reference group), even a small amount of missing data may have profound effects. For example, self-identified Black examinees commonly make up about 6% of the population taking the insurance practitioner licensure test used in our example, and nonresponse to the racial/ethnicity question is about 9%. Thus, if a major part of the nonresponding population is Black, the introduction of this large number of nonrespondents into the Black group can have a substantial effect on any inference made.

First, we present a model for the missing data in this setting. Then the major part of the chapter examines the effects of two interesting sets of assumptions about the missing data. We show that, when the nonresponse to the group identification question is ignorable, the Mantel–Haenszel odds ratio estimate is appropriate, whereas the standardized P-DIF statistic should be adjusted to take the nonresponse into account. We also consider a special type of nonignorable nonresponse where both the Mantel–Haenszel statistic and the standardized P-DIF statistic can be estimated without adjustments, using only the data from examinees who answered the group identification question. Finally, we comment on some side issues and give an example.

The goal in our work is to provide a framework for considering the effect of different assumptions about missing group identification information on current DIF analyses. This provides a way to incorporate additional information about group membership from follow-up studies and allows us to do sensitivity studies to examine the effects of different assumptions about nonresponse.

SOME NOTATION

If all examinees answered the group identification question, the data available for use in a DIF study are:

1. G = group = r (reference), f (focal), o (other).
2. X = score on the studied item = 0, 1.
3. S = score on the matching variable.

Because not all examinees respond to the group identification question, we require notation to reflect this. Let the variable R denote response to the group identification question; that is,

$$R = \begin{cases} 1 & \text{if the examinee responds to the group identification question} \\ 0 & \text{otherwise.} \end{cases}$$

In Mantel–Haenszel and standardization analyses of DIF (see chapter 3 of this volume), the probability that is estimated by using data from only those examinees that identify themselves as members of the reference or focal groups is

$$P(X = x \mid G = g \text{ and } S = s \text{ and } R = 1), \qquad (1)$$

where $x = 0,1$, $g = r$ or f, and S denotes the total score. Writing the probability in this way suggests that DIF analyses also might be based instead on

$$P(X = x \mid G = g \text{ and } S = s), \qquad (2)$$

the response probability for examinees regardless of whether they do or do not identify their group membership (r, f, or o). The issue of interest is what happens when respondents and nonrespondents differ in various ways? The purpose of the model described next is to allow us to study the effect of various types of nonresponse on (1) and (2). The model is an adaptation of the general approach to missing data described in Little and Rubin (1987).

THE MODEL

It is useful to think of this model as if it were describing a computer simulation that results in DIF data with group membership missing for some examinees.

We begin by generating N observations according to the joint distribution of X and S, $h(x,s)$; that is,

$$h(x,s) = P(X = x, S = s). \tag{3}$$

Suppose N_{xs} of the N generated cases have $X = x$ and $S = s$. Next, distribute these N_{xs} cases over their values of G according to a multinomial distribution. This results in n_{gxs} cases with $G = g$, $X = x$, and $S = s$ for $g = r, f$, and o. The parameters of this multinomial are N_{xs} and the probability vector $\underline{p}_{xs}$ where

$$\underline{p}_{xs} = (p_{r|xs}, p_{f|xs}, p_{o|xs}) \tag{4}$$

and

$$p_{g|xs} = P(G = g \mid X = x, S = s), \tag{5}$$

for $g = r, f, o$. Next, the missing data process is brought into play. Let $\rho(g,x,s)$ be defined as

$$\rho(g,x,s) = P(R = 1 \mid G = g, X = x, S = s). \tag{6}$$

Then $\rho(g,x,s)$ is the *selection function* that determines the missing data process.

We define R and G as follows: For each observation where $X = x$, $S = s$, and $G = g$, toss a biased coin with probability $\rho(g,x,s)$. If it comes up heads, set $R = 1$ (i.e., no missing data). If it comes up tails, set $R = 0$ (i.e., the value for G is deleted). This results in the conditional distribution of G and R given $X = x$ and $S = s$ being a multinomial distribution based on a total of N_{xs} with these four probability parameters that sum to one:

$$P(G = r, R = 1 | X = x, S = s) = p_{r|xs}\, \rho(r,x,s),$$
$$P(G = f, R = 1 | X = x, S = s) = p_{f|xs}\, \rho(f,x,s),$$
$$P(G = o, R = 1 | X = x, S = s) = p_{o|xs}\, \rho(o,x,s),$$
$$P(R = 0 \mid X = x, S = s) = 1 - \sum p_{g|xs}\, \rho(g,x,s), \tag{7}$$

where the sum in the final probability is over $g = r, f$, and o.

It should be emphasized that the model specified by making choices for $h(x,s)$, p_{xs} and $\rho(g,x,s)$ is completely general and can represent all possible missing data processes that result in missing data for G but not for X or S. Now let N_{gxs} denote the number of cases for which $G = g$, $X = x$, $S = s$, and $R = 1$, and N_{uxs} denote the number of cases for which $R = 0$, $X = x$, and $S = s$. The three-way array $\underline{N} = (N_{gxs})$ where $g = r, f, o$, or u classifies all N observations, including those where $G = u$ (unobserved). Then the likelihood function for all the data is

$$L(\underline{N}) = \prod_{xs} \left\{ \prod_{g} (\rho(g,x,s)p_{g|xs}h(x,s))^{N_{gxs}} \right\} \times$$

$$\left\{ (1 - \sum_{g} \rho(g,x,s)p_{g|xs})h(x,s))^{N_{uxs}} \right\} . \tag{8}$$

The product and sum in Equation 8 are only over $g = r, f,$ and o.

IGNORABLE CASE

The case of ignorable nonresponse (Little & Rubin, 1987) corresponds to $\rho(g,x,s)$ not depending on the value of the variable with missing values, that is, g. In the ignorable case we denote the selection function by $\rho(x,s)$ and the four probabilities in Equation 7 become

$$P(G = r, R = 1|X = x, S = s) = p_{r|xs} \, \rho(x,s) \, ,$$

$$P(G = f, R = 1|X = x, S = s) = p_{f|xs} \, \rho(x,s) \, ,$$

$$P(G = o, R = 1|X = x, S = s) = p_{o|xs} \, \rho(x,s) \, ,$$

$$P(R = 0|X = x, S = s) = 1 - \rho(x,s) \left(\text{because} \sum_{g} p_{g|xs} = 1 \right) . \tag{9}$$

We examine the consequences of Equation 9 in the two sections entitled Ignorable Nonresponse.

SIMPLE NONIGNORABLE NONRESPONSE CASES

A simple case of nonignorable nonresponse occurs when we say "suppose all of the nonrespondents are in the focal group." This corresponds to the following choice for $\rho(g,x,s)$:

$$\rho(r,x,s) = \rho(o,x,s) = 1 \text{ but } \rho(f,x,s) < 1. \tag{10}$$

Note that in Equation 10 $\rho(g,x,s)$ does depend on g. Likewise, we get "all the nonrespondents in the reference group" when

$$\rho(f,x,s) = \rho(o,x,s) = 1 \text{ but } \rho(r,x,s) < 1. \tag{11}$$

(See further examples of nonignorable nonresponse in the sections on forgettable nonresponse.)

THE MANTEL–HAENSZEL PROCEDURE

Although the Mantel–Haenszel (MH) procedure also includes a chi-square test, we consider the common odds ratio (α) for an item across the 2×2 tables for each score level. The log of this value is used as the MH measure of the amount of DIF. For each score level, s, the odds ratio based on all examinees can be expressed as

$$\alpha(s) = \frac{p_{r|1,s}}{p_{f|1,s}} \bigg/ \frac{p_{r|0,s}}{p_{f|0,s}} \tag{12}$$

For each score level, s, the odds ratio based only examinees with observed group membership is

$$\alpha_{\text{obs}}(s) = \frac{P(X=1|G=r,S=s,R=1)}{P(X=0|G=r,S=s,R=1)} \bigg/ \frac{P(X=1|G=f,S=s,R=1)}{P(X=0|G=f,S=s,R=1)}. \tag{13}$$

Written in terms of the probabilities that have been discussed previously, this value is seen to equal

$$\alpha_{\text{obs}}(s) = \frac{P(G=r,R=1|X=1,S=s)}{P(G=f,R=1|X=1,S=s)} \bigg/ \frac{P(G=r,R=1|X=0,S=s)}{P(G=f,R=1|X=0,S=s)}, \tag{14}$$

by applying Bayes' theorem to the four probabilities. Substituting Equation 7 into Equation 14 yields:

$$\alpha_{\text{obs}}(s) = \frac{p_{r|1,s}\,\rho(r,\,1,\,s)}{p_{f|1,s}\,\rho(f,\,1,\,s)} \bigg/ \frac{p_{r|0,s}\,\rho(r,\,0,\,s)}{p_{f|0,s}\,\rho(f,\,0,\,s)} \tag{15}$$

and

$$\alpha_{\text{obs}}(s) = \left[\frac{p_{r|1,s}}{p_{f|1,s}} \bigg/ \frac{p_{r|0,s}}{p_{f|0,s}} \right] \cdot \left[\frac{\rho(r,\,1,\,s)}{\rho(f,\,1,\,s)} \bigg/ \frac{\rho(r,\,0,\,s)}{\rho(f,\,0,\,s)} \right]. \tag{16}$$

In other words, the odds ratio that we ordinarily estimate for a score level ($\alpha_{\text{obs}}(s)$) in a DIF analysis is equal to the product of the odds ratio based on all examinees and a function of the selection function evaluated at different values of G and X; that is, the odds ratio can be written as

$$\alpha_{\text{obs}}(s) = \alpha(s)\,\beta(s), \tag{17}$$

where

$$\beta(s) = \frac{\rho(r,\,1,\,s)}{\rho(f,\,1,\,s)} \bigg/ \frac{\rho(r,\,0,\,s)}{\rho(f,\,0,\,s)}. \tag{18}$$

This relationship is important because it provides a way to find the odds ratio based on all examinees, not only on those who specified their group membership.

$$\alpha(s) = \alpha_{\text{obs}}(s)/\beta(s). \tag{19}$$

Note, however, that this odds ratio depends not only on what can be estimated from the observed data, but also on the selection function, $\rho(g,x,s)$, which we do not know.

Ignorable Nonresponse

When the nonresponse is ignorable we have

$$\rho(g,x,s) = \rho(x,s), \tag{20}$$

and then

$$\beta(s) = 1. \tag{21}$$

In this case, then, at each score level the odds ratio based on all examinees is exactly the same as the odds ratio based only on examinees specifying their group membership:

$$\alpha(s) = \alpha_{\text{obs}}(s) \tag{22}$$

Forgettable Nonresponse

The question that next arises is, "Are there other conditions under which $\alpha(s) = \alpha_{\text{obs}}(s)$?" In other words, what are the conditions under which $\beta(s) = 1$? For example, this occurs when

$$\rho(g,x,s) = \rho(g,s), \tag{23}$$

and more generally whenever the ratio,

$$\frac{\rho(r, x, s)}{\rho(f, x, s)}, \tag{24}$$

does not depend on the item response, x. The selection function in Equation 23 does not depend on whether examinees respond correctly to the item or not. We call this "forgettable nonresponse" because, although the nonresponse is not ignorable, it does not affect the value that we would like to estimate (i.e., we can "forget about" the nonrespondents). When either the assumption of ignorable nonresponse or the assumption of forgettable nonresponse is reasonable for every score level, the common odds ratio that is estimated from the complete data also can be estimated using only the examinees specifying their group membership. Under these conditions, the estimate we ordinarily calculate in a DIF analysis also estimates the common odds ratio for all examinees regardless of whether or not they reported their group membership.

THE STANDARDIZATION METHOD

At a score level, the quantity of interest in the standardization DIF measure is the difference score,

$$D(s) = P(X = 1 \mid G = f, S = s) - P(X = 1 \mid G = r, S = s), \quad (25)$$

where $P(X = 1 \mid G = g, S = s)$ is the probability for all examinees including those not reporting their group membership. The difference based on examinees for whom group membership is reported is the quantity that is estimated in a standardization DIF analysis and is given by

$$\begin{aligned} D_{obs}(s) = P(X = 1 \mid G = f, S = s, R = 1) \\ - P(X = 1 \mid G = r, S = s, R = 1). \end{aligned} \quad (26)$$

Using Bayes' theorem,

$$P(X = 1 \mid G = g, S = s, R = 1) =$$

$$\frac{\rho(g, 1, s)P(X = 1 \mid G = g, S = s)}{\rho(g, 1, s)P(X = 1, \mid G = g, S = s) + \rho(g, 0, s)P(X = 0 \mid G = g, S = s)}. \quad (27)$$

Solving Equation 27 for $P(X = 1 \mid G = g, S = s)$ gives us an explicit formula for the probabilities needed in Equation 25 in terms of the probabilities that enter into Equation 26 and the selection function, $\rho(g, x, s)$; that is,

$$P(X = 1 \mid G = g, S = s) =$$

$$\frac{\rho(g, 0, s)P(X = 1 \mid G = g, S = s, R = 1)}{\rho(g, 0, s)P(X = 1, \mid G = g, S = s, R = 1) + \rho(g, 1, s)P(X = 0 \mid G = g, S = s, R = 1)}. \quad (28)$$

Ignorable Nonresponse

When the nonresponse is ignorable, $\rho(g,x,s)$ is replaced by $\rho(x,s)$ in Equation 28, just cited. Note that in this case $D(s)$ need not equal $D_{obs}(s)$ in general; that is, it depends on the values of $\rho(1,s)$ and $\rho(0,s)$. Hence, in the ignorable case, estimating $D(s)$ is more complicated than just using an estimate for $D_{obs}(s)$ in place of an estimate of $D(s)$. We discuss this further in the Example section.

Forgettable Nonresponse

When Equation 23 holds, $\rho(g,x,s)$ is replaced by $\rho(g,s)$ in Equations 27 and 28. In this case, $\rho(g,s)$ can be factored out of the denominator and the numerator, so that in the case of forgettable nonresponse we have the result

$$D(s) = D_{obs}(s). \tag{29}$$

So, as in the case of the Mantel–Haenszel odds ratio, if the assumption of forgettable nonresponse holds for every score level, the standardized P-DIF estimate for the complete data also can be estimated using only the data from examinees specifying their group membership.

SIDE ISSUES

There are two side issues about which comments should be made. The first is of particular importance for analyzing the data in the example. The second has to do with the testability of assumptions about the nonresponse to group identification questions.

Estimation of the Probabilities

In standard Mantel–Haenszel or standardization DIF analyses, the probabilities in Equations 13 and 26 are estimated from the data using simple proportions. They then are averaged across score levels using a weighting scheme particular to each method to estimate α and standardized P-DIF, respectively. Because of the variability of the proportions used to estimate these probabilities and because of the introduction of the additional probabilities, $\rho(g,x,s)$, into the analysis when estimating probabilities for all examinees regardless of their identification of group membership, other estimation procedures are possible. For instance,

$$P(X = 1 \mid G = g, S = s, R = 1) \tag{30}$$

and

$$\rho(x,s) = P(R = 1 \mid X = x, S = s) \tag{31}$$

can be estimated from the data using logistic regression techniques (Cox, 1970), and the conditioned score distribution,

$$P(S = s \mid G = f, R = 1), \tag{32}$$

can be estimated by log-linear models for score distributions (Holland & Thayer, 1987).

Testing Assumptions

Because testing the assumption of ignorable nonresponse questions whether group membership influences selection or not and because complete data about group membership are not known, the assumption of ignorable nonresponse cannot be tested in general. The reasonableness of the assumption of ignorable nonresponse can be determined only by deciding whether or not it makes sense that response to the group identification question depends on group membership over and above its dependence on the accuracy of the answer given to the studied item and on score level. Other assumptions about the nature of the nonresponse are difficult to test. The assumption of forgettable nonresponse can be tested, but it is not simple to do, even when probabilities are estimated by proportions.

EXAMPLE

We know from the previous development that our usual estimates of DIF, based on examinees who specified their group membership, are appropriate for Mantel–Haenszel analyses if the nonresponse is ignorable or forgettable and for standardization analyses if the nonresponse is forgettable. Because of this, our example focuses on estimating the amount of DIF using the standardization method when ignorable nonresponse is assumed. Incidentally, we test the assumption of common odds ratios across score level that is assumed when using the Mantel–Haenszel procedure.

In order to illustrate how to adjust the estimated value of standardized P-DIF if the nonresponse is ignorable, we examine estimates for three items, two of which were identified as having significant DIF during an operational analysis that ignored nonresponse to the group identification problem. The data consist of item response information for examinees who identified themselves as White, examinees who identified themselves as Black, examinees who identified themselves as members of other groups, and examinees who did not identify their ethnicity on the preliminary materials for a spring 1989 licensure test for insurance agents. The sample sizes and percentages of each subgroup are presented in Table 11.1. The nonresponse rate was about 9% for the examinees in the sample. In each case, items identified as having significant DIF, other than the item

TABLE 11.1
Sample Sizes and Percentages of Subgroups
of Examinees

Subgroups of Examinees	N	%
White Examinees	2,375	76
Black Examinees	194	6
Other Examinees	267	9
Examinees with No Response	270	9
TOTAL	3,106	100

studied, were deleted from the total score. The studied item always was included in finding an examinee's score level. The maximum total score was 59, for the analyses of each of the two items previously identified as having significant DIF. The maximum total score was 58 for the analysis of the third item.

In order to calculate the difference in Equation 25 and the probabilities for the reference and focal groups given in Equation 28 under the assumption of ignorable nonresponse, two sets of probabilities must be estimated. They are the probabilities given in Equations 30 and 31. In the analyses for the three sample items, Equation 30 was estimated by fitting the following logistic regression model to the data for the examinees that specified their ethnicity:

$$\text{LOGIT}\{P(X = 1 | G = g, S = s, R = 1)\} = \alpha_g + \sum_{k=1}^{p} \beta_{gk} s^k \quad (33)$$

where β_{gk} values may or may not depend on g. Note that if the best fitting model of the form in Equation 33 has β_{gk} values that depend on group membership, the odds ratio is not constant across score levels. This would indicate that the use of the Mantel–Haenszel procedure may be inappropriate.

In the example, the probability in Equation 31 also was estimated using logistic regression. This time the analysis was based on all examinees and the models fit were of the form

$$\text{LOGIT}\{P(R = 1 | X = x, S = s)\} = \alpha + \beta x + \sum_{k=1}^{p} \gamma_k s^k + \sum_{j=1}^{g} \delta_j x s^j. \quad (34)$$

Finally, the standardized differences at each score level were combined across score levels. For data with observed group membership, a way to combine the differences across score levels that is parallel to the method used in practice is

$$\text{P-DIF}_{\text{obs}} = \sum_{s} D_{\text{obs}}(s) \, P(S = s | G = f, R = 1) \quad (35)$$

where $D_{\text{obs}}(s)$ is calculated for each score level from Equation 26 and $P(S = s | G = f, R = 1)$ is estimated using a loglinear model for the score distribution. Similarly, for all examinees,

$$\text{P-DIF} = \sum_{s} D(s) \, P(S = s | G = f) \quad (36)$$

where $D(s)$ is calculated for each score level from Equations 25 and 28 and $P(S = s | G = f)$ is estimated using the formula:

$$P(S = s | G = f) = \frac{\sum_{x'} \left[\dfrac{P(X = x' | G = f, S = s, R = 1) P(S = s | G = f, R = 1)}{\rho(f, x', s)} \right]}{\sum_{x', s'} \left[\dfrac{P(X = x' | G = f, S = s', R = 1) P(S = s' | G = f, R = 1)}{\rho(f, x', s')} \right]}. \quad (37)$$

TABLE 11.2
Results for the Examples

	ITEM		
	1	*2*	*3*
STD P-DIF$_{obs}$	−.099(.032)*	−.176(.037)	.004(.030)
P-DIF$_{obs}$	−.104	−.176	.001
P-DIF	−.105	−.176	.001
Overall % Correct	.91	.65	.87
LOGISTIC Reg. Model I	$\alpha_g + \beta_1 s$	$\alpha_g + \beta_1 s + \beta_2 s^2$	$\alpha_g + \beta_1 s + \beta_2 s^2$
LOGISTIC Reg. Model II	$\alpha + \gamma_1 s$	$\alpha + \gamma_1 s + \beta x$	$\alpha + \gamma_1 s$
LOGLINEAR MODEL	2 Moments	3 Moments	3 Moments

*Standard errors, where available, are indicated in parentheses.

Note that the probabilities in Equation 37 are estimated by using the fitted values in Equations 33 and 34, because in the ignorable case $\rho(g,x,s) = \rho(x,s)$. Probabilities also were estimated for a loglinear model for $P(S = s \mid G = f, R = 1)$.

Table 11.2 summarizes the results for the three items of interest. The first row of results, labeled STD P-DIF$_{obs}$, is the result of the initial DIF analyses based only on the examinees who specified their group membership and calculated in the usual way using proportions. P-DIF$_{obs}$ labels the row of results based on Equation 35. These results are based on the examinees who specified their group membership and were calculated using logistic regressions and loglinear models to smooth the proportions to estimate the probabilities of interest. The next row, labeled P-DIF, contains the results based on Equation 36. These results are based on the item responses for all examinees. The lower part of Table 11.2 contains information about the best fitting models used to estimate the probabilities in Equations 35 and 36.

These results provide two messages, if they are representative of results for other items and other tests. The first is that the assumption of common odds ratios is reasonable. The second is that the nature of nonresponse to group identification questions is such that standardization methods adjusted for ignorable nonresponse give results similar to those assuming forgettable nonresponse.

Formula 37 shows that we were not quite correct in our claim that the usual unadjusted standardization DIF estimate gave appropriate results when the assumption of forgettable nonresponse holds. If $\rho(g,x,s) = \rho(g,s)$ then Equation 37 becomes

$$P(S = s | G = f) = \frac{\left[\dfrac{P(S = s | G = f, R = 1)}{\rho(f, s)} \right]}{\displaystyle\sum_{s'} \left[\dfrac{P(S = s' | G = f, R = 1)}{\rho(f, s')} \right]} \qquad (38)$$

which does not simplify to

$$P(S = s \mid G = f) = P(S = s \mid G = f, R = 1) \qquad (39)$$

in general. Equation 39 does hold under the even stronger assumption that $\rho(g,x,s) = \rho(g)$; that is, that given group membership, nonresponse is not affected by either score level (s) or response (x). This problem is due to the way the standardized differences, $D(s)$ or $D_{obs}(s)$, are combined across score levels. The way the odds ratios, $\alpha(s)$ or $\alpha_{obs}(s)$, are combined across score levels also affects estimates of the M-H statistics, but to a lesser extent, because the assumption of common odds ratios for all score levels is made.

SUMMARY

We have presented a framework for examining the effect of nonresponse to group identification questions in DIF analyses. This framework identified two sets of assumptions that arise naturally from the nonresponse problem: ignorable nonresponse and forgettable nonresponse. If the assumption of forgettable nonresponse is true, then the usual DIF estimates from Mantel–Haenszel and standardization analyses are appropriate. If the assumption of ignorable nonresponse is true, the usual Mantel–Haenszel DIF estimates are appropriate. However, standardization DIF estimates should be adjusted. Examples using real data indicate that, although this is true, the practical differences between adjusted and unadjusted values may be small.

III

PRACTICAL QUESTIONS AND EMPIRICAL INVESTIGATIONS

The previous two parts of the book dealt with the methodology of measuring DIF, and were basically statistical in character. Now we turn to the uses of this methodology to learn about DIF in extant tests and about the structure of test items. Do many test items show large amounts of DIF? What kinds of items are more DIF-prone than others? Do factors that seem to cause DIF actually produce it when introduced into a test item? What are the practical issues that arise when DIF analyses are integrated into ongoing testing programs?

In chapter 12, O'Neill and McPeek examine some of the data files associated with past administrations of some of the largest volume tests associated with ETS. They investigate the differences in average DIF values for various categories of items using these data, and identify several item types that consistently show DIF in a specific direction across several testing programs. They also point to the important finding that positive DIF (i.e., DIF that favors a focal group) occurs in cases that are understandable and might have been predicted. The chapter focuses its attention on those unusual items that do show some DIF. O'Neill and McPeek carefully categorize those items by format, content, and affected group in a search for structure—clues to increase our understanding of what yields DIF. These exploratory results are supplemented by more directed exploration in chapter 14 by Schmitt, Holland, and Dorans, who show how to use these findings to construct and test hypotheses about the causes of DIF in randomized DIF studies.

These attempts at understanding DIF are summarized and commented on by Lloyd Bond in chapter 13, who emphasizes the importance of both exploration and experimental confirmation. Charles Lewis' discussion in chapter 15 illuminates the study of DIF in his inimitable fashion by examining the properties of the simplest DIF model.

It is sometimes a long way from the theoretical development of a procedure to an operational form that can be implemented. The chapters in part II present theoretical reasons supporting various statistical techniques. These results aid in choosing the methodology to be employed. Michael Zieky, in chapter 17, tells us about the kinds of issues, which are not always obvious, that must be resolved before a method can be implemented practically. He explains what choices had to be made, how they were made at ETS, and why. In chapter 16, Elizabeth Burton and Nancy Burton describe what the practical effects of implementing formal DIF procedures has had on an operational test. Robert Linn provides us with a wider view of the wisdom of these choices in his discussion of them in chapter 18.

12

Item and Test Characteristics That Are Associated with Differential Item Functioning[1]

Kathleen A. O'Neill
W. Miles McPeek
Educational Testing Service

Increasingly over the past decade, standardized tests have come under public scrutiny for possible bias against various subgroups including ethnic, racial, and gender subgroups. (See chapter 20 by McAllister for a discussion of testing, differential item functioning, and public policy.) However, the issue of fairness in items and tests long has been a matter of great concern to test developers. At testing companies such as Educational Testing Service (ETS), judgmental review procedures are used to prevent offensive or stereotyped material from being included in any test and to ensure that the tests reflect the multicultural society in the United States to the extent allowed by test specifications. (See chapter 19 by Ramsey for a description of this process.) Reviews of tests for statistical evidence of differential item functioning (DIF) also are used to identify items that evidence differential performance by groups of examinees. In addition to these reviews, DIF research is conducted in an effort to improve the items included in every test. This research is a response to the concerns of test developers, test users, and examinees to identify characteristics of items that may cause significant group differences in difficulty.

The purpose of this chapter is to review recent research that investigates the relationship between DIF and item and test characteristics. This survey is based primarily on post hoc analyses of existing tests that were assembled before the Mantel–Haenszel procedures to screen test questions were established for test developers. In this chapter, the findings of greatest general significance are emphasized although other salient findings limited to a single testing program also are discussed.

---

[1]Presented at the conference entitled Differential Item Functioning: Theory and Practice, October 1989, Educational Testing Service, Princeton, New Jersey.

255

Before the research results are presented, it is profitable to review briefly how DIF operates. The fundamental principle of DIF is simple: Examinees who know the same amount about a topic should perform about equally well on an item testing that topic regardless of their sex, race, or ethnicity. (See chapter 3 by Dorans and Holland and chapter 4 by Thissen, Steinberg, and Wainer for more detailed explanations of DIF statistics; see chapter 1 by Angoff for a review of other methods of estimating bias.) If two groups of examinees could be matched on the knowledge and skills measured by the test, then people in the matched groups should perform similarly on individual test items. In the operational use of indices of differential item functioning,[2] examinees from one of the focal or target groups such as women or Black examinees often are matched with examinees from a reference group such as men or White examinees on the basis of the total test score or subscore. The test score customarily is selected as the matching criterion for several reasons. First, the test is a reliable and valid measure administered under standard conditions. Second, a unifactor test measures the same ability as the items in it. Third, test scores are readily accessible for analysis. Although it is the best measure available to test developers, the test score still will be an imperfect criterion because no test is perfectly reliable or perfectly valid. (See chapter 17 by Zieky and chapter 18 by Linn for a detailed discussion of this issue.) If a test contains many different areas of knowledge or skill, examinees matched on the total test score are not necessarily matched on each separate area contained in the test.[3]

Because the DIF procedure matches people on the knowledge and skills included in the test, test questions that have high DIF values need to be investigated to see whether the difference in difficulty may be caused by factors from one of three broad areas: (a) surface features or content characteristics of the question, (b) real differences in the groups' knowledge and skills (such as those resulting from different educational experiences), or (c) the nature of the criterion used for matching. In and of itself, a high DIF value does not indicate an unfair question; it simply indicates that matched groups of examinees perform differently on an item without offering any information about the cause(s) of the difference in performance.

An additional reason to be careful in any interpretation of DIF results is that data for most testing programs are only available for one or two group comparisons because most tests are taken by too few focal group examinees to yield reliable information. In addition, the accuracy of DIF statistics can be affected if some examinees do not identify or misidentify their ethnic group and/or language competence. (See chapter 11 by Allen and Holland for a model on infor-

---

[2]The two indices used most often at ETS are the Mantel–Haenszel procedure (Holland & Thayer, 1988) and the standardization procedure (Dorans & Kulick, 1986).

[3]In such cases, a decision can be made to use a relevant subset of the items as the matching criterion.

mation missing about examinees' ethnic group.) Moreover, DIF results for one focal group are frequently inconsistent with results for another focal group. Due to these concerns, the research reported in this review is limited to recent studies that had large samples and that used Mantel–Haenszel, standardization, or IRT methods of determining bias. This means that most of the results reported are based on the American College Testing Program Assessment Test (ACT), the Graduate Management Admission Test (GMAT), the Graduate Record Examinations (GRE) General Test, the NTE Core Battery (NTE), and the Scholastic Aptitude Test (SAT).

For much of the research reported, a set of item characteristics that might result in differential performance by group was hypothesized. The items were classified according to each characteristic, and F tests were performed to determine if there were differences in mean DIF values for the categories within each characteristic. For example, "minority stimulus"[4] was one of the hypothesized characteristics. Items for the GMAT, GRE, and NTE were categorized as follows:

1. Stimulus material refers to Black people.
2. Stimulus material refers to Hispanic people.
3. Stimulus material refers to other minorities.
4. Stimulus material refers to people of no specified ethnic origin.
5. Stimulus material does not refer to people.

For the major testing programs, items were classified on at least 30 characteristics. Because of these multiple classifications, many within-characteristic categories were small or empty, and there was great overlap among some of the characteristics. For this reason, the discussion focuses on results that are significant in more than one major testing program. The decision to focus on results that are found in more than one program is intended simply to concentrate attention on findings most likely to be generalizable.

FINDINGS AND DISCUSSION

With appropriate cautions in mind, the first general point to be made is that relatively few items have DIF values that are considered high.[5] Even though the

---

[4]The word *stimulus* refers to information upon which several test questions typically are based, such as a reading passage.

[5]In the work reported by ETS researchers using the Mantel–Haenszel procedure, the conservative value used to flag high DIF items for research frequently has been a difference between the two groups of approximately one delta point (which is very approximately .08 difference in the proportion correct rates for the two matched groups). This difference can be represented by the formula

exact numbers vary on different programs, the number of items identified on admissions tests is small for any one focal group (generally less than 10% of the items contributing to a test score) and includes items on which the focal group performs worse than the matched comparison group and items on which the focal group performs better (e.g., Wild & McPeek, 1986). That the number of items is small indicates that it is important not to overgeneralize from the results.

In the following presentation of the research, the results are ordered so that findings from verbal tests are presented before those from quantitative tests. Within each type of test, gender-group results are presented before ethnic-group results.

Verbal Tests

Content Characteristics of Verbal items Associated with DIF for Women.   The reading sections of the GRE, NTE, and SAT include passages on a variety of topics such as humanities, social sciences, biological science, and so forth. Results from a number of studies show that, when women are compared to a matched group of men, they typically perform less well than men on reading comprehension items with science-related content. For instance, in the GRE General Test, items based on science passages were generally differentially more difficult for women than for a matched group of men, and items based on social science and humanities passages were generally differentially easier for women than for a matched group of men (Scheuneman & Gerritz, 1990; Wild & McPeek, 1986).

Research on SAT reading passages has shown that content related to technical aspects of science (as opposed to the history or philosophy of science) appears to be more difficult for women than for a matched group of men (Lawrence & Curley, 1989; Lawrence, Curley, & McHale, 1988). This difference is found despite the fact that all of the information necessary to answer the reading comprehension questions in the GRE General Test and the SAT is present in the reading passages.

SAT and GRE discrete verbal items are not based on reading passages. These items, which include sentence completion items and vocabulary item types such as antonyms and analogies, are classified into four general content areas: aesthetics/philosophy, practical affairs, science, or human relationships. Aesthetics/philosophy content includes topics related to music, art, architecture, literature, or philosophy. Practical affairs content includes items that relate to everyday life (e.g., money and its uses, tools and their uses, mechanical objects, sports, historical topics, etc.). Human relationships content includes material

---

| $P_{(Ref|Score)} - P_{(Focal|Score)} | \approx .08$. ETS researchers using the standardization procedure frequently have used a .05 difference in performance between the matched groups to flag items for study.

IMPETUOUS:

(A)   appropriate

(B)   respectful

(C)   uninteresting

FIG. 12.1. Antonym item that   (D)   voracious
has content classified as human
relationships.   *(E)   deliberate

related to how a person thinks, feels, or reacts. Specific knowledge of these areas is not tested, but items are distributed relatively equally across these areas in order to ensure that students are neither advantaged nor disadvantaged by exposure to or comfort with any one field.

On both the SAT and the GRE General Test, women perform better than a matched group of men on antonyms and analogies that are classified as aesthetics/philosophy or human relationships (Carlton & Harris, 1989b; O'Neill, Wild, & McPeek, 1989). Figure 12.1 shows an antonym item that has content classified as human relationships; on this item women performed better than men of similar verbal ability.

Women perform less well than a matched group of men on SAT and GRE antonyms and analogies that are classified as science or world of practical affairs. It is important to note that no specific scientific knowledge is necessary to answer SAT and GRE General Test vocabulary items classified as science items. In these items the science terminology used is generally accessible to all students. For example, Figure 12.2 contains science content on which women performed worse than the matched group of men.

The science results for both the vocabulary items and the reading comprehension items may well reflect differences in attitudes about science for men and women. Differences in the proportions of men and women taking courses in science and planning careers in science have been widely documented (e.g., Ramist & Arbeiter, 1986). It may be that there are differences between the groups in their interest in science topics, their confidence in their abilities to understand scientific subject matter, and their comfort level with science passages.

FATHOM : DEPTH ::

*(A)   kilometer : distance
 (B)   circumstance : line

 (C)   wavelength : receiver

FIG. 12.2. Item that contains
science content on which wom-   (D)   scale : note
en performed worse than the
matched group of men.   (E)   mass : weight

As noted, the performance of women on science content has been linked most often to their levels of interest and coursetaking. These conventional interpretations of the underrepresentation and marginal position of women in science have been based on the idea that sex role stereotypes inhibit women from entering a scientific career. However, such stereotypes may act as a selective filter rather than a barrier, because they are probably not equally discouraging to all women. It was argued recently by Bar-Haim and Wilkes (1989) that prevailing sex role definitions tend to discourage especially the potential empiricists among women from attempting a career in science. Although these are the women most likely to thrive on a traditional empirically based scientific career, they are fairly traditional women and less likely to aspire to such a career in the face of societal discouragement. Bar-Heim and Wilkes also argued that the women least likely to be deterred by the stereotypes are either ill-equipped for empirical research or unlikely to be content with a whole career of such circumscribed activity. If such speculation is close to the mark, it is not surprising that there seem to be special difficulties in the ways that women tend to relate to science and science-related verbal questions.

Reading comprehension questions that refer to both men and women (as opposed to referring to men only or to not mentioning people at all) show better performance by women than by a matched group of men.[6] This result has been found in analyses of the GMAT, SAT, and NTE, but the effect was not significant in the GRE General Test (Carlton & Harris, 1989b; O'Neill, McPeek, & Wild, in preparation; O'Neill, Wild, & McPeek, in preparation; Wild & McPeek, in preparation). This result may be analogous to the superior performance of minority examinees compared to matched White examinees on minority-oriented passages to be discussed later: test material likely to be of greater interest to a particular group often is found to be easier for that group than for its matched reference group.

Table 12.1 summarizes the results for women of content characteristics of verbal items that are related to differential item performance.

At the individual item level, the particular causes of DIF for men and women generally remain elusive. A few items that show large amounts of differential item performance seem relatively easy to explain. Words pertaining to stereotypically male pursuits such as *hunting* or *ice hockey* frequently are found to be harder for women than for a matched group of men.[7] The Preliminary Scholastic Aptitude Test item shown in Fig. 12.3 is such an item. Similarly, words related to

---

[6]Women do not appear to perform better than matched men on discrete items that refer to women (Carlton & Harris, in preparation; O'Neill, McPeek, & Wild, in preparation).

[7]For major skills tests, it has become our practice at ETS either (a) to eliminate problem items from item pools at the pretest stage if the volume of examinees is high enough to perform DIF analyses, or (b) to avoid writing items on these topics when there is sufficient evidence to lead us to believe that a topic is related to differences in group performance unless the topic is useful for measuring the construct being tested.

TABLE 12.1
Major Content Findings for Verbal Characteristics
in Female/Male Analyses

Content Areas	Performance Pattern
Reading Comprehension	
Science	—
Humanities	+
Analogy/Antonym/Sentence Completion	
Science	—
Social Science/Everyday Life	—
Aesthetics/Philosophy	+
Human Relationships	+
Analogy	
Concrete	—
Abstract	+

Note. The + indicates areas in which women perform better than the matched reference group of men; the — indicates the reverse.

stereotypically female pursuits such as *sewing* or *embroidery* frequently are found to be easier for women than for a matched group of men. Figure 12.4 shows a GRE item that contains content that stereotypically interests women. Despite examples of stereotypical content, it is also usually possible to find a few counterexamples of such generalizations. For example, the GRE item in Fig. 12.5 contains content related to war, but there is essentially no difference in performance on this item for men and women of similar verbal ability.

It seems possible that, for most items exhibiting a substantial amount of DIF, the DIF may result from the accumulation of effects of several individual characteristics of the items. These unidentified characteristics individually might have only small effects that are not ordinarily apparent. Also, the item characteristics causing DIF might do so only when certain combinations of them are present.

HOCKEY : ICE ::

*(A) soccer : grass

(B) diving : board

(C) skiing : lodge

(D) baseball : bat

(E) archery : target

FIG. 12.3. Item that contains content that stereotypically interests men.

TILE : MOSAIC ::

(A)   wood : totem

*(B)   stitch : sampler

(C)   ink : scroll

FIG. 12.4. Item that contains content that stereotypically interests women.

(D)   pedestal : column

(E)   tapestry : rug

Such a situation would account for the general lack of success in hypothesizing the causes of DIF for the majority of individual items that show extreme DIF.

Content Characteristics of Verbal Items Associated with DIF for Minority Group Examinees.   Unlike the science content results for women, research on the relationship between Black/White DIF and the content of reading passages presents a mixed picture. On the GRE General Test, Black examinees generally performed less well on questions associated with science passages than did a matched group of White examinees. On the SAT and the NTE, there was no relationship between DIF and reading passage content for Black examinees. The GRE findings may be due to particular characteristics of the test forms studied or of GRE examinees.

One very well-established finding is the superior performance of Black and Hispanic examinees, compared to matched White examinees, on items based on reading passages that are intended to be especially relevant to minority interests or concerns. This result has been found on the GRE, GMAT, NTE, and SAT (Carlton & Harris, 1989b; McPeek & Wild, 1986; Medley & Quirk, 1974; Wild & McPeek, 1986, in preparation). On the SAT, Black examinees performed better than matched White examinees on questions based on passages that contained references to Black Americans (Carlton & Harris, 1989a), and Hispanic examinees performed better than matched White examinees on questions based on a passage about Mexican-American women and on questions based on a passage that contained references to a Black mathematician (Schmitt, 1986). It appears that when test material is of especial interest to one ethnic group, that

TORPEDO : WEAPON ::

(A)   cannonball : gun

(B)   tractor : farm

(C)   submarine : fleet

FIG. 12.5. Item that contains stereotypical content, but has no DIF.

(D)   fin : swimmer

*(E)   boat : vehicle

group may perform better than its matched reference group, possibly due to the ethnic group's greater interest, knowledge, or self-confidence with the subject matter.

Possibly the most widely reported aspect of verbal tests has been the differential functioning of analogy items (e.g., Carlton & Harris, 1989b; Pearlman, 1987; Schmitt, 1986; Schmitt & Bleistein, 1987; Schmitt & Dorans, 1987a, 1987b; Wendler & Carlton, 1987). These studies have suggested that Black and Hispanic examinees may be responding to different cues on analogy items and that these examinees perform less well than matched White examinees on analogy items containing homographs. (Homographs are words that are spelled the same, but have significantly different meanings, e.g., *bear* as a noun and as a verb.)

As mentioned earlier, SAT and GRE General Test discrete questions (analogies, antonyms, and sentence completions) are classified into four areas: aesthetics/philosophy, practical affairs, science, and human relationships. In both the SAT and the GRE General Test, Black examinees perform better than matched White examinees on analogy items dealing with human relationships, and less well than matched White examinees on science analogies. Figure 12.6 shows an analogy with human relationships content that Black examinees found easier than did matched White examinees and an analogy with science content that Black examinees found more difficult than did matched White examinees. It should be

Human Relationships Content

REPRIMAND : REPROVE ::

(A) inquiry : respond

*(B) eulogy : praise

(C) document : sign

(D) confession : indict

(E) sermon : worship

Science Content

BARK : TREE ::

*(A) skin : fruit

(B) dew : grass

(C) seed : flower

(D) peak : hill

(E) wake : boat

FIG. 12.6. An analogy with human relationships content that Black examinees found easier than matched White examinees and an analogy with science content that Black examinees found more difficult than matched White examinees.

noted again that science knowledge is not necessary to answer the analogy items classified as science related. In contrast to these DIF results, Freedle and Kostin (1987, 1988) found that science content on analogies does not contribute independent variance in the prediction of DIF values. Rather, item difficulty and aspects of the analogical relationship were identified as predictors.

Analogies in the GRE General Test and the SAT are also classified as concrete, abstract, or mixed. In concrete analogies, the terms involve nouns that refer to entities that can be perceived by at least one of the primary senses (e.g., "hen:rooster"); in abstract analogies the terms cannot be perceived by one of the primary senses (e.g., "frugal:penurious"). On both the GRE General Test and the SAT, Black and Hispanic examinees perform less well than matched White examinees on concrete analogies, and better than matched White examinees on abstract analogies. Figure 12.7 shows an abstract analogy item on which Black examinees perform better than White examinees of similar ability and a concrete analogy item on which Black examinees perform worse than matched White examinees. It is important to note, however, that item difficulty may be confounded with the concrete characteristic because the category of concrete analogies generally contains more easy items (and fewer hard items) than the abstract analogy category. In addition, it is true that the easy and concrete analogies more often contain science content, and the more difficult and abstract analogies often may focus on human relationships.

Abstract Anology

INFINITESIMAL : QUANTITY ::

*(A)   inappreciable : value

(B)   unknown : anonymity

(C)   imprecise : meaning

(D)   indecisive : mind

(E)   unexpected : surprise

Concrete Anology

GEYSER : STEAM ::

(A)   fountain : coin

*(B)   volcano : lava

(C)   glacier : iceberg

(D)   avalanche : trees

(E)   mudslide : rocks

FIG. 12.7. An abstract analogy item on which Black examinees perform better than matched White examinees and a concrete analogy item on which Black examinees perform worse than matched White examinees.

The inclusion of homographs in the distractors of analogies on both the SAT and GRE General Test seems to be related to Black and Hispanic examinees performing less well than matched White examinees (Carlton & Harris, 1989b; O'Neill, McPeek, & Wild, in preparation; Schmitt, 1986). For example, Fig. 12.8 shows an analogy item on which both Black and Hispanic examinees perform more poorly than the matched group of White examinees. In this item, the homograph *hide* can mean the skin of an animal or the action of seeking concealment. Schmitt and Bleistein (1987) hypothesized that Black examinees responding to SAT analogies that they find difficult or confusing may be using different answering strategies such as searching for vertical relationships, that is, looking for similar content among terms of the stem and options rather than analyzing the relationship between the terms in the stem. The answer pattern that might result if such a strategy is used is found in the item in Fig. 12.9. Black examinees are selecting the correct response less frequently than are the matched White examinees, and instead they are selecting more frequently Choice C, which also talks about boats. If the use of a vertical relationship strategy is more likely with minority examinees, then homographs may be adding differentially more to the complexity of the relationship to be identified for Black and Hispanic examinees than for matched White examinees.

In Hispanic/White analyses, the presence of cognates also can be related to differential performance. As Schmitt (1986) noted, there are both true cognates (words that have similar meanings in English and Spanish) and false cognates (words for which there are different meanings in English and Spanish). Her research shows that, in general, Hispanic examinees (Mexican Americans and Puerto Ricans) perform better than matched White examinees when items contain true cognates, especially in the stem-key combination. The item in Fig. 12.10 contains five true cognates out of the six words, and this item is much easier for Hispanic examinees than for the matched comparison group.

Table 12.2 summarizes the findings of DIF analyses of the performance of minority examinees on content characteristics of verbal items.

In addition to DIF found for content aspects of items, there appears to be a modest positive correlation between item difficulty and DIF in Black/White analyses of verbal questions on the GRE General Test and SAT, but not on the

ANIMAL : HIDE ::

(A)   egg : yolk

(B)   deer : hunt

FIG. 12.8. An analogy item with a homograph on which both Black and Hispanic examinees perform more poorly than matched White examinees.

(C)   desk : top

(D)   fugitive : shelter

*(E)   fruit : rind

CANOE : RAPIDS ::

*(A)   plane : turbulence

(B)   truck : garage

(C)   oar : rowboat

(D)   factory : automation

(E)   pond : stream

FIG. 12.9. Analogy item on which Black examinees may be using a "vertical relationship" answering strategy.

GMAT. On GRE and SAT verbal items, Black examinees tend to perform better than matched White examinees on the more difficult items, and matched White examinees tend to perform better than Black examinees on easier items. On the SAT and GRE General Test, the correlation between DIF and item difficulty appears to be higher for antonyms and analogies than for the reading comprehension and sentence completion items (Freedle & Kostin, 1987, 1988; O'Neill, McPeek, & Wild, 1989). The greater spread of item difficulty among the antonym and analogy items in the GRE General Test and in the SAT, as compared to reading comprehension and sentence completion items, appears to account for only part of the higher correlation between DIF and item difficulty found for antonyms and analogies. In the discussion of their research, Freedle and Kostin (1988) suggested that the degree of context in items (antonym and analogy items have the least context, whereas reading comprehension questions have the greatest amount of context) may be an important modulator of the magnitude of the relationship between DIF and item difficulty. For items with minimal context, the magnitude of the correlation between DIF and difficulty is greater than for items with more verbal context.

Quantitative Tests

Content Characteristics of Quantitative Items Associated with DIF for Women. In addition to the content features of verbal tests, several features of quantitative items also are related to high DIF values. The mathematical content of

TURBULENT :

(A)   aerial

(B)   compact

*(C)   pacific

(D)   chilled

(E)   sanitary

FIG. 12.10. Item containing true cognates that is much easier for Hispanic examinees than for the matched comparison group.

TABLE 12.2
Major Content Findings for Verbal Characteristics in Minority/White Analyses

Verbal Characteristics	Science	Human Relationships	Minority-interest	Concrete	Homographs	True Cognates	False Cognates
Black/White							
Reading Comprehension	—	N/A	+	N/A	N/A	Not studied	Not studied
Analogies	—	+	N/A	—	—	Not studied	Not studied
Antonyms	—	+	N/A	N/A	Not sig.	Not studied	Not studied
Hispanic/White							
Reading Comprehension	—	N/A	+	N/A	N/A	Not studied	Not studied
Analogies	—	Not Sig.	N/A	—	—	+	—
Antonyms	Not Sig.	Not Sig.	N/A	N/A	Not studied	+	—

Note. The + indicates areas in which the focal group (Black or Hispanic) performs better than the matched reference group; the — indicates the reverse. N/A indicates not applicable. Not Sig. indicates a nonsignificant result.

items is related to differential difficulty in that women perform better on algebra items than do men matched on quantitative test score; men perform better on geometry and mathematics problem-solving items than do women matched on quantitative test score. This result, which has been found on several admissions tests at ETS (Carlton & Harris, 1989b; O'Neill, Wild, & McPeek, 1989) and on the ACT Assessment examination (Doolittle, 1989), may reflect the nature and quantity of the mathematics coursework taken by women, the attitudes that women have about the field of mathematics, or the experiences that women have in extracurricular activities.

Because algebra content often requires symbols to represent mathematical quantities, items using symbols are also easier for women than for men matched on total test score (McPeek & Wild, 1987; O'Neill, Wild, & McPeek, 1989).

Another difference in quantitative performance is noted for the way in which a problem is presented—whether items are word problems framed in terms of an actual situation or whether they are problems related to a purely mathematical presentation such as those involving a formula, equation, or theory. In general, men perform better on the word problems than do their matched female counterparts, and women perform better on the more abstract pure mathematics items than do their matched male counterparts. Figure 12.11 shows a pure mathematics problem on which women perform better and a word problem on which women perform worse than men of similar quantitative ability. This difference in performance on word problems has been found on GRE and GMAT items (O'Neill, Wild, & McPeek, 1989; Smith, 1988), SAT items (Carlton & Harris, 1989b), and ACT Assessment items (Doolittle & Cleary, 1987). Although the explanation for this result is not obvious, one area of exploration is suggested by an item characteristic studied in the SAT quantitative test, the relationship of the item to the curriculum, which identifies items as being more or less like textbook and homework problems. For this variable, the focal group (women or minorities) outperforms the matched reference group (men or Whites) when the item is very similar to problems found in textbooks, but not otherwise (Carlton & Harris, in preparation).

Before men and women are matched for a DIF analysis on these tests, women have a lower mean quantitative score than men do and they have a mean verbal score approximately equal to that of men. Because there is a large positive correlation between verbal and quantitative scores, the women in the matched group at each quantitative score level usually have higher verbal scores than the men who receive the same quantitative score. This makes it surprising to find consistently that women perform less well than matched men do on quantitative word problems. These word problems have a setting in the real world, do not usually resemble problems ordinarily found in textbooks, and may involve insightful or novel solutions. Additional research is needed to determine what aspect(s) of word problems are especially difficult for women.

Pure Mathematics Problem

$$\frac{23}{2} + \frac{23}{3} + \frac{23}{6} =$$

*(A)   23

(B) $23 \frac{1}{12}$

(C) $23 \frac{1}{6}$

(D) $23 \frac{5}{6}$

(E)   24

Word Problem

The rectangular bed of a truck is 6 feet wide and 7 feet long and has sides $1\frac{1}{2}$ feet high. A type of gravel weighs about 95 pounds per cubic foot. If the truck bed were filled level to the top of its sides with this gravel, approximately how many *tons* would the gravel weigh? (1 ton = 2,000 pounds)

(A) $\frac{1}{2}$

(B) $\frac{2}{3}$

*(C)   3

(D)   8

(E)   36

FIG. 12.11.   A pure mathematics problem on which women perform better than the matched group of men and a word problem on which women perform worse than the matched group of men.

Content Characteristics of Quantitative Items Associated with DIF for Minority-Group Examinees.   A finding related to mathematical content also occurs in some minority-group analyses: Black and Hispanic examinees tend to perform better on algebra items than does a matched group of White examinees on graduate admissions tests although not on the SAT (O'Neill, McPeek, & Wild, in preparation; O'Neill, Wild, & McPeek, in preparation). Figure 12.12 illustrates an algebra item of this type. As noted earlier, algebra items more often involve symbols for mathematical quantities than do arithmetic or geometry items, and items using symbols are also easier for Black examinees than for White examinees matched on test score (O'Neill, McPeek, & Wild, in preparation; O'Neill, Wild, & McPeek, in preparation). Thus, the results for algebra content and the use of symbols for mathematical quantities may well be confounded. When items contain geometry content, Hispanic examinees perform better than matched White examinees, but there is no appreciable difference in

$$(2x)^2 - (\sqrt{3}x)^2 + x^2 =$$

(A)   0

(B) x^2

FIG. 12.12. Algebra item on   *(C) $2x^2$
which Black and Hispanic exam-
inees tend to perform better   (D) $(3 - \sqrt{3})x^2$
than a matched group of White
examinees.   (E) $(5 - \sqrt{3})x^2$

the performance of matched Black and White examinees (Carlton & Harris, in preparation).

As in the female/male comparisons, the presentation of the problem as a word problem or an abstract problem shows differences between Black and White examinees. White examinees perform better than do matched Black examinees on word problems, and Black examinees perform better on the purer mathematics items than do matched White examinees. Figure 12.13 shows a pure mathematics problem on which Black examinees perform better than matched White examinees and a word problem on which Black examinees perform worse than matched White examinees. In addition to the results for Black/White analyses (O'Neill, Wild, & McPeek, 1989; Shepard, Camilli, & Williams, 1984), similar findings of lower minority group performance on word problems have been noted for Hispanic examinees and for Asian-American examinees for whom English is their best language (Carlton & Harris, in preparation) as well as for Asian-American examinees for whom English is not their best language (Bleistein & Wright, 1986). As noted earlier, this difference may be related to the similarity of pure mathematics items to textbook problems. Education for minorities may well differ in the amount of emphasis that is placed on such textbook exercises. Several Black educators who have examined relevant test items and considered these findings have mentioned to the authors that schools with heavy minority enrollments often have a larger number of novice teachers. These educators hypothesized that because these teachers do not have an extensive file of lesson plans, they are more likely to rely on textbook problems as assignments.

A final characteristic of quantitative items is that there is generally a moderate relationship between difficulty and DIF in the Black/White analyses, as noted earlier. Black examinees tend to perform better than matched White examinees on the more difficult quantitative items, and White examinees tend to perform better than matched Black examinees on the easier quantitative items.

Table 12.3 summarizes the findings for both female/male analyses and minority/White analyses of the relationship of DIF to characteristics of quantitative items.

Pure Mathematics Problem

If e, I, k, n, and p are positive and if $I = \dfrac{ne}{k + np}$, then $n =$

(A) $\dfrac{I(k + p)}{e}$

(B) $\dfrac{Ie}{k + Ip}$

*(C) $\dfrac{Ik}{e - Ip}$

(D) $\dfrac{Ik}{e + Ip}$

(E) $\dfrac{Ik}{Ip - e}$

Word Problem

A certain culture of bacteria quadruples every hour. If a container with these bacteria was half full at 10:00 a.m., at what time was it one-eighth full?

*(A)   9:00 a.m.

(B)   7:00 a.m.

(C)   6:00 a.m.

(D)   4:00 a.m.

(E)   2:00 a.m.

FIG. 12.13.   Pure mathematics problem on which Black examinees perform better than matched White examinees and a word problem on which Black examinees perform worse than matched White examinees.

Format Characteristics of Verbal and Quantitative Items Associated with DIF

In some DIF research, more than item content was analyzed; characteristics related to the format of items also have been considered, and two have proved noteworthy. The first is a format variable that identifies an item's set of responses as a vertical list or as a wraparound series. In a vertical list format, each answer choice begins on a separate line; in a wraparound format, the answer choices follow each other without line breaks indicating a new choice. The difference between those two formats is illustrated in Fig. 12.14. The decision about which

TABLE 12.3
Major Content Findings for Quantitative Characteristics

Item Type	Algebra	Geometry	Real	Pure	Resemble Textbook Items
Female/Male	+	—	—	+	+
Black/White	+	Not Sig.	—	+	+
Hispanic/White	+	+	—	+	+

Note. The + indicates areas in which the focal group (Black, Hispanic, or Female) performs better than the matched reference group; the — indicates the reverse. Not Sig. indicates a nonsignificant result.

of these two formats to use for a specific item typically is made by test production staff who specialize in page design. There is some evidence that on analogy items, White examinees may perform better than matched groups of Black, Hispanic, and Asian examinees when the wraparound format is used (Carlton & Harris, 1989a; O'Neill, Wild, & McPeek, in preparation). Because other SAT verbal item types and quantitative items did not show such a difference, further research is needed.

The second format characteristic identifies mathematics items that use visual material such as graphs, charts, or diagrams. On a quantitative item type such as GRE data interpretation items, all of the stimulus information may be presented in graph or table form; on other item types such as SAT regular math and GRE problem-solving items, items with visual material usually are accompanied by some written material. On both of these item types, Black examinees perform

Vertical Format

SAP :

*(A)   fortify

(B)   alleviate

(C)   lend credence

(D)   hold fast

(E)   draw out

Wraparound Format

SAP : *(A) fortify   (B) alleviate   (C) lend credence   (D) hold fast
(E) draw out

FIG. 12.14.   Vertical and wraparound formats.

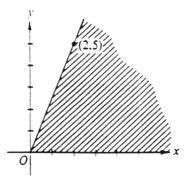

Which of the following points with coordinates (x, y) does NOT lie in the shaded region above?

(A) (1, 1)

*(B) (1, 3)

(C) (2, 3)

(D) (3, 1)

(E) (3, 3)

FIG. 12.15.   Item with visual material on which Black examinees performed more poorly than matched White examinees.

more poorly than do matched White examinees (Carlton & Harris, in preparation; McPeek & Wild, in preparation; O'Neill, Wild, & McPeek, in preparation).
Fig. 12.15 shows an item on which Black examinees performed more poorly
than White examinees of similar ability. Hispanic examinees perform more
poorly than matched White examinees on GRE data interpretation items but not
on SAT items with figures or graphs (Carlton & Harris, in preparation).

Consistent with the results for Black examinees, there is a strong correlation
of difficulty and DIF for data interpretation items for Black/White analyses
(O'Neill, Wild, & McPeek, in preparation). Similar findings that Black examinees perform more poorly than matched White examinees on items with visual
material also have been noted on social science items that use maps and charts
(Johnson, 1988; McPeek & Wild, in preparation).

In the female/male DIF analyses, there is a moderate correlation between DIF
and the difficulty of quantitative items that use visual material in the stimulus on
some tests such as GRE (O'Neill, Wild, & McPeek, in preparation) but not on
other tests such as GMAT (O'Neill, McPeek, & Wild, in preparation). Female
examinees tend to perform better than the matched group of men on difficult
items, but they tend to perform less well than the matched comparison group on
easy items. Insofar as the visual material relates to mathematics achievement

If x is an odd integer and if y is an even integer, then $x^2 - y^2$ is always which of the following?

    I.   An odd integer
    II. An even integer
    III. The square of an integer

*(A) I only
 (B) II only
 (C) III only
 (D) I and III only
 (E) II and III only

FIG. 12.16. Roman numeral item.

tests, researchers such as Benbow and Stanley (1980) hypothesized that gender differences in spatial ability may be contributing to the differential performance. However, Linn and Hyde (1989) argued that meta-analyses of gender differences provide no evidence for this hypothesis.

It is interesting to note certain format variables that do not relate to DIF. On tests where format has been studied, neither Roman numeral (k-type) items nor items with negatively worded stems have been shown to disadvantage female or minority group examinees. Figure 12.16 shows a Roman numeral item on which women performed better than the matched group of men.

Table 12.4 summarizes the findings for minority examinees when the relationship between DIF and format aspects of items is considered.

For all the recounting of item characteristics that are consistent across one or more major testing programs, there are many characteristics for which the results are mixed, as also has been noted for verbal tests. For example, using a matched group of White examinees as a reference group, the length of an item's stem is related sometimes to higher Black performance on longer stems (SAT Quantitative test) and sometimes to higher Black performance on shorter stems (GRE Quantitative test). As this example indicates, single item characteristics do not

TABLE 12.4
Major Content Findings for Format Characteristics

	Verbal		Quantitative
	Wraparound	Analogies	Visuals
Black/White	—		—
Hispanic/White	—		—

Note. The — indicates that the matched reference group performs better than the focal group (Black or Hispanic).

provide all the answers, and further investigations into combinations of characteristics are appropriate.

Test Characteristics Associated with DIF

A recent study of SAT verbal tests by Dorans, Schmitt, and Curley (1988)
showed that some differential item performance for Black examinees may be
caused by item position within a test. However, this result has not been found for
female or Black examinees on the GRE nor for Black examinees on the NTE
(DeMauro & Olson, 1989). The discrepant results for essentially similar item
types on the GRE and SAT may be related to a combination of (a) differences in
the proportion of examinees finishing the test, and (b) the fact that the SAT is a
formula-scored test (where wrong answers are taken into account as part of the
scoring formula) and the GRE is a rights-only test (where only correct answers
are used in the scoring formula).

CONCLUSION

These preliminary results underscore clearly the need for continued research and
some of the directions that the research might take. Thus far, single characteristics of items do not explain DIF results very adequately, and additional research
may help to identify whether combinations of variables such as those related to
problem-solving mathematics items will correlate consistently with DIF. Further
research also could help to establish whether changes in the quantity and nature
of visual material (e.g., table or graph versus text) would affect minority performance on items and whether other format issues may be involved in differential
item difficulty.

At issue also is research on items that evidence a high DIF value in favor of
the focal groups. Attention rightly has been paid to the items on which these
groups are disfavored, but more systematic investigation of the items that greatly
favor these groups also may be instructive in identifying differences in test taking
skills, cognitive styles, testwiseness, and so forth.

It should be pointed out that for each item characteristic that is associated with
differential item performance, the results are based on the mean of all items that
have been classified. Few individual items have a high DIF value. These results,
based on post hoc analyses of existing tests, need to be confirmed by experimental studies that systematically manipulate "suspect" characteristics before they
can be considered as firmly established.

Whether or not these early results are confirmed, it is appropriate to consider
the larger societal issues surrounding DIF, including the interpretation of DIF
results. Instead of seeing the test items as the sole cause of differential performance, we also must consider the issue of educational equity in our society. We

know that not all schools offer the same opportunities to their students; there are differences in staff, equipment, and course offerings. In addition, research has shown that teachers offer different amounts and kinds of attention to female and minority students than to male and White students (Campbell, 1986; Sadker & Sadker, 1986). Scott-Jones and Clark (1986) noted that ". . . male students receive more attention, praise, encouragement, and criticism from teachers than do their female counterparts" (p. 524). Differential treatment of minority students by teachers also occurs and may be related to teachers' expectations (Baron, Tom, & Cooper, 1985). Thus, the educational experience for female and minority students can differ from male and White students' experience even when all students are enrolled in the same class.

Until we recognize that these educational inequities exist, we will not be able to understand DIF results in the proper context.

13

Comments on the O'Neill & McPeek Paper

Lloyd Bond
University of North Carolina, Greensboro

Sigmund Freud was notorious for his peculiar approach to science: He could explain everything, but he could predict nothing. I think just such an approach characterized *item bias* research 15 to 20 years ago, in its infancy. We could invent elaborate and persuasive reasons for why a particular item was biased, but could not apply this reasoning to new items and predict whether or not they would be biased. At that time we found ourselves in just the opposite position of the Supreme Court justice who, in a celebrated court decision, wrote "I cannot define pornography, but I know it when I see it." We could define precisely (that is, mathematically) an item that was performing differentially for two specified groups of examinees, but, unlike the Supreme Court justice, we could not recognize it when we saw it.

The aforementioned point was brought home painfully to me some years ago while working with a graduate student. She and I spent the better part of an afternoon devising elaborate and ostensibly convincing theories about why six particular items on the Metropolitan Achievement Test were behaving differentially for Black examinees, only to discover that, because of a programming error, we had been examining the wrong items. What was especially painful was the realization that in subsequent theorizing about the correct set of items showing differential item functioning (DIF), we found ourselves making arguments that were diametrically opposed to our earlier reasoning.

It is perhaps useful to recount briefly the conclusions of O'Neill and McPeek (see chapter 12 of this text):

1. Compared to a matched sample of men, women perform less well on (a) reading passages with science-related content, (b) antonyms and analogies

classified as "science" or "world of practical affairs," (c) geometry and mathematics problem-solving items and "story" items, and (d) easy items.

2. Compared to a matched sample of women, men perform less well on (a) antonyms and analogies that are classified as "aesthetics/philosophy" or "human relationships," (b) reading comprehension questions that refer to both men and women (as opposed to referring to men only or to not mentioning people at all), (c) purely mathematical, "nonstory" algebra items involving formulas, equations, or theory, (d) quantitative items similar to those found in high school text books, and (e) difficult items.

3. Compared to a matched sample of Whites, Blacks perform less well on (a) GRE questions associated with science passages, (b) analogy items containing homographs, (c) concrete analogies, (d) "story" items, (e) quantitative items using graphs and other visual material, and (f) easy items (both quantitative and verbal).

4. Compared to a matched sample of Blacks, Whites perform less well on (a) items based on reading passages that are relevant to Black interests or concerns, (b) analogy items dealing with human relationships (as distinct from science analogies), (c) abstract analogies, (d) GRE algebra items; (e) "pure" mathematics items involving formulas, equations, or theory, and (f) difficult items (both quantitative and verbal).

5. Compared to a matched sample of Whites, Hispanics examinees perform less well on (a) analogy items containing homographs and "false" cognates, and story problems.

6. Compared to a matched sample of Hispanics, White examinees perform less well on (a) verbal items containing true cognates, and (b) items based on reading passages with a heavy minority emphasis (e.g., Mexican-American women, minority figures in history, etc.).

A few, very tentative conclusions are also possible with respect to Asian-Americans associated primarily with verbal items.

What can be said of the previous summary? O'Neill and McPeek have made a tentative (and admirable) attempt at generalization and integration that will require further, preferably experimental confirmation. I have no quarrel with their preliminary foray into what is admittedly murky waters. Many of their hypotheses seem eminently reasonable (e.g., the relatively better performance of minorities on reading passages of particular interest to them and the relatively better performance of Hispanics on vocabulary and verbal analogy items involving true Latin cognates). In general, however, theories about why items behave differentially across groups can be described only as primitive. Part of the problem, as I see it, is that the very notion of differential item functioning by groups implies a homogeneous set of life experiences on the part of the focal group that are qualitatively different from the reference group and that affect verbal and mathematical reasoning. As I have indicated elsewhere (Bond, 1980, 1981), we are still far from a coherent theory that relates life experiences to how knowledge is organized in long-term memory, how it is retrieved, and how it is used in problem solving.

The DIF work being undertaken at the Educational Testing Service (ETS) under the policy leadership of Greg Anrig and the technical leadership of Paul Holland is certainly exciting stuff. Its impact upon the profession is immense. One has only to examine any recent program catalogue of the American Educational Research Association to get some idea of the effect ETS research on differential item functioning is having on the profession and on psychometric research. My concern about the current looseness of theorizing on the reasons for differential item functioning notwithstanding, I am optimistic that research being conducted here and elsewhere will reap significant psychometric benefits and will result ultimately in tests of better quality.

14

Evaluating Hypotheses About Differential Item Functioning

Alicia P. Schmitt
Paul W. Holland
Neil J. Dorans
Educational Testing Service

Differential item functioning (DIF) research has had as one of its major goals the identification of the causes of DIF. Typically, DIF research has focused on determining characteristics of test items that related differentially to subgroups of examinees and thus might explain or be a cause of DIF in an item. The premise has been that, after identifying specific DIF-related factors, test development guidelines could be generated to prevent their future occurrence. With the elimination of these DIF factors, the items would not exhibit DIF and, thus, the total score would provide a better estimate of the true abilities of examinees from any subpopulation. The reality is that, to date, only a limited number of hypothesized DIF factors seem to hold consistently and that even these factors need to be better understood so that test construction guidelines can address them with the needed specificity.

There are several reasons why progress in the identification of DIF-related factors has been slow. First, the study of DIF is relatively new and so the initial emphasis has been on the development of statistical methods to identify DIF. Chapter 3, by Dorans and Holland, and chapter 4, by Thissen, Steinberg, and Wainer, provide good descriptions of the state-of-the-art statistical methods used to detect DIF.

Second identification of DIF-related factors requires a theory of *differential item difficulty* in a field in which theories of item difficulty are not well developed. Related to this is the fact that the reference and focal groups used to date—Blacks, Hispanics, Asian-Americans, and women, for example—are very heterogeneous and their differences are not easy to describe.

Third, the identification process is complex. Because more than one factor could be related to DIF in a given item, zeroing in on the specific cause of DIF for one item is not a simple process and confirming studies designed to test hypotheses about the causes of DIF are rare. We hope this chapter helps to stimulate further empirical work in this area.

The purpose of this chapter is to present and propose procedures for the systematic evaluation and corroboration of DIF-related factors or hypotheses. Descriptions of procedures to undertake observational DIF studies, to develop hypotheses, and to evaluate and construct items with the hypothesized factors are presented. Analytical comparison analyses are described and examples provided.

The systematic evaluation of DIF hypotheses involves a two-step process. The first step entails measuring DIF on regular operational items and using this information to generate hypotheses. The second step is a confirmatory evaluation of those hypotheses generated in step one. Thus, the main focus of the second step is the randomized DIF study, in which specially constructed items are developed to test specific hypotheses. These items are administered under conditions that permit appropriate statistical analyses to assess the efficacy of the hypotheses.

OBSERVATIONAL STUDIES: EVALUATING OPERATIONAL ITEMS

Hypotheses about factors related to DIF can be generated on the basis of theoretical or empirical considerations. Theoretical DIF hypotheses are founded on prior knowledge pertaining to cognitive processes that could be related to differential performance of test items. Although theoretical generation of DIF hypotheses is conceptually the first and most reasonable way to postulate logical reasons for DIF, it has not been very fruitful. Most test construction practices are carefully developed to avoid obvious factors that are known or suspected to be possible sources of discrimination toward any subpopulation of examinees. Processes such as the Test Sensitivity Review Process used at Educational Testing Service are used to evaluate developed items to ensure fairness to women and ethnic groups. This process is discussed in chapter 19. Evaluation criteria for such sensitivity review procedures are designed so that items included in a test "measure factors unrelated to such groups (minorities and women)" (Hunter and Slaughter, 1980, p. 8). Therefore, logical or theoretical causes of DIF due to discrimination against women or ethnic minorities are supposed to be excluded from test instruments and thus cannot be evaluated.

Empirical DIF hypotheses, generated after analyses of DIF data, may suggest that certain characteristics of items are differentially related to one or more subgroups of the population. Observational studies refer to investigations that make use of data and items constructed and administered under operational conditions. DIF analyses are conducted for all items in these tests to evaluate whether any item exhibits differential functioning by women or minority examinees. Performance of women on each item is compared to the performance of matched men (reference group for the female focal group) and the item performance of each minority group (e.g., Asian-American, Black, Hispanic, and Native American examinees) is contrasted to that of comparable White examinees (reference group for each minority focal group). Results of these DIF analyses can provide empirical information to generate DIF hypotheses.

Development of Hypotheses: Extreme DIF Items

Evaluation of items with extreme DIF can provide insight into factors that might be related to DIF. Such a process involves a careful examination of the items with extreme DIF by a variety of experts. The speculation about or insight into possible causes of DIF for these items from test developers, researchers, focal group members, cognitive psychologists, and subject specialists can be used to generate hypotheses. Differential distractor information can engender additional insight into causes of DIF. Knowledge about which distractors differentially attract a specific subgroup may help researchers understand the respondents' cognitive processes. Differential distractor analyses are described in the chapters on statistical DIF methods (chapters 3 and 4). Usually, analyses of more than one test form might be required in order to observe commonalities across items identified as having extreme differential performance. Some of the generated hypotheses might only consist of a general speculation or "story" about sources of DIF. It is important to consider any possible explanation. Because this stage is a generation-of-ideas phase, it can be considered almost a brainstorming process. Those possible explanations deemed most reasonable can then be developed into hypotheses to be tested.

Evaluation of Hypotheses Through Observational Data

Once a number of possible hypotheses have been identified, the next step is to evaluate the efficacy of these hypotheses. Following are the procedural steps to evaluate DIF hypotheses using observational data:

Classification of Items

In order to evaluate the hypotheses, all items of a test form under study need to be classified with respect to the various hypothesized item factors or characteristics. A clear and precise definition of the factors to be studied needs to be provided. At least two experts or judges should classify each item according to each hypothesized factor. In cases where the two judges disagree, a third expert should be consulted. In this fashion, each item is identified as containing or not containing the factor or item characteristic under evaluation. Typically, a dichotomous classification is coded for each item factor. In those cases when a factor might consist of gradients or levels, a more continuous classification is appropriate. In addition, information about related variables might also be identified and coded. For example, the location of the item factor of interest (i.e., in the stem, key, or distractors) or the item type (e.g., antonyms, analogies, sentence completion, or reading comprehension for verbal items) might provide information relevant to the relation of the factor to DIF. In fact, current research has shown that the greatest relationship between true cognates and DIF for Hispanic examinees is found when all components of an item have true cognates and the next greatest effect is found for those items with true cognates in the stem and/or key. On the SAT, these relationships were found to be most notable for antonym and analogy item types (Schmitt, 1988; Schmitt, Curley, Bleistein, & Dorans, 1988; Schmitt & Dorans, 1991).

Sampling Procedures

Groups. DIF factors can be postulated to be related to the differential item performance between two groups of examinees. In some instances, a postulated factor might not be specific to any one group. In such cases, more than one focal group might be of interest in a particular study. Typically, focal and reference groups have been determined on the basis of their gender and/or race or ethnic origin (i.e., females as focal group with males as reference group and Asian-Americans, Blacks, Hispanics, or Native Americans as focal groups with Whites as reference group). Nevertheless, other characteristics (e.g., income level, educational background, or language knowledge) can serve to either further delimit ethnic or gender groups or to define other distinctive groups of interest. How focal and reference groups are determined and delimited depends both on the population characteristics of the examinees for whom the test is designed and on hypothesized group characteristics. Circumspection on the number of characteristics chosen to determine the groups under study is recommended. As the number of group-delimiting variables increases, the sample size of these groups is consequently restricted. Moreover, when several variables determine a group, findings about factors related to DIF are harder to interpret and their effect harder to ascribe to specific group variables.

Sample Size. All possible examinees in each focal and reference group should be used when doing DIF research. Because the comparison of comparable groups of examinees is an important component in the calculation of DIF statistics, differences on item performance of focal and reference groups are calculated at each ability level. Ability levels based on a predetermined criterion (e.g., total test score or another related ability measure) are used in the computation of DIF indices in a fashion analogous to how a blocking variable is used in a randomized block or in a split-plot design. For this reason, a reasonable number of examinees at each ability level is essential. The largest possible number of examinees in both the reference and focal groups should be used to render stable DIF estimates and to ensure sufficient power to detect DIF effects. The standard error of the DIF statistic should be examined to help interpret results when samples are small. Chapters 3 and 7 of this volume discuss the standard error formulas and their accuracy.

DIF Analyses Procedures

Statistical Procedures.   Which statistical measure of DIF to use when conducting observational DIF studies is no longer the controversial decision it once was. The notable development and comparison of several DIF statistical methods during this decade have produced methods that not only are reliable, but that generally have good agreement (Donoghue, Holland, & Thayer, chapter 7, this volume; Dorans, 1989; Dorans & Holland, chapter 3, this volume; Dorans & Kulick, 1983, 1986; Holland, 1985; Holland & Thayer, 1988; Scheuneman & Bleistein, 1989; Thissen, Steinberg, & Wainer, chapter 4, this volume). Moreover, use of more than one statistical method may be recommended. Currently, the operational assessment of DIF at Educational Testing Service uses the Mantel–Haenszel procedure to flag items for DIF and the closely related standardization procedure as a statistical tool to generate and assess content-based explanations for DIF. As mentioned previously, in addition to statistical indicants of DIF for the correct response, the development and evaluation of DIF hypotheses benefit from differential information on distractor selection, omitted responses, and speededness. Similarly, evaluation of empirical option-test regression curves and conditional differential response-rate plots for all these responses can indicate whether any DIF effect is dependent on ability. Refer to chapter 3, this volume, and to Dorans, Schmitt, and Bleistein (1988) for descriptions of how to apply the standardization method to the computation of differential distractor, omit, and speededness functioning. Use of a loglinear model to examine DIF through the analysis of distractor choices by examinees who answered an item incorrectly is described by Green, Crone, and Folk (1989). Also see chapter 4, this volume, for a discussion of differential alternative functioning (DAF).

Matching Criterion.   The comparability of the focal and reference groups is achieved by matching them on the basis of a measure of test performance. Typically, this measure is the total score on the test to be evaluated for DIF and is sometimes referred to as an *internal matching criterion*.

The major consideration in the selection of an appropriate DIF matching criterion is the degree of relationship between the construct of interest and the criterion. For DIF analyses, the construct of interest is what the test item is constructed to measure. If the total score matching criterion is multidimensional, it will be measuring more than the construct of interest and may not be highly related to the item. Use of such a multidimensional total score criterion could compromise the comparability of the groups for a specific test item.

Another possible source of error in the estimation of a comparable total DIF matching criterion for the focal and reference groups is differential speededness (Dorans, Schmitt, & Bleistein, 1988). Several studies are currently evaluating the effect of differential speededness and are considering this proposed speededness refinement (Schmitt, Dorans, Crone, & Maneckshana, 1991).

Differential Response Style Factors. Different examinees approach the test-taking experience differently and these different response style factors may have an impact on DIF assessment, particularly for items at the end of test sections. These response style factors are *differential speededness* and *differential omission* (Schmitt & Dorans, 1990). When an examinee does not respond to an item and does not respond to any subsequent items in a timed test section, all those items are referred to as *not reached*. Differential speededness refers to the existence of differential response rates between comparable focal and reference group examinees to items appearing at the end of a test section. When an examinee does not respond to an item, but responds to subsequent items, that lack of response is referred to as an *omit*. Differential omission refers to the occurrence of differential omit rates between comparable focal and reference group examinees. Adjustments for these differential response styles are important when evaluating DIF hypotheses because their occurrence can confound results.

Descriptive Statistics

After all items have been classified and DIF indices estimated, DIF summary statistics are computed for each level of the factor. The unit of analysis in this step is the *item*. Means, medians, minimum and maximum values, and standard deviations can help evaluate the impact of the postulated factor. Examination of all items classified as containing the factor under study allows for the identification of items that differ from the positive or negative pattern expected for the factor. Closer examination of such items can provide valuable information about possible exceptions to the expected effect. Although correlation analysis can render useful associative information, use of this descriptive statistic is limited. The dichotomous nature of most of the hypothesized factors and the limited number of naturally occurring items with such factors restrict the usefulness of statistical significance tests. Furthermore, the lack of controls particular to naturalistic studies also hampers the evaluation of DIF hypotheses. Nevertheless, naturalistic studies are a good first step, providing information valuable for the postulation of DIF hypotheses and data for their evaluation and refinement.

Confirmatory studies are a natural next step in the evaluation of DIF hypotheses. These studies require the construction of items with the postulated characteristics and use scientific methods to ensure that extraneous factors are controlled so that the factors of interest can be accurately evaluated.

EXAMPLES OF OBSERVATIONAL DIF STUDIES

Two observational studies that have evaluated DIF hypotheses previously postulated on the basis of DIF information are now described and findings reported.

Language and Cultural Characteristics Related to Hispanic DIF

An in-depth analysis of the extreme DIF items for Hispanic examinees on one form of the Verbal Scholastic Aptitude Test (SAT-V) helped identify characteristics of the items that might explain the differential functioning by two Hispanic subgroups. Four hypotheses were generated about the differential item functioning of Hispanic examinees on verbal aptitude test items. These hypotheses were:

1. True cognates, or words with a common root in English and Spanish, will tend to favor Hispanic examinees. Example: *music* (musica).
2. False cognates, or words whose meaning is not the same in both languages, will tend to impede the performance of Hispanic examinees. Example: *enviable*—which means *sendable* in Spanish.
3. Homographs, or words that are spelled alike but which have different meanings, will tend to impede the performance of Hispanic examinees. Example: *bark*.
4. Items with content of special interest to Hispanics will tend to favor their performance. Most special-interest items will tend to be reading comprehension item types. Example: reading passage about Mexican-American women.

(For a detailed description of the study, see Schmitt [1985, 1988].)

Although some of the hypotheses were supported by the data (i.e., true cognates and special interest specific to the Hispanic subgroup), the low frequencies of false cognates and homographs in the two test editions studied precluded their evaluation. Construction of forms where the occurrence of the postulated factors could be controlled, and thus evaluated, was proposed as a follow-up to this investigation. The Schmitt et al. (1988) follow-up study remedied the limited naturally occurring item factors by developing items with these factors and administering them in non-operational SAT-V sections. Procedures and results of this confirmatory investigation are described and reported in a later section on examples of special confirmatory studies.

Differential Speededness

In an effort to identify factors that might contribute to DIF, Schmitt and Bleistein (1987) conducted an investigation of DIF for Blacks on SAT analogy items. Possible factors were drawn from the literature on analogical reasoning and previous DIF research on Black examinees (Dorans, 1982; Echternacht, 1972; Kulick, 1984; Rogers, Dorans, & Schmitt, 1986; Rogers & Kulick, 1987; Scheuneman, 1978; 1981b; and Stricker, 1982). Schmitt and Bleistein performed their research in two steps. Hypotheses about analogical DIF were developed after close examination of the three 85-item SAT-V test forms studied by Rogers and Kulick (1987). Following these analyses, two additional test forms were studied to validate the hypothesized factors. Standardization analyses were conducted in which the key, all distractors, not reached, and omitted items ("omits") all served as dependent variables.

The major finding was that Black students do not complete SAT-V sections at the same rate as White students with comparable SAT-V scores. This differential speededness effect appeared to account for much of the negative DIF for Blacks on SAT verbal analogy items. When examinees who did not reach the item were excluded from the calculation of the standardized response rate differences, only a few analogy items exhibited DIF.

Dorans, Schmitt, and Bleistein (1988) set out to document the differential speededness phenomenon for Blacks, Asian-Americans, and Hispanics on several SAT test editions, including some studied by Schmitt and Bleistein (1987). They found that differential speededness was most noticeable for Blacks and virtually nonexistent for Asian-Americans when compared with matched groups of Whites. A randomized DIF study to evaluate differential speededness under controlled conditions is described in the section on examples of special confirmatory studies.

EVALUATING SPECIALLY CONSTRUCTED ITEMS

we have not yet proved that antecedent to be the cause until we have reversed the process and produced the effect by means of that antecedent artificially, and if, when we do so, the effect follows, the induction is complete. (Mill, 1843, p. 252)

In contrast to observational studies that evaluate operational data and can only draw associational inferences about DIF and item characteristics, well-designed randomized studies using specially constructed test items can be used to draw causal inferences about DIF and postulated item factors. It is not until we can confirm an associated relation between item factors and DIF by verifying that the expected DIF is found on specially constructed items with these characteristics, that we can ascribe these factors to be a cause of DIF. The basic features of these randomized DIF studies is the use of control or comparison items and randomized exposure of examinees to these items. The purpose of this section is to describe procedures for constructing these items, for designing these systematic investigations, and for analyzing their results. Examples of two studies where these techniques have been applied are presented.

Method and Design

Variables

The variables used in randomized DIF studies may be described by the following terminology adapted from experimental design: *response variables, treatment variables,* and *covariates.* The response (or dependent) variable is the measure of the behavior predicted by a DIF hypothesis (e.g., choosing a predicted response). The treatment variable indicates the extent to which the item has the postulated DIF characteristics. Covariates are subject characteristics that are not affected by exposure to a particular treatment, that is, measures of performance on related types of items or measures of education level and English language proficiency.

Instrument Development

Some of the treatments in a randomized DIF study consist of exposure to test items that have been specially constructed to disadvantage one or more groups of examinees. For this reason great care must be exercised in the construction of these testing instruments to conform to test sensitivity and human subject guidelines as well as to test specifications and sound test development practice. These constraints on the final testing instruments ensure that operational scores are not affected by the study.

At least two levels of the treatment are needed in order to compare the effect of the DIF factor of interest. Thus, two versions of each item are developed. Ideally, these two items are identical in every respect but for the factor to be tested. The item that includes the postulated DIF characteristic is the *treated* level (t) of the treatment variable. The other item (the version that excludes the DIF factor) is the *control* level (c) of the treatment variable. The goal of the construction of these pairs of items is to make them as similar as possible except for the factor that is being tested. Parallelism of the two item versions is an important requirement that may allow us to infer that differences in the differential performance on these two items are caused by the difference between the items, that is, the postulated factor. Achieving parallelism of the item pairs is often difficult to do in practice because test questions are complex stimulus material and a change in one aspect of an item often entails other changes as well.

In order to insure parallelism when constructing parallel items, it is important to control the following item characteristics: difficulty, discrimination, location in the test, item type, content, and the location of the key and distractors. The number of items used to test each factor is also an important consideration because the unit of analysis is the item itself. Thus, it is desirable to construct several item pairs testing each factor.

The items in a pair are constructed to test a specific DIF hypothesis and are designed so that the treatment item (t) is more likely to elicit a particular type of response than is the control item (c) in the pair, especially for members of the focal group of interest. Schmitt et al. (1988) give the following example of a pair of specially constructed antonym items used in their randomized DIF study, which is discussed further in the section on systematic evaluation of Hispanic DIF factors:

Item t	*Item c*
PALLID:	ASHEN:
(A) moist	(A) moist
(B) massive	(B) massive
(C)* vividly colored	(C)* vividly colored
(D) sweet smelling	(D) sweet smelling
(E) young and innocent	(E) young and innocent

These two items are identical except for their stem, that is, PALLID or ASHEN, which are synonyms of roughly equal frequency in English. The factor being varied in this item pair is the existence of a Spanish cognate for the stem word. In this case, *palido* is a common word in Spanish whereas the cognate, *pallid,* is a less common word in English. The DIF hypothesis for this item pair is that the existence of a common Spanish cognate for a relatively more rare English word that plays an essential role in the item (in this case the stem word) will help Spanish-speaking examinees select the correct answer and will not help non-Spanish-speaking examinees.

Samples

The relevant reference and focal groups are determined by the DIF factors that are postulated. In a randomized DIF study, the reference and focal groups are then divided at random into subgroups of examinees who are exposed to either the t or c version of each item. Because of this subdivision, it is important to have large samples of each of the target groups.

Controls

Randomized DIF studies are by definition controlled studies. The use of control or comparison items allows us to infer that differences in DIF between the item pairs is caused by differences between the items (the postulated factor) as long as other causative variables are not contaminating the results. There are three major types of extraneous variables that can contaminate results if not controlled: examinee-related differences, lack of parallelism of the item pairs, and differences in the testing conditions of examinees taking each of the item pairs. The control of these extraneous variables needs to be carefully considered. The types of controls that can be used for this purpose are: *randomization, constancy, balance,* and *counterbalance.*

Randomization.   If the examinees who are exposed to the t version of an item pair differ in important ways from those exposed to the c version, *confounding* is said to occur. Confounding makes it difficult to separate the effect of responding to the t versus the c version of the item pair from the characteristics of the examinees in these two groups. Randomization tends to equalize the distribution of examinee characteristics in the t and c groups. It may be achieved by spiraling subforms together, each containing only one number of each pair of special items. We discuss the effect of randomization more formally in a later section on using logistic regression to estimate effect sizes.

Constancy.   Some factors, such as the position of the key in a multiple-choice question, can affect examinee responses and should be the same for items t and c in a given pair. This is an example of constancy. Other factors that might be controlled using this technique are item position and response options. The PALLID/ASHEN item pair is an example with a great deal of constancy across the pair of items. A special case of constancy arises when a factor is eliminated in the sense that it is prevented by design from occurring. An example of a factor that can be eliminated in a randomized DIF study is differential speededness. It is removed by placing the specially constructed items at the beginning of the test section.

Balance.   Balance is used in two distinct ways. On the one hand, it can refer to equalizing the distribution of important examinee characteristics across the t and c versions of an item pair. Randomization will approximately balance the distribution of covariates in a large study, but in a small study the researcher may need to achieve balance in a more active way (i.e., blocking). On the other hand, balance can refer to the entire set of stimulus material that an examinee is exposed to. Subforms are usually balanced with respect to content and item type so that they will not appear unusual to the examinees and thereby will not elicit unrepresentative responses.

Counterbalance.   Counterbalance refers to the stimulus material presented to the examinees. A factor that is appropriate to counterbalance across the subforms used in the study is the total number of occurrences of t and c items in each subform. When this is counterbalanced, all the subforms will have the same number of t and c items even though they cannot contain the *same* t and c items. This will tend to reduce the overall effect of each subform on differences in subgroup performance.

Other Considerations. The form of control used has an effect on the generality of the inferences made from the study. For example, if only one level of item difficulty is used in the evaluation of a hypothesis (i.e., constancy), then any resulting effect of the hypothesized DIF factor under study may be restricted to items with the tested level of difficulty. It is, therefore, important to select the method of control (i.e., balancing, etc.) based on the level of generality that is desired.

Another way to deal with extraneous variables is to control them in the design of the study. In such cases, the DIF factor will be one independent variable and another variable, such as item difficulty, will be a second independent variable. For example, item pairs that have similar difficulty within a pair, but varying difficulty across pairs. When more than one independent variable is being studied at one time, evaluation of their interactive effect is a part of the study. If an interaction is found, then analyses should proceed to see how the effect of the DIF factor varies across the levels of the interacting variables. Because the outcome measures in DIF studies are usually response probabilities, the scale in which these are measured, P or logit, may affect the study of interactions.

A major constraint on using several independent variables in designing the item pairs is that the number of items has to be increased accordingly, making the study more complex. Several items need to be constructed to evaluate each possible combined effect. For example, if the DIF factor under study consists of two levels (DIF factor present or absent) and the other independent variable consists of three levels (e.g., item difficulty: hard, medium, and easy) then the total number of subgroups of items testing all possible combinations is six. If there are then at least two examples of each item, there are at least 12 items involved in the study of a single DIF factor. Because of practical testing constraints, it may be necessary to limit the number of independent variables to be studied at a time in a randomized DIF study.

A Causal Inference Perspective On Randomized DIF Studies

This section adapts the formal model of Rubin (1974) and Holland (1986) to the analysis of randomized DIF studies.

Dependent Measures

In a randomized DIF study, the basic dependent measure is the response an examinee gives to the specially constructed test items. Assuming that we are considering multiple-choice tests, the responses of examinees are limited to choosing one of the response options or omitting the item. It is also possible that an examinee might not attempt to respond to some items, but our analysis will condition on responding to the special items. Depending on exactly what DIF hypothesis is being tested, the particular response of interest will vary. For many hypotheses, the behavior of interest is choosing the correct answer. For others, it might be choosing or not choosing a particular distractor, and for others it will be the decision to omit the item. We do not make an assumption on this and let the outcome variable, Y, be dichotomous with

$$Y = \begin{cases} 1 & \text{if the examinee makes the predicted re-} \\ & \text{sponse relevant to the DIF hypothesis,} \\ 0 & \text{otherwise} \end{cases}$$

(In all of our examples, however, we use $Y = 1$ to denote choosing the correct answer to the special items.)

There are two potential responses that could be observed for an examinee, Y_t, or Y_c, where

Y_t = the value of Y that will be observed if the examinee is asked to respond to item t of the pair,

Y_c = the value of Y that will be observed if the examinee is asked to respond to item c of the pair.

The difference, $Y_t - Y_c$, is the *causal effect* for a given examinee of being asked to respond to item t rather than to item c in the pair. Let S denote the member of the pair of special items to which the examinee is asked to respond, that is, $S = t$ or $S = c$. Then Y_S is the actual response that the examinee gives in the study. The notation Y_S means the following:

$$Y_S = \begin{cases} Y_t \text{ if } S = t \\ Y_c \text{ if } S = c. \end{cases}$$

The problem of causal inference in a randomized DIF study is to say as much as we can about the *unobservable* causal effect, $Y_t - Y_c$, for each examinee, from the *observable* data. For example, if $Y_t - Y_c = 0$, then the examinee would make the same response regardless of the version of the item to which he or she is exposed. When $Y_t - Y_c = 1$, then the examinee would make the predicted response to t but not to c, and so forth.

The Data

So far we have mentioned two pieces of information that are available from each examinee with respect to a given pair of items: the observed response Y_S and the member of the pair of special items to which the examinee responded, S. In addition, there is other important information. First of all, the examinee may belong to the focal or the reference group of interest, or possibly to neither one. Denote group membership by $G = r$ or f (reference or focal). In addition, there may be other test scores available for the examinee. For example, the special items may be part of a larger test. Let X denote an additional score obtained from part or all of this larger test. We must distinguish two important cases. If it is possible to assume that the score X is unaffected by whether or not the examinee was asked to respond to item t or to item c of the item pair of interest, then X is called a *covariate score*. For example, if the items that are part of the X-score are all asked prior to the examinees being asked to respond to the special items, then it is usually plausible to assume that X is a covariate score. On the other hand, if the special item is included in the X-score, then X is not a covariate score. In our examples, we will use covariate scores to group examinees.

In summary, the data observed for a given examinee can be expressed as

$$Y_S, S, G, \text{ and } X.$$

The Average Causal Effect

The individual-level causal effect, $Y_t - Y_c$, is not directly observable for a single examinee because we only observe Y_t or Y_c (but not both) on each examinee. An average causal effect (ACE) is found by averaging the individual-level causal effects over various groups of examinees. For example, we might consider

$$E(Y_t - Y_c) \tag{1}$$

the average over everyone in the study, or

$$E(Y_t - Y_c \mid G = f) \tag{2}$$

the average over everyone in the focal group, or

$$E(Y_t - Y_c \mid G = r) \tag{3}$$

the average over everyone in the reference group. Finally, we might consider

$$E(Y_t - Y_c \mid G = g, X = s) \tag{4}$$

the average over everyone in group g with covariate score x. We show later that average causal effects can be estimated by the data obtained in a randomized DIF study, even though the examinee-level causal effects cannot be estimated.

Let us consider the ACEs in Equations (1)–(4) further. Because Y_t and Y_c are dichotomous, the expectations in (1)–(4) may be expressed in terms of probabilities, that is,

$$E(Y_t - Y_c) = P(Y_t = 1) - P(Y_c = 1), \tag{5}$$
$$E(Y_t - Y_c \mid G = g) = P(Y_t = 1 \mid G = g) - P(Y_c = 1 \mid G = g), \tag{6}$$
$$E(Y_t - Y_c \mid G = g, X = x) = P(Y_t = 1 \mid G = g, X = x)$$
$$- P(Y_c = 1 \mid G = g, X = x). \tag{7}$$

The ACE, $E(Y_t - Y_c)$, averages over all examinees and as such represents the *main effect* of item t relative to item c over all examinees. Although this main effect is important, it is not the primary parameter of interest in a randomized DIF study. When Y represents choosing the correct option in a multiple-choice test, the main effect (Equation [5]) is simply the difference in the percentage correct for items t and c over the examinees in the study. As we see later, it is desirable to construct t and c so that the main effect (Equation [5]) is small.

In general, the idea behind a randomized DIF study is that item t will elicit a bigger change in the probability of the predicted response relative to item c for members of the focal groups than it does for members of the reference group. This leads us to examine the ACE-difference or *interaction parameter* defined by

$$T = E(Y_t - Y_c \mid G = f) - E(Y_t - Y_c \mid G = r), \tag{8}$$
$$= [P(Y_t = 1 \mid G = f) - P(Y_t = 1 \mid G = r)]$$
$$- [P(Y_c = 1 \mid G = f) - P(Y_c = 1 \mid G = r)]. \tag{9}$$

It is useful to remember the two ways of writing T in Equations (8) and (9). In Equation (8), T is expressed as the difference between the ACE in the focal group and ACE in the reference group. In Equation (9), T is expressed as the difference between the t and c items in their respective differences in the probability that $Y = 1$ between the focal and reference groups. When $Y = 1$ indicates a correct answer, the difference in the probability that $Y = 1$ between the focal and reference groups is called the *impact* of the item (Holland, 1985). Thus, in this case T may be viewed as the difference in the impact of item t and item c.

When T in Equation (8) is positive it means that the change in the probability of the predicted responses caused by t (relative to c) is larger for the focal group than it is for the reference group (i.e., the ACE for f is larger than the ACE for r). Typically, this is the type of prediction made in a DIF hypothesis.

One problem with a parameter like T is that the probability of the predicted behavior measured by Y_t or Y_c will often differ between the reference and focal group, that is, $P(Y_j = 1 \mid G = r)$ and $P(Y_j = 1 \mid G = f)$ will not be the same. It may also differ between item t and c, that is, if there is a main effect of items in the pair. When these differences are large, the interpretation of the magnitude of T is complicated by the boundedness of the probability scale (i.e., the fact that Y is a 0/1 variable). Consider these four examples in which Y denotes selection of the correct response for a pair of items, (t, c).

Example A:
$P(Y_t = 1 \mid G = r) = P(Y_c = 1 \mid G = r) = P(Y_t = 1 \mid G = f) = .5$,
and $P(Y_c = 1 \mid G = f) = .4$,

then

$$T = (.5 - .4) - (.5 - .5) = .1.$$

The ACE in the reference group is 0, whereas in the focal group it is .1, so that T is .1. In this case, items c and t are equally difficult for the reference group and t is equal in difficulty for the reference and focal groups. Furthermore, c is more difficult than t for the focal group. This is an ideal type of example in which some characteristic of item c causes it to be harder for members of the focal group, and when this is altered to item t the item is equally difficult for both the reference and focal groups.

Example B: $P(Y_t = 1 \mid G = r) = .55, P(Y_c = 1 \mid G = r) = .45,$
$P(Y_t = 1 \mid G = f) = .50, P(Y_c = 1 \mid G = f) = .30,$

then the ACE for r is .1 and the ACE for f is .2, so that $T = .2 - .1 = .1$, again.

This is a more realistic example than Example A because there is both a group difference and an item difference. Still, it is evident in this example that the change from item c to item t has a bigger average causal effect on members of the focal group than it has for members of the reference group.

Example C: $P(Y_t = 1 \mid G = r) = .95, P(Y_c = 1 \mid G = r) = .85,$
$P(Y_t = 1 \mid G = f) = .70, P(Y_c = 1 \mid G = f) = .50,$

then

$$T = (.70 - .50) - (.95 - .85) = .20 - .10 = .1,$$
once more.

The value of T is the same as in Examples A and B, but the context is quite different. Both c and t are much easier for the reference group than they are for the focal group and for both groups item t is somewhat easier than item c. The ACE for f is $.70 - .50 = .20$, but the ACE for r is only $.95 - .85 = .10$. However, the boundedness of the probability scale makes it impossible for $P(Y_t = 1 \mid G = r)$ to exceed $P(Y_c = 1 \mid G = r)$ by .20 when the latter probability is .85, as in this example. Does $T = .1$ mean that the change from c to t had a bigger effect for members of f than for members of r, or was c already so easy for members of r that the change to t could not improve their performance as much as it did for members of f? This ambiguity stems from the large difference in performance on c and t between the reference and focal group. The use of covariate scores is aimed at removing some of this confusion—as we discuss later.

Example D: $P(Y_t = 1 \mid G = r) = .95, P(Y_c = 1 \mid G = r) = .60,$

and

$$P(Y_t = 1 \mid G = f) = .85, P(Y_c = 1 \mid G = f) = .40.$$

In this case

$$T = (.85 - .40) - (.95 - .60) = .1,$$

as in the other examples. This example is like Example C except that the roles of the groups and the items have been reversed. In this example, there is a large main effect of items—item t is much easier for both groups than is item c. The consequence of this large main effect is that it confuses the interpretation of T. The ACE for f is $.85 - .40 = .45$, whereas the ACE for r is $.95 - .60 = .35$. However, starting with $P(Y_c = 1 \mid G = r) = .60$, it is impossible for the ACE for r to exceed $.40$. Again, the boundedness of the probability scale is a source of confusion in the interpretation of T.

The Use of Covariate Scores

Examples C and D show that the boundedness of the probability scale can confuse the interpretation of the parameter T when there are large differences between the reference and focal groups in their probabilities of producing the predicted response for items t, or when there is a large main effect of items. The introduction of a covariate score can help alleviate this problem when there are large group differences. Large main effects of items are generally a sign of a poorly designed item pair for a DIF study.

Suppose X is a covariate score in the sense described earlier, that is, X is measured on each examinee in the study and is not affected by exposure of the examinee to items t or c. Suppose further that examinees with the same X-score have similar probabilities of making the predicted response to items t and c regardless of whether they are in the reference or focal group. That is, suppose that $P(Y_t = 1 \mid G = r, X = x)$ and $P(Y_t = 1 \mid G = f, X = x)$ are similar in value and that $P(Y_c = 1 \mid G = r, X = x)$ and $P(Y_c = 1 \mid G = f, X = x)$ are also similar in value. This latter assumption is what we mean by a *useful* covariate score. If the predicted behavior is choosing the correct response to items t and c, then candidates for useful covariate scores are number right or formula scores based on sets of items that measure the same ability that is measured by items t and c. When the predicted behavior is choosing a particular distractor or omitting the item, number right or formula scores on other items may not produce a sufficiently useful covariate score and it may be necessary to augment test scores with other variables, or to define scores based on special choices of distractors.

When X is a covariate score, we can examine a third parameter based on the ACEs in Equation (7). Define $T(x)$ by

$$T(x) = E(Y_t - Y_c \mid G = f, X = x) - E(Y_t - Y_c \mid G = r, X = x), \quad (10)$$
$$= [P(Y_t = 1 \mid G = f, X = x) - P(Y_c = 1 \mid G = f, X = x)]$$
$$- [P(Y_t = 1 \mid G = r, X = x) - P(Y_c = 1 \mid G = r, X = x)]. \quad (11)$$

The causal parameter, $T(x)$, is an interaction like T but is conditional on each X-score. When X is a useful covariate score and the main effect in Equation (1) is small, the four probabilities in Equation (11) will be similar and the boundedness of the probability scale will not confuse the interpretation of $T(x)$ to the degree that it can for T.

Even though $T(x)$ can help clarify the results of a comparison of responses to t and c for members of the reference and focal group, it does introduce the added complexity of a whole set of parameter values, one for each value of X, rather than just a single value. When X is a univariate score, this plethora of parameters can be handled by a graph of $T(x)$ versus x. When X is a multivariate set of covariate scores, this solution is not as helpful.

One way around this plethora of parameters is to average $T(x)$ over some distribution of X-values, $w(x)$, where $w(x) \geq 0$, $\Sigma_x w(x) = 1$. This results in a new parameter T_w defined by

$$T_w = \sum T(x)\, w(x) \tag{12}$$

$$= \sum_x [P(Y_t = 1|G = f, X = x) - P(Y_t = 1|G = r, X = x)]\, w(x)$$

$$- \sum_x [P(Y_c = 1|G = f, X = x) - P(Y_c = 1|G = r, X = x]\, w(x). \tag{13}$$

The choice of $w(x)$ matters, and is somewhat arbitrary. In the standardization DIF procedure, described in chapter 3 of this volume, the distribution of X in the focal group is often used as weights, that is,

$$w(x) = P(X = x \mid G = f).$$

This leads to the parameter that we denote by T_f given by

$$T_f = \sum_x T(x)\, P(X = x|G = f) \tag{14}$$

$$= \sum_x [P(Y_t = 1|G = f, X = x) - P(Y_t = 1|G = r, X = x)]\, P(X = x|G = f),$$

$$- \sum_x [P(Y_c = 1|G = f, X = x) - P(Y_c = 1|G = r, X = x]\, P(X = x|G = f). \tag{15}$$

If we let

$$\Delta_t = \sum_x [P(Y_t = 1|G = f, X = x) - P(Y_t = 1|G = r, X = x]\, P(X = x|G = f) \tag{16}$$

$$\Delta_c = \sum_x [P(Y_c = 1|G = f, X = x) - P(Y_c = 1|G = r, X = x]\, P(X = x|G = f) \tag{17}$$

then

$$T_f = \Delta_t - \Delta_c. \tag{18}$$

In the case where X is a number right or formula score and the predicted behavior is selecting the correct response for items t and c, Δ_t and Δ_c are the parameters estimated by the standardization DIF procedure. Hence, T_f may be interpreted as the difference between standardization DIF parameters for items t and c.

At this point, it is worth stopping for a moment and asking why we pay so much attention to the ACE parameters given in Equations (1)–(4). After all, in computing a DIF measure for an item, we compare the performance of matched focal and reference group members on the studied item, and this is not an ACE parameter. To make the comparison sharper, in computing a DIF measure for an item using the standardization methodology, the basic parameters are the differences

$$P(Y_j = 1 \mid G = f, X^* = x) - P(Y_j = 1 \mid G = r, X^* = x) \qquad (19)$$

for a fixed item $j = t$ or c and a score X^* that *includes* the score on the studied item 1.[1] In contrast, the corresponding ACE is

$$P(Y_t = 1 \mid G = g, X = x) - P(Y_c = 1 \mid G = g, X = x) \qquad (20)$$

where g is a particular group, reference or focal, and X is a covariate score that does *not* include the studied items.

The motivation for our emphasis on the ACE parameters is a causal model that underlies the observations. Consider the joint distribution of the two variables (Y_t, Y_c) over the set of examinees for which $G = g$ and $X = x$. Let this (conditional) joint distribution be denoted by

$$p_{uvgx} = P(Y_t = u, Y_c = v \mid G = g, X = x). \qquad (21)$$

Thus, for example, p_{10fx} is the probability that a focal group member with covariate score $X = x$ will give the predicted response if responding to item t but will not give it if responding to item c. In this sense, then p_{10fx} is the probability that item t *causes* the predicted response for focal group examinees with covariate score $X = x$. The values of p_{uvgx} are *causal parameters* in this special, but clear-cut, sense. Notice that

$$P(Y_t = 1 \mid G = g, X = x) = p_{11gx} + p_{10gx}. \qquad (22)$$

Hence, the ACE parameter given in Equation (4) can be expressed in terms of the causal parameters in Equation (21) in the following way:

$$\begin{aligned} E(Y_t - Y_c \mid G = g, X = x) \\ = (p_{11gx} + p_{10gx}) - (p_{11gx} + p_{01gx}) \\ = p_{10gx} - p_{01gx}. \end{aligned} \qquad (23)$$

---

[1]See Holland and Thayer (1988) and Donoghue, Holland, and Thayer (chapter 7, this volume) for a discussion of why inclusion of the studied item in the matching variable is important for both the Mantel–Haenszel and the standardization procedures.

Finally, this gives us an important formula that relates the conditional-on-X ACE-difference, $T(x)$, to the causal parameters, that is,

$$T(x) = p_{10fx} - p_{01fx} - (p_{10rx} - p_{01rx}) \tag{24}$$

Equation (24) can be used to justify our emphasis on the ACE parameter in the following way. Suppose item c is just as likely to cause members of f to make the predicted response as it is to cause members of r to do this for examinees with $X = x$. This means that

$$p_{01fx} = p_{01rx}. \tag{25}$$

It follows that if Equation (25) holds then

$$T(x) = p_{10fx} - p_{10rx}, \tag{26}$$

so that in this case $T(x)$ is the excess of the probability that t causes the predicted response in the focal group over this probability in the reference group. Assumptions about the causal parameters, p_{uvgx}, are generally untestable, but, depending on the degree of control exercised in the design of the (t, c) item pair, some assumptions can be made plausible and then give a direct causal interpretation to $T(x)$. We emphasize that Equation (25) is not the only type of assumption that can arise in a randomized DIF study.

EXAMPLES OF SPECIAL CONFIRMATORY STUDIES

Randomized DIF that grew out of the two examples of observational studies discussed previously are described in this section. These studies either constructed items with the postulated factors or varied the location of the items. Other examples of DIF research evaluating effects of specially constructed items are: Bleistein, Schmitt, and Curley (1990) and Scheuneman (1987).

Systematic Evaluation of Hispanic DIF Factors

The purpose of the Schmitt et al. (1988) investigation was to provide a follow-up to the Schmitt (1985, 1988) studies through analysis of specially constructed SAT-V items in which the occurrence of postulated factors (true cognates, false cognates, homographs, and special interest) was rigorously controlled and manipulated. Two parallel 40-item non-operational sections were constructed so that each item in one form is a revised but very similar version of the same-position item in the other form. The standardization method was used to compare the performance of the White reference group and each Hispanic focal group for each item in each of the two special forms. An external matching criterion was used: the 85-item SAT-V operational examination, taken in the same booklet as the specially constructed section under study. Hence, the studied items were *not* included in the matching criterion, which is the appropriate course of action for a randomized DIF study. (Refer to the previous section's causal inference perspective on randomized DIF studies for an explanation of why a studied item is not included as part of the matching criterion or covariate.) Estimations of DIF were corrected for speededness by including only those examinees who reached the item. In addition to calculating DIF values for the key, differences in the standardized proportion of responses for each distractor were computed and evaluated in order to further understand the effects of the hypothesized factors on Hispanic DIF. Empirical-option response curves and conditional differential response-rate plots were also evaluated for each item comparison.

Comparison of the DIF value obtained for one item version versus the DIF value obtained for the other item version indicated whether or not the postulated factor effect was supported or not. The most convincing support was found for the hypothesis that the true cognates facilitate the performance of Hispanic examinees. Striking effects were found for two antonym item pairs where the true cognates produced positive DIF values that exceeded 10% for nearly all Hispanic subgroups, whereas the DIF value for the alternate neutral item indicated that the Hispanic groups preformed slightly worse than the reference White group. The PALLID/ASHEN item pair (#7 in Fig. 14.1) presented earlier was one of these two antonym item pairs. Figure 14.1 presents differences in standardization DIF values (STD P-DIF) between the item pairs testing the true cognate factors for the total Hispanic group. Confidence bands are drawn on this figure to indicate that differences greater than 3% between the DIF values of the item pairs are statistically significant. Although only the two antonym item pairs had differences (17% and 15% for all Hispanics) that fell outside the confidence band for all the Hispanic subgroups, some of the other item pairs had differences in the postulated direction. Comparison of the true cognates with differences in the postulated direction versus those with no apparent DIF effect indicates that the true cognates that consistently made the items differentially easier for Hispanics were words with a higher frequency of usage in the Spanish language. Because of these results, the true cognate hypothesis was revised to restrict the positive effect of true cognates to true cognates with a higher usage in the Spanish language than their usage in the English language (Schmitt & Dorans, 1991). Because mixed or marginal results were found for the other hypothesized factors, the authors counseled that "more research is needed before prescriptive or proscriptive rules can be devised to guide item writers. The true cognate items demonstrate clearly, however, that DIF can be manipulated, at least some of the time" (Schmitt et al., 1988, p. 20).

Using Logistic Regression to Estimate Effect Sizes

The earlier section of this chapter that discussed the parameters of interest in a randomized DIF study at the population level did not discuss the details of how to

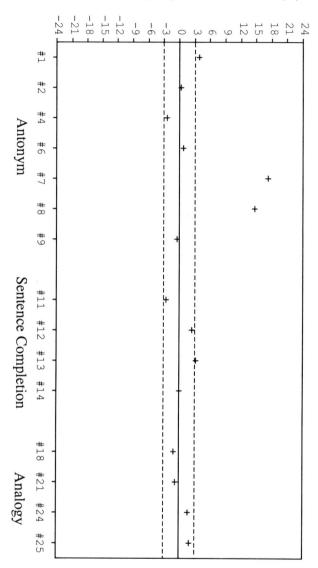

FIG. 14.1. True cognate item effects for all Hispanics

estimate them. We now consider the problem of estimation. There are two parts to this discussion. The first concerns how random assignment of the special items to examinees allows the basic probabilities in Equations (5)–(7) to be estimated from the data collected in a randomized DIF study. The second concerns how to use modern discrete data models to estimate the causal parameters of interest. We discuss each in turn, using the data from the randomized DIF study for Hispanics, described in the previous section, to illustrate how the procedure is used and to compare its estimates of effect size to those produced by standardization.

Randomization and the Causal Parameters

To reiterate, the various ACEs defined in Equations (1)–(4) and the ACE-difference or interaction parameters, T and $T(x)$, defined in Equations (8) and (10), are based on these probabilities:

$$P(Y_j = 1), P(Y_j = 1 \mid G = g) \text{ and } P(Y_j = 1 \mid G = g, X = x) \quad (27)$$

for $j = c,t$ and $g = f,r$.

However, the data that is obtained in a randomized DIF study is Y_S, S, G, and X on each examinee. Hence, the parameters that can be directly estimated in a randomized DIF study are not those in Equation (27), but are, instead,

$$P(Y_S = 1 \mid S = j), P(Y_S = 1 \mid S = j, G = g)$$
$$\text{and } P(Y_S = 1 \mid S = j, G = g, X = x), \quad (28)$$

which can also be expressed as

$$P(Y_j = 1 \mid S = j), P(Y_j = 1 \mid S = j, G = g)$$
$$\text{and } P(Y_j = 1 \mid S = j, G = g, X = s). \quad (29)$$

(Note that in Equations (28) and (29) we have made use of the fact that X is a covariate score—otherwise it would be subscripted by j.)

The role of random assignment of examinees to item t or c is that it makes the variable S statistically independent of Y_t, Y_c, G, and X. Hence, randomization results in the probabilities in (29) being respectively equal to those in (27) that underlie the ACEs and ACE-differences of interest to us. Thus, we may use estimates of the probabilities in (28) as the basis of our inferences of the causal parameter T, $T(x)$, and T_w. If random assignment fails for some reason, then this is not true. There are a variety of ways that random assignment can fail to be executed in any randomized study. An important class of such failure is *differential dropout* between the units assigned to each condition. In randomized DIF studies *drop-out* means that the examinee does not attempt to answer the special test items. Differential drop-out might occur between examinees assigned to item t and to item c if the location of these items in the overall test form is very different, for example, if t is the first item in its test form but c is the last item of its test form.

Estimating the Main Effect Parameter

Useful estimation strategies always depend on the type and extent of the available data. We now describe an approach, based on logistic regression, that can be used in a variety of situations. The main effect parameter

$$E(Y_t - Y_c) = P(Y_t = 1) - P(Y_c = 1)$$

can also be expressed, by the argument given previously, as the treatment-control difference,

$$P(Y_t = 1 \mid S = t) - P(Y_c = 1 \mid S = c), \tag{30}$$

in a randomized DIF study. Let $\hat{p}_t$ denote the proportion of examinees who made the predicted response among those asked to respond to item t and let $\hat{p}_c$ be similarly defined for item c. Then the difference, $\hat{p}_t - \hat{p}_c$, estimates the difference in Equation (30). For example, consider the PALLID/ASHEN item discussed earlier. A sample of 42,033 White or Hispanic examinees answered the PALLID item (t) and 45,960 White or Hispanic examinees answered the ASHEN item (c). The proportions answering the two items correctly are, respectively, .51 and .50. The estimate of the main effect of items is the difference, .01. Thus, we see that, in fact, the two items are nearly of equal difficulty, over the subpopulation consisting of proportional representations of self-identified White and Hispanic examinees. There were 84,852 White examinees and 3,141 Hispanic examinees in this sample.

It is useful to set up our notation for logistic regression now so that we can show its relationship to the main-effect parameter in Equation (30). Let S^* and G^* be indicator variables defined by

$$S^* = \begin{cases} 1 & \text{if } S = t, \\ 0 & \text{if } S = c, \end{cases} \quad G^* = \begin{cases} 1 & \text{if } G = f, \\ 0 & \text{if } G = r. \end{cases} \tag{31}$$

We set up a logistic regression model of the following fairly general form:

$$\text{logit}[P(Y_S = 1 \mid S, G, X)]$$

$$= \alpha_0 + \sum_{k=1}^{a} \alpha_k X^k + \beta_0 S^* + \gamma_0 G^* + \lambda_0 S^* G^*$$

$$+ \sum_{k=1}^{a} \beta_k S^* X^k + \sum_{k=1}^{a} \gamma_k G^* X^k + \sum_{k=1}^{a} \lambda_k S^* G^* X^k, \tag{32}$$

where

$$\text{logit}(p) = \log \left(\frac{p}{1 - p} \right)$$

and α_k, β_k and λ_k are the model parameters.

In Equation (32) the logit is assumed to be a polynomial of degree at most a in the covariates score X and this polynomial is possibly different for each of the four combinations of S and G. Simplification of this general model is achieved by data analysis in which various submodels of Equation (32) are examined. Polynomials in X of degree 2 or more may be used to allow for curvilinear logit functions. For example, in the PALLID/ASHEN example the following logistic regression models were found to give satisfactory fits to the data in which X is the operational SAT-V score that does not include the studied item:

ASHEN, White examinees:

$$\text{logit } P(Y_S = 1 \mid S = c, G = r, \text{SAT-V})$$
$$= -1.970 - 0.458 \, (\text{SAT-V}) + 0.581 \, (\text{SAT-V})^2.$$

PALLID, White examinees:

$$\text{logit } P(Y_S = 1 \mid S = t, G = r, \text{SAT-V})$$
$$= -3.885 + 3.081 \, (\text{SAT-V}) - 1.184 \, (\text{SAT-V})^2 + 0.255 \, (\text{SAT-V})^3.$$

ASHEN, Hispanic examinees:

$$\text{logit } P(Y_S = 1 \mid S = c, G = f, \text{SAT-V})$$
$$= -0.621 - 1.907 \, (\text{SAT-V}) + 0.917 \, (\text{SAT-V})^2.$$

PALLID, Hispanic examinees:

$$\text{logit } P(Y_S = 1 \mid S = t, G = f, \text{SAT-V})$$
$$= -1.194 + 0.174 \, (\text{SAT-V}) + 0.273 \, (\text{SAT-V})^2.$$

Let $\bar{p}(j,g,x)$ denote the estimated conditional probability (or fitted probability) that results from the logistic regression analysis. The fitted probabilities are related to the estimated logits in Equation (32) according to the following formula:

$$\tilde{L}(j,g,x) = \text{estimated logit } [(P(Y_S = 1 \mid S = j, G = g, X = x))],$$

then

$$\bar{p}(j,g,x) = \exp(\tilde{L}(j,g,x))/(1 + \exp(\tilde{L}(j,g,x))).$$

The four fitted probability functions for the estimated logits just given are displayed in Fig. 14.2. We see that the predicted probabilities for the PALLID item for the Hispanic group are quite different from the other three.

Once a satisfactory logistic regression model is selected, we may use it to obtain various covariate adjusted estimates. The fitted probabilities, $\bar{p}(j,g,x)$ are estimates of the conditional probability,

$$p(j,g,x) = P(Y_S = 1 \mid S = j, G = g, X = x). \tag{33}$$

Define $\bar{p}_j$ by

$$\bar{p}_j = \sum_{x,g} \bar{p}(j,\ g,\ x)\ n_{jgx} \Bigg/ \left(\sum_{x,g} n_{jgx} \right), \tag{34}$$

where n_{jgx} is the number of examinees in the study with $S = j$, $G = g$, and $X = x$. Thus, $\bar{p}_j$ may be viewed as an estimate of p_j, the proportion of examinees in the population who give the predicted response to item j in the pair $(t,\ c)$, that is based on the smoothed predicted probabilities, $\bar{p}(j,g,x)$. However, if the sub-model of Equation (32) that is selected to represent the data contains α_0 and β_0 as

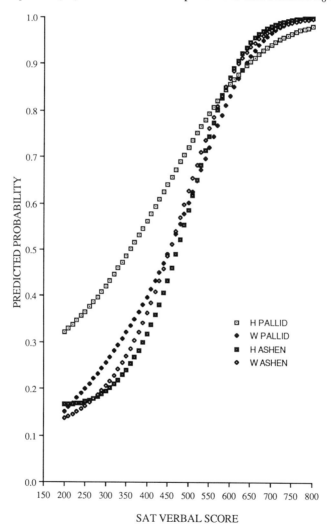

FIG. 14.2.   Fitted probabilities for the PALLID/ASHEN item pair: Reference group is White (N), focal group is Hispanic (H).

free parameters, it may be shown that $\bar{p}_j$ and the raw proportion, $\hat{p}_j$, are equal. Because we allowed α_0 and β_0 to be free in our analysis, covariance adjustment does not change our estimate of the main effect parameter.

Estimating T

The interaction parameter T defined in Equation (8) can be estimated directly or by the use of covariate adjustments. Let $\hat{p}_{jg}$ denote the proportion of examinees making the predicted response among all those exposed to item $j = t$ or c in group $g(g = f,r)$. The argument given in the earlier section shows that the difference of sample differences in proportions,

$$\hat{T} = \hat{p}_{tf} - \hat{p}_{cf} - (\hat{p}_{tr} - \hat{p}_{cr}), \tag{35}$$

estimates the ACE-differences, T. In the PALLID/ASHEN example, the four proportions that make up $\hat{T}$ are as follows:

	(t) PALLID	(c) ASHEN
Whites (r)	.51	.50
Hispanics (f)	.56	.36

the value of $\hat{T}$ is therefore

$$\begin{aligned} \hat{T} &= (.56 - .36) - (.51 - .50) \tag{36} \\ &= .19. \end{aligned}$$

A covariate adjusted estimate of T can also be obtained from the fitted probabilities resulting from a logistic regression analysis. Let $\bar{p}_{jg}$ be defined by

$$\bar{p}_{jg} = \sum_x \bar{p}(j, g, x)\, n_{jgx} \bigg/ \left(\sum_x n_{jgx} \right) \tag{37}$$

where $\bar{p}(j, g, x)$ and n_{jgx} are as defined earlier. Then, the covariate adjusted estimate of T is

$$\tilde{T} = \bar{p}_{tf} - \bar{p}_{cf} - (\bar{p}_{tr} - \bar{p}_{cr}). \tag{38}$$

If the submodel of Equation (32) that is selected to represent the data contains α_0, β_0, γ_0, and λ_0 as free parameters, then it may be shown that $\bar{p}_{jg}$ and $\hat{p}_{jg}$ are equal. Because we have done this in the models fit to the data in the PALLID/ASHEN example, our estimates, $\tilde{T}$ and $\hat{T}$, are equal.

Estimating T(x)

When sample sizes are very large, a useful direct estimate of $T(x)$ is available. In analogy with Equation (35) it is

$$\hat{T}(x) = \hat{p}_{tfx} - \hat{p}_{cfx} - (\hat{p}_{trx} - \hat{p}_{crx}) \tag{39}$$

where $\tilde{p}_{jgx}$ is the proportion of examinees who made the predicted response among all those for whom $S = j$, $G = g$ and $X = x$. However, in practice, where samples are often small, Equation (39) yields very noisy estimates of $T(x)$ that can mask trends. Instead, a more useful approach is to use the fitted probabilities from the logistic regression analysis, $\tilde{p}(j, g, x)$. This yields

$$\tilde{T}(x) = \tilde{p}(t,f,x) - \tilde{p}(c,f,x) - (\tilde{p}(t,r,x) - \tilde{p}(c,r,x)). \tag{40}$$

When x is a univariate score, a graph of $\tilde{T}(x)$ versus x is a useful summary of the results for items t and c of the randomized DIF study. Figure 14.3 shows a plot of

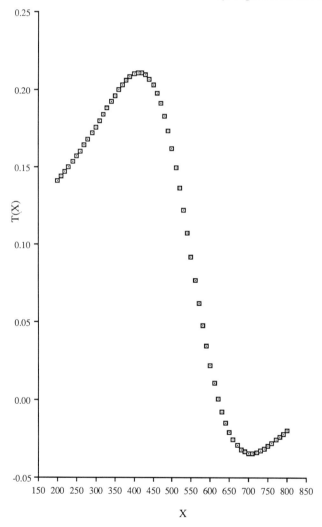

FIG. 14.3. Plot of $T(x)$ versus X, where X is SAT Verbal Score, for PALLID/ASHEN item pair.

$T(x)$ versus x for the PALLID/ASHEN example in which the covariate is the SAT-V score.

Estimates of T_w are easily derived from Equation (40) via the formula

$$\bar{T}_w = \sum_x \bar{T}(x) \, w(x) \qquad (41)$$

for any set of weights $w(x)$. In particular, when

$$w(x) = \frac{\sum_j n_{jfx}}{\sum_{j,x} n_{jfx}}, \qquad (42)$$

we obtain an estimate of T_f, $T(x)$ weighted by the distribution of X in the focal group. It is

$$\bar{T}_f = \sum_x \bar{T}(x) \; \frac{\sum_j n_{jfx}}{\sum_{j,x} n_{jfx}}. \qquad (43)$$

For the PALLID/ASHEN example, $\bar{T}_f$ is .17, which agrees with the difference in standardization parameters reported in Schmitt et al. (1988). This agreement is due to several factors. Most importantly, the sample sizes for the Hispanic groups who responded to the t and c items were sufficiently large (1,619 and 1,522, respectively) that the distribution of the covariate scores in these two groups was similar to the distribution obtained by pooling them. In addition, the curves reported in Fig. 14.2 are the result of careful data analysis and represent the noisy raw proportions in the data very well. Finally, the estimate of the standardization parameter is based on an *external* matching criterion that is the same as that used in the logistic regression analyses reported here—the SAT-V score. We note that the use of an external matching criterion that does not include the studied item is generally not an appropriate procedure for measuring the amount of DIF exhibited in an item, but in this case it is appropriate because the parameter of ultimate interest is the average interaction parameter, T_f, given in Equation (18), rather than the DIF values just mentioned.

Summary of Steps for Using Logistic Regression in a Randomized DIF Study

The theory and practice of logistic regression are now fairly well established. The discussions in Cox (1970) and Hosmer and Lemeshow (1989) are very helpful and software is available in the SAS, SPSS, and BMDP packages. We suggest the following checklist for the use of logistic regression in the analysis of data from randomized DIF studies:

- Be sure that the variables used as covariate scores are, in fact, covariates— that is, they are unaffected by whether the examinee was exposed to the t or c item.
- Consider including as many covariate scores as possible in the analysis— for example, math as well as verbal scores, or subscores such as rights *and* omits on formula-scored tests.
- Consider including powers higher than linear or quadratic terms in order to improve the fit of the model.
- Start with a large model like that in Equation (32), then simplify it to the point where there are as few parameters as possible without a degradation in the fit.
- Check the fit of the model in at least the following two ways:
  1. See if the inclusion of a term in the model adds substantially to its fit as measured by the standard one-degree-of-freedom likelihood ratio test.
  2. Plot the fitted proportions from the model along with the observed proportions as functions of the covariate scores for each combination of group (f or r) and item (t or c). The fitted proportions should go through the middle of the scatter of observed proportions.
- In addition, check residuals from the model for outliers, remove them to see if they are responsible for unusual features of the resulting model.
- Remember that the point of this careful data analysis is to find a smooth function of the covariate score(s) that adequately smoothes the noisy observed proportions, $\tilde{p}_{jgx}$.
- Use the fitted proportions, $\tilde{p}(j,g,x)$, to compute $\tilde{T}(x)$ and single-number summaries like $\tilde{T}_f$.
- Do not concentrate on interpreting the coefficients of the finally selected logistic regression model, that is, $\hat{\alpha}_k$, $\hat{\beta}_k$, $\hat{\gamma}_k$ or $\hat{\lambda}_k$, because these are in the logit scale. Rather, compare the four functions $\tilde{p}(t, r, x)$, $\tilde{p}(c, r, x)$, $\tilde{p}(t, f, x)$ and $\tilde{p}(c, f, x)$ via plots, as in Fig. 14.2, and interpret these differences.

Differential Speededness Assessed Under Controlled Conditions

An example of a special confirmatory study where the location of the items was varied is found in Dorans, Schmitt, and Curley (1988). This study examined directly how differential speededness affects the magnitude of DIF. In addition, it evaluated how well the procedure of excluding not-reached examinees from the calculation of the DIF statistic adjusts for the effects of differential speededness. The purpose of the study was to answer two questions:

- Does an item's DIF value depend on its location in the test?
- If so, can the item location effect be removed via a statistical adjustment of the DIF statistic?

(For a detailed description of the study see Dorans, Schmitt, & Curley [1988]).

For the purposes of their study, one non-operational 45-item and one non-operational 40-item SAT-Verbal pretests were labeled *Form A* and *Form B*, respectively. The 10 analogy items appearing in Form A in positions 36 to 45 were combined with the antonyms, sentence completions, and reading comprehension items from Form B to create *Form C*, a 40-item section in which the 10 analogies appeared in positions 16 to 25. Similarly, the analogy items from Form B in positions 16 to 25 were combined with the antonyms, sentence completions, and reading comprehension items from Form A to create *Form D*, a 45-item test in which the 10 analogies were shifted to the end of the section in positions 36 to 45.

This particular design afforded an opportunity to examine how differential speededness for Blacks affects the magnitude of DIF statistics on two sets of analogy items. As a control analysis, Dorans, Schmitt, and Curley (1988) also conducted differential speededness and DIF analyses for females on the same sets of analogy items. Standardized distractor analyses (see chapter 3, this volume) that focused on not-reached items were used to assess differential speededness.

Figures 14.4 and 14.5 depict the degree of differential speededness observed for Blacks and females on the Form A and Form D analogy items, respectively. In these figures, the standardized difference in not-reached performance (STD P-DIF(NR)) values, in percentage units, are plotted against item number. Absolute values of 5% or greater indicate a sizeable degree of differential speededness. A positive STD P-DIF(NR) value means that the focal group, Blacks or females, is not reaching the item to the degree that the base or reference group, Whites or males, is. Conversely, a negative STD P-DIF(NR) value means the focal group is reaching the item in greater proportions than the matched base group.

In Fig. 14.4, there is little evidence of differential speededness for females. For Blacks, there is some evidence, particularly on items 42 and 43, and possibly 40 and 41. In Fig. 14.5, for females, item 44 is approaching the 5% cutoff. For Blacks, differential speededness is quite pronounced. Items 41, 42, 43, and 44 are at or above the 5% value, and items 38, 39, and 40 are approaching the 5% value. Note that across Figs. 14.4 and 14.5 all but one item has a positive STD P-DIF(NR) value for Blacks, indicating that Blacks reach items at the end of the 45-item section at a slower rate than a matched group of Whites, as reported by Dorans, Schmitt, and Bleistein (1988). In contrast, the STD P-DIF(NR) values for females are either at 0 (9 of 20 items), or slightly negative, indicating that females get further into the test than a matched group of males.

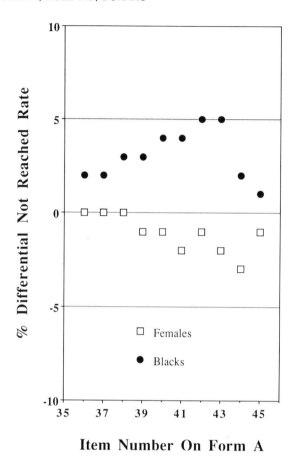

FIG. 14.4.   Differential speededness on Form A.

There are no figures for the analogy items on Forms B or C because there is no differential speededness on the analogy items in positions 16 to 25 of the 40-item format. In fact, all examinees reached these items.

A major goal of the Dorans, Schmitt, and Curley (1988) research was to ascertain whether or not there was a position effect on DIF statistics. Evidence has been presented for a differential speededness effect on Blacks, and of negative DIF, predominantly for Blacks on the earlier, easier analogy items. In addition item position effects were reported.

Does an item's DIF value depend on its location in the test? Dorans, Schmitt, and Curley (1988) reported that the answer is yes for some items, particularly when one position is subject to a differential speededness effect and the other is not.

The second question to be addressed by the Dorans, Schmitt, and Curley (1988) research was: Can the item location effect be removed via a statistical

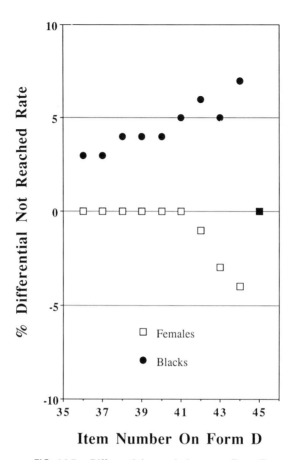

FIG. 14.5.   Differential speededness on Form D.

adjustment? In particular, does exclusion of the candidates who do not reach the item from calculation of the DIF statistic produce a statistic that is less sensitive to position? All things considered, the adjustment for not-reached items tended to dampen the position effect for most items. It did not, however, completely remove statistically the speededness effect.

SUMMARY

This chapter provided prescriptions for the practice of conducting research into the evaluation of DIF hypotheses. Advice was given for both observational studies with operational item data and controlled studies with specially constructed items. The following checklist can be used to guide the conduct of observational studies:

Summary of Steps in the Evaluation of DIF
Hypotheses Using Observational Data

• Operationalize the definition of the postulated DIF factors in order to permit the objective classification of items.

• Classify all items in accordance with postulated DIF factors.

• Define the appropriate focal and reference groups.

• Select appropriate samples.

• Determine the matching criterion, considering dimensionality, reliability, and criterion refinement issues.

• Determine what statistical adjustments are relevant (e.g., speededness and omission).

• Select an appropriate DIF estimate based on the foregoing considerations.

• Calculate DIF statistics for the key, distractors, and response style factors.

• Evaluate relevant information provided by distractor and difference plots.

• Summarize DIF information by the postulated factors; use descriptive statistics (e.g., correlate comparable DIF outcomes with hypothesized factors using appropriate statistical methods).

• Determine whether the DIF information supports the hypothesized DIF factors.

Described in this chapter were the rudiments of a theory of causal inference, the success of which hinges on putting the J. S. Mill quotation from nearly 150 years ago into action by measuring causation through experimental manipulation. The section on using logistic regression to estimate effect sizes described the specifics of one approach toward accomplishing this. The following checklist can be used to guide future randomized DIF studies:

Summary of Steps in the Confirmatory Evaluation
of DIF Hypotheses Using Specially Constructed Items

• Construct sets of items (treatment and control) in accordance with postulated DIF factors; control extraneous factors to the extent possible.

• Define the focal and reference groups and randomly determine control and treatment subgroups.

• Select appropriate sample sizes; replicate administrations when needed in order to obtain sufficient sample sizes.

• Determine the matching criterion that is a covariate in the sense used here; use an external matching criterion when possible. Consider dimensionality and criterion refinement issues.

- Specify what statistical adjustments are relevant (e.g., speededness and omission).
- Calculate DIF statistics for the key, distractors, and response style factors.
- Evaluate relevant information provided by distractor and difference plots.
- Summarize DIF information by the postulated factors; use descriptive and inferential statistics.
- Determine whether the DIF information supports the hypothesized DIF factors.

These randomized DIF studies are distinguished by the careful construction of hypothesis items and their controls, the control of extraneous factors, the use of randomization, and the quest for adequate samples to achieve enough statistical power to detect effects related to the DIF hypotheses. If these conditions are met in practice, then DIF findings, if replicated, may suggest changes in educational assessment and practice. Evaluation of DIF hypotheses is complicated, however, by a variety of practical and ethical considerations. Sound scientific method needs to operate within these constraints and achieve success in advancing knowledge that will affect test development practice, assessment, and educational practice.

15
A Note on the Value of Including the Studied Item in the Test Score When Analyzing Test Items for DIF

Charles Lewis
Educational Testing Service

We all know that, when using test score as a matching variable with a Mantel–Haenszel analysis for differential item functioning (DIF), the item under study should be included. But do we know why? Holland and Thayer (1988) proved this result for items following the Rasch model, and Zwick (1990) established the degree of its applicability for more general item response models. In her discussion, Zwick illustrated the appropriateness of the total test score as a matching variable for the binomial test model (which may be thought of as a special case of the Rasch model with all items of equal difficulty). It is this illustration that I would like to review and develop here (generally following her notation). My motivation for doing this is that the binomial model is both simple and familiar, so that it may help improve our intuitions regarding the role of a matching variable in DIF analyses.

To begin, let us rephrase the binomial model in item response theory (IRT) terms, specifically, what might be called the zero-parameter logistic model or 0PL:

$$P(X_i = 1|\theta) = \Psi(\theta), \ i = 1(1)n, \tag{1}$$

with mutual independence among the X_i, given θ. Here, $\Psi(\cdot)$ denotes the logistic distribution function. This may be thought of as a special case of the Rasch model, with all item difficulty parameters set equal to zero.

Suppose our interest is in item j, and define two scores, respectively excluding and including this item:

$$S' = \sum_{i \neq j}^{n} X_i \tag{2}$$

and

$$S = \sum_{i=1}^{n} X_i. \tag{3}$$

Finally, let G ($= 0$ or 1) denote membership in the groups to be compared. Under the null hypothesis, G is independent of the X_i, given θ.

Our interest, when taking the Mantel–Haenszel approach to analyzing DIF, is in the probability that $X_j = 1$, given values for S' and G, or for S and G. Following Zwick (1990), we first consider this probability conditioning on θ as well:

$$P(X_j = 1|\theta,s',g) \tag{4}$$

and

$$P(X_j = 1|\theta,s,g) . \tag{5}$$

Because X_j is independent of G (under the null hypothesis of no DIF) and the other X_i, given θ, we may rewrite the first of these probabilities as

$$P(X_j = 1|\theta,s',g) = P(X_j = 1|\theta) = \Psi(\theta) . \tag{6}$$

Thus, if we condition on both θ and s', the latter piece of information is made irrelevant by the former when it comes to the probability of success on item j.

How does this change when we use the score including X_j? Again, if the null hypothesis is true, we may rewrite the original probability as

$$P(X_j = 1|\theta,s,g) = P(X_j = 1|\theta,s) . \tag{7}$$

Now, however, the roles of θ and the score are reversed, compared with the previous case: X_j and θ are independent, given s. To see this, think of a series of n Bernoulli trials, each with the same success probability. If s of these trials are a success, what is the probability that trial j is a success? Clearly, the answer is s/n, a result that is independent of the success probability. Thus, for our problem,

$$P(X_j = 1|\theta,s) = P(X_j = 1|s) = \frac{s}{n}. \tag{8}$$

To find the probabilities of interest in a Mantel–Haenszel analysis, we must average the probabilities just obtained with respect to the appropriate posterior distribution for θ. For the case where X_j is not included in the score, the result is

$$P(X_j = 1|s',g) = \int \Psi(\theta)p(\theta|s',g)d\theta \tag{9}$$

and, for the case where the item is included, because θ does not appear in the probability already derived, we may write the result immediately as

$$P(X_j = 1|s,g) = \frac{s}{n}. \qquad (10)$$

It should be clear that the first of these expressions may differ from one group to the other, whereas the second is invariant over groups. Thus, when there is no DIF present (i.e., when the item response function for the studied item is identical for the two groups), conditioning on the score without the item under study (S') may lead to an odds ratio between groups for success on the item that differs from unity, whereas conditioning on the score that includes that item (S) is guaranteed to give an odds ratio of 1. Because this last is a requirement for the Mantel–Haenszel analysis, such an analysis should be carried out only based on S.

Of course, the point of the aforementioned development was not to find out what should be done for the binomial model, but rather to help improve our intuitions about the choice between S' and S. In particular, it should be clear at this point that the virtue of using S is not that it does a perfect job of matching individuals from the two groups. Indeed, with a short test and groups whose distributions of θ differ markedly, S may do a very poor job of matching. The point is that conditioning on the full score removes the dependence of X_j on θ, so that group differences in the distribution of θ become irrelevant. As Zwick (1990) pointed out, this happens with the binomial model and with the Rasch model, but not with any IRT model more complex than Rasch.

16

The Effect of Item Screening on Test Scores and Test Characteristics

Elizabeth Burton
University of Colorado

Nancy W. Burton
Educational Testing Service

Differential item functioning (DIF) statistics identify SAT test items that are unusually difficult for members of particular population subgroups. Such items usually are considered undesirable because they appear to be measuring slightly different constructs for different subgroups. These items may not be removed from the test, however, when the construct being measured is an explicit part of the intended domain of the test. For example, the College Board science achievement tests require some mathematical skills, and sometimes the required math skills are differentially difficult for women or non-Asian minority students, who on average take fewer advanced mathematics courses. Although differentially difficult questions are avoided when possible, they are used when necessary to meet test specifications. Note that such results are found when the test measures more than one dimension of skill or knowledge (such as science knowledge and math skill), and those dimensions are distributed differentially in the two groups being compared.

Since March 1989, all SATs introduced have been constructed from item pools screened for DIF. Because SAT items are pretested in actual SAT administrations, it is possible to compute DIF indices on the testing population under normal administration conditions. Because pretest samples include 5,000 or more students, it is possible to accurately screen for even small subgroups, such as Native Americans (DIF screening requires a minimum of 100 students in the smaller group and 500 in the two groups combined; Petersen, 1987).

The purpose of this study was to answer two related questions about the effect of DIF screening on the psychometric quality of the SAT. The first general question is (a) How does DIF screening affect the psychometric quality of the pretest pool available for use in building final SAT editions? How many items are

lost? What are their characteristics? Are certain content areas particularly suscep-
tible to DIF? The second, and somewhat separable question, is (b) How does DIF
screening affect the psychometric quality of actual SAT editions? Is it still possible to meet content and difficulty specifications? And what happens to students'
scores after test editions are screened for DIF?

Our major finding was that there is very little extreme DIF in the SAT. In the
pretest pool, about 7% of verbal items and 2% of mathematical items were
flagged for unusual levels of DIF. As a result of the small incidence of DIF items
in the pool, the screening of DIF items had little effect on the psychometric
quality of the final SAT editions. Test editions published after DIF screening
began met all content and statistical specifications, so they were indistinguishable from test editions published before DIF screening began. Furthermore, test
scores for population subgroups did not change as a result of DIF screening. The
small number of differentially functioning items that were removed were not
enough to change the relative standing of minority students compared to White
students, or female students compared to male students.

We discuss several details of interest. In looking for the kinds of verbal items
that exhibit DIF, we noticed that there was a slight tendency for the DIF statistic
to be correlated with both item difficulty measures and with item discrimination
measures. The correlation of DIF with item difficulty also was found by Schmitt
and Bleistein (1987) and Kulick and Hu (1989). The correlation of DIF with item
discrimination relates to a finding by Camilli and Smith (1990) and Donoghue
and Allen (1991); it was not supported, however, in Kulick and Hu (1989). These
correlations were somewhat higher when we compared African American students with White students than they were for the sex comparisons. In addition, it
appeared that reading items exhibited less DIF than did the more abstract, con-
textless, analogy and antonym questions (see also Wendler & Carlton, 1987).
Although this study allows only a preliminary description of such findings, it
raises some interesting questions.

For example, average scores for African American and White students are
very different. Do large score differences complicate the interpretation of DIF
results? Is it possible that floor and ceiling effects for these two groups of very
different average proficiency may be affecting the DIF statistics? Or could it be
that DIF statistics are telling us that individual items have very different characteristics for groups of very different abilities? (See Camilli & Smith, 1990, for a
discussion of the problems that may be raised by large differences in the distributions of proficiency for focal and reference groups.)

HOW DOES DIF AFFECT PRETEST POOLS?

The SAT given in March 1989 was the first SAT edition screened for DIF prior to
publication; since that time, DIF information has been considered in assembling

TABLE 16.1
DIF and Item Difficulty for 1987–1988 SAT-Verbal Pretest Items

Difficulty (Delta)	Annual Need N	1987–1988 Pretest Total N	DIF Category					1987–1988 Pretest Not "C"	
			−C N	−B N	A N	+B N	+C N	N	%
hard 18 up		7	0	0	3	3	1	6	86
17–17.9		40	0	0	32	6	2	38	95
16–16.9	30	97	0	3	72	21	1	96	99
15–15.9	72	198	1	7	139	43	8	189	96
14–14.9	168	261	7	17	201	34	2	252	97
13–13.9	120	310	5	25	239	32	9	296	96
12–12.9	96	320	6	25	261	22	6	308	96
11–11.9	87	344	16	37	252	33	6	322	94
10–10.9	87	289	27	33	192	33	4	258	89
9– 9.9	120	211	10	44	138	12	7	194	92
8– 8.9	96	150	12	37	82	15	4	134	89
7– 7.9	72	88	14	24	44	5	1	73	83
6– 6.9	48	49	7	13	25	1	3	39	80
easy 5.9 down	39	18	5	6	6	1	0	13	72
Total N	1,035	2,382	110	271	1,686	261	54	2,218	93
%		100	5	11	71	11	2	93	

all SATs. Pretest items are analyzed for DIF to identify those items that have an unacceptably high positive or negative DIF value (C-items).[1] The C-items are removed from the item pool unless the inclusion of an item is necessary to meet test specifications for a particular edition. After the SAT has been administered, the items are analyzed again for DIF and, ideally, no C-items will be found. In the discussion that follows, the DIF characteristics of items from the 1987–1988 pretest pool (all items pretested during that testing year) are examined as well as the relationship between DIF value and other item characteristics such as difficulty and discrimination.

Table 16.1 shows the distributions of the Mantel–Haenszel[2] delta difference statistic for each item by item difficulty[3] for the 1987–1988 verbal pretest pool (the DIF statistic for the group comparison with the largest absolute DIF value was included for each item). Table 16.1 also includes the marginal totals by DIF category, by difficulty category, and the collapsed distribution of all non-C-items

---

[1]For a summary of the development of ETS DIF standards, see Zieky (1987); for ETS DIF statistical procedures, see Petersen (1987).

[2]See Holland & Thayer, 1988.

[3]Item delta difficulty is expressed as a normal transformation of percent correct, scaled to have a mean of 13 and standard deviation 3.

in the pool (that is, all items with acceptable DIF levels.) Finally, the total number of items needed annually in each range of difficulty is given. Note from the distributions in Table 16.1 that, although the number of middle-difficulty items pretested far exceeds the annual need, and the number of high-difficulty items is adequate, the number of low-difficulty items falls below or only just meets the annual need.

In the distribution across DIF values in Table 16.1, a fairly strong positive relationship between item difficulty and DIF value can be discerned. Upon closer examination, it becomes apparent that this relationship is due largely to the fact that there are no items with negative DIF values at the high end of the difficulty range. This relationship does not hold for the non-negative-DIF items, which are distributed fairly evenly across difficulty values. The pattern is even more striking when just the analogy items are examined, as can be seen in Figs. 16.1 and 16.2. In these figures, item difficulty is plotted against DIF value for 607 verbal analogy items; each plot represents a particular group comparison. In Fig. 16.1, for which women are the focal and men the reference group, item difficulty and DIF value have a low positive correlation of .10. However, in Fig. 16.2, the correlation for the Black/White comparison group, the comparison for which the mean score difference between groups is greatest, is .58. Kulick and Hu (1989) found similar results for Asian-American and Hispanic comparisons with Whites

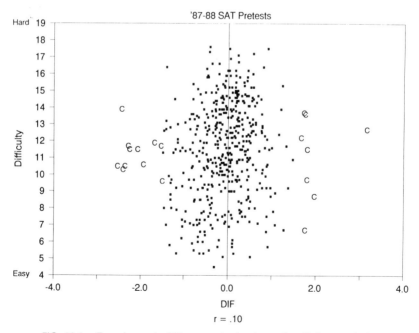

FIG. 16.1.   Female–male DIF on anologies items has little correlation with item difficulty.

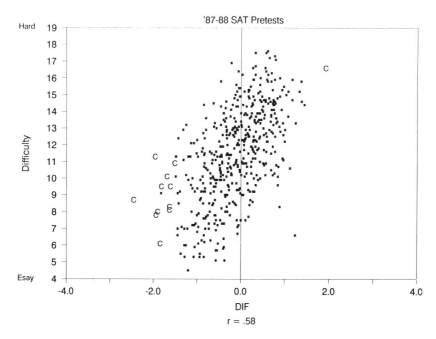

FIG. 16.2.   Black–White DIF on anologies items is correlated with diffi-culty.

and, like the current study, found little correlation for the female/male com-parison.

It is not possible to explain fully the relationship between item difficulty and DIF value, especially the striking correlation seen in the plot of the Black/White data in Fig. 16.2. However, there are factors that might contribute to these patterns. The tendency for negative C-items to cluster at the low end of the difficulty scale might be due partly to floor and ceiling effects. In other words, because the reference group proportion correct is fairly high for low-difficulty items, there is more room for the focal group to score differentially lower on those items. Following the same logic, there would be little room for the focal group to perform differentially lower at the high end of the difficulty scale because the proportion correct for the reference group would be fairly low. The difference in proportions correct for these items, therefore, easily could be lower than the average difference in performance of the two groups which might give the item a positive DIF value. Although the Mantel–Haenszel weighted odds-ratio is corrected for continuity when it is calculated, the patterns observed in Table 16.1 and Figs. 16.1 and 16.2 suggest that the correction may not be sufficient to entirely adjust for floor and ceiling effects.

It also should be noted that the mean DIF values for the comparisons exhibited in the figures range between $-.1$ and $-.2$ for particular focal groups. Because

TABLE 16.2
DIF and Reading Content for 1987–1988 SAT-Verbal Pretest Items

Item Content	1987–1988 Pretest Total N	DIF Category					1987–1988 Pretest Not "C"	
		−C N	−B N	A N	+B N	+C N	N	%
Argumentative	97	0	1	85	11	0	97	100
Humanities	150	0	7	127	16	0	150	100
Narrative	131	0	10	104	13	4	127	97
Biological Science	159	1	9	144	5	0	158	99
Physical Science	93	5	14	69	5	0	88	95
Social Studies	70	0	2	60	7	1	69	99
Total N	700	6	43	589	57	5	689	98
%	100	1	6	84	8	1	98	

the average DIF value across all verbal items in a DIF computation must equal zero, it is clear that this set of analogies items exhibits more negative DIF than would the other item types used in the calculation. (The score on the actual verbal test administered at the same time as the pretests is used as the DIF criterion.) It seems likely, therefore, that if the plots included all verbal items, the relationship that is currently obvious in the plots would not be as apparent.

Tables 16.2 and 16.3 give distributions of DIF value by item content. Although there are few content differences immediately apparent, it does seem clear that the reading items consistently show lower levels of DIF than do the other three formats. None of the reading content categories shows more than 5% C-items, although the combination of antonym, analogy, and sentence items in Table 16.3 shows between 6% and 11% C-items. The reading items also have

TABLE 16.3
DIF and Verbal Content on Antonyms, Analogies,
and Sentence Completion Items

Item Content	1987–1988 Pretest Total N	DIF Category					1987–1988 Pretest Not "C"	
		−C N	−B N	A N	+B N	+C N	N	%
Aesthetic/Philosophical	398	10	36	289	49	14	374	94
World of Practical Affairs	421	34	65	269	41	12	375	89
Science	447	44	97	265	35	6	397	89
Human Relationships	414	16	29	273	79	17	381	92
Total N	1,680	104	227	1,096	204	49	1,527	91
%	100	6	14	65	12	3	91	

slightly lower proportions of B-items (that is, items with a moderate level of DIF).

Table 16.4 shows distributions of the DIF statistic for each item by discrimination, again including the statistic with the highest absolute value across group comparisons for each item. Here, a pattern opposite to that in Table 16.1 can be discerned, although it is not as pronounced. The apparently negative relationship between r-biserial and DIF category suggests that those items that are most discriminating are also more likely to be differentially more difficult for focal than for reference group members. Analogous to the item difficulty information in Table 16.1, r-biserials cluster somewhat in the upper left corner of the distribution whereas no items at the low end of the r-biserial scale have negative DIF values. Plots of r-biserial with DIF value for the analogy items appear in Figs. 16.3 and 16.4. As with the corresponding plots for item difficulty, the relationship between item discrimination and DIF is most apparent for the Black/White comparison group (Fig. 16.4), again, the comparison that has the greatest mean score difference between groups. The correlation for this group is −.33 and for the female/male comparison, plotted in Fig. 16.3, is −.10. Although these correlations are negative, the ordering is the same as that for the item difficulty information with the Black/White group having the most and the female/male group the least extreme value. Again, as noted earlier, the mean DIF values for the data exhibited in Figs. 16.3 and 16.4 range from −.1 to −.2, indicating that the analogies items are more likely to exhibit negative DIF values than would other verbal item types.

It may be that these difficulty and discrimination effects are related, especially for the groups displaying large ability differences. The most extreme results have

TABLE 16.4
DIF and Item Discrimination for 1987–1988 SAT-Verbal Pretest Items

Discrimination (r-biserial)	1987–1988 Pretest Total N	DIF Category					1987–1988 Pretest Not "C"	
		−C N	−B N	A N	+B N	+C N	N	%
.70–.79	17	7	1	8	1	0	10	59
.60–.69	203	33	36	104	22	8	162	80
.50–.59	515	33	86	323	61	12	470	91
.40–.49	618	24	84	441	52	17	577	93
.30–.39	510	10	43	386	63	8	492	96
.20–.29	285	2	15	227	35	6	277	97
.10–.19	159	1	5	133	19	1	157	99
.00–.09	55	0	1	47	5	2	53	96
negative	20	0	0	17	3	0	20	100
Total N	2,382	110	271	1,686	261	54	2,218	93
%	100	5	11	71	11	2	93	

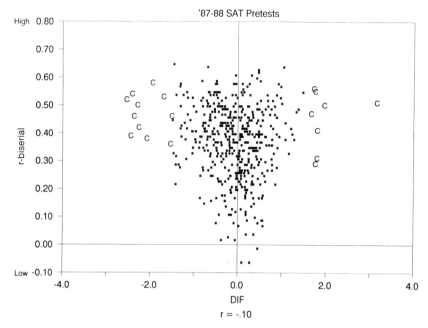

FIG. 16.3. Female–male DIF on anologies items has little correlation with item discrimination.

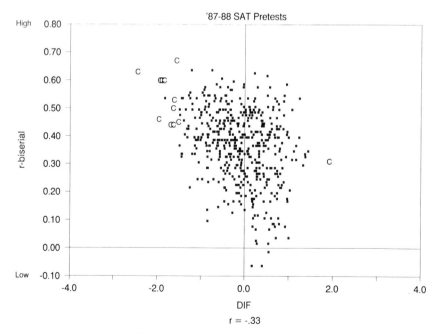

FIG. 16.4. Black–White DIF on anologies items is moderately correlated with item discrimination.

328

been observed for African-American students, who are also most different from the reference group in average scores. Items that are relatively easy for the total testing population will be of average difficulty for lower scoring students. Because middle-difficulty items are capable of the greatest discrimination, it follows that items that are relatively easy for the testing population as a whole may be most discriminating for the African-American subgroup. Suppose that the items most likely to show DIF are those items that are most discriminating for the focal group. Thus an effect that is based on discrimination could masquerade as an effect of difficulty. Our analysis was based on difficulty and discrimination indices computed on all test takers. However, for understanding DIF results, it may be useful also to evaluate difficulty and discrimination indices for each focal group.

HOW DOES DIF SCREENING AFFECT SAT TEST CHARACTERISTICS?

Tables 16.5 through 16.8 show information about DIF and item characteristics for four tests assembled before DIF statistics were available for the pretested item pool (one March, one May, and two June editions administered in 1988) and four tests assembled after DIF screening was implemented (editions given at the same administrations in 1989). Table 16.5 shows SAT-Verbal and SAT-Mathematical DIF values for the 2 years. As would be expected, the percentage of B- and C-items decreases from 1988 to 1989 in both cases. For Verbal, which consistently has a greater percentage of non-A-items than Math, the change is more

TABLE 16.5
DIF Information for Tests Built Without DIF Screening (1988)
and with DIF Screening (1989)—Distribution of Largest
(Absolute) DIF Value for Each Item

| DIF Category | Verbal | | | | Math | | | |
| | 1988 | | 1989 | | 1988 | | 1989 | |
	N	%	N	%	N	%	N	%
+C	6	2	3	1	0	0	0	0
+B	22	6	14	4	12	5	7	3
A	267	79	302	89	210	87	220	92
−B	25	7	19	6	16	7	12	6
−C	20	6	2	1	2	1	1	0
Total	340	100%	340	100%	240	100%	240	100%

Note. Information is collapsed across March, May, and June (two administrations) for each of the two groups.

TABLE 16.6
DIF Information for Tests Built Without DIF Screening (1988)
and With DIF Screening (1988)—DIF Values for Five Focal Groups

	Female/Male		Black/White		Hispanic/White		Asian/White		Native Amer./White	
	1988	1989	1988	1989	1988	1989	1988	1989	1988	1989
Verbal										
Mean	−.04	.02	−.02	−.01	−.03	.03	−.09	−.04	.01	.02
SD	.70	.51	.44	.41	.51	.40	.55	.46	.20	.17
Maximums										
Positive	2.23	1.78	1.06	1.17	1.59	1.73	1.40	1.33	0.98	0.59
Negative	−3.34	−1.57	−1.92	−1.42	−2.51	−1.46	−2.64	−1.94	−0.73	−0.52
Mathematical										
Mean	.00	−.02	.00	.00	.02	.02	.00	−.02	.01	.02
SD	.51	.48	.45	.40	.29	.23	.53	.47	.17	.14
Maximum										
Positive	1.30	1.09	0.98	0.94	0.82	0.59	1.23	1.14	0.45	0.41
Negative	−1.71	−1.14	−1.74	−1.51	−1.14	−0.76	−1.70	−1.70	−0.71	−1.14

Note. Information is collapsed across March, May, and June (two administrations) for each of the groups.

pronounced. The percentage of non-A-items for Verbal decreased from 21% to 11%; for Math, the percentage decreased from 13% to 8%. Of particular interest is the change in number of C-items. For Verbal, 26 of the 1988 items were C-items whereas only 5 were classified as C-items in 1989. For Math, two items were classified as C-items in 1988 and one in 1989.

TABLE 16.7
Item Difficulty for Test Built Without DIF Screening (1988)
and with DIF Screening (1989)

		Verbal		Math	
		1988	1989	1988	1989
March	Mean	11.3	11.2	12.1	12.0
	SD	2.8	2.9	3.1	3.2
May	Mean	11.2	11.5	12.4	12.1
	SD	3.0	3.0	3.0	3.1
June	Mean	11.3	11.4	12.2	12.1
(1st Form)	SD	2.7	2.9	3.3	3.3
June	Mean	11.5	11.4	12.2	12.1
(2nd Form)	SD	3.0	2.9	3.4	3.2
Specified	Mean	11.4		12.2	
	SD	3.0		3.3	

TABLE 16.8
Item Discrimination for Tests Built Without DIF Screening (1988)
and with DIF Screening (1989)

		Verbal		Math	
		1988	1989	1988	1989
March	Mean	.48	.49	.57	.56
	SD	.13	.11	.10	.11
May	Mean	.49	.50	.54	.54
	SD	.10	.11	.10	.09
June	Mean	.48	.47	.53	.57
(1st Form)	SD	.12	.13	.11	.11
June	Mean	.46	.49	.54	.54
(2nd Form)	SD	.13	.12	.11	.10
Specified	Mean	.43		.47	

Table 16.6 shows the means, standard deviations, and maximum and minimum DIF values for each of the comparison groups for the 2 years. For both years, as would be expected, the mean DIF values are very close to zero.[4]

For both Verbal and Mathematical sections, the standard deviations of the DIF values decrease between 1988 and 1989 for all focal groups. Because, in general, math sections exhibit less DIF, the decrease in the standard deviations is more extreme for Verbal. The decreases in standard deviation for Verbal range from .03 for both the Black/White and Native American/White comparisons to .19 for the female/male comparison. For Math, the decreases range from .03 for the female/male and Native American/White comparisons to .06 for the Hispanic/ White and Asian/White comparisons.

Although most of the changes are moderate, DIF screening was successful in its goal of reducing the differential difficulty of final SAT forms. Furthermore, not surprisingly, the largest changes in standard deviation tended to correspond to comparison groups that had the most extreme negative or positive DIF values. For example, the largest change in standard deviation occurred for Verbal for the male/female comparison which had unusually extreme maximum positive and negative DIF values. For the Native American/White comparison, on the other hand, the change in standard deviation for both Verbal and Math was quite small, consistent with the relatively small maximum DIF values.

The pattern of changes in the maximum positive and negative DIF values is not as consistent. In general, the maximum values in 1989 are less extreme than the corresponding values in 1988; this is not the case in every instance, however. Specifically, the maximum positive value for the Black/White comparison for

---

[4]The fact that the means are not exactly zero is due to a slight problem in the current DIF computation, which assumes a rights-scored test. There are slight errors for formula-scored tests like the SAT.

Verbal increased from 1.06 to 1.17, the maximum positive value for the Hispanic/White comparison for Verbal increased from 1.59 to 1.73, and the maximum negative value for the Native American/White comparison for Math decreased from -0.71 to -1.14. Because the greatest effect that performing DIF analyses has results from the identification and removal of items for which the focal group does differentially worse than the reference group (i.e., items with negative DIF values) and because the increases in the maximum positive values for the Black/White and Hispanic/White comparisons are very slight, these increases are neither surprising nor problematic.

The increase in positive maximum value for each focal group is probably due to the removal of one or more items that had negative DIF values. The maximum positive values may have increased slightly because the mean DIF value must be at or near zero. Although the DIF values for the final form are calculated on a different set of items than the pretest values, the removal of the large, predominantly negative DIF items would lead to a final distribution with a somewhat higher center (if an absolute scale of DIF were available) and with an altered distribution of high and low DIF values.

The increase in the negative DIF value for Verbal for Native Americans is interesting, because it only can be a secondary effect of DIF screening (if it is an effect of DIF screening at all). At the time these first tests were assembled, no Verbal C-items had been identified for Native Americans. Thus, DIF screening would not have affected directly values for Native Americans, though items that were removed for other groups also would have a (presumably modified) effect on the values for Native Americans. This effect raises a question as to what degree of correlation of DIF values exists between different subgroups.

The decrease in the maximum negative DIF value for Math for the Native American/White comparison is somewhat more problematic, both because it represents greater differential difficulty for the focal group and because the magnitude of the decrease is large compared to the standard deviation of the DIF values. However, three points should be kept in mind: First, the maximum negative value of -1.14 for this group is not unusually extreme when compared to the other maximum negative values for Math; second, the group of Native Americans on which these values are based is likely to be very small and the values, therefore, are likely to be less reliable and more prone to substantial changes in different samples; and, third, when the first few SATs were assembled, only about 65% to 75% of the item pool had been screened for DIF, so each of these tests included a substantial minority of unscreened items.

In summary, in all but three instances the maximum positive and negative DIF values became less extreme or, in one case, remained the same as a result of screening for DIF. The effect on negative DIF was larger than the effect on positive DIF: For the Verbal sections, the median extreme value changed from -2.51 to -1.46 (a third of a standard deviation on the delta scale of 3); for the Mathematical sections, the median changed from -1.70 to -1.14 (.2 SD). For both Verbal and Math, the changes in the positive median were in the second decimal.

Tables 16.7 and 16.8 give difficulty and discrimination information for SATs administered in 1988 (without DIF screening) and 1989 (with DIF screening). Information is included on four test editions—one given in March, one in May, and two in June—for each year. Table 16.7 gives item difficulty means and standard deviations for each edition by year and test content. The information given shows that means and standard deviations changed only slightly between 1988 and 1989, indicating that DIF screening had no appreciable effect on the item difficulty characteristics of the test forms. Table 16.8 gives item discrimination (r-biserial) means and standard deviations for each form by year and test content. Again, the slight changes indicate that DIF screening had no appreciable effect on the item discrimination characteristics of these forms.

Because we observed moderate relationships between DIF values and both difficulty and discrimination in the pretest pool, it follows that the statistical specifications of the test were maintained because the SAT item pools were large enough to permit some loss.

HOW DOES DIF SCREENING AFFECT AVERAGE TEST SCORES?

The final question we could answer in this analysis is whether DIF screening affects average scores. Figure 16.5 shows Verbal and Mathematical mean scores expressed as effect sizes (the difference between the focal and reference group means divided by their pooled standard deviation). Effect sizes for tests administered in 1988 (without DIF screening) are plotted against tests administered in 1989 (with DIF screening). Because all of the points fall on or near the 45° line, it is clear that the relative performances of focal and reference groups did not change as a result of initial DIF implementation. In other words, any difference in performance between the focal and reference groups in 1988 was virtually unchanged in 1989. It should be noted, however, that although the changes were slight, the advantage in Mathematics scores for Asian Americans consistently decreased as a result of DIF implementation.

Why did not DIF screening improve focal groups' test scores? First, recall that items with large positive DIF (those that are differentially difficult for male or White test takers) are screened as well as those with large negative DIF. This policy results in a more unidimensional test, a test that is measuring the same construct for all groups analyzed. The policy also makes any large changes in group means unlikely. The final justification of this policy must await construct validation, emphasizing predictive studies, which soon will be possible. Students tested between March of 1989 and January of 1990, the high school class of 1990, will receive their freshman grades in the spring of 1991.

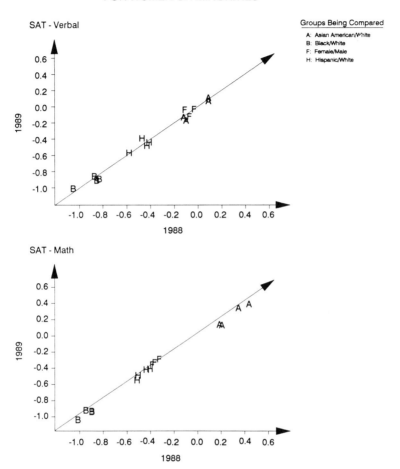

FIG. 16.5. Effect sizes for tests developed without DIF screening (1988) versus tests developed with DIF screening (1989). Note that points represent standardized differences between 1988 and 1989 group means for tests administered in March, May, and June (ethnic information for two June forms is included).

In fact, most of the DIF observed was negative (110 −C-items in Table 16.1, compared to 54 +C items), and one of the clearest changes in the DIF-screened final tests was in the balance of negative to positive DIF items. In this case, it would seem theoretically possible for DIF screening to increase average focal-group scores slightly. However, one must recall that there were relatively few C-DIF items. Table 16.5 shows that in four tests introduced before DIF screening, there were 20 verbal negative C-items and 2 math negative C-items. Under optimum conditions (assuming no change in positive items and that the replacements for negative DIF items had zero DIF) and allowing roughly 7 scaled-score points for each item, the maximum verbal gain from dropping five negative items per test would be about 5 scaled-score points, spread over five focal groups.

SUMMARY

The information presented in the tables and graphs and discussed in the preceding sections indicates that, although implementation of DIF analysis procedures did cause a reduction in the number of B- and C-items, this change did not have a substantial effect either on test characteristics such as item difficulty and item discrimination or on the average test scores of focal groups relative to their corresponding reference groups. Between 1988 and 1989, the percentage of non-A-items decreased, the standard deviations of the mean DIF values decreased, and the maximum DIF values, for the most part, became less extreme; however, item difficulty and discrimination changed very little. Furthermore, the performance of each focal group, relative to its corresponding reference group, did not change significantly between the 2 years. This, perhaps, should not be considered surprising because the number of C-items from the 1987–1988 pretest pool (prior to DIF implementation) was fairly small relative to the total number of items in the pool. The 1989 tests, therefore, were probably not significantly different than they would have been had DIF analyses not been done and the scores of the test takers would not be expected to have been greatly affected.

The appearance of a positive relationship between item difficulty and DIF and a negative relationship between item discrimination and DIF has not yet been explained adequately. Floor and ceiling effects may have contributed to some extent to the relationships. However, the fact that DIF statistics are corrected for continuity in order to lessen the impact of floor and ceiling effects suggests that there may be some other factor or factors involved.

17 Practical Questions in the Use of DIF Statistics in Test Development

Michael Zieky
Educational Testing Service

Measures of differential item functioning (DIF) can help test developers to identify questions that may be unfair for members of sampled groups. DIF can, therefore, be an extremely useful tool for test developers. The use of DIF in test development, however, raises many questions. DIF statistics are often difficult to interpret. They are used to make decisions in the controversial and emotionally charged contexts of item and test bias. Furthermore, the decisions associated with DIF are likely to be scrutinized in the adversarial arenas of legislation and litigation.

The purpose of this chapter is to explore the questions raised when DIF statistics are introduced as routine components in an ongoing, large-scale test development process. Our experiences at Educational Testing Service (ETS) are used to illustrate the questions that were raised and our current responses to those questions. Procedures for the use of DIF in test development are still evolving. As our knowledge and experience increase, we expect to make improvements to the procedures.

Other chapters of this book are devoted to the statistical aspects of DIF. This chapter focuses on the following practical questions:

- What should the matching criterion be?
- Should use of DIF be symmetrical?
- Should use of DIF to eliminate items be automatic or judgmental?
- Which groups should be analyzed and how should those groups be defined?
- How should DIF data be presented to test developers?
- When and how should DIF data be used in the test development process?

- How large should sample sizes for DIF analysis be?
- What have been the effects of using DIF on the test development process?

WHAT SHOULD THE MATCHING CRITERION BE?

DIF analyses require that examinees be matched in terms of relevant knowledge, skill, and ability before their performance on test items can be compared. A major question is what to use as a matching criterion. No perfect matching criterion exists. If one did, we would no longer need our admittedly imperfect tests. Course grades, for example, mean very different things in different schools. Even within the same school, grades mean different things in different courses. In fact, even in the same course in the same school, grades may mean different things if awarded by different teachers. If grades are not appropriate, what can be used?

To people trained in measurement, the use of test scores as a matching criterion is an obvious solution. Many discrimination indices use test scores as criteria, and we are comfortable with the concept of judging an item in the context of the test that includes the item. To people without training in measurement, however, the entire process may seem suspiciously circular. Using a "biased test" to help find "biased questions" may make the use of DIF seem pointless or misleading to them.

Test scores, however, are almost always the only available practical matching criteria. They are obviously relevant to whatever knowledge, skill, and ability are being measured by the test. Their reliability and validity can be empirically determined, and they are obtained under standardized conditions for all examinees. Operational use of DIF at ETS, therefore, employs test scores as the matching criteria.

To help reduce the problem of perceived circularity for DIF analyses done at ETS, the following procedures are used: Whenever it is technically feasible to do so, before operational use of a set of items as a matching criterion, a preliminary DIF analysis is done. Items that have elevated values of DIF are removed from the matching criterion before it is used in an operational DIF analysis. Test developers inspect the modified matching criterion to ensure that it is still reasonable in terms of the content and statistical aspects of the remaining items before it is used operationally.

If, for example, a test consists of 100 items, 3 items may be removed from the test as a result of the preliminary DIF analysis before scores on the test are used as operational matching criteria. On the basis of the remaining 97 items, the people who have taken the test can be divided into clusters determined by their scores: one cluster containing people with scores of 97; another cluster containing people with scores of 96; and so on. The people in each cluster are certainly not identical because no test can be a perfect measure of any knowledge or skill.

However, the people in each cluster will be quite closely matched in terms of what the test is measuring, if the test is reasonably unidimensional.

SHOULD USE OF DIF BE SYMMETRICAL?

When DIF statistics are applied to items, differences in difficulty that *favor* minority groups and women are found as well as the more conventionally expected differences that favor White and male examinees. For example, a verbal aptitude item containing the word *emollient* was found to favor female examinees, and a verbal aptitude item containing the word *commodious* was found to favor Hispanic examinees. Should items that favor minority group members or women be identified by DIF statistics as well as items that favor majority group members or men?

The response to the question is based on the meaning that is assigned to the word *bias*. If bias is thought of as negatively affecting only minority group members or women, then the use of DIF statistics to identify items that are differentially difficult for only those groups is sensible. If, however, bias is seen as any invalid difference between groups, then a symmetrical use of DIF is more appropriate. The decision made at ETS was to treat DIF symmetrically to identify items. The procedures for use of DIF described in a later section of this chapter deal with items that are differentially more difficult for the members of *any* group for which DIF data are available.

It is important to note that using DIF symmetrically to identify items does not necessarily mean that all identified items will be treated in the same way. In the example just cited, Hispanic examinees found the word *commodious* easier than did a matched group of White examinees because there is a similar word in Spanish with a similar meaning. The fact that knowledge of Spanish makes the meaning of an English word more easily recognized does not necessarily make the item unfair for non-Spanish speakers, as long as the word is a valid sample of the content the test is intended to measure. The use of judgment in evaluating the fairness of such items is discussed in the next section.

SHOULD USE OF DIF TO ELIMINATE ITEMS BE AUTOMATIC OR JUDGMENTAL?

If a statistic existed that could *prove* that a test item was biased, then it would be quite reasonable, even laudable, to forbid the use of items that had been so proven. However, no such statistic exists. Raw differences in percentages correct between groups confound real group differences in relevant knowledge, skill, and ability with differences that may have been caused by unfairness in the item. Raw differences, therefore, can not be used as proof of bias.

It is important to realize that DIF is *not* a synonym for *bias*. The item response theory based methods, as well as the Mantel–Haenszel and standardization methods of DIF detection, will identify questions that are not measuring the same dimension(s) as the bulk of the items in the matching criterion. Certainly, multidimensionality is not synonymous with bias. For example, a quantitative test may consist primarily of algebra items with relatively few geometry items. If matching is done on the basis of the total score, the geometry items are likely to be identified as having elevated values of the DIF statistic. If the test consisted primarily of geometry items with a few algebra items, then the algebra items would be so identified. Another reason why DIF is not synonymous with bias is that DIF statistics are unstable when sample sizes are small. A certain number of items will be identified as having elevated levels of DIF by chance alone.

Therefore, judgment is required to determine whether or not the difference in difficulty shown by the DIF index is *unfairly* related to group membership. The judgment of fairness is based on whether or not the difference in difficulty is believed to be related to the construct being measured. Consider the example of *commodious* again. A knowledge of Spanish, or any other Romance language, can improve a student's ability to define English words with Latin roots. A real improvement in a construct-related skill would exist because the items are intended to measure breadth of vocabulary in English. Thus, even though the item was identified as having elevated values of DIF, it would not necessarily be eliminated from an operational test. If, on the other hand, the word *commodious* had been part of the text used to state the problem in a mathematics item, the difference in difficulty would be unrelated to the construct of quantitative ability, and the item might be judged to be unfair and might be removed.

The fairness of an item depends directly on the purpose for which a test is being used. For example, a science item that is differentially difficult for women may be judged to be fair in a test designed for the certification of science teachers because the item measures a topic that every entry-level science teacher should know. However, that same item, with the same DIF value, may be judged to be unfair in a test of general knowledge designed for all entry-level teachers. The decision made at ETS, therefore, was that appropriate use of DIF requires procedures that incorporate the judgments of trained test developers and subject-matter specialists.

WHICH GROUPS SHOULD BE ANALYZED AND HOW SHOULD THOSE GROUPS BE DEFINED?

Routine use of DIF requires precise definitions of the groups to be analyzed. Because the purpose of DIF is to identify questions that may be unfair, the obvious groups to be analyzed are those for which fairness has become a societal concern: Asian, Black, Hispanic, Native American, and female examinees. DIF analyses have also been performed for examinees with disabilities.

The current policy at ETS is that the groups used for DIF analyses should consist predominantly, though not necessarily entirely, of the type of people for whom the test is intended. Therefore, except for tests designed for special populations and for tests of foreign languages, the samples are to consist predominantly of people who have been educated primarily in schools in the United States and whose ability to comprehend English is within the range expected of native English speakers. If an overwhelming majority of those sampled meet the criteria of U.S. education and competence in English, ETS procedures do not require further refinement of the samples by excluding all others.

HOW SHOULD DIF DATA BE PRESENTED
TO TEST DEVELOPERS?

Test developers at ETS often work with large amounts of quantitative data on each item: difficulty, discrimination, number of people choosing each option, mean score of the people choosing each option, omit rate, and so forth. The addition of DIF data on as many as five groups per item could result in information overload. For that reason, the DIF statistics at ETS are presented on scales that are familiar to test developers, and the items are grouped into three categories to highlight important distinctions.

Two measures of DIF are routinely used at ETS: the Mantel–Haenszel (MH) statistic and the standardized P-Difference. (See chapter 3 by Dorans & Holland for more details on these measures). The Mantel–Haenszel statistic can be defined as the average factor by which the odds that members of one group will answer an item correctly exceed the corresponding odds for *comparable* members of the other group. The Mantel–Haenszel statistic is, therefore, in the form of an odds–ratio. Even though odds–ratios have certain desirable statistical properties, the numbers are not intuitively meaningful for most people. (Is an odds ratio of 1.23 big or small?)

To obtain a statistic that is more meaningful to staff at ETS, the odds–ratios have been transformed to an index that can be interpreted directly in terms of differences in the difficulty of items. The DIF statistic is expressed as differences on the delta scale, which is commonly used by test developers at ETS to indicate the difficulty of test questions.[1] For that statistic, known as Mantel Haenszel delta difference (*MH D-DIF*), a value of 1.00 means that one of the two groups being analyzed found the item to be one delta point harder than did comparable members of the other group. (Except for hard or easy items, a difference of one delta is very roughly equal to a difference of 10 points in percentage correct between groups.) The Standardized P-Difference can be interpreted directly as the difference in proportion correct on the question between matched members of

---

[1]The delta scale is an inverse normal transformation of percentage correct to a linear scale with a mean of 13 and standard deviation of 4.

the groups being compared. Although the Mantel–Haenszel statistic is preferred for detecting DIF statistically, the Standardized P-Difference is preferred for describing the size of the DIF that has been found. (See chapter 6 by Wainer for more information on this issue.) The two measures of DIF are, of course, highly related to one another because they measure the same phenomenon. By using the two measures of DIF, however, test developers at ETS are able to capitalize on the particular strengths of each one.

At ETS, we have adopted the convention of having negative values of MH D-DIF or Standardized P-Difference mean that the question is differentially more difficult for the *focal group* (generally Asian, Black, Hispanic, Native American, or female examinees). Positive values of MH D-DIF or Standardized P-Difference mean that the question is differentially more difficult for the *reference group* (generally White or male examinees). Both positive and negative values of the DIF statistic are found and are taken into account by our procedures.

On the basis of MH D-DIF, items are classified into three categories. The category into which an item will be placed depends on two factors: the absolute value of MH D-DIF and whether or not the value is statistically significant. It is important to use absolute value in addition to significance because even an extremely small DIF value could be statistically significant merely because the analysis had been based on a large number of examinees.

The three categories carry the labels *A, B,* and *C*. Category A contains the items with negligible or nonsignificant DIF. Categories B and C contain items with statistically significant values of DIF. Category B contains the items with slight to moderate values of DIF, and Category C contains the items with moderate to large values of DIF. The procedures for using DIF described here are based on the categories into which the items have been classified. The exact definitions of the categories follow:

Category A)   MH D-DIF not significantly different from zero
OR
absolute value less than 1.0

Category B)   MH D-DIF significantly different from zero and absolute value of at least 1.0
AND EITHER
(1) less than 1.5
OR
(2) not significantly greater than 1.0

Category C)   MH D-DIF significantly greater than 1.0
AND
absolute value 1.5 or more

Because every item may have as many as five different DIF statistics (one for each of the groups being analyzed), the decision was made that the category of an item would depend on the worst case. For example, if an item is in Category A for three groups, Category B for one group, and Category C for one group, the item would be classified as Category C. As a result, each item will fall into only one category.

The categories allow test developers to use DIF efficiently. In addition, the complete set of DIF data are available for any test developers who care to use them.

WHEN AND HOW SHOULD DIF DATA BE USED?

DIF data may be applied throughout the test development process. At ETS, DIF may be used in setting specifications for tests, assembling tests, before reporting scores, and after score reporting.

One of the most important stages of the entire test development process is that of setting specifications—establishing the blueprint that will guide the rest of the developmental effort. Test specifications detail the content and skills that are to be measured and indicate how those attributes are to be measured. The setting of specifications is most often done by committees of subject-matter experts, instructors, and job incumbents, all of whom may use data from curriculum surveys, task analyses of behavior on the job, inspection of widely used texts, mail surveys, and interviews.

As more DIF data are gathered over time and as more research is performed, certain reasonably consistent relationships between aspects of the contents of items and the size and direction of their DIF values are becoming known. (See chapter 14 by Schmitt, Holland, & Dorans for examples of these findings.) These relationships will be made available to the committee members as they determine the content and skills to be measured. At ETS, a feedback loop has been established between the DIF data-gathering and analysis activities and the establishment of specifications for new or revised tests. For each program that gathers DIF data, an experienced test developer has been given the responsibility of preparing summary reports for use by the committees.

As described by Ramsey in chapter 8 of this volume, every item in every test developed at ETS is scrutinized by specially trained reviewers who follow an extensive set of guidelines to ensure that items are not offensive, do not reinforce negative stereotypes, and that the questions are appropriate for our multicultural society. It is important to note that DIF is *not* a replacement for that sort of scrutiny. Even if an item shows no differential difficulty, it should not be included in a test if it fails the review criteria. The appropriate use of DIF data is as an additional safeguard to help ensure the fairness of test items, not as a replacement for reviews of items for appropriateness.

Once items have been written and reviewed, they may be administered to students in a pretest to gather data before the items are scored in a final form. Ideally, for the largest testing programs, the pretest samples will include enough focal and reference group members to justify the computation of DIF statistics. Eventually, for some testing programs, a large number of pretested items will be available in a pool from which the test assembler will select the best set of items to meet the specifications that have been set for a final form.

To ensure that DIF will be used appropriately in building final forms from pretested items, the following procedures have been instituted at ETS:

- The content and statistical specifications for the test must be met.

- Large form-to-form variations in DIF in tests made from the same pool of items must be avoided. Test assemblers making more than one test from a pool of items should not use up all of the questions in Category A or the items in Category B with the lowest DIF values in the first tests to be assembled, thereby forcing later tests to have progressively larger DIF values.

- Within the previously mentioned constraints, items from Category A should be selected in preference to items from Categories B or C.

- For items in Category B, when there is a choice among otherwise equally appropriate questions and the equivalence of tests made from the pool can be maintained, items with smaller absolute DIF values should be selected in preference to items with larger values.

- Items from Category C will *not* be used unless they are judged to be fair and essential to meet test specifications.

- If Category C items must be used, the test assembler will document the reason and will explain why the items are not unfairly related to group membership. A reviewer will check to make sure that the use of Category C items was indeed necessary and that the items are fair.

The procedures have been designed to result in the selection of the most appropriate set of items in a final form that meets all of the content and statistical specifications that have been established while allowing the assembly of parallel forms over time.

Using DIF data to help in the selection of items is the most appropriate way to employ DIF. However, not all testing programs are able to pretest items before they are used in a final form. Even those that administer pretests may not have large enough samples of focal and reference group members to compute useful statistics. Such programs must still apply DIF if sufficient samples of examinees in the various groups can be obtained during the brief period after the test has been administered, but before the scores have been released. The analyses performed at that stage require the identification and review of all Category C items. In addition, many test developers choose to exceed the requirements and review the Category B items that are almost in Category C.

One of the difficult decisions that must be made is how to treat the flagged items at that stage. One possibility is to treat all the Category C items as subject to removal unless they can be shown to be essential to meet important test specifications as well as judged to be fair. The other possibility is to treat the Category C items as subject to retention unless they are judged to be unfairly related to group membership or found to be flawed in some other way. Because the test has already been administered, examinees have spent time responding to the flagged items. As a result, they may not have reached other items in the test. For that reason, items should not be eliminated lightly. The decision made at ETS, therefore, was to eliminate only those items that have been judged to be unfairly related to group membership or have been found to be otherwise flawed. To avoid the possibility that test developers may be too lenient in judging items that they have previously selected for inclusion, the procedures established at ETS require that the items identified at that stage pass multiple reviews by people who have not worked on the test before, if the items are to be retained for scoring. As an additional safeguard, external reviewers who are not affiliated with ETS participate in review sessions when possible.

Once test scores have been released, further DIF analyses may be performed if sufficient additional samples of people are available to provide significantly more information than was previously obtained. These post-hoc analyses provide the most stable data because they are performed on the largest samples. The analyses are rich sources of data for the generation and confirmation of hypotheses about DIF.

HOW LARGE SHOULD SAMPLE SIZES BE?

There is a need to decide how many people must be available in the groups being compared before a testing program will be required to perform DIF analyses. If large sample sizes are required, the resulting DIF statistics will be more stable. However, because DIF by its very nature depends on the analysis of minority groups, setting the sample sizes too high will limit the use of DIF to only the largest testing programs.

ETS has selected rather small sample sizes to trigger the need to do DIF analyses. The decision to do so was made after weighing the harm that could be caused by relatively unstable statistics against the harm that could be caused by failure to do any analyses at all.

If the sample sizes are small, then some items with no real DIF may be misclassified as having DIF. Other items with real DIF will be misclassified as having no DIF. Even though some items with real DIF may be missed, they would certainly have been missed if no analyses had been done. The only loss associated with using small samples, therefore, is that some items will be given additional reviews or unnecessarily be given lower priority in selection for operational forms.

The sample sizes currently in force at ETS are:

- For use of DIF statistics in test assembly, at least 100 people must be available in the smaller of the groups being compared, and the smaller and larger groups together must sum to at least 500 people.
- For use of DIF statistics after tests have been administered but before scores are reported, at least 200 people must be available in the smaller of the groups being compared, and the smaller and larger groups together must sum to at least 600 people.
- For use after score reporting, at least 500 people should be available in the smaller group for the analyses of previously unanalyzed groups. Analyses done earlier should be repeated if the sample is sufficiently larger than the one previously analyzed to cut the earlier standard error of the DIF statistic in half. (That takes roughly about four times as many people in the sample.)

WHAT HAVE BEEN THE EFFECTS OF USING DIF ON THE TEST DEVELOPMENT PROCESS?

The effects of using DIF on the statistical characteristics of tests have been discussed in other chapters. The use of DIF has had effects on test developers as well as on tests. The most evident effect has been to sensitize item writers and test assemblers to the effects on various groups of the settings and contexts of items. A grammar item that is based on a sentence dealing with weapons may have different DIF values than a grammar item based on a sentence about children, even if the items are measuring exactly the same grammatical point. Reading passages concerning focal group members tend to be differentially easier for members of the focal groups discussed in the passages. DIF has pointed to areas in which specifications could be improved. For example, some words with Latin roots tend to have different DIF values than words with Germanic roots. Specifications could be enhanced by determining the most appropriate mix of words with the two types of roots.

The use of DIF statistics has been compared to turning a microscope on the test development process. The use of DIF procedures has caused us to focus more clearly on exactly what knowledge, skills, and abilities we are trying to measure. In the long run, the continued use of DIF statistics will result in more valid as well as fairer tests.

CONCLUSION

In all of our work with the index of differential item functioning, as with any other statistic, we must constantly keep in mind the fact that numbers cannot make decisions for us. The subject of differential item functioning is extremely complicated and it touches on some very sensitive issues. We must take great care not to allow some quantitative system to take the place of informed judgment. We have an obligation to test-takers, to test-users, and to the public to ensure to the best of our ability that tests developed by ETS are free of questions that are inappropriately difficult for members of different groups.

18 The Use of Differential Item Functioning Statistics: A Discussion of Current Practice and Future Implications

Robert L. Linn
University of Colorado at Boulder

Michael Zieky (chapter 17 of this text) considered eight practical questions regarding the use of differential item functioning (DIF) in test development. Each of these questions has important implications for test development practice. Answers to these questions obviously are needed in order for DIF to be used as part of the test development, form assembly, scoring, and reporting processes of an operational testing program. The answers also may have implications for the development and justification of the content specifications of future tests and for the construct validity of the resulting measures.

The following discussion is organized around the eight practical questions posed by Zieky. Brief consideration then is given to possible artifacts in the DIF categorization of items.

WHAT SHOULD THE MATCHING CRITERION BE?

As Zieky indicated, the Educational Testing Service (ETS) uses test scores, where feasible, with some removal of items with large DIF prior to the operational computations. Three obvious bases for judging this choice of a matching criterion are (a) practicality, (b) relative superiority among available alternatives, and (c) acceptability to the public and to test critics.

Practicality.   Evaluation with regard to the first of these characteristics is simple and clear. Because test scores now are being used as the matching criterion in the routine computation of DIF statistics, it is obvious that they do provide a matching criterion that is practical for operational use.

Relative Superiority. Although practical, it is less obvious that test scores provide the best available matching criterion. In my judgment, however, test scores probably are the best available alternative for matching in most cases. The ideal matching variable would be a perfectly valid and reliable, unbiased measure of the developed ability the test is intended to measure. Such a measure obviously is unavailable and test scores are generally the closest approximation that is available.

Even in the case of the aforementioned unrealistic ideal matching variable, there would be a need to be concerned about the dimensionality of the domain being assessed. In other words, unidimensionality should be added to the list of characteristics for the ideal matching criterion. Otherwise, DIF may be associated with valid differences along different dimensions. The same may be said for the use of test scores. To the extent that the content domain of the test is relatively heterogeneous and spans more than a single dimension, there is apt to be a need to use separate subscores as the matching criteria for different subsets of items. With this caveat, however, test scores are probably the best available matching criterion for operational use in most cases.

Nonetheless, there are some situations where other criteria may be of interest. The addition of measures of prior instructional experiences or demographic characteristics other than those used to define reference and focal groups in a DIF analysis, for example, may lead to better understanding of DIF patterns. For some purposes, it also may be desirable to use variables other than the test being analyzed for matching. A recent study by Angoff and Johnson (1988) provides an illustration of use of measures other than the test under study to match. Angoff and Johnson used DIF analyses to study the differential performance of groups of people with different college experiences on the items of the Graduate Record Examination after matching on Verbal and Mathematics scores obtained four years earlier on the Scholastic Aptitude Test. Such work is necessarily quite separate from the immediate operational demands of test development, however.

Acceptability to the Public and to Critics.   I agree with Zieky's concern that the process of using a test that is perceived to be "biased" to control for differences in overall performance before looking for biased items does seem "suspiciously circular." Test scores may be the best available practical matching variable, but it does not follow necessarily that they will be viewed as acceptable for this purpose by test critics or a broader public. On the contrary, test critics already have attacked the use of test scores as the matching criterion and I expect they will continue to do so. But this is not unique to the area of DIF.

It is unrealistic to expect that there is a technical solution—better statistical techniques, better matching criteria, and so forth—that would lead to ready acceptability. We cannot expect DIF to satisfy someone who does not want tests to be used or someone whose major concern is "impact," rather than with items that function differently for groups that are equivalent in terms of the knowledge and skills that the test is intended to measure.

We should recognize that DIF techniques, whether based on the Mantel–Haenszel, the standardization, or an item response theory (IRT) procedure, all suffer from the serious limitation that they can detect only items that show large differences in one direction or the other relative to the total set of items. One cannot expect DIF procedures to detect "pervasive bias." Critics have a point when they argue that there is a kind of circularity. To trust the procedures you need to have some general level of acceptance of the overall test. Studies of predictive bias also require the acceptance of the criterion measure, or more specifically, an assumption that the criterion is unbiased. However, the corresponding assumption for DIF procedures that depend on an internal criterion rather than an external criterion is harder to defend.

The fact that DIF procedures cannot be expected to detect pervasive bias should not be interpreted to mean that the procedures are of no value. Rather, it suggests that alone they are insufficient. DIF analyses need to be used in conjunction with judgmental review of test content such as those described by Ramsey (see chapter 8 of this text), by investigations of relationships to external criterion measures for focal and reference groups, and investigations of the construct validity of the measures for these different groups.

SHOULD USE OF DIF BE SYMMETRICAL?

Zieky reported that the ETS practice is to treat items symmetrically to identify items—that is, to flag items that have either large negative (lower average performance for the focal group than for matched reference group members) or large positive (higher average performance the focal group) DIF values. There are bound to be both positive and negative DIF values. Large negative DIF values must be balanced by positive DIF values and will have an average of approximately zero. Although this does not mean necessarily that there will be equal numbers of positive and negative "C" items (i.e., items with the most extreme DIF values), in practice, both positive and negative C flags do occur.

According to ETS policy, both types of flagged items have to be reviewed. However, this does not imply that the flagged items will be treated the same way. A decision may be made to retain an item with large DIF, based on review of an item in terms of what the test is intended to measure. Zieky gave an example, where the word *commodious* was retained despite a large DIF value favoring Hispanic test takers.

What Zieky's examples does not indicate is what happens most often in practice. What percentage of items in the C+ category are retained after review? What percentage of the items in C− category are retained? Can the rationales for retaining the two categories of large DIF items be characterized? If so, do the rationales differ?

My expectation is that items with positive DIF are more likely to be retained than items with negative DIF. The retention of positive DIF items is less likely to cause problems with external reviewers such as the New York Advisory Committee for Bias in Standardized Testing than the retention of negative DIF items. But this is a pragmatic reason for my expectation and begs the question of whether DIF should be treated symmetrically, not only in the categorization of items, but in the bottom-line decisions to retain or eliminate an item from a test and in the longer term use of DIF information to reevaluate the content specifications of tests.

I believe this issue is linked to Zieky's third question and is best considered in that context.

SHOULD USE OF DIF TO ELIMINATE ITEMS BE AUTOMATIC OR JUDGMENTAL?

Zieky made a key point with regard to this question. DIF does not prove bias. For that matter, the lack of DIF does not prove lack of bias. As was indicated earlier, DIF cannot be expected to detect pervasive bias. The procedures are designed to detect items that function differently than the set of items that comprise the test. Although DIF can be operationally defined, whether by the use of the Mantel–Haenszel, a standardization procedure, or an IRT-based procedure, bias cannot. Nonetheless, there is always some informal, possibly quite variable, notion of bias lurking behind the DIF analyses.

In his introductory comments at the start of this conference on DIF, Greg Anrig noted that a high-priority goal for ETS is to do the best job possible to make tests "bias free." DIF procedures were introduced not merely as another general item analysis tool, but because of a concern about the possibility that factors that are irrelevant to the developed abilities that tests are intended to measure may place members of one gender or of one racial/ethnic group at an unfair disadvantage relative to another. It was hoped, in fact, that DIF would help ETS to do the best job it can to make tests bias free.

Although admittedly vague, I believe there is a general concept that biased items are ones that place a particular group at an unfair disadvantage that is due to group differences other than the knowledge, skills, and developed abilities that the test is intended to measure. We do not have a way of operationalizing this concept directly, but the idea of an item that functions differently for groups that have been matched on total score is related. The problem is just that, however. DIF is related to the general concept of an item that should be called biased to a particular group in light of the intended purpose of the test, but as Zieky said, DIF and bias are not synonymous.

Because DIF is not synonymous with bias, I do not think that the use of DIF to eliminate items should be an automatic process. Judgment as well as DIF statistics are needed.

The test is an imperfect matching criterion. Consequently, an item may have a large DIF value because it is revealing differences in knowledge or skill that the test, in fact, is intended to measure, but the total test score has not provided an adequate match on that aspect of the construct being measured.

It has been found fairly consistently, for example, that items based on reading passages dealing with technical science material tend to have DIF statistics indicating that on average women do worse than men after controlling for total score (e.g., Lawrence, Curley, & HcHale, 1988; see also O'Neill & McPeek, chapter 12 of this text). Does this mean that such passages should be excluded from reading comprehension tests? I do not think so. Such passages are a legitimate part of the reading materials that students are expected to encounter in high school and college and it is reasonable to expect that they will need to be able to comprehend such reading material in college.

Such findings do pose serious questions about what the specifications for a test should be, however. What proportion of the passages should involve technical science material? How technical should such passages be? Should the proportion of such passages be controlled tightly from form to form of the test? I return to such questions later. But for now let me just note that I agree with the decision to "incorporate judgments of trained test developers and subject-matter specialists" in the use of DIF statistics to make decisions about item elimination.

I would assume that the burden should be on those who want to retain an item with high DIF to provide a justification in terms of the intended purposes of the test. In the previous example of technical science passages, for instance, I would think that evidence that men tend to take more science courses than women would be relevant. The scope of reading materials contained in the test specifications also would be relevant, though the latter should be the focus of critical review in light of accumulated evidence from DIF analyses and the subject matter coverage expected in high school and college.

With regard to the previous question about the symmetrical use of DIF, I think that it is quite reasonable to review both positive and negative DIF items. Because the primary motivation for conducting DIF analyses comes from concerns about possible bias against the focal groups, however, I believe it should be much easier to retain an item with positive DIF (e.g., a C+ item) than an item with equal negative DIF.

WHICH GROUPS SHOULD BE ANALYZED AND HOW SHOULD THOSE GROUPS BE DEFINED?

The protected class groups that are now the focus are the most obvious choice for DIF analyses conducted as part of operational testing programs. Zieky called our attention to the fact that even this question is not quite as simple as it may appear initially. The use of screens for English language dominance, for example, represents one type of complication or refinement. Another possible refinement is the use of more specific criteria to define reference and focal groups. The most obvious example of the latter extension would be to make distinctions among Puerto Rican, Mexican-American, Cuban, and other Hispanic groups. Distinctions also might be made using combinations of currently used characteristics or on the basis on other characteristics (gender by racial/ethnic group, urban vs. rural).

Breakdowns such as urban/rural are unlikely candidates for routine item analyses as part of test development, in part because such breakdowns are not focused on protected classes, and in part because of the practical difficulties of obtaining defensible definitions and dealing with the overload of results. For understanding factors that contribute to DIF, however, we may have more to learn from studying groups defined on characteristics other than those now in use. DIF analyses for groups that have had different numbers of years of high school science or that differed in other educationally relevant background experiences, for example, are apt to be more informative about the experiential factors that contribute to DIF than are the current DIF analyses.

For operational use of DIF, I would guess that there are already about as many groups as can be considered reasonably at this time. Special studies using more refined groups (e.g., Puerto Rican, Mexican American, Cuban American, and other Hispanic) are worth pursuing, however, and could lead to a recognition that the approach needs to be expanded at some time in the future.

HOW SHOULD DIF BE PRESENTED TO TEST DEVELOPERS?

As Zieky indicated, information overload is a real concern. The use of the A, B, C category labels with an indication of direction, strikes me as a reasonable attempt to get the critical information to test developers without overwhelming them. Whether this is an effective way of reporting from the test development perspective, however, is something that test developers are better suited to judge than I am. My personal preference would be for some type of graphical presentation of the DIF results, but the level of information provided by the A, B, C categories seems about right.

WHEN SHOULD DIF DATA BE USED?

Zieky indicated that DIF may be used at various stages, including the setting of test specifications, test assembly, before scores are reported, and after scores are reported. In the long run, I think that the most significant of these may be in the setting of test specifications.

As DIF results accumulate, they are likely to raise basic questions about the specifications of test content that are fundamentally issues of construct validity. An early indication of the type of difficult question that an accumulation of DIF results may pose for the setting and justification of test specifications was provided by the results of a study conducted with the National Teacher Examination (NTE) by Medley and Quirk (1974).

The Medley and Quirk (1974) study differed from most DIF analyses in that it involved the construction of experimental subtests for the NTE Common Examination. The 60-item test used in the Medley and Quirk study consisted of 15 fine arts items, 15 literature items, and 30 social studies items. Within each of these three content categories, one third of the times was selected to meet the usual test specifications. Items in this first third were referred to as the *traditional* items. Another third of the items was selected to meet the general content specifications, but, in addition, the items were required to reflect the experiences, accomplishments, or concerns of Blacks. They involved "black authors, artists, writers, musicians, and important historical and political black figures" (Medley & Quirk, 1974, p. 236). The remaining third of the items in each of the three general content areas, in addition to meeting the other content specifications, consisted of items that were required to reflect "modern" culture, that is, to ask questions about contemporary music, art, culture, literature, philosophy, and politics.

The test with its 20 traditional, 20 Black, and 20 modern items then was administered to approximately 500 Black and 500 White examinees at NTE testing centers. Medley and Quirk (1974) found a significant interaction between item category and group. The group means on the three 20-item subtests formed by item category are plotted in Fig. 18.1. In keeping with other information, the mean for Whites is substantially higher—by a bit less than standard deviation—than the mean for Blacks on the traditional items. The group differences are somewhat smaller on the modern items, but still favor the White group by a substantial amount. On the items dealing with contributions of Blacks, however, the Black group has a mean that is higher than the mean for Whites.

The Medley and Quirk (1974) results are more extreme than those from DIF analyses, in part because of the experimental manipulation of item content. However, the results are not the only ones that have shown a relative advantage on the average for minority students on items dealing with contributions of minority group members or on topics of particular relevance to minority group members.

According to content specifications for the Verbal Scholastic Aptitude Test (SAT-V) reported in the 1984 Technical Handbook (Donlon, 1984), each form of the SAT-V is required to contain six reading comprehension passages. The content categories for these six passages are: narrative, biological science, argu-

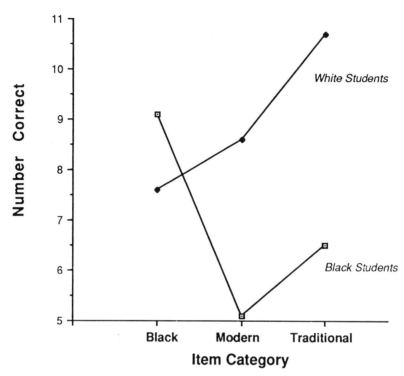

FIG. 18.1.   Black standards do markedly better on items dealing with contribution of Blacks. Data taken from Medley and Quirk (1974).

mentative, humanities, social sciences, and physical sciences. It also is specified that one of the six passages "must have a minority orientation." This requirement for a minority-oriented passage has been in place since December 1977—quite some time before the introduction of DIF on a routine basis.

In 1980 the sensitivity review guidelines were implemented (see Ramsey, chapter 8 of this text, for a description of these guidelines). The guidelines are intended to eliminate materials that women or minority group members are likely to find offensive or patronizing. The guidelines also encourage the use of materials that acknowledge the contributions of women and minority group members.

There is a suggestion in the guidelines that there should be some "balance that acknowledges the cultural diversity of the test-taking population" (ETS, 1987, p. 5). This seems to imply that contributions of women and minorities should be represented adequately in testing materials. But what constitutes adequate representation? Should the contributions of Blacks and Hispanics both be represented in each form of the test or is it sufficient to represent one group on one form and the other on the next? How about Native Americans and Asian-Americans? Answers to questions such as these are not provided in the test specifications.

However, the DIF results suggest that the relative advantage that minority group members have on the average on passages with a minority orientation is specific to the particular minority in question (e.g., O'Neill & McPeek, chapter 12 of this text). For example, a passage concerning contributions of a Black leader is likely to have positive DIF for Black students but not for Hispanic, Asian-American, or Native-American students. This poses a difficult challenge for test development and the creation of more detailed test specifications.

With only six reading passages on an SAT-V, the degrees of freedom are quite limited. Thus there is a need also to consider the discrete verbal items in considering how best to achieve adequate representation and an acceptable balance. The sentence completion items, which are divided into four content areas (aesthetics/philosophy, world of practical affairs, science, and human relations) would seem to provide the best opportunity here, but it is unclear how many of the 15 sentence-completion items would need to involve contributions of women, or of specified minority groups in order to achieve adequate representation or balance.

It obviously is not for me to say what is the right balance. The issue is worthy of serious consideration when the content specifications of a test are reviewed. The accumulation of evidence from DIF studies should help inform that debate, but such evidence cannot be expected to provide an answer.

I believe that available DIF results already pose some difficult questions regarding the specifications of the antonym and analogies sections. Tendencies for homographs (words that are spelled alike but have different meanings) to be more difficult for Asian-Americans, Blacks, and Hispanics than matched Whites (O'Neill & McPeek, chapter 12 of this text) do not imply that homographs should be excluded. Many homographs are part of the vocabulary that a college student needs. But knowing the result should force consideration of questions about the relative frequency of such words, and, more generally, about the basis for selecting and rejecting words for antonyms and analogies. A similar comment could be made about the tendency for true cognates to have DIF values favoring Hispanics, whereas those with false cognates tend to have negative DIF for Hispanics (e.g., O'Neil & McPeek, chapter 12 of this text; Schmitt, Holland, & Dorans, chapter 14 of this text).

HOW LARGE SHOULD SAMPLE SIZES BE?

Compared to the other questions that Zieky addressed, this seems like a fairly simple one. Although there is no clear cutting point below which DIF analyses are not worth doing and above which they are, this is at least a question that has to do with technical questions of sampling error and the relative seriousness of false negative and false positive flags.

The ETS decision to use what strike me as rather small sample sizes was based apparently on the reasoning that false positives—that is, items that are flagged that would not be flagged if data were available, say, for all potential test takers—cause little harm. This is reflected in Zieky's statement that "The only loss associated with using small samples . . . is that some items will be given additional reviews or unnecessarily be given lower priority in selection for operational forms" (see chapter 17 of this text, section entitled How Large Should Sample Sizes Be?).

This position seems reasonable, but it seems to me that the accumulation of a large number of false positives based on small samples may have other disadvantages. Far fewer general principles about test construction have been derived as the result of DIF analyses than most researchers expected when DIF analyses first were being investigated. The majority of items with large DIF values seem to defy explanation of the kind that can lead to more general principles of sound test development practice. More often than not the explanations are post hoc and judges have a rather poor record of predicting which items will or will not be flagged.

The College Board press release in September 1989 that described the release of question-by-question data to the New York Advisory Committee for Bias in Standardized Testing made the difficulty of rationalizing items with large DIF values quite apparent. The press release indicated that 29 of the 955 items on seven forms of the SAT and the Preliminary Scholastic Aptitude Test (PSAT) that were administered in New York State in 1988–1989 showed DIF in the "C" category for one or more of the five group comparisons (see Table 18.1).

Although these flags are only based on New York State test takers, which may explain the lack of flagged items for Native Americans, the number of items identified for any focal group is quite small. Furthermore, a review of the content of the 29 items provides few clues as to the reasons for identification, and no obvious principles, except that DIF is found more on the verbal than math and more on the antonyms than the other verbal item types.

Seventeen of the 29 flagged items involved antonyms, 4 were analogies items, 3 were sentence-completion items, 1 was a reading-comprehension item, and the remaining 4 were math items. All the flagged math items were regular math items rather than quantitative comparisons, but we are talking about a small number of exemplars for any generalizations.

The link between statistical identification of items by DIF analyses and substantive interpretations or judgmental ratings of items is, at best, quite weak. It should be noted that the 29 items found to have large DIF for one or more groups in New York come from operational versions of the SAT and PSAT. Hence, they already have passed many screens, including, I assume, at least for some of the 955 items administered in New York State during 1988–1989, DIF analyses from pretesting or previous operational administrations of the items.

Where items have not passed so many screens or where they are designed intentionally to test hypotheses such as was done in the Medley and Quirk (1974)

TABLE 18.1
Cross-Tabulation of Items Flagged
as Showing DIF in 1989 Report to New York
State by Focal Group and Direction of DIF

Focal Group	Number of Items and Relative Difficulty for Focal Group	
	Easier	Harder
Female	3	8
Native American	0	0
Asian-American	3	4
Black	2	4
Hispanic	3	3

Note. Based on September 1989 College Board Press Release. There were a total of 29 of the 955 items from seven forms of the SAT and PSAT administered in New York State in 1988–1989 that were categorized as having large DIF. The total above is 30 because 1 item was harder for two focal groups (Hispanic and Black).

example and has been done by Scheuneman (1987), the links are stronger than are seen in these SAT and PSAT antonym items. Nonetheless, we still are left with relatively few general principles.

Given the weak link between DIF results and substantively defensible interpretations, I wonder if routine DIF analyses with samples as small as 100 in the focal group will just add more noise to an already noisy system. Consideration needs to be given to the tradeoffs between Type I and Type II errors and the power of the DIF procedures for differences judged to be of practical importance.

WHAT HAVE BEEN THE EFFECTS OF USING DIF ON THE TEST DEVELOPMENT PROCESS?

I would have liked to have heard more in response to this question. The points that Zieky made are intriguing. He suggested, for example, that test "specifications could be enhanced by determining the most valid mix of words" with Latin and Germanic roots. Such a suggestion is getting at what seems to me to be one of the central issues that needs further thought and discussion. That is, how can the accumulated evidence be used to alter test specifications? How should the test specifications be altered as the result of DIF findings? And, what is the process for deciding what, if any, changes in the test specifications should be made?

I could imagine that analyses of the distributions of word frequencies for words with Latin and Germanic roots on some clearly defined corpus of high school or college textbooks and other works likely to be assigned to students might provide an appropriate data base for making such judgments. The Carroll, Davies, and Richman (1971) *Word Frequency Book,* for example, might provide a place to test such an idea, however, the corpus of words used by Carroll et al. is a bit out of date. More important, it is not targeted right for most of the ETS tests and therefore does not include many of the words that appear on tests such as the SAT.

Zieky's suggestion raises much broader questions than the proportion of words with Latin and Germanic roots. His phrase, "the most valid mix," seems to imply that there is an agreed-upon way of judging the most valid mix. Word frequency analyses, for example, could be used to guide the selection of vocabulary on a variety of characteristics in addition to the root of the word. This would lead to tighter test specifications and provide a better basis for judging the content validity of the tests. But Messick (1989), among others, would prefer the label *content relevance* for such judgments and would consider it a weak basis for claiming that validity had been enhanced. More explicit consideration of how the construct validity would be affected by such changes in test specifications is needed.

POSSIBLE ARTIFACTS

Although it does not fall neatly into one of Zieky's questions, I would like to close with a brief consideration of an issue that I believe is of considerable importance for the practical use of DIF results. That is the degree to which DIF statistics are the result of statistical artifacts.

Speededness.   Several reports (e.g., Schmitt & Dorans, 1988) have found evidence of differential speededness and omits. The possible effects of differential speededness and tendencies to omit on DIF seem worthy of more detailed investigation. In addition, however, the fact that differential speededness is observed may have implications for test specifications. Are more generous time limits needed? Would more generous time limits benefit minority test takers as much or more than the elimination of a few items on the basis of DIF results?

Nonresponse to Background Questions.   DIF analyses depend on self-reports of group membership. Allen and Holland (chapter 11 of this text) demonstrated that the DIF results can be quite sensitive to assumptions that are made about nonrespondents. Because of this sensitivity and the relatively high nonresponse rate to racial/ethnic group membership questions, it seems clear that more attention needs to be given to approaches that may reduce the nonresponse rates.

Item Difficulty and Item Discrimination.   DIF statistics are related strongly to more familiar item statistics: overall item difficulty, the biserial correlation of the item with the total test score, and the reference and focal group difference in difficulty. These relationships, particularly the first two, are of concern because they suggest that what is being identified by DIF analyses may be, at least in part, a statistical artifact having to do with differences in item discrimination, and floor and ceiling effects related to item difficulty.

Burton and Burton (chapter 16) provided summaries of DIF statistics for 2,382 items that were pretested for the SAT-V in 1987–1988. From those results it is possible to compute the percentage of items with DIF values in each of the five categories used for reporting test development (C−, B−, A, B+, and C+) as a function of several characteristics, including item difficulty using the ETS delta statistic and the biserial correlation of the item scores with the total test scores.

Figure 18.2 provides a plot of the percentage of items that are categorized as negative C and the percentage of items that are categorized either as negative B

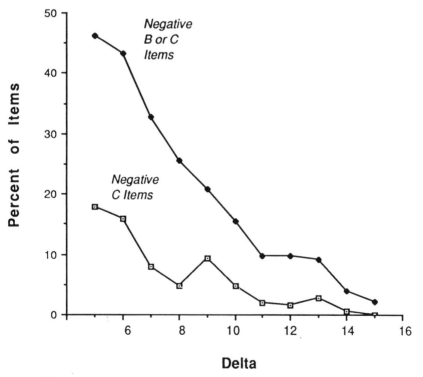

FIG. 18.2.   Percentage of items with negative DIF decreases as item difficulty increases. Data taken from Burton and Burton, chapter 16 of this volume.

or negative C as a function of Delta. As can be seen, relatively easy items are much more likely to be flagged for having negative DIF values of B or C than are difficult items. Although this result may run counter to the naive expectation of test critics who often assume that it is the more esoteric vocabulary that places minority test takers at a greater disadvantage, the results are consistent with what would be expected on psychometric grounds.

Because the items are all multiple choice, it is clear that test takers, regardless of level of knowledge or developed ability, have a nonzero probability of answering an item correctly if they respond to the item. Consider, for example, an IRT model that allows for a nonzero lower asymptote (e.g., the three-parameter logistic model). If item response curves for both the reference and focal groups have the same lower asymptote (pseudochance level) then there will be little chance of detecting DIF for very difficult items because the curves will coincide over much of the range of proficiency levels of the lower scoring group even though they might diverge at higher proficiency levels due to differences in the difficulty or discrimination parameters. Such items only discriminate at the high end of the scale. Very easy items, on the other hand, will discriminate best at the low end of the scale.

DIF values not only are related strongly to item difficulty but also are related to item discrimination as measured by the biserial correlation with total test score. As can be seen in Fig. 18.3, the percentage of negative B or C and the percentage of negative C items increases as a function of the biserial correlation. Items that are related most strongly to total test scores are also most likely to be flagged for having large negative DIF values.

A total of 220 of the 2,382 items summarized by Burton and Burton in chapter 16 of this text had biserial correlations of .60 or higher. Forty (18.2%) of those items with biserials greater than .60 had DIF statistics in the negative C category for one or more focal groups and an additional 37 items (16.8%) had DIF statistics in the negative B category. Thus, slightly over a third of the most highly discriminating items, items that generally would be preferred on classical psychometric grounds, are flagged as having negative B or negative C DIF values and therefore would be given lower priority for use in operational tests. On the other hand, only 2.0% of the 510 items with modest biserials in the .30 to .39 range had DIF values in the negative C category and only 10.4% fell in either the negative B or negative C categories. The percentages are still lower for items with biserials below .30, but presumably those items would receive relatively low priority for inclusion in operational tests on grounds other than DIF.

It may be, as Masters (1988; see also Camilli, chapter 21 of this volume) suggested, that high item discrimination sometimes may be obtained for the wrong reasons and thus items with lower biserials sometimes may be preferred for certain measurement purposes to those with higher biserials. However, it also may be that items with high biserials have a greater tendency to have negative DIF than items with low biserials because the former items provide more valid

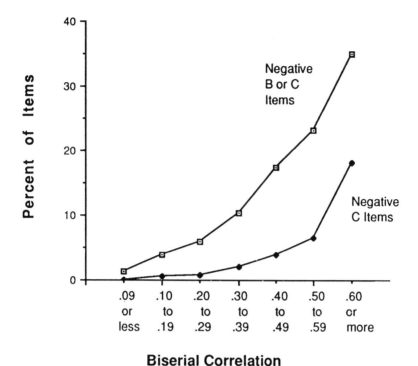

Biserial Correlation

FIG. 18.3.   Percentage of items with negative DIF increases with item-test biserial correlation. Data taken from Burton and Burton, chapter 16 of this volume.

measurement of group differences in the developed abilities than the test is designed to measure. This is an issue that deserves more detailed analysis and review. It also suggests that consideration may need to be given to the use of DIF procedures that do not confound DIF with between-item differences in discrimination level.

CONCLUSION

Greg Anrig opened the October 1989 conference on Differential Item Functioning: Theory and Practice with two questions related to DIF: "What have we learned? What should we do about it?" Although still far less complete than would be desired, the chapters resulting from the conference presentations provide a good set of responses to the first of these questions. A great deal has been learned about the statistical techniques from the simulations conducted by Longford, Holland and Thayer (chapter 9) and from the analyses of sampling and self-selection issue (Allen & Holland, chapter 11). Complicated though they may be, there are some patterns concerned with item content and item type that are identified in the review reported by O'Neill and McPeek (chapter 12) and the approaches described by Schmitt, Holland, and Dorans (chapter 14) promise to strengthen some of the conclusions about item characteristics in the future.

Anrig's second question, however, is the more important question, and not surprisingly, the more difficult to answer. Summarizing and disseminating information about what is known as the result of work with DIF is one response, and the conference and publication of the proceedings is a positive step in that direction. Answering the eight questions posed by Zieky that make DIF a part of the operational test development process is another and I already have commented on those questions and answers. In my judgment, however, the central answer to Anrig's second question has to do with an analysis and rethinking of test specifications.

I believe that enough information has accumulated to make it timely to begin the process of rethinking test specifications and the role that DIF results should have in determining those specifications. Future DIF analyses and refinements of techniques surely will provide additional grist for that mill, but that will continue to be true for some time and substantial changes in test specifications cannot take place overnight anyway. Thus, it is not too early for ETS and its major clients to begin the process of opening up test specifications for a major review, taking into account not only what has been learned from DIF analysis but what has been learned from the past several years of sensitivity reviews. Experienced test development staff and other staff with experience with the sensitivity reviews and DIF research should have an opportunity to have a significant voice in the process. In addition, however, it seems essential for the test specification review process to include significant representation of all of the focal groups involved in current DIF analyses as well as other emphasized in the sensitivity review process.

IV
ANCILLARY ISSUES

This section contains three chapters that are related to DIF but are, in different ways, apart from the main thrust of this book. Nevertheless, they address issues important enough for our understanding of the context of the development of fair tests that we felt it vital to include them.

The first of these chapters is a discussion of test sensitivity review; it is not about DIF. It is, however, intimately related to the broader purposes of DIF studies. It is about test fairness and thus, ultimately, about test validity. All aspects of the testing process must be attuned to the often subtle aspects of life in modern society. The history of testing is littered with instances where sensitivity to issues associated with the backgrounds of examinees was lacking. This is now in the process of changing. The past decade has seen the emergence of a serious attempt to sensitize everyone associated with the production of tests to these issues. In chapter 19, Paul Ramsey presents, as a case study, the experience of the Educational Testing Service in the development of standards for sensitivity review and training. He points out that there is an uncertain relationship between the results of a sensitivity review and a DIF study, that they are both tools used to ensure that the tests given, as well as their supporting documentation, are fair. This may be done to make tests more valid, but irrespective of any changes in validity that such reviews yield, it is done because it is proper that it should be done.

Chapter 20 places the theme of this book into a broader perspective. Much of what is discussed in this volume addresses scientific issues in an analytic way. But this is only part of the picture. The results obtained from even the most carefully conceived and executed studies will only be part of the input that is used in public policymaking. Policy decisions are made in the real world of competing interests and values from which most scientists are somewhat removed. In her chapter, Patricia McAllister carefully traces some of the legislative issues that swirl around testing in general and the study of differential performance of tests and items in particular. Research can be better structured if those doing it maintain an awareness of the larger world. This chapter provides a very good start toward the development of such an awareness.

Gregory Camilli, in chapter 21, contrasts the statistical methods discussed in this volume—DIF methods—and what they are designed to measure, with the concept of item bias. He concludes that they are not necessarily the same thing. He emphasizes the importance of not confusing the two.

19 Sensitivity Review: The ETS Experience as a Case Study

Paul A. Ramsey
Educational Testing Service

THE HISTORY

In September of 1980, Educational Testing Service (ETS) formalized a review process for test items that had been evolving for at least a decade. The codification of this process warranted a publication, the *ETS Test Sensitivity Review Process* (ETS, 1980), developed by a White assistant director of the Office of Corporate Quality Assurance, Ronald Hunter, and a Black test developer, Carole Slaughter, and reviewed by pretty much everyone within the corporation who could read. The introduction to this document, quoting from the *Principles, Policies and Procedural Guidelines Regarding ETS Products and Services* (ETS, 1979)—the immediate forerunner of the current *ETS Standards for Quality and Fairness* (ETS, 1987)—gives two goals for the sensitivity review process: It was to ensure that "specifications for tests [w]ould require material reflecting the cultural background and contributions of women, minorities, and other subgroups" (p. 24), and it committed the company to producing tests that contain no "language, symbols or content which are generally considered potentially offensive, inappropriate for major subgroups of the test-taking population or serving to perpetuate any negative attitude which may be conveyed toward these subgroups" (p. 25). The 1980 *Guidelines* go on to acknowledge that although they "can be applied to any population group, experience has shown that a particularly vigilant effort must be made to evaluate . . . tests from the perspectives of the following groups: Asian Americans, Black Americans, Hispanic Americans, Native Americans, and women" (p. 5).

In 1986, when the *Guidelines* were revised and reissued, the targeted groups were expanded to include "individuals with disabilities" (ETS, 1986). Indeed,

367

as we look at the sensitivity review process over its 10 formalized years, and even before, we see that it is always becoming more inclusive: In 1984, what formerly had been the ETS test sensitivity review process became the ETS sensitivity review process (hereinafter referred to as "the process") when the corporation mandated that all program publications receive a sensitivity review. In 1986, the *Guidelines* were expanded, as noted previously, to cover people with disabilities and also nonprint materials. In 1988, research and statistical reports came under the purview of the process. A review of the process that is currently underway will culminate in the publication of a revised set of guidelines that I suspect again will expand the terrain covered by the process.

A look at the forerunners of the *ETS Test Sensitivity Review Process* (ETS, 1980) suggests the same growth pattern: In 1974, the *ETS Guidelines for Testing Minorities* was published internally. In 1976, the sensitivity arena was enlarged with the distribution of the *ETS Guidelines for Sex Fairness in Tests and Testing Programs*. But the real parent of the current *Guidelines* in terms of tone and content is a series of tracts published by the McGraw-Hill Book Company that has been revised and compiled into the *Guidelines for Bias-Free Publishing* (undated).

The immediate predecessor of sensitivity reviews were minority reviews. These were optional reviews of tests that a testing program director could ask a staff member of color or a woman to perform. There were no promulgated criteria; basically, minority and women staff would read through a test to see if there were "respect signals" in the test, that is, questions about women and/or people of color, or anything in the test that might offend these groups. It was at the discretion of a testing program whether to have these reviews done and whether to act on the findings of the reviewer.

With the issuance of the *ETS Test Sensitivity Review Process* in 1980, what had been "minority reviews" were expanded semantically to include women; thus, they became "sensitivity reviews" (ETS, 1980). These minority reviews that had been optional became mandatory; opinions that minority and women staff members had expressed about tests under the minority review process became judgments informed by corporate-sanctioned criteria made by staff of both genders and any color; and what had been a fairly informal, loose process became, as one might expect at ETS, standardized with forms, rules, and rulers.

THE PROCESSES

The test sensitivity review process, the parent process, has spawned similar processes that I discuss briefly, for the sake of thoroughness, in the publications, research, and statistical areas. All reviews, regardless of the area, must be performed by trained sensitivity reviewers. Even if trained, the author of a document may not perform a sensitivity review on his or her own work. Sen-

sitivity reviewers trained to review tests also may review publications and research reports, but the reverse is not the case because the specialized training
needed to review tests is touched upon only lightly in the training for publications
and research reviewers.

By and large, peers review the work of each other; that is, test assemblers tend
to perform sensitivity reviews of tests, and researchers of research reports. The
organization insists that all in an area be trained but does not require all to
perform sensitivity reviews. Some people feel that they just cannot do a good job
whereas others are opposed to the process on philosophical grounds, seeing it as
a form of censorship. But those who do not do reviews are by far the exception
rather than the rule. The decision to train all has had a fortuitous effect on the
process in that rather than an elite or abhorred, as the case may be, cadre of
people performing sensitivity reviews, sensitivity reviewing has become a part of
the fabric of the organization. On one document a staff member may be a
reviewer whereas on another he or she is the recipient of a review. Another
positive outcome of the decision to train all in the process is that all staff,
regardless of gender or race, are involved in the process. Minority reviews were
the problem and work of minority and women staff; sensitivity reviews, the
responsibility of all ETS staff.

Because it is the most comprehensive, let me begin by describing the test
sensitivity review process. Once a test is assembled in draft form and ready for
the numerous reviews it will receive, a test assembler may ask for a preliminary
or optional sensitivity review to get a reading on whether there are likely to be
any sensitivity problems with the test. This optional review is, understandably,
generally more necessary for verbal than for quantitative or scientific tests. In the
area of reading, test assemblers often ask a sensitivity reviewer to review a
passage before they begin writing questions on it, because it really makes no
sense to write questions on a passage that ultimately will be rejected because it is
not in conformity with the *Guidelines*. A few programs, ostensibly to save
money, bypass this preliminary review and wait for the mandatory sensitivity
review that comes immediately before the test is ready to be printed. Some
programs that originally bypassed this review, only to find as a test went to
publication that some question or passage was not in conformity with the *Guidelines,* now insist on it. It is costly, time consuming, and infuriating to have done
all the work necessary to publish a test only to have it stopped at the 11th hour
because there is a sensitivity problem.

The sensitivity reviewer receives a test from the area test sensitivity review
router who chooses the reviewers. The test assembler may not choose the sensitivity reviewer for his or her test, although the assembler may indicate that the
test is to be reviewed by someone who is a specialist in the content area. When
the reviewer receives a test, he or she is to review the test within 48 hours and
note on an official form any sensitivity review comments he or she has on the
test. There are levels of comments: Some are on the order of "this test would be

better if . . ."; others signal major problems. An example of the former might be found in a review of a mathematics test that has only a few word problems, let us say two, that refer to human beings. These items are balanced in that one refers to men and one to women, but the sensitivity reviewer notices that the item referring to women portrays them in passive or stereotypical roles, for example, cooking. Because there are too few items really to establish a pattern, the sensitivity reviewer would note the concern on the form but would not hold the test up even if the test assembler for some reason did not want to change the item. But if there were a test with a number of questions that refer to people, and the references to men and women were not balanced or there were a pattern of stereotyping, the sensitivity reviewer would not sign off on the test.

Once the sensitivity reviewer performs the review, the test and sensitivity review form are returned to the test assembler, who must respond on the form to each of the reviewer's comments. The assembler and reviewer then meet to discuss the review. Virtually all of the differences, if there are any, are reconciled during this tête-à-tête. In those cases where they are not, the assembler and reviewer meet with a sensitivity review area coordinator whose job it is to suggest strategies for resolving the issue; it is not his or her job to tell colleagues what to do. If the coordinator has done his or her job, the assembler and reviewer leave that meeting never knowing the coordinator's personal opinion about the matter under discussion.

More than 9 times out of 10 the tests that go to the coordinator are reconciled after this meeting. In those instances where this is not the case, the assembler, the reviewer, and the coordinator together take the test to the division director. The role of the division director at this meeting is analogous to that of the coordinator at the previous meeting: to try to help the parties reconcile their differences. The role of the coordinator at this meeting is to ensure that no undue pressure is brought on either the reviewer or assembler to "give in."

In those few instances—seven in 8 years—in which the parties are not able to reconcile their differences while meeting with the division director, the test in question is sent to binding arbitration. The coordinator contacts the sensitivity review steering committee, a group of three who oversee the process for the corporation; they assemble three arbiters. There are five arbiters in the corporation, but only three serve on any given arbitration panel. There are always more than three arbiters because an arbiter must disqualify him- or herself if he or she has any involvement with the test in question.

None of those who have been involved with the disputed test meets with the arbiters. The test, a memorandum from the reviewer explaining why he or she believes the test is in violation of the *Guidelines,* and a memorandum from the test assembler explaining why he or she believes that it is not, are all that the arbiters receive. On the basis of these, they decide whether or not the item or passage in question is in violation. If it is, then it must be deleted from the test; if it is not, the test goes immediately into production. Of the seven tests that have gone to arbitration, five were judged to be in violation of the *Guidelines* and two in conformity.

It was in an attempt to undercut any effects that personalities might have on these arbitration decisions that it was decided that the arbiters would base their decisions on written rather than oral presentations. To further distance the arbiters from their colleagues involved in the dispute, the written materials for arbitration come via the steering committee and without names. But arbitration cases are so rare and so worthy of office gossip that it is hard to imagine that the arbiters do not know who at least some of the parties involved with a disputed test are before they render their decision. Even so, the process is designed to keep the arbiters at a distance from the disputants.

In 1988, in response to a recommendation that was *not* made in the second audit of the sensitivity review process by the ETS Office of Quality Assurance and Control, it was decided to suspend the arbitration process for 2 years. Understandably, line management has never been at ease with the fact that the sensitivity review process was outside the line. One of the 1988 audit recommendations was that the line take more responsibility for the smooth working of the process. It was this recommendation that led to the suspension of arbitration. Basically, the line managers reasoned that if they were to be more responsible for the process, they needed to be able to make decisions about it. One salutary effect of the suspension of arbitration has been that line managers, who now might have to make decisions previously made by the arbitration panel, have almost all been trained in the process. Under the current system, if, after meeting with the sensitivity review coordinator, the sensitivity reviewer and test assembler still disagree, the coordinator convenes a panel that he or she chairs, consisting of the test assembler's immediate supervisor and the division director. The reviewer and assembler prepare their respective explanatory position memoranda and also meet with the panel. The panel is to come to a consensus on whether or not the test is in conformity with the *Guidelines*. If they cannot reach consensus, the ranking line manager, the division director, makes a decision that any of the other panel members, the reviewer, or the assembler can ask the area vice president to revisit. Anyone involved could continue to ask the line to review the decision until it reaches the president of ETS whose decision is, of course, final. This new adjudication procedure has yet to be tried, and after 2 years the corporation will have to decide which, if either, of the aforementioned procedures—arbitration or adjudication—it will opt for.

Between 1984, when the sensitivity review process was expanded to nontest publications, and 1986, when the *Guidelines* (ETS, 1986) were reissued, the publication process did not have an arbitration component. Trained editors performed sensitivity reviews as part of their standard editorial reviews. They completed a sensitivity review form confirming that they had done the required review and noting any sensitivity problems. The text and reviews were returned to the program director responsible for the publication who decided whether to accept the suggestions of the sensitivity reviewer. Of course, most people accepted most suggestions. In those instances in which the person responsible for the publication believed it was not appropriate to accept the suggestions of the sensitivity reviewer, the reviewer sent to the publications sensitivity review coordinator a copy of the review with a memorandum outlining in greater detail his or her objections and noting that the publication was being printed without the suggested changes having been made.

When the *Guidelines* were reissued in 1986, they included an arbitration process for publications like the one for tests. No editor has ever invoked arbitration, and now, as is the case with tests, publications arbitration has been suspended for 2 years, the resolution of disputes becoming a line responsibility.

As stated earlier, research and statistical reports came under the purview of the sensitivity review process in 1988 when researchers and statistical analysts were trained in the process. As part of their review of each other's work, they, as do the editors with publications, perform sensitivity reviews, noting concerns on a sensitivity review form that is returned to the author with the manuscript. If the reviewer and author cannot reconcile their differences, the research sensitivity review coordinator is consulted. If no agreement is reached after this consultation, the issue goes before one of the research vice presidents who convenes a panel composed of him- or herself, the sensitivity review coordinator, and one other research manager. As is the case in the other areas, the sensitivity reviewer and test assembler prepare memoranda outlining their respective positions. The panel, after reviewing the memoranda and meeting with the parties, decides whether or not they believe the document in question to be in conformity with the *Guidelines*. Unlike the process in the other areas, the research process places the responsibility for accepting or rejecting the opinion of the management panel on the author of a report who, if he or she chooses, may decline the panel's advice. There is no further appeal procedure in the research process. The decision to have no appeal procedure and to have the author as the final judge was made in the name of academic freedom. To date, all differences have apparently been settled at the author-reviewer level.

TRAINING

The key to having a successful sensitivity review process is in the training of the reviewers. Trainees by and large are presented with written and audio-visual material relevant to their work, most of which has some sensitivity-related problems that they are to find and make suggestions for remedying.

Sensitivity training is based on a method of consensus building derived from the training used to teach essay readers to score papers holistically: Training or sample papers are given to readers who must decide where along a scale each essay fits. After a training paper is read, a show of hands indicates how each reader rated the paper. Aberrant readers quickly see that their readings are "off," and, at least in theory, begin to modify their standards to conform to those of the group.

During sensitivity review training, the prospective reviewers have to decide whether a training paper is or is not in conformity with the *Guidelines*. If it is not, they have to cite the guideline it violates, and, if possible, make suggestions for remedying the problem. This training lasts for a whole day for editors, statisticians, and researchers, and for a day and a half for test developers. In addition, every 5 years a sensitivity reviewer must take a half-day refresher course. "If," to quote the 16th-century English poet Sir Walter Ralegh when speaking of an ideal, "all the world and love were young,/ And truth in every shepherd's tongue," and we did indeed live or at least work in a pastoral world or utopia, we would have ongoing training, for example, lunchtime seminars to ensure that reviewers were reviewing consistently according to the standards they learned in their initial training; but there simply is not the staff and time for such training. Even so, the two audits of the process, one in 1982 and one in 1988, and the two studies of the process in 1987 and 1988—one on consistency of reviews and one on the attitude of reviewers—suggest that although there are areas that could use shoring up, by and large the process is working well.

The sensitivity review training papers are chosen carefully to give prospective reviewers an opportunity to apply the criteria outlined in the *Guidelines*. The training also attempts to instill in the reviewers a sense of proportion about the gravity of a problem. With each sample, the trainers are asked four questions:

1. Is there a problem?
2. If there is, to which guideline does it relate?
3. Can you suggest a revision?
4. Would you sign off on this document if the author felt he or she did not want to make the suggested change?

It is this last question, as one might well expect, that it is most difficult for the training to give some practical guidance in, and it is in considering this question that we see a major difference between the sensitivity review process and the differential item functioning (DIF) process. DIF is a statistical process, whereas sensitivity review is a judgmental one. Many of the judgments the sensitivity review process demands are very difficult to make, in large part because they must be made in culturally very touchy areas, the areas of race and gender. The training does all that it can to help the reviewer to objectify his or her judgments, to sanitize the encounters between the sensitivity reviewer and author, but every author knows when he or she hands over a document, he or she may be judged to be lacking in sensitivity; and every sensitivity reviewer knows that if he or she finds a problem, an author may feel that he or she is being judged a racist or sexist. The training works hard to dispel these fears on both sides: "Just apply the *Guidelines*"; "the sensitivity review process has nothing to do with your own sensitivity towards minorities or women or people with disabilities" (Then why, one might ask, the name "sensitivity"?), but these fears are larger than the process. They tap into the very racial and gender fabric of our society.

As part of the training, minority- and women-relevant passages that are in conformity with the *Guidelines* are included among the samples to dispel the tendency of the neophyte reviewer to see problems everywhere. The training tries to emphasize that most of what one reviews will be fine; perhaps a quarter of what is reviewed will fall into a gray area where it simply is not clear how the *Guidelines* apply, and in a small percentage of cases a reviewer will come across texts that are clearly inappropriate. The goal of the training is to help all reviewers agree on what is clearly contrary to the *Guidelines* and, therefore, unacceptable. Take, for example, the pie chart in Fig. 19.1, which is used in training (note that not only words but also pictures and graphs have always come under the umbrella of the *Guidelines*).

This chart is clearly in violation of the *Guidelines* because *housewife* is classified in the *Guidelines* (p. 21) as an "unacceptable term" in that it defines a person, in this case a woman, in terms of her marital status: "wife." Housewife unequivocally puts this chart at odds with the *Guidelines*. The acceptable term here is *homemaker*. It is virtually inconceivable that the author would not be willing to make this change, but if he or she were not willing, the reviewer could not sign off on the document.

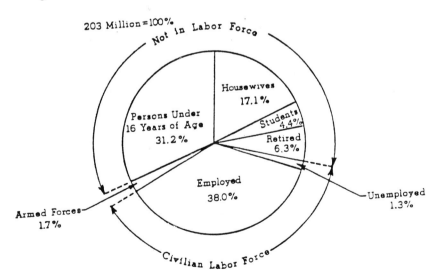

FIG. 19.1.   Employment status of the population of the United States, May 1969. Reprinted by permission of the National Industrial Conference Board.

Also, some reviewers believe that in the terminology *not in labor force,* there is a sexist underlying assumption that women who stay at home and care for the house and, perhaps, children do not do real work. This problem is remedied easily by inserting the word *paid* before *labor.* But what if, for some reason, the author did not want to make this change? Should the sensitivity reviewer sign off on the document? This case clearly falls within the gray area. Some might argue that the original wording is not sexist or that, if sexist, it reflects the terminology economists use. In training, we explain that the reviewer of such a document should try to convince the author to change the wording, but if he or she refuses, the consensus among the trainers is that the caption is not a clear enough violation of the *Guidelines* to merit the reviewer's not signing off on the document. Reviewers always want rules like *"Housewife* is an unacceptable term," but by and large the *Guidelines* are just that: guides that have to be interpreted, rather than rules that apply for all seasons.

THE CRITERIA

The *Guidelines* set forth six criteria, three of which apply to all ETS documents and three that apply exclusively to tests:

All ETS documents (a) should be balanced, (b) should not foster stereotypes, and (c) should not contain ethnocentric or gender-based underlying assumptions. In addition, all ETS tests (d) should not be offensive when viewed from an examinee's perspective, (e) should not contain controversial material that the subject matter does not demand, and (f) should not be elitist or ethnocentric.

Balance

"In general, the sensitivity reviewer should determine whether there is a suitable balance of multicultural material . . . [, and] the number of references to males and females in items that refer to people should be approximately equal" (ETS, 1986, p. 14). At the most simple and superficial level, balance means counting. It means making sure that you do not refer to hes and hims more often than you do to shes and hers. Related to this issue is the *generic he,* which, the *Guidelines* (ETS, 1986, p. 23) tell us, "is unacceptable" although "here, as elsewhere, historical context and/or direct quotations must be considered when evaluating materials." The generic he guideline means that you probably could not say in an ETS document, "The average American drinks his coffee black," if what you mean is that the average person from the United States drinks black coffee. Generic hes are fairly easy for reviewers to revise because their training includes a three-page document entitled "Gracefully Eliminating the Generic He" that covers almost any case one conceivably could come across with the generic he and explains how to eliminate it.

Related to generic hes are the "man" words. The *Guidelines* (ETS, 1986b, p. 23) explain that "the word *man* . . . is no longer considered broad enough to be applied to a person of either gender." Thus, the grammar item that follows is unacceptable:

> Owing to her detailed and perceptive study of the modern female, Germaine Greer has become a recognized spokesman of the women's liberation movement. If you begin with *her detailed,* which of the following is the correct verb form?
> A. having made
> * B. has made
> C. made of
> D. became
> E. is becoming

In short, the *Guidelines* prohibit all that has come to be known as sexist language.

The aforementioned guidelines related to balance I have called "simple and superficial," and I believe they are, although they are by no means unimportant. But documents, like life, seldom present us with problems that are solved as easily as those just discussed. Even the supposedly straightforward guideline on generic hes nods to complexity with its caveat about "historical context and/or direct quotations." It is fairly easy (sometimes) to balance the hes and shes in a document or in a skills or learned-ability test where the test developer is not limited in the content from which he or she may draw, but what of the achievement or professional test where the content defines the test—say a history or law test? Although the *Guidelines* do not call for a 50-50 balance between male and female or between minority and nonminority references in such tests, they do insist, even when the test specifications do not, that, where possible, such tests acknowledge that many different types of people have contributed to the canon:

> Tests that largely assess content should meet their own specifications on sex-referenced and multicultural material. If the test's specifications do not refer to women and minority groups, ETS's corporate guideline requiring "the inclusion of material reflecting the cultural background and contributions of major population subgroups" should be followed. (ETS, 1986, p. 14)

One of the most recent and acrimonious arbitration cases centered on this complex issue of balance: When is *some* good enough. The test was a literature test that, the test assemblers explained in their memorandum to the arbitration panel, was "to document that a candidate has developed the ability to analyze and interpret literature." The sensitivity reviewers, arguing that all literature can be analyzed and interpreted, suggested that the test include more material by and about women. They were also concerned that the test, when read as a whole, gave a particularly homocentric view of the world. They said in their memorandum to the arbitration panel that "the test presents a universe primarily peopled by and written about men. Women, for the most part, are background figures." The assemblers, on the other hand, argued that "the test contain[ed] a reasonable number of passages by women writers given the nature of the curriculum":

> The purpose of the test is not to reflect a particular kind of universe or to represent groups of people but to provide passages from a range of literary works that test a student's ability to analyze and interpret prose, poetry, and drama of different historical periods. When works are chosen to represent the Classical, Renaissance, and other literature written before the late twentieth century, depicting women in "non-traditional," or heroic roles or in specific numbers presents a significant obstacle to the main purpose of the test. The test does, nevertheless, contain a number of women characters, although the Guidelines do not require their inclusion.

Further, they argued, the passage selections had been informed "by an extensive curriculum survey of some 230 colleges."

The reviewers countered with:

> [The assemblers of this test have] indicated that the selection of the texts is based on a curriculum survey carried out by the program. [They argue] that the [test development] committee would think that the test would not represent the curriculum as defined by professionals in the field if other women writers were included in the test. While it is true that the number of literary works written by men exceeds that written by women, the test does not require the candidate to identify the author. Therefore, the inclusion of women writers would not disadvantage students who had taken literature courses that did not include women writers. If, however, it is important to maintain such links with the curriculum for the purposes of face validity, [we] would then *strongly* argue for the inclusion of women characters to correct the imbalance.

The world of sensitivity review is indeed complex.

The arbitration panel found:

> In assembling the test, gender balance could have been achieved by including passages written by women, passages about women, or passages that contain references to women. Of course, passages of the latter two types should not be disparaging or negative. In a ninety-item test, having only seventeen or even twenty references to women is unbalanced and, therefore, unacceptable.
>
> In reviewing the test, the arbitration panel discussed the curriculum survey at length. We noted that few women writers were included in the survey and that many prominent women writers were not listed. . . . In summary, we feel that the curriculum survey is not sufficient justification for the nature of the test.

The panel ended their memorandum with the reminder:

> The arbitration panel believes that the Test Sensitivity Review Guidelines have served ETS well. We recognize that there are areas of ambiguity in the Guidelines and room for different interpretations of the spirit and the process of sensitivity reviews. . . . An arbitration decision represents a perspective. It should not be interpreted as a decision in favor of or against any individual. An arbitration decision does not create winners or losers. We realize that test developers, assemblers, reviewers, and arbitrators may differ in their views on balance and sensitivity, while being equally committed to the principles upon which they are based.

Stereotypes

"Sensitivity reviewers must ensure that no test implies that a population group is culturally or biologically inferior or superior to any other group. Thus, the review should ensure that no material contains language or symbols that reinforce offensive stereotypes" (*Guidelines*, 1986, p. 15). Figure 19.2 was included in a history test. The text of the question is as follows:

> The cartoon pictured here from the early 1960s depicts
> A. A newly revived tribal dance
> B. Communist anger at American involvement in Vietnam
> C. The displeasure of Communist leaders over the closing of the Suez Canal
> * D. Efforts to increase Communist influence in Africa
> E. The resentment of Mao and Khrushchev at African attempts to mediate the Israeli-Arab conflict

This item would not pass sensitivity review because of the prohibition against stereotyping. As the commentary to the *Guidelines* explains, "The cartoon is offensive because it stereotypes Africans as primitive, spear-carrying people in grass skirts or leopard skins" (*The ETS Sensitivity Review Process: A Commentary for Test Assemblers*, 1986, p. 9). The *Guidelines* (pp. 17–26) go into detail in an attempt to help reviewers recognize the most prevalent stereotypes associated with each of the six targeted groups, but it is precisely in the consideration of this criterion that the *Guidelines* make it most clear that they "can and should be applied to any population group" (p. 3). Certainly the reading passage that follows is unacceptable, although its "quintessential Russian peasant" is nowhere singled out by the *Guidelines*:

> Khrushchev's gift to history is, and always was, himself. Khrushchev's greatest qualities, those that distinguished him from all other Soviet leaders, were his energy, his enthusiasm, his confidence in himself and in others. It was his prodigal personality, his ability to confess a mistake and reverse himself, his explosive

FIG. 19.2.   A cartoon from the early 1960s.

unpredictability, that did more than anything else to spring the genie of spontaneity out of the bottle of repression in which Stalin had contained the Russian spirit for thirty years.

Khrushchev was the quintessential Russian peasant. He was cunning and sly. He was given to the charming fantastical Russian kind of lying called *Vranyo,* and to extremes, like the *Muzhik* who works hard and then spends days on a drinking spree. Coming at the moment of Russian history when he did, Khrushchev's great contribution was his confidence in the Russian people and his effort to give them confidence in themselves.

This passage has proven to be a particularly rich training piece because the group to which it refers is fairly far from the average sensitivity reviewer's everyday considerations. But one of the suggestions we make to reviewers during training is that when they are unsure about whether or not a document is in conformity with the *Guidelines,* they substitute in the document a group about which they feel strongly. If the passage is offensive with this substitution, it is almost surely not in conformity with the *Guidelines.* The Khrushchev passage makes this point extremely well. Think of saying about women or persons of color what is said in this passage about Russians. Of course, when it was socially acceptable to be sexist or racist, similar things were said; therefore, the need for the sensitivity review process.

Examinee Perspective

"All group reference questions are viewed from the perspective of test takers who may not have access to the correct answers" (ETS, 1986, p. 14). Closely aligned with the stereotyping criterion is one on examinee perspective. Basically this guideline, that applies only to tests, means that no part of a test question, not even the wrong answers or distractors, should support a stereotype about any group. This criterion flies in the face of traditional item writing wisdom that suggests that one way to make plausible wrong answers is to incorporate stereotypes into the distractors. The problem with this practice, of course, is that potentially negative stereotypes can be supported in the minds of those test takers who choose options with negative stereotypes, thinking they are correct. Take, for example, the following social studies test item designed for elementary school children:

1. The people are very simple and would be good servants, for I saw they do not know better than to do what they are told; and I think that they would very quickly become Christians, as they seem to have no religion or beliefs. (1492)

2. Many of the French are married to Indian women and are settled in villages where they hunt, fish, and lead lives like those of the Indians. (1818)

3. On what is the Indian claim to American lands founded? Occupancy! What do these painted people make of the soil? Do they till it? They do not! I believe that the Indians, not having made better use of the soil for many hundred years, have given up all claims to the land and ought to be driven from it. (1867)

4. Unlike other people, the Indian has never done anything to improve his life. The Indian's life will always remain harsher than it has to be unless he adopts our ways of housing, feeding, and clothing himself. (1897)

Each passage expresses a prejudiced or biased view of Indian culture EXCEPT:

   A. 1
* B. 2
   C. 3
   D. 4

This is a particularly complicated question because of its Except format, but even if we assume that young examinees understand what they are being asked, those who choose passages 1, 3, or 4 are supported in thinking that the views in those passages are *not* examples of prejudice. This item potentially supports stereo-types about Native Americans' being "simple," "painted people" who have "never done anything" and have "no religion," most unfortunate views to rein-force; and think of the Native American child taking a test with this question in it!

Controversial Material

"Highly controversial issues, such as legalized abortion or hypotheses about genetic inferiority, must not be included in any test question unless such issues are both relevant and essential to the content validity of the test" (ETS, 1986, p. 14). The controversial material guideline is very difficult to apply to a test because interpreting it calls for a great deal of subjectivity. Reviewers are cau-tioned to stand on this criterion only after they have discussed the item or passage in question with a number of other reviewers to see if they too judge the matter in question to be too controversial. This criterion is interpreted quite strictly in skills tests like writing or reading, so although a test for doctors may have to ask questions about abortion, there is no way a reading test, in light of this guideline, could include a passage or question on this most controversial subject. And whereas a biology test will assume that the theory of evolution is correct, a reading passage that has our forefathers or, for that matter, foremothers climbing out of the sea or walking on all fours almost surely will be rejected because of this guideline, although a more subtle evolution passage, say one on fossils, will not be judged too hot for a reading test.

This guideline assumes that what we hear from test takers is true: Some topics are upsetting to them. Our fear is that if test takers are agitated by a passage or question, their performance may be adversely affected. This guideline hopes to identify those topics that are likely to be most upsetting to most test takers and eliminate them from tests where possible. Some critics of this guideline have argued that it makes for bland tests. The corporation has not denied this crit-icism, but its actions have said that if we must choose, better bland than offen-sive.

As can be seen from the aforementioned, the acceptability of controversial material vis-à-vis the *Guidelines* is informed by the context and purpose of the test. When testing content, the canon must be assessed even if portions of it are disturbing, although great care must be taken in how this disturbing material is tested. But, as has been implied throughout this paper, when a skill, for example, reading, is being assessed, and virtually anything in the world that is readable and at the appropriate level may be drawn from, there certainly is no need to choose controversial material that may upset a test taker. So although a history test may demand a question about Hitler's Germany, the grammatical point tested in the following item in no way demands the controversial subject matter in which it is clothed:

Ferencz shows how, as the war progressed, concentration-camp labor increasingly *becomes an essential ingredient of both the Nazi war effort and of* private German industrial production.

   A. becomes an essential ingredient of both the Nazi war effort and of
* B. became an essential ingredient of both the Nazi war effort and
   C. was an ingredient essential to both the Nazi war effort and to
   D. had become an ingredient essential to both the Nazi war effort and for
   E. was essential to both the Nazi war effort and to

The question always before the sensitivity reviewer of a subject area test is, "Does the content demand that this subject matter, although controversial, be covered?"

Elitism and Ethnocentricity

> To eliminate concepts, words, phrases, or examples that may upset or otherwise disadvantage a test taker, every effort is made not to include expressions that might be more familiar to members of a particular social class or ethnic group than the general population . . . unless they are defined or knowledge of them is relevant to the purpose of the test. (ETS, 1986, p. 16)

Let me here state the obvious: The test sensitivity review process is about making tests as fair to all test takers as possible. Thus, every attempt is made not to include questions that may unfairly favor one group over another for any reason other than mastery of the subject matter that is being tested. Take, for example, the set of questions in the Appendix written for a humanities test. Although no one of these questions is in and of itself in any way problematic, when taken as a group at least five (questions 5–9) and perhaps six (questions 4–9) of them draw on the Christian tradition for answers. As the commentary to the *Guidelines* (ETS, 1986, p. 11) explains, the question the sensitivity reviewer must answer is, "Is such emphasis on detailed knowledge of Christian tradition justifiable?" Because no case on elitism or ethnocentricity—in this case Christiocentricity— has ever gone to arbitration, the corporation has yet to answer this question. It is one with which the process continues to struggle.

One other issue the items just discussed highlight is how items can play against each other. Items that individually are fine can, when juxtaposed, present problems. For this reason the organization decided to approve tests rather than items. When the process was being formulated, some argued for an item rather than a test review. An item review seemed less time consuming and, therefore, less costly, but test developers, who know the strange things that can happen when items are put together, insisted that tests, not just items, be reviewed.

Underlying Assumptions

"Sensitivity reviewers should attempt to eliminate ethnocentric or gender-based beliefs and prejudices" (ETS, 1986, p. 16). Perhaps the most important guideline is this one that in effect prohibits solipsism. It is so important because it protects the reader from having to do the impossible, that is, get into the mind of the author before he or she can answer a question correctly or understand a document. It is really unfair to insist that people share our world view before we can communicate with them. Although the underlying assumption criterion may be the most important guideline, it is also the most difficult to train reviewers to apply. The reason for this is obvious: It is difficult, sometimes impossible, to get an objective perspective on the way we perceive the world. Take, for the sake of example, the following excerpt:

> The reading comprehension item set from the November 1983 SAT concerned the life-style of migrant Mexican-American families. Four out of five items on this passage have positive DSTD2 values for the Mexican-American test-takers, indicating that all items are generally easier for the migrants when compared to a matched White group.

This paragraph makes sense only if we assent with the author that the two groups, Mexican Americans and migrants, are the same, that all Mexican Americans are migrants.

The next item, designed for a test for social workers, is used to teach about unacceptable underlying assumptions in the context of a test:

> In order to work effectively with members of a minority group, the most important consideration is for the social worker to:
> * A. Be aware of his or her own self, values, and biases
>   B. Study the language of the minority group
>   C. Be sympathetic and nondiscriminating
>   D. Live among or close to the minority-group members

The only way one can possibly answer this item is if he or she pictures the world as has the writer of this question: Social workers are not minority people; minority people are the people whom social workers help. How difficult it must be for a test taker of color to make sense of such a question.

When prospective reviewers are able to see the ethnocentrism at the heart of the next statement, they are on their way to becoming able sensitivity reviewers:

> The 3,000 Innuvialuit, what the Eskimos of Canada's western Arctic prefer that they themselves be called, live in the treeless tundra around the Bering Sea.

The underlying assumption here, of course, is that the real name of these people is "Eskimos" even though they call themselves something else. The practice of putting one's own group in a passage if unsure of its acceptability works very well here. When, say, a White reviewer puts his or her group in this sentence and has it read, "The 3,000 Anglos, what the gringos of the United States prefer that they themselves be called, live in the . . . ," it is easy to see why this apparently innocuous sentence is at odds with all the *Guidelines* stand for.

SENSITIVITY REVIEW AND DIF

Although this chapter has said little about DIF, its thrust points to the differences between the sensitivity review and DIF processes. Discussed previously is the judgmental nature of the former, whereas all the other chapters in this volume enlighten us about the statistical nature of the latter. The sensitivity review process comes before a test is ever administered to a single test taker; the DIF process after it has been taken by a relatively large number of examinees. The processes are very different and no attempt has been made at ETS to link them. *The ETS Sensitivity Review Process: An Overview* (1987) clearly stated that "the importance attached to sensitivity review does not imply a measurable relationship between material considered offensive by some test takers and the scores of test takers" (p. 4). There is no promise to anyone that the sensitivity review process will raise the scores of, say, minority test takers, and there are many items with significant negative DIF values that are in absolute conformity with the *Guidelines*. If the sensitivity review process does not necessarily lead to better scores for certain test takers, then why do it? I think the answer to this question is simply, "Because it's right." It is right to try to create tests that acknowledge and respect diversity through the inclusion of some material and the exclusion of other. Some attempt to undercut the process by defining it primarily as a public relations document, and indeed it is such a document. ETS likes to be able to say that all of its tests receive sensitivity reviews (what testing company wouldn't?), but I contend, as does scripture, that it is better to do than to say. If it is good to say that we do these reviews, then it is better actually to do them. Why? Because they make for better tests. It is indeed fortuitous and rare when public relations and the public good are one.

Although previously I emphasized the differences between the two processes, I am struck by the fact that once you have the DIF statistic before you, the two processes begin to look more alike than different. They are both then judgmental processes. Once the numbers are run, the heretofore objective DIF statistical process becomes totally judgmental as mere mortals look at that statistic and try to hypothesize why an item has performed as it has.

Even though the organization is wise to make a clear distinction between the sensitivity and DIF processes, lest someone claim for one what is the province of the other, it is unfortunate that the processes do not inform each other more on a day-to-day basis. I think sensitivity reviewers could profit from seeing which types of items tend to have negative DIF values, just as DIF reviewers have profited from having been trained in the sensitivity review process. Often sensitivity criteria have formed the basis of a hypothesis about a DIF item. Even so, there is no consistent effort to inform sensitivity reviewers about what we are learning from DIF. Many of them, because they are test developers, know which items are receiving significant DIF values on the tests they develop, but as sensitivity reviewers, they review many tests they do not develop, and the DIF information on these tests is more often than not lost to them.

RESEARCH

There is much need for research in the area of the sensitivity review process. It would be most helpful to have research information about the effect of including minority- or women-relevant materials in a test. Does it make a DIF difference? If it does, to whom? And how much difference does it make? Do we find, as I suspect, that if we build the optimal test for one group as defined by the relevance of its content or the DIF statistics of its items, we build a less optimal test for another group? How "biased" is such a test against that other group? If there is no optimal test for all groups, how do we balance a test so that it is as fair as possible to all test takers?

Although the sensitivity review process would not permit such items in a test, it would be useful to know whether and, if so, how negative or offensive items affect a test taker's performance. Perhaps we could do this research by performing sensitivity reviews and DIF analyses on tests that were developed before the process began; we then could see whether there is any pattern that suggests that those items in violation of the *Guidelines* have a negative DIF value for particular groups. It also would be informative to know whether a test taker's performance gets worse after he or she encounters offensive items. We know very little about the interaction between affectively positive and negative items and performance; to build better tests we need to know more (see Medley & Quirk, 1974; see also chapter 18 in this volume).

THE FUTURE

I began this chapter by recounting the history of the sensitivity review process; I would like to end it by guessing about its future. Of one thing I am sure: It will continue to be and to change. My guess is that the next major development will be in the area of raising our consciousness about people with disabilities. This group was mentioned specifically in the 1986 edition of the *Guidelines*, so all the criteria discussed earlier apply to people with disabilities as well, but our training materials in this area are weak and the discussion of this group in the *Guidelines* leaves much to be desired. The process is, in reference to this group, where it was with people of color and women 10 years ago.

I also think that those who are concerned that the *Guidelines* make for bland tests will be heard more, at least in the area of achievement testing. Three separate groups of outside content experts—in literature, in the social sciences, and in history—have been brought in to discuss the process. They all have suggested that we permit more provocative materials in the achievement tests designed for their respective areas. And unless the line managers prove very insensitive to the *Guidelines* or their involvement is criticized internally or externally as a conflict of interest, I would guess that the adjudication process will stay with them.

Although the process will be modified continually, I suspect that if in 10 years I am again asked to write about the sensitivity review process, I could dust this article off, make a modest number of changes, insert some new examples, and submit much the chapter you have just read; and that is not necessarily a bad thing. When a new writer was brought on to the then very successful *I Love Lucy Show,* he wanted to change the format. Lucy is said to have looked at him and exclaimed, in much more graphic language than the *Guidelines* will permit, something to the effect of, "Son, don't mess with success." Though far from perfect, we have a process that works well in that it commits us to creating documents that are reflective of the fact that we live in a heterogeneous society, and it gives us guidelines for identifying test questions that could impact negatively on student performance. I believe the next 10 years will involve fine-tuning this working instrument.

APPENDIX

1. Often read as a children's classic, it is in reality a scathing indictment of human meanness and greed. In its four books, the Lilliputians are deranged, the Yahoos obscene.

The passage above discusses

(A) *Tom Jones*   (B) *David Copperfield*   (C) *The Pilgrim's Progress*   * (D) *Gulliver's Travels*   (E) *Alice in Wonderland*

2. Which of the following deals with the bigotry an anguished Black family faces when it attempts to move into an all-White suburb?

(A) O'Neill's *Desire Under the Elms*
(B) Miller's *Death of a Salesman*
(C) Williams' *A Streetcar Named Desire*

(D) Albee's *Who's Afraid of Virginia Woolf?*
*   (E) Hansberry's *A Raisin in the Sun*

3. Which of the following has as its central theme the idea that wars are
    mass insanity and that armies are madhouses?

    * (A) *Catch-22*   (B) *Portnoy's Complaint*   (C) *Lord of the Flies*
    (D) *Heart of Darkness*   (E) *Vanity Fair*

4. Which of the following is often a symbol of new life arising from death?

    (A) A gorgon   (B) The minotaur   (C) A unicorn   (D) A griffin
*   (E) The phoenix

5. Which of the following musical forms is divided into the sections: Kyrie,
    Gloria, Credo, Sanctus, Benedictus, Agnus Dei?

    (A) A symphony   (B) A piano concerto   * (C) A mass
    (D) A madrigal   (E) A cantata

6. The work pictured above is

    * (A) a fresco   (B) a stabile   (C) a woodcut   (D) an illumination
    (E) an etching

7. The theme of the work is the

    (A) sacrifice of Isaac   (B) expulsion from Eden   (C) reincarnation of
    Vishnu   * (D) creation of Adam   (E) flight of Icarus

8. The work is located in the

(A) Alhambra   * (B) Sistine Chapel   (C) Parthenon   (D) palace of
Versailles   (E) Cathedral of Notre Dame

9. The sculpture pictured above is called

(A) The Annunciation   (B) The Flight into Egypt   (C) The Adoration of
the Magi   * (D) The Pietà   (E) The Visitation

20 Testing, DIF, and Public Policy

Patricia H. McAllister
Educational Testing Service

Over the past 10 years approximately 30 state legislatures and Congress have considered legislation related to procedures and policies of testing organizations. There is public concern about the importance placed on tests at all levels of the educational process but particularly as tests are used for admission to postsecondary educational institutions and for entry to various professions and occupations. Although calls have been made to focus testing more toward helping people learn, their use as a sorting mechanism remains dominant (Glaser, 1981). It is this use and the ever-growing public awareness of it that has drawn issues related to testing into the legislative forum as well as the courts.

This chapter examines and analyzes the issues that have been considered in the legislative forum with particular emphasis on recent state legislative initiatives directed at regulating the test development process and the difficulties encountered in discussing complex, technical procedures, such as differential item functioning (DIF), in the public domain.

WHY TESTING IS A LEGISLATIVE ISSUE

A number of factors have contributed to the sustained public interest in testing in our society. First, concern about a decline in standards and quality of education being provided to our children and citizens has resulted in more interest in methods of demonstrating knowledge and competency. Second, elected officials are increasingly interested in accountability of educational institutions and are looking for ways to demonstrate this accountability. Third, changing demographics in American society and the increasing number of minority citizens have caused many minority groups and organizations to continue to be legitimately concerned about the use of tests as they relate to equity and access to educational and professional opportunities. The convergence of these trends has magnified the focus on the fairness of tests and how tests are used to make decisions.

Self-appointed public interest groups such as FairTest and the Nader Public Interest Research Group (PIRG) are monitoring the activities of test companies and promoting the regulation of the standardized testing industry through litigation and legislative initiatives. During the past few years, legislative interest in regulating standardized testing has been confined to a few states where special interest groups have been able to sustain momentum on the issue.

THE EVOLUTION OF TESTING LEGISLATION

Legislation to regulate standardized testing first appeared in the late 1970s and was tied to the consumer rights movement spearheaded by Ralph Nader. Issues of concern at that time focused on access to information about tests and test results and openness in the testing process. The outcome that proponents of the legislation sought to achieve was "demystification" of the testing process.

In 1978, California enacted legislation requiring test sponsors to file facsimile postsecondary admissions tests with the California Postsecondary Education Commission. This was the first time a state passed a law specifically addressing policies of private testing agencies who developed standardized postsecondary admissions tests. In 1981, this law was amended to require that students be provided with a question and answer (Q & A) service for undergraduate admissions tests (ACT and SAT) for at least half of the regular Saturday administrations.

Exactly 10 years ago, New York State passed the so-called "Truth-in-Testing" law, which required full and immediate disclosure of postsecondary admissions tests. Essentially, this law requires that test agencies file copies of test questions and answers with the Commissioner of Education's office and that students be provided the opportunity to request copies of test questions, correct answer keys, scoring instructions, and their answer sheets. Following passage of the New York law, many other states and Congress introduced Truth-in-Testing bills. Subsequently, most testing agencies established voluntary, national test disclosure policies modeled after the New York law. This voluntary action seemed to dissipate the Truth-in-Testing movement, which was concerned primarily with making the testing process more open by increasing students' and the public's access to test questions and answers. It is interesting to note that fewer than 2% of test takers nationally were requesting the Q & A service in the first few years following the enactment of the legislation. Testing critics then began to direct their attention toward issues of test fairness and test use. Of these two issues, test fairness is the one that has received the most recent attention by the public, mass media, legislatures, and the courts.

During the last several years the most prevalent legislative initiatives have proceeded from the assumption that differences in correct answer rates between various subgroups and the majority population imply that the test is biased. Here the desired outcome seems to be the development of "fairer" tests that would minimize the differences in results among various groups. Legislative initiatives in this vein focused on requirements that test questions be selected or reviewed on the basis of minimal differences in correct answer rates between groups.

The focus on correct-answer rate differences became a legislative issue following an out-of-court settlement between Educational Testing Service (ETS) and the Golden Rule Insurance Company of Illinois in 1984. The settlement, which ended an 8-year lawsuit, applied to two of the four ETS insurance licensing tests used in Illinois. As part of the settlement, ETS agreed to select test questions for inclusion in the test based in part on the size of the percentage differences in correct answers between White and Black examinees. It is this particular selection method and variations of it that have been applied to admissions tests and other licensing tests and promoted in state legislatures.

Legislation including provisions similar to those agreed to in the settlement with the Golden Rule Insurance Company were considered in California, Massachusetts, New York, Rhode Island, Texas, and Wisconsin.

The key common provisions of such legislation include the following:

1. Constructing tests by using questions with the least differences first.
2. The establishment of study committees to analyze correct-answer rate differences between groups and to recommend methods for altering test items with potential bias.

In response to these initiatives, the professional measurement community, including the American Educational Research Association (AERA) and the National Council on Measurement in Education (NCME), publicly expressed serious concerns about the extension of the Golden Rule methodology to admissions tests and other licensing tests.

The January 6, 1987, issue of the American Psychological Association (APA) *Monitor* contained a letter by ETS President Gregory R. Anrig, which described his feelings and regrets about approving the Golden Rule settlement. Anrig stressed that, although the settlement did make sense in the limited context to which it applied, the transference of the concept to other standardized tests could undermine sound psychometric standards. This letter discussed the serious problems associated with extensions of the Golden Rule methodology to other types of tests. These problems include the following:

1. The implication that the mere existence of differences between groups is evidence of bias.
2. The removal or under-representation of content areas that are viewed as relevant.

3. The inclusion of questions with low reliability and validity for the sole purpose of reducing differences, which would result in poorer tests.

These problems with the Golden Rule procedure were most recently re-emphasized in the National Research Council's report *Fairness in Employment Testing,* which pointed out the "detrimental" effects of the procedure on the quality of tests.

In the wake of professional criticism of Golden Rule, legislative measures were dropped that originally had called for constructing tests by using questions with the least differences first. Instead, legislative initiatives became focused on establishing politically appointed committees to review tests for fairness and equity.

In 1987, legislation was passed in New York State that required test companies to collect voluminous data on hundreds of test questions for a study of tests used in the process of admission to college and graduate schools and to determine if tests are fair with respect to race, ethnicity, gender, and linguistic background. This law specified that DIF data also be collected when the available number of examinees are large enough. Test agencies, including ETS, were required to submit data to the New York Study Committee on September 1, 1989. The committee will review correct-answer rates and biserial correlations for all test subjects combined and separately by race, ethnicity, gender, or linguistic background. The committee also will review DIF data, where available, and consider this information in relation to its findings and recommendations.

The testing profession supports studying the effects of tests on various subgroups of the population and has done so for many years. However, it is very important to collect and analyze factors associated with real differences in knowledge and skills in various groups. Such factors include socioeconomic status, high school academic background, intended major in college, and so forth. Unfortunately, the study committee in New York is mandated to look at differences in test scores and not other information that might explain those differences. The committee itself now realizes that the issues are much broader than just correct-answer rate differences. In spite of this awareness, and because of the legislative mandate, it is likely that this study will show that there are indeed differences in the performance of majority and minority test takers, but other important factors, such as real differences in knowledge and skill, may not be taken into account (although such factors will be provided for ETS tests administered in New York). This incomplete study may become the basis for future legislation to further regulate the development of tests or the use of tests and may make it increasingly difficult for test companies to continue providing quality services at reasonable costs. The passage of legislation in Rhode Island, which is similar to the New York law, supports this point.

In 1987, Rhode Island enacted a law requiring a study of teacher competency tests to determine if they have the effect of discriminating against test takers on the basis of race, ethnic background, or gender. Like the New York law, the Rhode Island statute required test agencies to collect ethnic data and to provide this to the State Board of Regents for transmittal to the Advisory Commission. Unlike the New York law, the Rhode Island statute did not include language requiring the reporting of DIF data where available and appropriate.

The Advisory Commission submitted their study concerning the effects of the NTE on test subjects of varying backgrounds to the legislature in January of 1989. Significant findings and recommendations included the following:

Findings

1. The number of minority candidates in the population was too small to have any confidence in the results.
2. The performance of minorities in Rhode Island was worse than the national average. Sixty-two percent of Blacks did not pass the Communications Skills component.
3. The failure rates for Blacks and Hispanics on the Professional Knowledge component was markedly worse than the failure rates for all test takers nationally and in Rhode Island.

Recommendations

1. Use of the NTE as an absolute criterion in granting initial certification should be suspended for 5 years, but the test should continue to be administered during this time.
2. Individuals who score below a preset level on the test should be given provisional certification for 3 years during which time they will undergo a performance evaluation to maintain certification.

Legislation embodying these recommendations was introduced in the Rhode Island Assembly and passed by that body in the spring of 1989 (Rhode Island H. 6121). Similar legislation establishing an advisory committee to study the effects of the NTE and other licensing tests has been considered in New York.

PUBLISHING TEST AND ITEM-LEVEL DATA
IN THE POLITICAL DOMAIN

We have reviewed the evolution of testing legislation from procedural issues such as disclosure toward more fundamental issues such as what questions should be included in a test and what criteria should be used to make the decision. The major concern for psychometricians is control of the test development process. Should this process be controlled by educators, psychometricians, and testing experts or by politicians and judges? How can political concerns be addressed without giving up control?

Certainly the testing profession recognizes the public interest and right to obtain information concerning standardized tests and their use. Disclosure of test contents and providing information about tests to the public are standard operating procedures at most testing organizations.

It is important to differentiate these positive initiatives from the negative ones that restrict the testing profession's ability to provide a quality product and that would not result in any benefit to test takers or the society at large. On the contrary, increasing educational achievement could be hampered seriously by the use of tests that masked real differences.

Those concerned about measures directed at the test development process have consistently stressed the fact that differences in correct-answer rates do not imply that a question is biased, and that an adequate analysis of test fairness must include information on indicators of real differences in knowledge and skills among various groups.

The testing profession has embraced DIF as the preferred method for detecting potential bias in tests and enhancing the development of fair tests. However, the DIF methodology has been labeled by testing critics as an unacceptable alternative to the Golden Rule approach (Shapiro, Slutsky, Watt, 1989, p. 263). Critics assert that the method of matching examinees on their total test scores presumes the collective fairness of all test questions. Advocates of the use of DIF have the responsibility to explain in clear, nontechnical language why using total test scores to match examinees in terms of knowledge and ability is preferable to other criteria, and why professional judgment is necessary to determine ultimately whether a question is truly biased. In the testing community, differences in correct answer rates, total scores, and so on do not mean bias. In the political realm, the exact opposite perception is found; differences mean bias. It may be that a semantic problem exists with the use of the word bias. In a general context, the word *bias* connotes having a particular mental inclination or learning. In the context of testing, the word *bias* is generally associated with disadvantage; that is, large differences in correct answer rates between minorities and the majority population mean bias because minorities are disadvantaged by the question. To focus instead on fairness and how various procedures like DIF promote fairness might be a way around the problem created by the different perceptions that exist about bias.

Gender differences in test scores on postsecondary admissions tests (particularly SAT) are used increasingly in the political domain to emphasize bias. Testing critics and women's organizations emphatically assert that standardized tests are biased against women whose scores are lower than male scores, and that women as a result are being discriminated against, especially in the award of scholarships. Similarly, many minority groups contend that standardized tests are a barrier to entry into postsecondary equation and the professions. This year legislation was introduced in California to strongly encourage the University of California and California State University to discontinue the use of standardized test scores as part of the requirements for admission. Other legislation in that state sought to establish a statewide test preparation program to assist minority students in preparing to take college entrance tests (California S. 1599, California A. 33). These two legislative initiatives in the same state illustrate the conflicting attitude toward testing that often exists in the public domain. The dilemma concerns whether to accept the standard of achievement represented by standardized tests or to do away with the standard altogether. Those who favor elimination of the standard embrace the notion that differences mean bias, and they may seek to use the existence of these differences as a reason to alter the criteria for deciding what questions to include in tests. The testing profession is faced with the difficult but important task of explaining why standards of achievement exemplified by tests are important to our society and that we need the information provided by tests to improve our educational process.

The testing profession should be encouraged by the fact that its message concerning appropriate tests score use has had an impact. Several states, which had been awarding scholarships based solely on tests scores, have adopted multiple criteria, often including test scores, as the preferred criteria. Leaders of testing agencies were quite vocal concerning the inappropriateness of using test scores as the sole criteria for scholarship awards.

A similar stance is appropriate and necessary concerning the issue of test bias (or fairness). The study underway in New York affords an opportunity. Indications are that the study committee may embrace the approach used by Phyllis Rosser, which equates raw group differences with bias as its model (Rosser, 1989). This approach is similar to the Golden Rule and the same criticisms apply. It is crucial that members of the testing profession try to ensure that the New York Study Committee focuses on more relevant data, such as item content and associated DIF statistics. Where large differences in correct percentages among different groups on tests or items are found, these must be correlated with educational preparation, grades, college major, and so forth. Inclusion of these other factors should help in the conduct of a valid study of unintended bias. Like passage of the New York Truth-in-Testing law in 1979, the New York Study Committee report is likely to be widely publicized. It is crucial that the committee's report not be focused narrowly on only correct-answer rate differences for subgroups. In the meantime, the more we can learn about why score differences exist, the better we can inform the public debate.

In addition, the testing profession must continue its efforts to promote proper test use. The question as to whether a test or a particular item is fair cannot be answered by using only a statistical procedure. Issues such as validity and proper test use must be emphasized continually. Although standards exist to promote proper test use, how tests are used and how test scores are interpreted are not within the control of test agencies or any other specific entity. Equitable test use is not a statistical or technical issue but a value judgment (Dwyer, 1987).

21

The Case Against Item Bias Detection Techniques Based on Internal Criteria: Do Item Bias Procedures Obscure Test Fairness Issues?

Gregory Camilli
Rutgers University

In which directions has item bias research evolved in the last decade? This question is best approached with a good description of how social scientists originally conceived "item bias," and why they sought to identify biased test items. The current definition of *item bias* is highly restrictive: It is a technical term that carries few of the connotations of everyday language. It is argued later that the modern definition of item bias is quite different from previous conceptions, but that archetypes of the earlier thinking are abundant in the research literature of the 1980s. This mixture of the old and the new has resulted in confusion regarding the purpose of item bias research and some exaggerated claims of efficacy.

The purpose of this chapter is to contrast recent with earlier concepts of item bias. Currently, item bias techniques do not address directly the fairness of a test. Rather, when items show a larger than average gap in the performance of two groups, expert reviewers may recognize this gap to be the result of factors irrelevant to the aims of the test. As a result of this review, an item may be labeled as biased and either modified or removed from the test. The earlier approach was concerned chiefly with the systematic underestimation of intelligence test scores for minority populations. The major issue was one of opportunity to learn, and consequently, group differences arising from unequal training.

Although the term *item bias* now largely has been supplanted by *differential item functioning* or simply DIF, these terms are not equivalent. The distinction is as follows. An item is said to "function differently" for two or more groups if the probability of a correct answer to a test item is associated with group membership for examinees of comparable ability. Statistical indices of DIF are designed to identify such test items. If the degree of DIF is determined to be practically significant for an item and the DIF can be attributed plausibly to a feature of the item that is irrelevant to the test construct, then the presence of this item on the test biases the ability estimates of some individuals. This compound condition, when satisfied, indicates item bias. The goal of most item analyses employing DIF techniques is to detect and remediate item bias, and therefore item bias is the central concern of this chapter. It is important to note, however, that the terms DIF and item bias have been used inconsistently in the literature, especially because the latter term preceded the former by about 35 years.

In many cases the purpose of an item bias analysis is to detect and eliminate biased items, and thus to create a fair test. However, statistical techniques are only appropriate for detecting potential bias in an item, and it must be stressed that a biased item does not necessarily create an unfair test. Within the limited scope of differential item functioning, it is argued later that DIF techniques may detect *test bias* only when most items on a test do not create similar errors in the scores of certain examinees, and this is rarely known in practice without performing a validity study. Some argue that differential item functioning and test bias can be linked through expert judgment, but this process has not yet been demonstrated to be reliable. Thus, the degree to which item bias methods improve fairness by reducing test bias is probably quite modest. The framework and language for discussing these issues in this chapter is that of test validity, and the distinction between internal and external validation processes is treated in detail to provide a consistent lexicon.

The measurement community has not been careful enough with the definition of bias, and this lack of focus may create a rift with the public and public interest groups. An example of the lack of communication is discussed in connection to the Golden Rule settlement.

Original Objectives of Item Bias Research

Before examining the current meaning of such terms as *bias* and *impact,* it is useful to reconsider an earlier rationale for defining and operationalizing these constructs. Eells, Havighurst, Herrick, and Tyler (1951) were not the first researchers to address the question of socioeconomic differences on intelligence test items; however, they drew together much of the literature—nine studies from 1911 to 1947 were reviewed—and performed a primary analysis of more than 650 items from eight IQ tests. Moreover, they defined item bias precisely:

> By *cultural bias in test items* is meant differences in the extent to which the child being tested has the opportunity to know and become familiar with the specific subject matter or specific process required by the test item. If a test item requires, for example, familiarity with symphony instruments, those children who have opportunity to attend symphony concerts will presumably be able to answer the

question more readily than children who have never seen a symphony orchestra. To the extent that intelligence-test items are drawn from cultural materials of this sort, with which high status pupils have more opportunity for familiarity, status differences in I.Q.'s will be expected. (p. 58)

Eells et al. were interested in establishing the extent to which observed group differences in IQ scores were artifactual, that is, dependent on the specific content of the test items rather than an important underlying ability in pupils (p. 4). A test was considered to be fair if it was composed of items that were equally familiar or unfamiliar to all persons: "Those problems for whose solution the training of different socio-economic groups has been *unequal* cannot be used as constituting in themselves a test of the general mental activity of those cultural groups. . . . They may be used only as measures of the *present skills* of two individuals who almost certainly have different genetic equipment and who certainly have had different amounts of training on the skills tested" (p. 23). These researchers took the position that the flaws in IQ tests could be overcome only if items were included that relied on experiences generally available in the American culture (p. 25). Furthermore, they strongly objected to curricula and derivative tests that predominantly reflected the middle-class school culture (pp. 26–27).

The two major purposes of the Eells et al. (1951) study were to detect item bias, and then to discover "a) those kinds of test problems on which children from high socioeconomic backgrounds show the greatest superiority and b) those kinds of test problems on which children from low socioeconomic backgrounds do relatively well" (p. 6). This knowledge then would be used to eliminate *cultural bias,* favoring any particular socioeconomic group, from the test (p. 24), and it is apparent that such bias was considered to diminish the measured ability of students lacking opportunity. When items showing large group differences in performance were detected and analyzed for commonalities, Eells et al. (1951, chapter 8) concluded that "[v]ariations in opportunity for familiarity with specific cultural words, objects, or processes required for answering the test items seem to the writer to appear . . . as the most adequate general explanation for most of the findings" (p. 68).

By eliminating items that relied on opportunity to learn, Eells et al. (1951) believed that group differences then would reflect more accurately an important underlying ability. Scheuneman (1987) summarized this process as follows:

At one time an orderly progression of research was envisioned as follows: a) Devise procedures for reliably detecting items that are performing differently for the groups of interest; b) examine the items and identify causes for this differential performance; c) develop procedures for modifying these items so that the differential performance is reduced or eliminated where appropriate; and d) develop guidelines for item writers so that future items are free from such bias. (p. 97)

It must be added that Eells et al. (1951) were concerned primarily with intelligence tests. Thus, the lack of opportunity to learn created a problem for an individual attempting to show his or her potential, which was considered to be more fundamental than cultural skills acquired through learning. Achievement test scores, on the other hand, are highly influenced by the opportunity to learn. Eells et al. may not have insisted that the *opportunity to learn* was a necessary ingredient for item bias on tests geared more toward achievement than aptitude. In addition, their definition of cultural item bias suggests that material causing bias is highly specific in content, and is not a more general skill such as reading comprehension.

Current Notions of Item Bias Research

How does this compare to more current thinking about item bias research? To facilitate a comparison, four recent views are given in the following sections. They were chosen not as definitions of item bias per se, but as illustrations of the commonality of today's approach to research and development with the one previously discussed. (But note that the concepts of item bias and DIF are not clearly distinguished in these views.) There is an important difference, as is evident, that concerns what Eells et al. (1951) referred to as the opportunity to learn, or equality of training. This is discussed later.

According to Linn, Levine, Hastings, and Wardrop (1980):

> If items on a test differ in their dependence on the characteristic that is incidental to the skill being assessed, then the biasing effects of that incidental characteristic would be expected to result in an interaction between the items and the characteristics of the examinees. In other words, the magnitude of group differences in performance would be expected to vary as a function of the extent to which items were dependent on the incidental characteristics. Once identified, the offending items could be revised or replaced in an effort to eliminate their biasing effects. (p. 4)

Osterlind (1983) observed:

> For the legitimate use of tests, it is crucial that all examinees be assured of equality in test items as far as their achievement or ability may be reliably assessed. Tests should be constructed so that when an inequality exists between the groups' test scores, the disparity is due primarily to differences in whatever it is the test purports to measure. By detection and elimination of biased items, tests can be constructed to this standard. (p. 8)

As Shepard (1981) put it:

> The logical connections established initially between test items and the construct domain must be reexamined in light of the new evidence of differential group

performance . . . the overarching question to be deliberated is whether the "bias" index signals a distortion in the meaning between groups, hence real bias, or a true difference in knowledge that legitimately should be addressed in keeping with the purpose of the test. The conclusion of bias and the decision to throw items out of the test will depend on what abilities the test was intended to represent. (p. 99)

Mellenbergh (1989) put it this way:

In many applications the user is satisfied with the detection of items that are biased with respect to certain groups. The items are removed from the test and it is claimed that the test is fair with respect to the groups that have been investigated. But, an important question remains: Why are these items biased? The answer to this question is not only of academic interest, but also has relevance for test construction. If the biasing factors are known the test constructor can prevent the occurrence of biased items. (p. 139)

The first three authors implied either directly or indirectly that the result of statistical screening of tests for biased items may help to weed out the kind of bias, if it exists, that inflates the difference in average ability between cultural groups. This appears to coincide with the intentions of Eells et al. (1951) that bias in test items distorts groups differences. Mellenbergh (1988) also seemed to agree that once such items are eliminated, and the "test is fair," it still remains to develop a set of item development principles. However, the notion of opportunity to learn has undergone a transformation. An item now is biased if the opportunity to learn is associated with a "characteristic that is incidental to the skill being assessed." In particular, "It is not considered to be an instance of bias when a well-constructed test reflects real differences in what groups have been taught. Bias can creep in, however, when differences in opportunity to learn in different subject areas are mixed together, as, for example, when group differences in math are confounded by reading abilities" (Shepard, 1981, pp. 83–84).

Furthermore, it is suggested that opportunity to learn is only a sufficient condition; it is not a necessary condition. Rather, the critical requirement is that group differences on an item reflect differences only on the intended construct. An observed difference due in part to any irrelevant but related construct, on which groups are unequal for any reason, is then the basis for identifying an item as biased. The Office for Minority Education at Educational Testing Service (ETS, 1980) made the historical commentary:

Over the years of research on item bias, the definition of the problem has taken several forms. . . . The current status is a curious one, however, in some ways similar to the differential prediction situation. While the intent of the investigations originally was to find items that are unfair for minority group members, the definition being urged at present is a more broad one, namely that any item should be regarded as biased if it measures something different in different groups. (p. 2)

Before discussing problems associated with this change, however, it is necessary to present a set of modern definitions that have replaced terms such as cultural item bias and opportunity to learn.

DEFINITIONS AND LANGUAGE CONVENTIONS

The language used herein concerning item bias comes from the literature on test validity rather than item validity. This language is used for two reasons. First, the literature on test validity is more mature, which has allowed a greater conceptual clarity to develop. Second, it is more natural to talk about test validity, because item validity generally is recognized as supporting evidence for test validity. In this context, items frequently are thought of as "little" tests, although items rarely are validated by the same means as tests. Specifically, I attempt to conform to the language used by Jensen in his 1980 book *Bias in Mental Testing,* although it is clear that others do not conform.

Fairness

Fairness refers to ethical questions about how a test is used, and the fairness of test scores used in selection situations is a familiar problem. There is not a neutral mechanism for determining whether a test is fair; rather, according to Jensen (1980 fairness refers:

> to the ways in which test scores (whether of biased or unbiased tests) are used in any selection situation. The concepts of fairness, social justice, and "equal protection of the laws" are moral, legal, and philosophical ideas and therefore must be evaluated in these terms. Consequently, persons holding divergent philosophies about these matters will understandably differ in their interpretations of "fairness" and "unfairness" in selection procedures based on tests. They will legitimately disagree about the criteria for deciding the fairness of a selection procedure involving members of different racial, social, or cultural groups. This in itself is not a statistical decision. . . . [It] must remain a policy decision based on philosophic, legal, or practical considerations. . . . (p. 376)

Test Bias

Bias is one of the most misunderstood words in modern psychometrics. Unlike the term fairness, bias has a narrow technical definition and I believe that it is difficult for any native speaker of English to use the word with a uniform connotation. And even if this were possible, it would be difficult for any native speaker of English to hear such a uniform connotation. It is helpful to present Jensen's (1980) definition of test bias:

In mathematical statistics, "bias" refers to a systematic under- or overestimation of a population parameter by a statistic based on samples drawn from the population. In psychometrics, "bias" refers to systematic errors in the predictive validity or construct validity of test scores of individuals that are associated with the individual's group membership. "Bias" is a general term and is not limited to "culture bias." It can involve any type of group membership—race social class, nationality, sex, religion, age. The assessment of bias is a purely objective, empirical, statistical and quantitative matter entirely independent of subjective value judgments and ethical issues concerning fairness or unfairness of tests and the uses to which they are put. *Psychometric bias is a set of statistical attributes conjointly of a given test and two or more specified subpopulations.* (p. 375)

Consider another definition of test bias by Shepard (1981): "Bias in a test is a slant in the way a test measures what it is intended to measure; it is a systematic error that disadvantages the test performance of one group to another" (p. 80). This is different from Jensen's (1980) definition. Test bias, according to Shepard, disadvantages one group. The use of disadvantage implies a test that is biased is unfair. Along these lines, Shepard, Camilli, and Averill (1981) argued that "Bias is a kind of invalidity that harms one group more than another. On an achievement test, carefully constructed to sample the content domain accurately, bias may nevertheless occur because the format of the questions or the mode of presentation is unfair to one group . . ." (p. 318).

Green (1975) used an example of a word knowledge test used as an indication of intelligence to illustrate bias. For whites, measured individual differences might approximate differences in reasoning ability, but for Blacks, such differences might reflect to a greater degree the opportunity to learn. In this example, the equivalence of the measured construct for two groups is challenged, and it also is suggested that the lack of equivalence has a social meaning, one that leads to the threshold of fairness. Indeed, this concept of bias is highly similar to the one of Eells et al. (1951), although the latter authors did not make a clear-cut distinction between item bias and test bias. Needless to say, the research literature has not maintained a crisp distinction between the concepts of bias and fairness.

Differential Item Functioning

Definitions of DIF fall generally into two broad categories: definitions related to an item-by-group interaction concept and definitions that are conditional on ability (Scheuneman, 1981a). In the item-by-group-interaction definition, an item functioning differently shows a relatively larger performance difference than other items—this is the standard analysis of variance (ANOVA) definition of interaction. A roughly equivalent way of saying this is that the group difference on an item showing DIF is either more or less than the average item difference on the total test. The conditional definition of item bias specifies that given two comparable groups, the probability of a correct response is not the same. (Often, comparability means equivalent ability on the test construct.)

The categories are much closer than they would appear. In fact, if one equates groups on ability, the definitions are nearly identical (see Angoff & Ford, 1973). This is because the probability of correct response can be conceptualized as the average difference between a 1-response and a 0-response. Thus, requiring the probabilities of a correct response from two groups to be the same for all items is equivalent to requiring no interaction. This leads to one standard definition of DIF: the systematic under- or overestimation of a parameter, which in the case of a dichotomously scored item is a probability. Both types of definition retain the ethically neutral connotation of test bias.

Variation in the Meaning of DIF and Item Bias

Some examples of actual definitions appearing in the literature may serve to illustrate the range of different connotations that currently exists. These examples are not exhaustive, but are well-known and have been influential:

According to Angoff (1982), "The items falling some distance from the [delta] plot may be regarded as contributing to the item-by-group interaction. These are items that are especially more difficult for one group than for another, *relative* to the other items" (p. 97). He went on to say:

> It may therefore be useful to work toward diffusing the bias issue by acknowledging that what we are considering here are not necessarily *item-bias* methodologies but only *item-discrepancy* methodologies. It should be understood that the presence or absence of bias is unavoidably a matter for human judgment, for which the statistical analysis is only a useful tool. It would probably clear the air considerably if we reserved the use of "bias" for its important social role and referred to the methods under present consideration in appropriately parsimonious terms. These methods are, after all, only item-discrepancy methods; they should not be credited with a higher function than they are capable of serving. (p. 114)

Holland and Thayer (1988) provided the following definition:

> The study of items that function differently for two groups of examinees has a long history. Originally called "item bias" research, modern approaches focus on the fact that different groups of [comparable] examinees may react differently to the same questions. These differences are worth exploring since they may shed light both on the test question and on the experiences and backgrounds of different groups of examinees. We prefer the more neutral terms, differential item performance or *differential item functioning*, (i.e., DIF), to item bias since in many examples that exhibit DIF the term "bias" does not accurately describe the situation. (p. 129)

And, as Cole and Moss (1989) put it:

Consider a geometry item on a mathematics survey test on which female students score considerably lower than male students, although the total test score difference is fairly small. Suppose that the use of the test score is to identify high-achieving mathematics students for placement in an honors mathematics class, and students who are ready for the advanced material are being sought. If that honors class requires prior knowledge of geometry, the result on the geometry item might be relevant to whether the student is adequately prepared for the honors class, regardless of the group difference on it. If, however, a student who had not learned geometry would be minimally affected in the particular honors class, the geometry item could be said to introduce an irrelevant effect and could be labeled as biased. (p. 211)

Angoff (1982) tempted to distinguish *item discrepancies* from item bias. He felt the latter term played a social role whereas discrepancy carried a neutral connotation. Item bias eventually would come into play when considering test fairness, but this judgment required something beyond item statistics. Holland and Thayer (1988) rendered a useful service in changing a well-defined, but a prone-to-be-misinterpreted term, namely item bias. The term DIF has displaced item bias to a large degree and admirably reflects the broad and neutral question of current item bias research: Does an item have the same probability of being correct for comparable groups? Bias, in the sense used by Jensen (1980), had a similar neutral connotation.

Cole and Moss (1989), to the contrary, showed that a reasonable interpretation exists to the effect that item bias methods either will or should ensure that the overall group difference on an observed item score accurately reflects the overall difference on the construct. This definition is not so different from that of Eells et al. (1951), and is also not so different from the language of Linn et al. (1980), Shepard (1981), and Osterlind (1983). However, Cole and Moss treated the term item bias in relation to the cause of the DIF; that is, there is a difference on the item that is caused by something irrelevant to the purpose of the test. Holland and Thayer (1988) used the term DIF to describe an observed effect. This is consistent with other works of Holland where he emphasized "*measuring the effects of causes* because this seems to be a place where statistics, which is concerned with measurement, has contributions to make" (1986, p. 945), and, similarly,

I do not mean to imply that the search for the causes of a phenomenon is useless endeavor: indeed, it is a driving force that motivates much of science. Rather I mean that a logical analysis of the search for causes follows from an analysis of the measurement of causal effects and it is not logically prior to this more basic activity. Defensible inferences about the *causes* of an effect are always made against a backdrop of measured causal effects and relevant theories. (1988, p. 3)

The modern notion of DIF separates unadjusted group differences, such as those arising from the unequal opportunity to learn, from unexpected effects that are observed between comparable groups. Relative, not absolute, effects are sought. The machinery of causal inference is concerned with estimating effects in situations in which units (examinees for instance) could have been exposed to different treatments, and this limits the range of hypotheses and causes to situations in which comparability can be defined sharply. This, however, is not necessarily congruent with an interest in test fairness. Before returning to this issue, the rationale for separating unadjusted and adjusted group differences is examined.

THE EGALITARIAN FALLACY AND IMPACT

Jensen (1980) described the *egalitarian fallacy* as

> . . . the gratuitous assumption that all human populations are essentially identical or equal in whatever ability or trait the test purports to measure. Therefore, any difference between populations in the distribution of test score . . . is taken as evidence that the test is biased. . . . with respect to scholastic performance, there is now general agreement that group differences in *achievement test* scores are not wholly due to test bias. The achievement differences between groups are more often attributed primarily to inequalities in schooling and home background. (p. 370)

Achievement differences that result from unequal opportunity to learn generally are not considered to be fair in our society. However, according to Jensen the test is the messenger, not the enemy. It could be argued that an unfair test is one that conceals this information. Thus, we need a term to describe global or unadjusted differences in ability between groups. Holland and Thayer (1988) defined *impact* as follows:

> If both examinee ability and item characteristics are confounded by simply measuring the difference in performance on an item between unmatched reference and focal group members [majority and minority groups], the result is a measure of *impact* rather than differential item performance. . . . In this chapter we do not discuss impact, since the confounding of differences in examinee ability with characteristics of items is of little utility in attempting to identify items that may truly disadvantage some populations of examinees. (p. 130)

Large differences between certain groups do indicate inequality or lack of opportunity, which no one denies. However, this is an issue well beyond the narrow scope of test bias, and even farther beyond the scope of DIF. The disadvantage that DIF techniques address has to do with the relative probabilities of correctly answering an item for comparable examinees. Test developers and psychometricians are concerned with group differences that have their source in the item, not the environment. Such items are the ones that truly disadvantage some examinees. What then, if anything, links DIF to test bias and fairness which are functions of test use? When items showing large DIF indices are eliminated from a test, are group differences reduced? Does the test become more highly correlated with a criterion?

THE CONNECTION BETWEEN DIF AND TEST VALIDITY

The basic reason for performing DIF analysis has to do with test validity. But the crucial question is how it fits into the network of validation. Certainly, there is no direct connection between DIF and predictive validity, or DIF and fairness. For example, as Scheuneman (1981a) explained, "The bias that has been found to exist in items, however, has not been clearly tied to bias in tests. In general, while the presence of biased items seems to decrease the likelihood that the test as a whole is unbiased, failure to detect item bias cannot conversely be considered as evidence that [test] bias does not exist but only that, if [test] bias exists the amount is much the same for all items" (p. 20). But the relationship of validity and DIF must begin somewhere, and we can look for the connection by examining modern motives for studying DIF. Berk (1982) wrote, "Since the item is the most fundamental level of content analysis and the foundation for these inferences, item bias studies are necessary for all tests" (p. 3). Berk continued:

> Other reasons for concentrating on item bias methods include the following: (1) item bias studies can be incorporated into the early stages of test construction and item analysis to minimize the chances of bias accusations arising later; (2) the elimination of item bias may decrease the likelihood of test bias, although research evidence is needed to verify this relationship; and (3) the regression and factor analytic methods employed in test bias studies of predictive and construct bias questions are not particularly troublesome compared to proposed item bias methods. (p. 3)

I interpret (unconfidently) the third reason to mean that the item bias methods are not particularly troublesome compared to regression and factor analytic methods. Berk recognized, however, that:

> In some cases, item biases may tend to cancel one another when viewed in terms of subtest or total test scores. Even if the item biases balance out across the test or the bias effects only account for a minute proportion of the total variance, the test should still be regarded as biased. Biases of any kind are socially and psychometrically undesirable, and every effort should be expended to minimize if not completely eliminate bias. (pp. 3–4)

Berk advocated the modern idea that DIF is undesirable because it implies a test item does not measure the same ability in two groups. This falls under the broad notion of differential validity (Jensen, 1980). The other reasons for studying DIF I interpret to be (a) to help deflect criticisms of unfairness ("bias accusations"), (b) to reduce test bias, although this is an unproven possibility, and (c) that some DIF methods are relatively easy to perform.

A common rationale for item bias studies is that "bias in testing" foments ubiquitous social and political controversy; hence, considerable effort should be devoted toward the development and validation of statistical techniques for detecting culturally biased items. Does not this reasoning suggest that the true intentions of some who perform item bias research is to decrease test bias? It is therefore important to understand in detail why DIF is not strongly related to test bias.

THE CONNECTION BETWEEN DIF AND TEST BIAS

By examining a number of definitions, it was argued previously that the term DIF does not necessarily imply bias. It is a measure of an effect, and does not suggest the cause. In itself, DIF most often has no external referent except the particular data set used: It is primarily an interaction of test items given to a particular group of examinees. This lack of external referent, also known as the *circularity problem,* now is reviewed. Following this, the role of experts in connecting DIF to test bias is explored.

DIF Statistics are Ipsative

When comparable groups are formed on the basis of scores on the test in question, a confounding occurs. Shepard (1982) wrote, "A major limitation of all the bias detection approaches employed in the research to date is that they are all based on a criterion internal to the test in question. They cannot escape the circulatory inherent in using the total score on the test or average item to identify individuals of equal ability and hence specify the standard of unbiasedness" (pp. 23–24). This internal circularity is manifest as the inability to detect pervasive bias. Thus, DIF statistics do not distinguish pervasive bias from impact. According to Scheuneman (1981a), ". . . the mean bias effect across items appears as part of the apparent differences between groups on item difficulty. What remains to be detected is only the variation across items" (pp. 24–25).

It is helpful to look at the actual results of DIF analyses to understand this limitation. For example, Linn et al. (1980) found that items showing large unexpected differences did not always favor White students. They found that one out of three items (showing consistent group differences) seemed to favor Blacks. Scheuneman (1981a) reviewed several studies: "Cotter and Berk (1981) found seven items that appeared to be biased against blacks and six that seemed to favor them. Sinnot (1980) reported results at two levels of disparity. Of the more extreme items, nine were for blacks, and eight were against blacks, while at the less restrictive level, fifteen items were for blacks, and ten were against" (p. 25). Furthermore, Holland, Longford, and Thayer (1989) reported that the average log-odds (the Mantel–Haenszel measure of effect size) was "usually close to zero." I would argue, partly on the basis of this information, that the theoretical mean is zero, and an observed nonzero mean is an estimation artifact. (More mathematical arguments also may be made.) For example, the average log-odds ratio for a 30-item test (13 with significant DIF) analyzed by Camilli and Smith (1990) was $\bar{x} = .004$ with $s = .389$. Holland et al. referred to this property as "self-norming." The *ipsative* property of DIF indices perhaps is seen most clearly in the computer program BIMAIN (Bock, Muraki, & Pfeiffenberger, 1988), in which DIF indices are explicitly constrained to sum to zero.

The circulatory problem is exemplified by the fact that the average DIF index on a test is zero. Internal methods of DIF are ipsative: Holding ability constant, if one group of examinees tends to miss some items unexpectedly, it must unexpectedly answer other items correctly. In other words, items that disfavor the minority group are canceled by items that favor the minority group. If DIF is linked to test bias, it is not by way of indicating a systematic underestimation of test scores for a particular group. It must be linked by an unbiased external criterion, or by expert judgment. However, because unbiased external criteria are generally unavailable or nonexistent, expert review has more potential in practice.

It is important to emphasize that the instances of DIF in favor of a minority group cannot be ignored when considering items for modification or deletion. A DIF analysis provides no empirical basis for this action. The studies cited earlier indicated that with real tests, DIF tends to be symmetric. Thus to close the gap in group performance, additional arguments would have to be made through expert review for retaining items that favored one group while discarding oppositely biased items. I have argued previously that DIF indices are normed with an arbitrary zero point, so the deletion of items with DIF indices of the same sign could be justified by transforming this scale to one with a nonarbitrary zero point. This is equivalent in some respects to the problem of providing a criterion-referenced interpretation to the value of an otherwise norm-referenced scale.

The Role of Experts

Experts might solve the circularity problem by indicating a true zero point for a set of DIF indices conditioned on total score. A measure of bias thus would be obtained that is not ipsative. For example, individuals who combine expertise in the subject matter of test items with expertise in instruction and child development might be able to sort achievement items into groups that should exhibit positive, negative, and no DIF (relative to two demographic groups). A link between item bias and test bias then could be established if this predictive classification showed a strong relationship to empirical measures of DIF. The accuracy of judges is critical in this process. Lacking this ability, it would be desirable if experts could explain (rather than predict) patterns of statistical bias in items to a satisfactory degree. The case also might be made that a weaker version of these two conditions is sufficient, namely, whether judges can be internally consistent in identifying items that are biased. But it is obvious that such permissiveness simply would shift the circularity to another set of indices. Intersubjective agreement alone cannot constitute evidence for bias.

How well can judges confirm empirical patterns of DIF? There are some bright spots in the research; for example, see Scheuneman (1987) and Schmitt (1988) who confirmed a limited number of predictions concerning DIF with quasi-experimental designs. However, in a review of three studies, Reynolds (1982) found that judges are consistently unable to find biased test items. More recently, Engelhard (1989) performed a study on a teacher certification test with 42 judges described as follows:

> The judges included in this study are the actual members of item bias review committees. The individuals are highly motivated professionals who were recommended by their colleagues for this judgmental task. Since the judges themselves are primarily teachers, it may be safe to assume that they will be able to provide more accurate estimates of differential item performance than individuals who are not practitioners. Further, they received a 45 minute training session on item bias. (p. 5)

After an analysis of the agreement of judges with statistical indices, Engelhard concluded that "The data suggest that it is probably unreasonable to expect judges to flag the same items that are identified by empirical procedures" (p. 19).

In many cases of test development, though, no prior hypotheses are made. Instead, a post hoc analysis of DIF is performed. Perhaps DIF can be recognized more readily than predicted. There are few data available on which to evaluate the effectiveness of this process, although it is doubtlessly true that post hoc analyses are the most prevalent kind. It is not even clear what standards could be used to measure the effectiveness of judges in this situation.

Still, there is a role for judgmental review. The Office for Minority Education at ETS (Office for Minority Education, 1980) concluded that DIF studies have not led to a consistency "that would generalize into a principle that could be followed by practitioners, and the prospects of one emerging are not bright. Instead, a less quantitative approach, that of minority review, seems to have the most promise for providing appropriate specific steps to take in test construction" (p. 3). One such approach is *sensitivity review,* which is important for creating tests that are socially balanced and even-handed. It is meant to remove stereotypic implications and insulting or derogatory language from the manner in which questions are posed, but not necessarily to remove DIF.

Researchers agree that expert judgment studies eventually may have the direct effect of screening out items that are biased, or would contribute to a systematic misestimation of ability. However, there is precious little evidence that such technology is currently available. This is a valuable direction for those interested in DIF, but is likely to be tough research. For example, Scheuneman (1987) concluded recently in a study with some positive findings that "What emerges most clearly . . . is how little we know about the mechanisms that produce differential performance between black and white examinees" (p. 117).

DIF ANALYSIS AS THE STUDY
OF CONSTRUCT REPRESENTATION

Although there seems to be a consensus that no direct path exists from DIF to test bias, this is considered to be a limitation, not a fatal flaw. After all, predictive validity always refers in part to a criterion being predicted, but often there is no clear-cut external criterion for what the test is intended to measure. Thus there is some justification to concentrate on the internal validity of a test. At this point it is useful to discuss DIF analysis as an analysis of construct representation.

It may be argued that DIF analyses address the problem of construct representation that concerns the internal validity of a test. Other activities that fall into this area, for example, are reliability and factor analysis. Construct representation can be studied by task decomposition methods (Embretson, 1985), and to stretch Embretson's meaning a little, a task should not be decomposable by ethnic (or whatever) group membership for examinees of equal ability. The variable "group" here can be thought of as a proxy for cognitive variables that are determined by different educational histories. Construct representation, though, should be distinguished from *nomothetic* span. The latter concerns the utility of a test as a measure of individual differences (Embretson, 1985).

It is important to understand the relationship between these two facets of validity. Embretson (1985) explained:

> . . . the relationship between construct representation and nomothetic span is crucial to the construct validity of a test and to test design. Specifically, it is important to determine how individual differences in performing the underlying cognitive variables influence the test's variance and covariance with other measures.

> It is important to note that the cognitive variables that are identified by construct representation research *may* or *may not* be sources of individual differences in the test score. The cognitive variables are not necessarily sources of individual differences in the test score because they may not vary systematically over individuals or they may be too highly correlated with other cognitive variables to contribute uniquely to test variance. (p. 196)

Item bias technology as a tool for construct representation research currently has useful applications in the study of group differences in cross-cultural psychology, if not test bias. For example, Schmitt (1988) studied language differences between Hispanic and native speakers of English. Potentially useful results also have been demonstrated in the area of instructional sensitivity (Miller & Linn, 1988; Muthén, Kao, & Burstein, 1988). Because DIF statistics can be obtained to examine these and other aspects of a test construct, they "should not be thought of as impoverished substitutes for predictive validity methods. They answer a different question, more fundamental to an improved understanding of what a test measures. The predictive validity paradigm is a limited model to emulate, because it focuses on only one element in a more demanding schema of validity and does not, by itself, enlighten us about the meaning of obtained correlations" (Shepard, 1982, p. 24).

CONCLUSIONS

One original purpose of item bias research was to rid IQ tests of group differences that resulted from unequal opportunity to learn. This did not necessarily involve, as Jensen (1980) described, the assumption that all human populations are equal on a particular trait. Rather, the assumption was that unequal opportunity distorts the measurement of group differences in aptitude. When dealing with achievement in contrast to potential, the definition of item bias by Eells et al. (1951) is not necessarily inconsistent with the modern definition.

Apparent differences in usage of the terms item bias and DIF arise in the current literature depending on whether one is emphasizing cause (namely, lack of relevant cause), in which case the term item bias often is used, or effect, in which case the term DIF often is used. It is clear that Eells et al. (1951) were more concerned with cause. However, it is also apparent that some believe that a test showing no DIF is likely to be an unbiased test, and perhaps a fair test. This juxtaposition of terms is problematic.

As a means of demonstrating test fairness, the use of DIF analyses is by no means straightforward. It must be understood at the outset that a test showing little DIF is not necessarily unbiased. A systematic bias in test scores cannot be detected; DIF techniques are only sufficient for demonstrating the relative strengths of groups of examinees. Furthermore, an unbiased test may or may not exhibit differential item performance. If a more indirect route to making a fair test is accepted, it first needs to be established that the presence of DIF can be explained as due to factors that are extraneous to the test construct, that is, such items are biased. Second, all items showing either positive or negative bias must be removed. However, the link between the statistical index of DIF and the judgment of a test item as biased is weak—regardless of whether the bias is considered to be relative (item bias) or absolute (test bias). As Cronbach (1982) wrote:

The causal statements for which internal validity can be claimed are peculiarly restricted. Causal conclusions are conditional, and the conditions may severely limit the application of such conclusions. . . . the reasoning leading [to external validation] is not exclusively formal or statistical. Many statements, only a few of them explicit, link formal reasoning to the real world; their plausibility determines the force of the argument. Internal inference, then, is much less rigorous and deductive than others have suggested. (p. 112)

Finally, the removal or modification of items judged as biased may or may not result in a fairer test: Fairness must take into account the external circumstances of test use.

It is difficult to evaluate DIF analyses that are based on internal criteria, and it is not yet clear how external criteria should be utilized in defining comparability. Strong signals of DIF do not imply a test is unfair, on one hand, and the deletion of a few items rarely makes a perceptible difference in test score distributions, on the other (e.g., see Hu & Dorans, 1989). The analysis of DIF has served a useful function in construct representation research. However, the technical sophistication involved (e.g., log-odds, chi-squares, item response theory) should not unintentionally serve the purpose of deflecting claims of unfairness. As Angoff (1982) wrote, "These methods are, after all, only item-discrepancy methods; they should not be credited with a higher function than they are capable of serving."

Appendix

FAIRNESS, BIAS, IMPACT AND ISSUES
SURROUNDING THE "GOLDEN RULE"

The "Golden Rule" is a strategy intended to reduce the performance differential directly by choosing items that are limited in terms of the difference in pass rates for White and Black examinees. The Golden Rule (GR) settlement is far more complex, of course, but this is an important and controversial component. In terms of the aforementioned definitions, the GR is intended to directly reduce our impression of impact, and has been criticized widely for this purpose.

In opposing the GR several points are central. First, if group differences on items are not controlled for ability, they reflect *impact* and not bias. Equating impact with bias is, in effect, blaming the test for real environmental differences, or, from another point of view, holding a testing agency responsible for conditions well beyond its control. What suffers with the GR selection procedure is the link between the real-life situation and the test score. But the efficiency of the measuring process also is lowered; in many instances, only less reliable items show group differences that fall into the required range. This may increase the "lottery" effect if the error component of the test score is increased.

I want to examine the contention that DIF methods provide a more appropriate methodology for selecting test items than the GR requirements. The major issue is "Why is it more appropriate? What problems are solved by DIF methods?" To answer these questions, first consider three observations made by major players in the GR controversy. Linn and Drasgow (1987) wrote, "Some of the concerns that have led to support for the Golden Rule procedure are legitimate. The possibility of item bias deserves continued attention. However, this needs to be

415

done using more justifiable techniques" (p. 17) Linn and Drasgow were referring to techniques based on item characteristic curve (ICC) differences, and approximations such as the Mantel–Haenszel procedure. Faggen (1987) wrote, "The Mantel–Haenszel statistic helps to identify differences in performance on an item-by-item basis that may reflect potentially irrelevant characteristics of certain test questions that may be unfair to certain groups" (p. 7). Anrig (1988) elaborated more on the use of Mantel–Haenszel statistics: "Test items whose differential difficulty statistics suggest that these items may be biased for one or more subgroups are subjected to intensive reviews by test-development and subject matter specialists. Items whose fairness remains in doubt are rewritten or replaced" (p. 21). It appears that the GR procedure has the aim of reducing item bias, according to Linn and Drasgow. However, is the aim of the GR to reduce item bias, or is it to create a fairer test? This is an absurd question: Reducing item bias in this context is only useful to the degree that it is related to increasing test fairness. Unfortunately, the connection is not strong. Thus, Faggen was not being modest in weakly connecting the use of the Mantel–Haenszel statistic to detecting potentially unfair test items; note the double use of the word *may.*

The connection between item bias and fairness is not clear in Anrig's statement. One possible interpretation is that an unfair item may show a noticeable amount of DIF. Consequently, such an item would be reviewed to see if the DIF could be explained by an extraneous feature of the item. If so, the item is rewritten or replaced. However, is it also suggested that all (or even most) unfair (as opposed to biased) items would be rewritten or removed? This is a strong claim for bias detection technology, but more important, creating fair test items—in the limited sense of unbiased items—does not necessarily create a fair test. Fairness is a property of test use that exceeds the narrow confines of the item and the engine of causal inference. It is also a criterion that exceeds (but does not preclude) the responsibility of the test developer.

The selection of unbiased items was not the ultimate objective advocated by supporters of the GR procedure. For example, Rooney (1987) wrote that the procedure requires test developers "to take specific, verifiable steps to reduce unnecessary racial differences" (p. 19). The word *unnecessary* plays a key role here, as Rooney explained,

> By "unnecessary racial differences," I refer to differences which arise from the use of specific test questions whose racial differences in correct answer rates are greater than that of other questions, *in the same content area, having the same content validity.* In other words, in a given content area . . . , where several possible questions have been determined to be content valid, failing to select questions having the least racial difference in correct answer rates results in unnecessary racial differences. (p. 23)

It is believed by many psychometricians and educators that the *impact* on a test should be used to justify remedial interventions. Eventually this may validly reduce the impact. The GR procedure, however, was an attempt to adjust *current* conditions. Rooney's (1987) stated motivation for seeking a different procedure for selecting test items was a belief that an insurance test was "for all practical purposes excluding blacks entirely from the occupation of insurance agent." I do not think Rooney was really very concerned about DIF, but about seeking fairness in terms of his own system of political, social, and moral beliefs. By excluding unnecessary differences from a test, Rooney believed that more Blacks would be allowed to be insurance agents.

A more technical argument can be made for not automatically choosing among items of equal quality by selecting those with higher discrimination. Such a strategy will boost group differences as well as reliability. Masters (1988) presented an argument that this may be a source of systematic bias if the item attains some of its discriminating power on a secondary ability. Let the primary and secondary abilities be labeled P and S, and the two groups in question be labeled R and F. Now assume that (a) If R and F were equated on P, then they would have different averages on S, and (b) P and S are highly correlated. The *observed* test score 0 will have two components: P and S. Thus, equating groups on O will confound some of $S_R - S_F$ with $O_R - O_F$. That is, some of the irrelevant difference will be confused with impact. To understand why a correlated ability S can be considered irrelevant, consider a test intended to measure achievement. Let P be the relevant construct and S be test wiseness. It seems likely that these abilities are correlated but also that it is highly desirable to measure as little of S as possible.

Can this type of bias be detected by the Mantel–Haenszel technique or current ICC methods, and will such items be discarded when appropriate? Hunter (1975) showed that unidimensional test models do not deal adequately with group differences in the distribution of secondary abilities, but research on this problem is only in a preliminary stage. Furthermore, although highly discriminating items result in a reliable test, they do not necessarily increase the test's predictive validity: Reliability does not imply validity. Therefore, I do not find Rooney's (1987) reasoning without merit; and it would be quite interesting to examine the range of difficulty and discrimination values for items in a particular content area judged equally valid by experts.

The actual effectiveness of the GR for increasing the number of Black insurance agents (or any other purpose) is a matter that should be unrelated to the appropriate methods for choosing test items. It is inappropriate, in my mind, that the discussion of fairness—and the tradeoffs that might ensue—should be relegated to a mechanical rule. To balance our social accounts, should we resort to tinkering with the technical aspects of test scores or test items? The most simple and direct method would be too explicate the social utilities of various outcomes (Petersen & Novick, 1976) based on the most valid predictors of success we can muster. But this is such an intractable debate in our society that the tradeoff usually occurs at a highly technical level. This obfuscates the compromise as well as the predictive validity of the test.

V

CONCLUDING REMARKS AND SUGGESTIONS

Say, do you have any good ideas for a thesis topic?
Anonymous graduate student, anytime.

DIF analyses contribute important quantitative information to the study of the fairness of a test or a test item. It is not the only information that can inform such issues, but it is directly relevant to questions of differences in the performance of subgroups of examinees, and it provides information that is different from the historically older measures of reliability and of predictive and face validity.

The term *testing instrument* is only the most obvious term-of-art that signifies the measuring instrument view of tests. In this view, tests are created in order to measure some cognitive aspect of a person, and then used to compare examinees. DIF (as well as other quantitative) analyses turn things around and use the responses of those being measured to say something about the measuring instrument itself. Does the measurer measure up?

In our view, DIF analyses should be broadly conceived as using information about the differential performance of groups of examinees to study, in detail, the ingredients of the test itself. For the most part, the current use of DIF analyses involves groups of examinees that are very heterogeneous—Blacks versus Whites, females versus males. This is a useful place to start because of the social significance of these large groups of examinees on Ameri-

419

can society. However, because of their heterogeneity, the information obtained from these analyses is less useful to the test development process than it would be if it were obtained from more closely circumscribed comparisons that involved carefully considered educational and experiential aspects of examinees. We encourage further research along these lines.

The methods for performing DIF analyses that are discussed in this book are the logical consequence of work started at least as long ago as the 1970s, and represent, in our opinion, the standard against which all future DIF methods should be compared. We are no longer in the position where any new idea for measuring DIF can be considered on its own merits. New methods need to show that they improve upon the Mantel–Haenszel, standardization, and likelihood ratio IRT methods discussed here. Improvement can take many forms but high on the list are improved statistical properties like power and robustness, decreased sensitivity to nuisance factors, and the ability to handle more complex item responses while losing neither the good standards already achieved for multiple-choice items nor the practical cost levels that current DIF methods enjoy.

It is unlikely that the basic parameters that are estimated by DIF methods will change much in the future (although the new method proposed in chapter 5 expands on those described in chapter 3 and suggests additional parameters that might be usefully estimated without ignoring the role of those in current use). Unadjusted differences in item performance that do not compare the performance of comparable examinees are not measures of DIF but of impact and only serve to confound differential performance on an item with differential examinee ability that the item is supposed to measure. Concentrating on measures of impact can hide true DIF, direct attention to the wrong items, and does not lead to improved measurement. We expect that measures of impact will cease to have any direct interest to those interested in improving tests, and will be replaced with more appropriate DIF measures when the questions of interest involve the performance of different groups of examinees. For example, we don't believe that the measure of impact used in the Golden Rule Insurance Company/ETS settlement of 1984, described in chapter 20, will have an important role in the improvement of tests. At the major testing organizations it is DIF analyses and not measures of impact that have become routine in many testing programs.

Being related to test fairness, DIF is also usefully considered from the "contest" view of tests. In many uses of tests there is an implicit or explicit contest that the examinees are in—most obviously to win a college scholarship or to gain admittance to a limited number of places in a competitive college's freshman class. However, one can sometimes think of professional licensure or admission to special education programs as contests. Test fairness is commonly related to the idea that fair contests must take place on level playing fields. In tests that are contests, certain items exhibiting DIF may tilt the field. Within this metaphor, we can consider the methods described in this book as crucial tools for the assiduous keeper of the grounds.

We think that one of the most important practical lessons that emerges from DIF studies of real test items is that a test item can exhibit DIF, that is, comparable examinees in different groups can perform differently on the item, but the item need not be biased in any reasonable sense. That is, DIF is a measurable quantity associated with a test item in a given context, but *bias* is a judgment that involves the intended use of the test as well as complex issues of fairness. DIF is not bias. On the other hand, "biased" test items that do not exhibit appropriate DIF are "biased" without empirical consequences for examinees and it is possible that concern over them might be better spent on other testing issues.

We have presented in this book what we believe to be the two most important approaches to measuring DIF, both of which emphasize comparing the item performance of comparable examinees in two groups. One set of methods, the Mantel–Haenszel and the standardization methods, compare examinees who are comparable on observed scores and possibly other data. These two methods are closely related and, we believe, are the best available observed score methods for measuring DIF. They both have the three ingredients that we think a respectable DIF procedure should have—interpretable parameter estimates, associated standard errors, and powerful tests of the hypothesis of no DIF. The other method, based on parametric item response theory (IRT) models, compares examinees who are comparable on the unobserved latent variables that these models hypothesize to underlie the observed test scores. It should be emphasized that we have been very selective in our choice of IRT procedures to discuss in this book. We regard the approach in chapter 4 (simultaneously fitting IRT models by marginal maximum likelihood to both groups of examinees and using likelihood ratio tests, parameter estimates, and estimated standard errors based on these models to evaluate, sequentially, the equality of item parameters for different groups) as the proper use of these models to measure DIF. In our opinion, this is the standard to which other uses of IRT models to measure DIF should be compared. The older approach of fitting separate IRT models to the data from two different groups and then comparing the item parameters that result makes no allowance for the fact that the latent traits that are separately estimated may not have a common interpretation in the two groups and for this reason we believe that the methods of chapter 4 are more acceptable.

Are IRT methods or observed score methods to be preferred? In practice they have different strengths. Generally speaking, the observed score methods discussed in chapter 3 are more practical to apply in terms of costs and computing resources. They do not involve iterative numerical algorithms and yet for many purposes they yield sufficient information for action and understanding. IRT methods are more expensive, involve more complex computing resources, and depend on explicit models. However, when these models are reasonable they can give a more detailed look at the difference in the performance of different groups of examinees on test items. In addition, it is likely that IRT methods are not sensitive to some of the nuisance factors that can affect the observed score methods as described in chapter 7, although this is a question that needs more research. In short, we see a continued role for both observed score and IRT methods and encourage the continued development of both with the aim of improving those methods discussed here.

What might the future hold for DIF research? It can move forward on several fronts. Chapter 10, by Shealy and Stout, gives a formal theory of the origins of DIF in terms of the multidimensionality of the latent variables that underlie tests and test items. This research may stimulate new DIF detection methods based on multidimensional IRT models but may also stimulate others to develop other competing theories of the origins of DIF in test items. The use of randomized DIF studies, described in chapter 14, can shed light on such theories. In fact, we think that the use of randomized DIF studies should become more widely used to study the causes of DIF in real test items. This is not easy work, as chapter 14 illustrates, but only by the results of such studies can real progress be made on the question of why some items show DIF and others don't. Such experimental work is slow, but it inexorably leads to genuine knowledge that can improve the fairness of tests, and our knowledge of what test items really measure. However, randomized DIF studies are not the only way DIF research can progress. The analysis of extant DIF data by cross-classifying test items by factors thought relevant to DIF (as exemplified in chapter 12) is always a useful first step in the identification of the causes of DIF. We expect this work to continue and to build on the results reported here.

Chapter 9 considers a variety of issues about DIF measures that can be addressed best by considering DIF results for many test items at once. This is an important area for future work because the amount of DIF exhibited by a single item is often quite small and only by thoughtful aggregation across items or test administrations can useful and stable information be obtained. The use of random effect or random parameter models to accomplish this, as discussed in chapter 9, is an area full of exciting research potential.

Perhaps the most important conclusion from the many contributions in this book is that the study of differential item functioning is a well-defined research area with a principled methodology and a growing body of findings. It is a fruitful area of research on testing and one of the few empirical areas that can tell us new things about tests, what they measure and how well they do it. To the anonymous graduate student looking for suggestions for research we say, "go to it."

References

Alderman, D. L., & Holland, P. W. (1981). *Item performance across native language groups on the Test of English as a Foreign Language* (Research Rep. No. 81–16). Princeton, NJ: Educational Testing Service.

Allen, N., & Wainer, H. (1989). *Nonresponse in declared ethnicity and the identification of Differential Item Functioning* (Research Rep. No. 89–87). Princeton, NJ: Educational Testing Service.

Angoff, W. H. (Ed.). (1971). *The College Board Admissions Testing Program: A technical report on research and development activities relating to the Scholastic Aptitude Test and Achievement Tests.* New York: College Entrance Examination Board.

Angoff, W. H. (1972, Sept.). *A technique for the investigation of cultural differences.* Paper presented at the annual meeting of the American Psychological Association, Honolulu. (ERIC Document Reproduction Service No. ED 069686)

Angoff, W. H. (1982). Use of difficulty and discrimination indices for detecting item bias. In R. A. Berk (Ed.), *Handbook of methods for detecting test bias* (pp. 96–116). Baltimore: Johns Hopkins University Press.

Angoff, W. H., & Cook, L. L. (1988). *Equating the scores of the Prueba de Aptitud Academica and the Scholastic Aptitude Test.* New York: College Entrance Examination Board.

Angoff, W. H., & Ford, S. F. (1973). Item-race interaction on a test of scholastic aptitude. *Journal of Educational Measurement, 10,* 95–106.

Angoff, W. H., & Johnson, E. G. (1988). *A study of the differential impact of curriculum on aptitude test scores* (Research Rep. 88–46). Princeton, NJ: Educational Testing Service.

Angoff, W. H., & Modu, C. C. (1973). *Equating the scores of the Prueba de Aptitud Academica and the Scholastic Aptitude Test* (Research Rep. No. 3). New York: College Entrance Examination Board.

Angoff, W. H., & Sharon, A. T. (1974). The evaluation of differences in test performance of two or more groups. *Educational and Psychological Measurement, 34,* 807–816.

Anrig, G. R. (1987). ETS on "Golden Rule." *Educational Measurement: Issues and Practice, 6,* 24–27.

Anrig, G. R. (1987, January). "Golden Rule": Second thoughts. *APA Monitor,* p. 3.

Anrig, G. R. (1988). ETS replies to Golden Rule on "Golden Rule." *Educational Measurement: Issues and Practice, 7,* 20.

423

Ansley, T. N., & Forsyth, R. A. (1955). An examination of the characteristics of unidimensional IRT parameter estimated derived from two-dimensional data. *Applied Psychological Measurement, 9,* 37–48.

Baker, F. B. (1981). A criticism of Scheuneman's item bias technique. *Journal of Educational Measurement, 18,* 59–62.

Bar-Haim, G., & Wilkes, J. M. (1989). A cognitive interpretation of the marginality and under-representation of women in science. *Journal of Higher Education, 6,* 371–387.

Baron, R., Tom, D., & Cooper, H. (1985). Social class, race, and teacher expectations. In J. Dusek & G. Joseph (Eds.) *Teacher Expectancies* (pp. 251–269). Hillsdale, NJ: Lawrence Erlbaum Associates.

Benbow, C. P., & Stanley, J. C. (1980). Sex differences in mathematical ability: Fact or artifact? *Science, 20,* 1261–1264.

Berk, R. (Ed.). (1982). *Handbook of methods for detecting test bias.* Baltimore: Johns Hopkins University Press.

Bersoff, D. N. (1981). Testing and the law. *American Psychologist, 36,* 1047–1056.

Birnbaum, A. (1968). Some latent trait models and their use in inferring an examinee's ability. In F. M. Lord & M. R. Novick, *Statistical theories of mental test scores* (pp. 392–479). Reading, MA: Addison-Wesley.

Bishop, Y. M. M., Fienberg, S. E., & Holland, P. W. (1975). *Discrete multivariate analysis.* Cambridge, MA: MIT Press.

Bleistein, C. A., & Schmitt, A. P. (1989, March). *Criterion selection for evaluation of DIF for Chemistry Achievement tests.* Paper presented at the annual meeting of the National Council on Measurement in Education, San Francisco.

Bleistein, C. A., Schmitt, A. P., & Curley, W. E. (1990, April). *Factors hypothesized to affect the performance of Black examinees on SAT-Verbal analogy items.* Paper presented at the annual meeting of the National Council on Measurement in Education, Boston.

Bleistein, C. A., Schmitt, A. P., Curley, W. E., & Kubota, M. Y. (1990, April). *Factors affecting the performance of Black examinees on SAT analogy items.* Paper presented at the annual meeting of the National Council on Measurement in Education, Boston.

Bleistein, C. A., & Wright, D. J. (1985). *Assessing unexpected differential item performance of Asian-American candidates on SAT Form 3FSA08 and TSWE Form E47* (Statistical Rep. No. 85–123). Princeton, NJ: Educational Testing Service.

Bleistein, C. A., & Wright, D. J. (1986, April). *Assessment of unexpected differential item difficulty for Asian-American candidates on the Scholastic Aptitude Test.* Paper presented at the National Council on Measurement in Education annual meeting, San Francisco.

Bleistein, C. A., & Wright, D. J. (1987). Assessment of unexpected differential item difficulty for Asian-American candidates on the Scholastic Aptitude Test. In A. P. Schmitt & N. J. Dorans (Eds.) *Differential item functioning on the Scholastic Aptitude Test* (Research Memorandum No. 87–1). Princeton, NJ: Educational Testing Service.

Blyth, C. R. (1972). On Simpson's paradox and the sure-thing principle. *Journal of the American Statistical Association, 67,* 364–365.

Bock, R. D. (1975). *Multivariate statistical methods in behavioral research.* New York: McGraw Hill.

Bock, R. D., & Aitkin, M. (1981). Marginal maximum likelihood estimation of item parameters: An application of the EM algorithm. *Psychometrika, 46,* 443–449.

Bock, R. D., & Jones, L. V. (1968). *The measurement and prediction of judgement and choice.* San Francisco: Holden-Day.

Bock, R. D., & Lieberman, M. (1970). Fitting a response model for n dichotomously scored items. *Psychometrika, 35,* 179–197.

Bock, R. D., & Mislevy, R. J. (1981). *The profile of American youth: Data quality analysis of the Armed Services Vocational Aptitude Battery.* Chicago: National Opinion Research Center.

Bock, R. D., Muraki, E., & Pfeiffenberger, W. (1988). Item pool maintenance in the presence of item parameter drift. *Journal of Educational Measurement, 25,* 275–285.

Bock, R. D., & Yates, G. (1973). *MULTIQUAL: Log-linear analysis of nominal and ordinal qualitative data by the method of maximum likelihood.* Chicago: National Educational Resources.

Bond, L. (1980). Review of Bias in Mental Testing by A. R. Jensen. *Applied Psychological Measurement, 3,* 406–410.

Bond, L. (1981). Bias in mental tests. In B. F. Green & B. Schrader (Eds.). *New Directions for testing and measurement: Issues in testing—Coaching, disclosure, and ethnic bias. No. 11.* pp. 55–77. San Francisco: Jossey-Bass.

Bond, L. (1987). The Golden Rule settlement: A minority perspective. *Educational Measurement: Issues and Practice, 6,* 18–20.

Camilli, G., & Shepard, L. A. (1987). The inadequacy of ANOVA for detecting biased items. *Journal of Educational Statistics, 12,* 87–99.

Camilli, G., & Smith, J. K. (1990). Comparison of the Mantel-Haenszel Test with a randomized and a jackknife test for detecting biased items. *Journal of Educational Statistics, 15,* 53–67.

Campbell, P. B. (1986). What's a nice girl like you doing in a math class? *Phi Delta Kappan, 67,* 516–520.

Cardall, C., & Coffman, W. E. (1964). A method for comparing the performance of different groups on the same items of a test. *Research and Development Reports, 9,* 64–65. Princeton, NJ: Educational Testing Service.

Carlton, S. T., & Harris, A. M. (1989a, March). *Characteristics of differential item performance on the Scholastic Aptitude Test—selected ethnic group comparisons.* Paper presented at the annual meeting of the National Council on Measurement in Education, San Francisco.

Carlton, S. T., & Harris, A. M. (1989b, March). *Female/male performance differences on the SAT: Causes and correlates.* Paper presented at the annual meeting of the American Educational Research Association, San Francisco.

Carlton, S. T., & Harris, A. M. (In preparation). *Characteristics associated with differential item performance on the Scholastic Aptitude Test: Gender and majority/minority group comparisons.*

Carroll, J. B., Davies, P., & Richman, B. (1971). *Word frequency book.* New York: American Heritage Publishing.

Cattell, R. B. (1963). Theory of fluid and crystallized intelligence: A critical experiment. *Journal of Educational Psychology, 54,* 1–22.

Cleary, T. A. (1968). Test bias: prediction of grades of Negro and white students in integrated colleges. *Journal of Educational Measurement, 5,* 115–124.

Cleary, T. A., & Hilton, T. J. (1968). An investigation of item bias. *Educational and Psychological Measurement, 5,* 115–124.

Clogg, C. C. (1988). Latent class models for measuring. In R. Langeheine & J. Rost (Eds.). *Latent trait and latent class models* (pp. 173–205). New York: Plenum.

Cochran, W. G. (1954). Some methods for strengthening the common χ^2 test. *Biometrics, 10,* 417–451.

Cole, N. S. (1973). Bias in selection. *Journal of Educational Measurement, 10,* 237–255.

Cole, N. S. (1978). *Approaches to examining bias in achievement test items.* Paper presented at the national meeting of the American Personnel and Guidance Association, Washington, DC.

Cole, N. S. (1981). Bias in testing. *American Psychologist, 36,* 1067–1077.

Cole, N. S. (1984, April). *Testing and the 'crisis' in education.* Presidential address presented at the annual meeting of the National Council on Measurement in Education, New Orleans.

Cole, N. S., & Moss, P. A. (1989). Bias in test use. In R. L. Linn (Ed.). *Educational Measurement* (3rd Ed. pp. 201–219). New York: American Council on Education/Macmillan.

College Entrance Examination Board. (1980). *College Board releases question-by-question data on how New York students did on SAT and PSTA/NMSOT: No major differences on 97% of questions.* (Press release, September 1989). New York: Author.

Cotter, D. E., & Berk, R. (1981, April). *Item bias in the WISC-R using black, white and Hispanic learning disabled children*. Paper presented at the annual meeting of the American Educational Research Association, Los Angeles.

Cox, D. R. (1970). *Analysis of Binary Data*. Methuen and Co., Inc., London.

Cramér, H. (1928). On the composition of elementary errors. *Skandinaviske Aktuartidskrcongres, 11*, 141–180.

Cressie, N., & Holland, P. W. (1983). Characterizing the manifest probabilities of latent trait models. *Psychometrika, 48*, 129–141.

Cronbach, L. J. (1982). *Designing evaluations of educational and social programs*. San Francisco: Jossey-Bass.

Darling, D. A. (1957). The Kolmogorov-Smirnov, Cramér-von Mises tests. *Annals of Mathematical Statistics, 28*, 832–838.

de Leeuw, J., & Verhelst, N. (1986). Maximum likelihood estimation in generalized Rasch models. *Journal of Educational Statistics, 11*, 183–196.

DeMauro, G. E., & Olson, J. F. (1989, March). *The impact of differential speededness on DIF*. Paper presented at the annual meeting of the National Council on Measurement in Education, San Francisco.

Deming, W. E., & Stephan, F. F. (1940). On a least squares adjustment of a sample frequency table when the expected marginal totals are known. *Annals of Mathematical Statistics, 11*, 427–444.

Donoghue, J. R., & Allen, N. L. (1991, April). *"Thin" versus "Thick" matching in the Mantel-Haenszel procedure for detecting DIF*. Paper presented at the annual meeting of the National Council on Measurement in Education, Chicago.

Donlon, T. F. (Ed.). (1984). *The College Board technical handbook for the Scholastic Aptitude Test and achievement tests*. New York: College Entrance Examination Board.

Doolittle, A. E. (1989). Gender differences in performance on mathematics achievement items. *Applied Measurement in Education, 2*, 161–177.

Doolittle, A. E., & Cleary, T. A. (1987). Gender-based differential item performance in mathematics achievement items. *Journal of Educational Measurement, 24*, 157–166.

Dorans, N. J. (1982). *Technical review of item fairness studies: 1975–1979* (Statistical Rep. No. 82–90). Princeton, NJ: Educational Testing Service.

Dorans, N. J. (1989). Two new approaches to assessing differential item functioning: Standardization and the Mantel-Haenszel method. *Applied Measurement in Education, 2*, 217–233.

Dorans, N. J., & Kulick, E. (1983a). *Assessing unexpected differential item performance of female candidates on SAT and TSWE forms administered in December 1977: An application of the standardization approach* (Research Rep. No. 83–9). Princeton, NJ: Educational Testing Service.

Dorans, N. J., & Kulick, E. (1983b). *Assessing unexpected differential item performance of Oriental candidates on SAT Form CSA6 and TSWE Form E33: November 1980 Administration* (Unpublished Statistical Rep. No. SR 83–106). Princeton, NJ: Educational Testing Service.

Dorans, N. J., & Kulick, E. (1986). Demonstrating the utility of the standardization approach to assessing unexpected differential item performance on the Scholastic Aptitude Test. *Journal of Educational Measurement, 23*, 355–368.

Dorans, N. J., & Lawrence, I. M. (1987). *The internal construct validity of the SAT* (Research Rep. No. 87–35). Princeton, NJ: Educational Testing Service.

Dorans, N. J., & Schmitt, A. P. (1989, March). *The methods for dimensionality assessment and DIF detection*. Paper presented at the annual meeting of the National Council on Measurement in Education, San Francisco.

Dorans, N. J., Schmitt, A. P., & Bleistein, C. A. (1988). *The standardization approach to assessing differential speededness* (Research Rep. No. 88–31). Princeton, NJ: Educational Testing Service.

Dorans, N. J., Schmitt, A. P., Bleistein, C. A. (1989). *The standardization approach to differential distractor functioning: Assessing differential speededness*. Manuscript submitted for review.

Dorans, N. J., Schmitt, A. P., & Curley, W. E. (1988, April). *Differential speededness: Some items have DIF because of where they are, not of what they are.* Paper presented at the annual meeting of the National Council on Measurement in Education, New Orleans.

Duncan, O. D. (1984). Rasch measurement: Further examples and discussion. In C. F. Turner & E. Martin (Eds.), *Surveying subjective phenomena* (Vol. 2, pp. 367–403). New York: Russell Sage Foundation.

Dwyer, C. A. (1987, April). Testimony before the House Judiciary Committee, subcommittee on civil and constitutional rights. Hearing on fairness in standardized tests. U.S. Congress, Washington, DC.

Echternacht, G. (1972). *An examination of test bias and response characteristics of six candidate groups taking the ATGSB* (Research Rep. No. 72–4). Princeton, NJ: Educational Testing Service.

Educational Testing Service. (1980). *An approach for identifying and minimizing bias in standardized tests: A set of guidelines.* Princeton, NJ: Author.

Educational Testing Service. (1987). *ETS sensitivity review process: An overview.* Princeton, NJ: Author.

Eells, K., Havighurst, R. J., Herrick, V. E., & Tyler, R. W. (1951). *Intelligence and cultural differences.* Chicago: University of Chicago Press.

Efron, B. (1982). *The jackknife, the bootstrap and other resampling plans.* Philadelphia: Society for Industrial and Applied Mathematics.

Ellis, B. B. (1989). Differential item functioning: Implications for test translations. *Journal of Applied Psychology, 74,* 912–921.

Embretson, S. E. (1985). Multicomponent latent trait models for test design. In S. E. Embretson (Ed.), *Test design: Developments in psychology and psychometrics* (pp. 195–218). Orlando: Academic.

Engelhard, G. (1989). Accuracy of bias review judges in identifying teacher certification tests. *Applied Measurement in Education, 3,* 347–360.

Esary, J. D., Proschan, F., & Walkup, D. W. (1967). Association of random variables, with applications. *Annals of Mathematical Statistics, 38,* 1466–1474.

Eubank, R. L. (1988). *Spline smoothing and nonparametric regression.* New York: Marcel Dekker.

Faggen, J. (1987). Golden Rule revisited: Introduction. *Educational Measurement: Issues and Practice, 6,* 5–8.

Fisher, R. A., & Yates, F. (1963). *Statistical tables for biological, agricultural, and medical research* (6th ed.). New York: Holden-Day.

Flaugher, R. L. (1978). The many definitions of test bias. *American Psychologist, 33,* 671–679.

Freedle, R., & Kostin, I. (1987). *Semantic and structural factors affecting the performance of matched black and white examinees on analogies items from the Scholastic Aptitude Test.* Princeton, NJ: Educational Testing Service.

Freedle, R., & Kostin, I. (1988). *Relationship between item characteristics and an index of differential item functioning (DIF) for the four GRE verbal item types* (Research Rep. No. 88–29). Educational Testing Service, Princeton, NJ.

Glas, C. A. W. (1988). The derivation of some tests for the Rasch model from the multinominal distribution. *Psychometrika, 53,* 525–546.

Glaser, R. (1981). The future of testing. *American Psychologist, 36,* 923–936.

Green, B. F., Crone, C. R., & Folk, V. G. (1989). A method for studying differential distractor functioning. *Journal of Educational Measurement, 26,* 147–160.

Greer, D. G. (1986). *Truth in testing: An analysis of political and legal consequences, and prospects* (Monograph 83–6). Houston: Institute for Higher Education, Law & Governance.

Gulliksen, H. (1960). *Intercultural attitude comparisons and introductory remarks of the Princeton University Conference on preference analysis and subjective measurement* (Research Memorandum No. 60–8). Princeton, NJ: Educational Testing Service.

Haberman, S. J. (1979). *Analysis of qualitative data: Vol. 2: New developments.* New York: Academic.

Haley, D. C. (1952). *Estimation of the dosage mortality relationship when the dose is subject to error* (Technical Rep. No. 15). Stanford, CA: Stanford University, Applied Mathematics and Statistics Laboratory.

Hambleton, R. K., & Swaminathan, H. (1985). *Item response theory: Principles and applications.* Boston: Kluwer-Nijhoff.

Haney, W. (1981). Validity, vaudeville and values: A short history of social concerns over standardized testing. *American Psychologist, 36,* 1021–1034.

Hardle, W. (1990). *Applied nonparametric regression.* Cambridge, MA: Cambridge University Press.

Hartigan, J. A., & Wigdor, A. K. (Eds.). (1989). *Fairness in employment testing.* Report on the committee on the general aptitude test battery. Commission on behavioral and social sciences and education, National Research Council. Washington, DC: National Academy Press.

Hauck, W. H. (1979). The large-sample variance of the Mantel-Haenszel estimator of a common odds ratio. *Biometrics, 35,* 817–819.

Holland, P. W. (1985). *On the study of differential item performance without IRT. Proceedings of the 27th Annual Conference of the Military Testing Association* (Vol. 1, pp. 282–287). San Diego.

Holland, P. W. (1986). Statistics and causal inference. *Journal of the American Statistical Association, 81,* 945–970.

Holland, P. W. (1987). *The Dutch identity: A new tool for the study of item response models* (Technical Rep. No. 87–78). Princeton, NJ: Educational Testing Service.

Holland, P. W. (1988). GRITS is the pits. *Educational Measurement: Issues and Practice, 7,* 7.

Holland, P. W. (1989). A note on the covariance of the Mantel–Haenszel log-odds estimator and the sample marginal rates. *Biometrics, 45,* 1009–1015.

Holland, P. W., Longford, N. T., & Thayer, D. T. (1989). *Stability of the MH D-DIF statistics across populations.* Manuscript submitted for review.

Holland, P. W., & Thayer, D. T. (1985). *An alternative definition of the ETS delta scale of item difficulty* (Research Rep. No. 85–43). Princeton, NJ: Educational Testing Service.

Holland, P. W., & Thayer, D. T. (1986). *Differential item functioning and the Mantel–Haenszel procedure* (Technical Rep. No. 86–69). Princeton, NJ: Educational Testing Service.

Holland, P. W., & Thayer, D. T. (1987). *Notes on the use of log-linear models for fitting discrete probability distributions* (Research Rep. No. 87–31). Princeton, NJ: Educational Testing Service.

Holland, P. W., & Thayer, D. T. (1988). Differential item performance and the Mantel-Haenszel procedure. In H. Wainer & H. Braun (Eds.), *Test validity* (pp. 129–145). Hillsdale, NJ: Lawrence Erlbaum Associates.

Hosmer, D. W., & Lemeshow, S. (1989). *Applied logistic regression.* New York: Wiley.

Hout, M., Duncan, O. D., & Sobel, M. E. (1987). Association and heterogeneity: Structural models of similarities and differences. *Sociological Methodology, 17,* 145–184.

Hu, P. G., & Dorans, N. J. (1989, March). *The effects of deleting items with extreme differential item functioning on equating functions and reported score distributions.* Paper presented at the annual meeting of the American Educational Research Association, San Francisco.

Hu, P. G., & Schmitt, A. P. (1989, March). *Evaluation of matching criteria for differential item functioning analyses of Biology Achievement Tests.* Paper presented at the annual meeting of the National Council on Measurement in Education, San Francisco.

Hulin, C. L., Drasgow, F., & Komocar, J. (1982). Applications of item response theory to analysis of attitude scale translations. *Journal of Applied Psychology, 67,* 818–825.

Hulin, C. L., Drasgow, F., & Parsons, C. K. (1983). *Item response theory.* Homewood, IL: Dow Jones/Irwin.

Humphreys, L. G. (1984). *A theoretical and empirical study of the psychometric assessment of psychological test dimensionality and bias.* Office of Naval Research, Arlington, VA.

Humphreys, L. G. (1986). An analysis and evaluation of test and item bias in the predicting context. *Journal of Applied Psychology, 71,* 327–333.

Hunter, J. E. (1975). *A critical analysis of the use of item means and item-test correlations to determine the pressure or absence of content bias in achievement test items.* Paper presented at the National Institute of Education conference on test bias, Annapolis, MD.

Hunter, R. V., & Slaughter, C. D. (1980). *ETS test sensitivity review process.* Princeton, NJ: Educational Testing Service.

Ironson, G. H. (1982). Use of chi-square and latent trait approaches for detecting item bias. In R. A. Berk (Ed.), *Handbook of methods for detecting item bias* (pp. 117–155). Baltimore: Johns Hopkins University Press.

Ironson, G., Homan, S., Willis, R., & Signer, B. (1984). The validity of item bias techniques with math word problems. *Applied Psychological Measurement, 8,* 391–396.

Jensen, A. R. (1980). *Bias in mental testing.* New York: Free Press.

Johnson, S. T. (1988, June). *Some observations on differential item functioning procedures and use.* Presentation at Educational Testing Service, Princeton, NJ.

Judd, C. M., & McClelland, G. H. (1989). *Data analysis: A model comparison approach.* San Diego: Harcourt Brace Jovanovich.

Junker, B. (1989a). *Conditional association, essential independence, and monotone unidimensional item response models.* Manuscript submitted for publication.

Junker, B. (1989b). Essential independence and likelihood based ability estimation of polytomous items. *Psychometrika, 56,* 255–278.

Kelderman, H. (1984). Loglinear Rasch model tests. *Psychometrika, 49,* 223–245.

Kelderman, H. (1985, June). *Item bias detection using the loglinear Rasch model: Observed and unobserved subgroups.* Paper presented at the annual meeting of the Psychometric Society, Nashville.

Kelderman, H. (1987). *Estimating quasi-loglinear models for a Rasch table if the number of items is large* (Research Rep. No. 87–5). Enschede, The Netherlands: University of Twente.

Kelderman, H. (1988). *Loglinear multidimensional IRT models for polytomously scored items* (Research Rep. No. 88–17). Enschede, The Netherlands: University of Twente.

Kelderman, H. (1990). Item bias detection using loglinear IRT. *Psychometrika, 54,* 681–697.

Kelderman, H., & Macready, G. (1988). *Loglinear-latent-class models for detecting item bias* (Research Rep. No. 88–10). Enschede, The Netherlands: University of Twente.

Kelderman, H., & Steen, R. (1988). *LOGIMO: A program for loglinear IRT modeling.* Enschede, The Netherlands: University of Twente.

Kok, F. (1988). Item bias and test multidimensionality. In R. Langeheine & J. Rost (Eds.), *Latent trait and latent class models* (pp. 263–275). New York: Plenum.

Kulick, E. (1984). *Assessing unexpected differential item performance of Black candidates on SAT form CSA6 and TSWE form E33* (Statistical Rep. No. 84–80). Princeton, NJ: Educational Testing Service.

Kulick, E., & Dorans, N. J. (1983a). *Assessing unexpected differential item performance of candidates reporting different levels of father's education on SAT Form CSA2 and TSWE Form E29* (Statistical Rep. No. 83–27). Princeton, NJ: Educational Testing Service.

Kulick, E., & Dorans, N. J. (1983). *Assessing unexpected differential item functioning of Oriental candidates on SAT form CSAG and TSWE form E33* (Statistical Rep. No. 83–106). Princeton, NJ: Educational Testing Service.

Kulick, E., & Hu, P. G. (1989). *Examining the relationship between differential item functioning and item difficulty* (College Entrance Examination Board Report No. 89–5; Educational Testing Service Research Report No. 89–18). New York: College Entrance Examination Board.

Lawrence, I. M., & Curley, W. E. (1989, March). *Differential item functioning for males and females on SAT-Verbal reading subscore items: Follow-up study.* Paper presented at the annual meeting of the American Educational Research Association, San Francisco.

Lawrence, I. M., Curley, W. E., & McHale, F. J. (1988). *Differential item functioning for males and females on SAT-Verbal reading subscore items* (Report No. 88–4). New York: College Entrance Examination Board.

Lawrence, I. M., Curley, W. E., & McHale, F. J. (1988, April). *Differential item functioning of SAT-Verbal reading subscore items for male and female examinees.* Paper presented at the annual meeting of the American Educational Research Association, New Orleans.

Lazarsfeld, P. F. (1950). The logical and mathematical foundation of latent structure analysis. In S. A. Stouffer, L. Guttman, E. A. Suchman, P. F. Lazarsfeld, S. A. Star, & J. A. Clausen (Eds.), *Measurement and prediction* (pp. 362–412). New York: Wiley.

Lim, R. G., & Drasgow, F. (in press). An evaluation of two methods for estimating item response theory parameters when assessing differential item functioning. *Journal of Applied Psychology.*

Linn, R. L. (1989). Current perspectives and future directions. *Educational Measurement* (3rd ed.) Ed. by R. L. Linn. New York, N.Y.: Macmillan.

Linn, M. C., & Hyde, J. S. (1989). Gender, mathematics, and science. *Educational Researcher, 18*, 17–27.

Linn, R. L. (1986). Bias in college admissions. In *Measures in the college admissions process: A College Board colloquium* (pp. 80–86). New York: The College Entrance Examination Board.

Linn, R. L., & Drasgow, F. (1987). Implications of the Golden Rule settlement for test construction. *Educational Measurement: Issues and Practice, 6*, 13–17.

Linn, R. L., Levine, M. V., Hastings, C. N., & Wardrop, J. L. (1980). *An investigation of item bias in a test of reading comprehension* (Technical Rep. No. 163). Center for the Study of Reading, University of Illinois at Urbana-champaign.

Linn, R. L., Levine, M. V., Hastings, C. N., & Wardrop, J. L. (1981). Item bias in a test of reading comprehension. *Applied Psychological Measurement, 5*, 159–173.

Little, R. J. A., & Rubin, D. B. (1987). *Statistical analysis with missing data.* New York: Wiley.

Lord, F. M. (1952). A theory of test scores. *Psychometric Monographs* (Whole No. 7), Richmond, VA: William Byrd Press.

Lord, F. M. (1977). A study of item bias, using item characteristic curve theory. In Y. H. Poortinga (Ed.) *Basic problems in cross-cultural psychology* (pp. 19–29). Amsterdam: Swets & Zeitlinger.

Lord, F. M. (1980). *Applications of item response theory to practical testing problems.* Hillsdale, NJ: Lawrence Erlbaum Associates.

Lord, F. M., & Novick, M. R. (1968). *Statistical theories of mental test scores.* Reading, MA: Addison-Wesley.

Maccoby, E., & Jacklin, C. N. (1974). *Psychology of sex differences.* Palo Alto, CA: Stanford University Press.

Mahalanobis, P. C. (1930). On tests and measures of group divergence. *Journal and Proceedings of the Asiatic Society of Bengal, 26*, 541–588.

Mahalanobis, P. C. (1936). On the generalized distance in statistics. *Proceedings of the National Institute of Science of India, 12*, 49–55.

Mantel, N., & Haenszel, W. (1959). Statistical aspects of the analysis of data from retrospective studies of disease. *Journal of the National Cancer Institute, 22*, 719–748.

Marascuilo, L. A., & Slaughter, R. E. (1981). Statistical procedures for identifying possible sources of item bias based on chi-square statistics. *Journal of Educational Measurement, 18*, 229–248.

Masters, G. N. (1988). Item discrimination: When more is worse. *Journal of Educational Measurement, 25*, 15–30.

Mazzeo, J. (1989, March). *A study of the dimensionality of the ATP Achievement test in chemistry.* Paper presented at the annual meeting of the National Council on Measurement in Education, San Francisco.

McLaughlin, M. E., & Drasgow, F. (1987). Lord's chi-square test of item bias with estimated and with known person parameters. *Applied Psychological Measurement, 11*, 161–173.

McPeek, W. M., & Wild, C. L. (1986, April). *Performance of the Mantel-Haenszel statistic in a variety of situations.* Paper presented at the annual meeting of the American Educational Research Association, San Francisco.

McPeek, W. M., & Wild, C. L. (1987). *Characteristics of quantitative items that function differently for men and women.* Paper presented at the annual meeting of the American Psychological Association, New York.

McPeek, W. M., & Wild, C. L. (in preparation). *Identifying differentially functioning items in the NTE Core Battery.*

Medley, D. M., & Quirk, T. J. (1974). The application of a factorial design to the study of cultural bias in general culture items of the National Teacher Examination, *Journal of Educational Measurement, 11,* 235–245.

Mellenbergh, G. J. (1983). *Conditional item bias methods.* New York: Plenum.

Mellenbergh, G. J. (1989). Item bias and item response theory. *International Journal of Educational Research, 13,* 127–143.

Messick, S. (1989). Validity. In R. L. Linn (Ed.), *Educational Measurement* (3rd Ed., pp. 13–103). New York: Macmillan.

Mill, J. S. (1843). *A system of logic.*

Miller, M. D., & Linn, R. L. (1988). Invariance of item characteristic functions with variations in instructional coverage. *Journal of Educational Measurement, 25,* 205–220.

Millsap, R. E. (1989, July). *The detection of DIF: Why there is no free lunch.* Paper presented at the annual meeting of the Psychometric Society, Los Angeles.

Mislevy, R. J. (1984). Estimating latent distributions. *Psychometrika, 49,* 359–381.

Mislevy, R. J. (1986). Recent developments in the factor analysis of categorical variables. *Journal of Educational Statistics, 11,* 3–31.

Mislevy, R. J., & Bock, R. D. (1983). *BILOG: Item and test scoring with binary logistic models.* Mooresville, IN: Scientific Software.

Mislevy, R. J., & Bock, R. D. (1986). *PC-BILOG: Item analysis and test scoring with binary logistic models.* Mooresville, IN: Scientific Software.

Morgan, R. (1989, March). *An examination of the dimensional structure of the ATP Biology Achievement test.* Paper presented at the annual meeting of the National Council on Measurement in Education, San Francisco.

Mosteller, F., & Tukey, J. W. (1977). *Data analysis and regression.* Reading, MA: Addison-Wesley.

Muraki, E., & Engelhard, G. (1989, April). *Examining differential item functioning with BIMAIN.* Paper presented at the annual meeting of the American Educational Research Association, San Francisco.

Muraki, E., Mislevy, R. J., & Bock, R. D. (1987). *BIMAIN: A program for item pool maintenance in the presence of item parameter drift and item bias.* Mooresville, IN: Scientific Software.

Muthén, B. (1987). *LISCOMP: Analysis of linear structural relations with a comprehensive measurement model.* Mooresville, IN: Scientific Software.

Muthén, B., Kao, C., & Burstein, L. (1988, April). *Instructional sensitivity in mathematics achievement items: Application of a new IRT-based detection technique.* Paper presented at the annual meeting of the American Educational Research Association, New Orleans.

Muthén, B., & Lehman, J. (1985). Multiple group IRT modeling: Applications to item bias analysis. *Journal of Educational Statistics, 10,* 133–142.

Muthén, B., Shavelson, R., Hollis, M., Kao, C. F., Muthén, L., Tam, T. W. Y., Wu, S. T. & Yang, J. W. (1988). *Relationship between applicant characteristics, MBA program attributes, and student performance: Year 1 report, the psychometric study.* Los Angeles: Graduate Management Admission Council.

Nandakumar, R. (in press). *Simultaneous item bias amplification and cancellations: Shealy-Stout's test for bias/DIF.* To appear in *Journal of Educational Measurement.*

Neyman, J., & Pearson, E. S. (1928). On the use and interpretation of certain test criteria for purposes of statistical inference. *Biometrika, 20A,* 174–240, 263–294.

Novick, M. R., & Ellis, D. D. (1977). Equal opportunity in educational and employment selection. *American Psychologist, 22,* 306–320.

Novick, M. R., & Jackson, J. E. (1977). *Statistical methods for educational and psychological research*. New York: McGraw-Hill.

O'Neill, K. A., McPeek, W. M., & Wild, C. L. (1989, March). *Characteristics of GRE verbal test items that show differential item functioning for Black and White examinees*. Paper presented at the annual meeting of the American Educational Research Association, San Francisco.

O'Neill, K. A., McPeek, W. M., & Wild, C. L. (In preparation). *Identifying differentially functioning items on the Graduate Management Admission Test*.

O'Neill, K. A., Wild, C. L., & McPeek, W. M. (In preparation). *Identifying differentially functioning items on the Graduate Record Examinations General Test*.

O'Neill, K. A., Wild, C. L., & McPeek, W. M. (1989, March). *Gender-related differential item performance on graduate admissions tests*. Paper presented at the annual meeting of the National Council on Measurement in Education, San Francisco.

Osterlind, S. J. (1983). *Test item bias*. Sage University Papers: Quantitative applications in the social sciences. Beverly Hills, CA: Sage.

Pearlman, M. A. (1987, April). *Trends in women's total score and item performance on verbal measures*. Paper presented at the annual meeting of the American Educational Research Association, Washington, DC.

Pearson, E. S., & Hartley, H. O. (1972). *Biometrika tables for statisticians* (Vol. 2). Cambridge, MA: Cambridge University Press.

Petersen, N. S. (1987). *DIF procedures for use in statistical analysis*. Unpublished memorandum of September 25, Educational Testing Service, Princeton, NJ.

Petersen, N. S., & Novick, M. R. (1976). An evaluation of some models for culture-fair selection. *Journal of Educational Measurement, 13*, 3–29.

Phillips, A., & Holland, P. W. (1987). Estimation of the variance of the Mantel-Haenszel log-odds-ratio estimate. *Biometrics, 43*, 425–431.

Plake, B. S. (1980). A comparison of a statistical and subjective procedure to ascertain item validity: One step in the test validation process. *Educational and Psychological Measurement, 40*, 397–404.

Raju, N. S. (1988). The area between two item characteristic curves. *Psychometrika, 53*, 495–502.

Raju, N. S. (1989, March). *Asymptotic mean and variance of an estimate of the area between two ICC's*. Paper presented at the annual meeting of the American Educational Research Association, San Francisco.

Ramist, L., & Arbeiter, S. (1986). *Profiles, college-bound seniors, 1985*. New York, NY: College Entrance Examination Board.

Ramsay, J. O. (1982). When data are functions. *Psychometrika, 47*, 379–396.

Rao, C. R. (1973). *Linear statistical inference and its applications*. New York: Wiley.

Rasch, G. (1960). *Probabilistic models for some intelligence and attainment tests*. Copenhagen: Denmarks Paedagogiske Institut. (Republished in 1980 by the University of Chicago Press, Chicago).

Reckase, M. D., Carlson, J. E., Ackerman, T. A., & Spray, J. A. (1986, June). *The interpretation of unidimensional IRT parameters when estimated from multidimensional data*. Paper presented at the annual meeting of the Psychometric Society, Toronto.

Reynolds, C. R. (1982). The problem of bias in psychological assessment. In C. R. Reynolds & T. B. Gutkin (Eds.), *The handbook of school psychology* (pp. 178–201). New York: Wiley.

Rivera, C., & Schmitt, A. P. (1988). *A comparison of Hispanic and White students' omit patterns on the Scholastic Aptitude Test* (Research Rep. No. 88–44). Princeton, NJ: Educational Testing Service.

Robins, J., Breslow, N., & Greenland, S. (1986). Estimators of the Mantel–Haenszel variance consistent in both sparse data and large-strata limiting models. *Biometrics, 42*, 311–323.

Rogers, J., Dorans, N. J., & Schmitt, A. P. (1986). *Assessing unexpected differential item performance of Black candidates on SAT form 3GSA08 and TSWE form E43* (Statistical Rep. No. 86–22). Princeton, NJ: Educational Testing Service.

Rogers, J., & Kulick, E. (1987). An investigation of unexpected differences in item performance between Blacks and Whites taking the SAT. In A. P. Schmitt & N. J. Dorans (Eds.), *Differential item functioning on the Scholastic Aptitude Test*. (Research Memorandum No. 87–1, pp. 1–37). Princeton, NJ: Educational Testing Service.

Rogers, J., & Swaminathan, H. (1989, March). *A logistic regression procedure for detecting item bias*. Paper presented at the annual meeting of the American Educational Research Association, San Francisco.

Rooney, J. P. (1987). A response from Golden Rule to "ETS on 'Golden Rule.'" *Educational Measurement: Issues and Practice, 6*, 5–8.

Rosenbaum, P. (1985). Comparing distributions of item responses for two groups. *British Journal of Mathematical and Statistical Psychology, 38*, 206–215.

Rosenbaum, P. R., & Rubin, D. R. (1985). Constructing a control group using multivariate matched sampling methods that incorporate the propensity score. *American Statistician, 39*, 33–38.

Rosser, P. (1989). *The SAT gender gap-Identifying the causes*. Center for Women Policy Studies.

Roznowski, M. (1987). Use of tests manifesting sex differences as measures of intelligence: Implications for measurement bias. *Journal of Applied Psychology, 72*, 480–483.

Rubin, D. B. (1974). Estimating causal effects of treatments in randomized and nonrandomized studies. *Journal of Educational Psychology, 66*, 688–701.

Rubin, D. B. (1982). *Multiple imputation for sample surveys*. New York: Wiley.

Rubin, D. B. (1987). *Multiple imputation for nonresponse in surveys*. New York: Wiley.

Rudner, L. M. (1977, April). *An approach to biased item identification using latent trait measurement theory*. Paper presented at the annual meeting of the American Educational Research Association, New York.

Rudner, L. M., Getson, P. R., & Knight, D. L. (1980). Biased item detection techniques. *Journal of Educational Statistics, 5*, 213–233.

Sadker, M., & Sadker, D. (1986). Sexism in the classroom: From grade school to graduate school. *Phi Delta Kappan, 67*, 512–515.

Samejima, F. (1969). Estimation of latent ability using a response pattern of graded scores. *Psychometric Monograph No. 17*. Richmond, VA: William Byrd Press.

Samejima, F. (1979). *A new family of models for the multiple-choice item* (Research Rep. 79–4). Knoxville: University of Tennessee.

Scheuneman, J. D. (1975, April). *A new method of assessing bias in test items*. Paper presented at the annual meeting of the American Educational Research Association, Washington, DC. (ERIC Document Reproduction Service No. ED 106–359).

Scheuneman, J. D. (1978). Ethnic group bias in intelligence test items. In S. W. Lundsteen (Ed.), *Cultural factors in learning and instruction* (pp. 65–77). New York: ERIC Clearinghouse on Urban Education, Diversity Series, No. 56.

Scheuneman, J. D. (1979). A method of assessing bias in test items. *Journal of Educational Measurement, 16*, 143–152.

Scheuneman, J. D. (1981a). A new look at bias in aptitude tests. In P. Merrifield, (Ed.), *New Directions for Testing and Measurement: Measuring human abilities* (Vol. 12, pp. 3–33). San Francisco: Jossey-Bass.

Scheuneman, J. D. (1981b). A response to Baker's criticism. *Journal of Educational Measurement, 16*, 143–152.

Scheuneman, J. D. (1987). An experimental exploratory study of causes of bias in test items. *Journal of Educational Measurement, 24*, 97–118.

Scheuneman, J. D., & Bleistein, C. A. (1989). A consumer's guide to statistics for identifying differential item functioning. *Applied Measurement in Education, 2*, 255–275.

Scheuneman, J. D., & Gerritz, K. (1990). Using differential item functioning procedures to explore sources of item difficulty and group performance characteristics, *Journal of Educational Measurement, 27*, 109–131.

Schmitt, A. P. (1985). *Assessing unexpected differential item performance of Hispanic candidates on SAT form 3FSA08 and TSWE form E47.* (Statistical Rep. No. 85–169). Princeton, NJ: Educational Testing Service.

Schmitt, A. P. (1986, April). *Unexpected differential item performance of Hispanic Examinees.* Paper presented at the National Council on Measurement in Education, San Francisco.

Schmitt, A. P. (1988). Language and cultural characteristics that explain differential item functioning for Hispanic examinees on the Scholastic Aptitude Test. *Journal of Educational Measurement, 25,* 1–13.

Schmitt, A. P., & Bleistein, C. A. (1987). *Factors affecting differential item functioning for Black examinees on Scholastic Aptitude Test analogy items* (Research Rep. No. 87–23). Princeton, NJ: Educational Testing Service.

Schmitt, A. P., Curley, W. E., Bleistein, C. A., & Dorans, N. J. (1988, April). *Experimental evaluation of language and interest factors related to differential item functioning for Hispanic examinees on the SAT-Verbal.* Paper presented at the annual meeting of the National Council on Measurement in Education, New Orleans.

Schmitt, A. P., & Dorans, N. J. (1987a). *Differential item functioning for minority examinees on the Scholastic Aptitude Test.* Paper presented at the annual meeting of the American Psychological Association, New York.

Schmitt, A. P., & Dorans, N. J. (1987b). *Differential item functioning on the Scholastic Aptitude Test* (Research Memorandum No. 87–1). Princeton, NJ: Educational Testing Service.

Schmitt, A. P., & Dorans, N. J. (1988). *Differential item functioning for minority examinees on the SAT.* (Research Rep. No. 88–32). Princeton, NJ: Educational Testing Service.

Schmitt, A. P., & Dorans, N. J. (1990). Differential item functioning for minority examinees on the SAT. *Journal of Educational Measurement, 27,* 67–81.

Schmitt, A. P., & Dorans, N. J. (in press). Factors related to differential item functioning for Hispanic examinees on the Scholastic Aptitude Test. In J. Deneeu, G. Keller, & R. Magallan (Eds.), *Assessment and access: Hispanics in higher education.* New York: Suny Press.

Schmitt, A. P., Dorans, N. J., Crone, C. R., & Maneckshana, B. T. (1991). *Differential speededness and item omit patterns on the SAT* (Research Rep. No. 91–50). Princeton, NJ: Educational Testing Service.

Scott-Jones, D., & Clark, M. L. (1986). The school experiences of Black girls: The interaction of gender, race, and socioeconomic status. *Phi Delta Kappan, 67,* 520–526.

Serfling, R. (1980). *Approximation theorems of mathematical statistics.* New York: Wiley.

Shapiro, M. M., Slutsky, M. N., & Watt, R. F. (1989, Winter). Minimizing unnecessary differences in occupational testing. *Valparaiso University Law Review, 23.*

Shealy, R. (1989). *An item response theory based statistical procedure for detecting concurrent internal bias in ability tests.* University of Illinois, Department of Statistics doctoral thesis.

Shealy, R., & Stout, W. (in press). A model-based standardization approach that separates true bias/DIF from group ability differences and detects test bias/DIF as well as item bias. *Psychometrika.*

Shepard, L. A. (1981). Identifying bias in test items. In B. F. Green (Ed.). *New direction in testing and measurement: Issues in testing-Coaching, disclosure and test bias,* No. 11 (pp. 79–104). San Francisco: Jossey-Bass.

Shepard, L. A. (1982). Definitions of bias. In R. A. Berk (Ed.), *Handbook of methods for detecting test bias* (pp. 9–30). Baltimore: Johns Hopkins University Press.

Shepard, L. A. (1987a). The case for bias in tests of achievement and scholastic aptitude. In S. Modgil & C. Modgil (Eds.), *Arthur Jensen: Consensus and controversy* (pp. 177–190). New York: Falmer Press.

Shepard, L. A. (1987b). Discussant comments on the NCME Symposium: Unexpected differential item performance and its assessment among Black, Asian-American, and Hispanic students. In A. P. Schmitt & N. J. Dorans (Eds.), *Differential item functioning on the Scholastic Aptitude Test.* (Research Memorandum No. 87–1). Princeton, NJ: Educational Testing Service.

Shepard, L. A., Camilli, G., & Averill, M. (1981). Comparison of procedures for detecting test-item bias with both internal and external ability criteria. *Journal of Educational Statistics, 6,* 317–375.

Shepard, L. A., Camilli, G., & Williams, D. M. (1984). Accounting for statistical artifacts in item bias research. *Journal of Educational Statistics, 9,* 93–128.

Shepard, L. A., Camilli, G., & Williams, D. M. (1985). Validity of approximation techniques for detecting item bias. *Journal of Educational Measurement, 22,* 77–106.

Simpson, E. H. (1951). Interpretation of interaction contingency tables. *Journal of the Royal Statistical Society, (Series B), 13,* 238–241.

Sinnot, L. T. (1980). *Differences in item performance across groups.* Princeton, NJ: Educational Testing Service.

Smirnov, N. V. (1936). Sur la distribution de ω^2. *Compe-Rendu of the Academy of Science, 202,* 449–452.

Smith, R. M. (1988, April). *Differential item familiarity in graduate admissions mathematics tests.* Paper presented at the annual meeting of the National Council on Measurement in Education, New Orleans.

Sörbom, D. (1974). A general method for studying differences in factor means and factor structures between groups. *British Journal of Mathematical and Statistical Psychology, 37,* 222–239.

SPSS, Inc. (1988). *SPSS-X User's Guide* (3rd Ed.). Chicago: Statistical Package for the Social Sciences, Inc.

Stanley, J. C., & Porter, A. C. (1967). Correlation of Scholastic Aptitude Test scores with college grades for Negroes versus Whites. *Journal of Educational Measurement, 4,* 199–218.

Stout, W. (1987). A nonparametric approach for assessing latent trait unidimensionality. *Psychometrika, 52,* 589–617.

Stout, W. (1990). A new item response theory modeling approach with applications to unidimensionality assessment and ability estimation. *Psychometrika, 55,* 293–325.

Stricker, L. J. (1982). Identifying test items that perform differently in population subgroups: A partial correlation index. *Applied Psychological Measurement, 6,* 261–273.

Tatsuoka, K. K., Linn, R. L., Tatsuoka, M. M., & Yamamoto, K. (1988). Differential item functioning resulting from the use of different solution strategies. *Journal of Educational Measurement, 25,* 301–319.

Temp, G. (1971). Test bias: Validity of the SAT for Blacks and Whites in thirteen integrated institutions. *Journal of Educational Measurement, 8,* 245–251.

Thissen, D. (1982). Marginal maximum likelihood estimation for the one-parameter logistic model. *Psychometrika, 47,* 201–214.

Thissen, D. (1987). Discussant comments on the National Council on Measurement in Education symposium, Unexpected Differential Item Performance and its Assessment Among Black, Asian-American, and Hispanic Students. In A. P. Schmitt & N. J. Dorans (Eds.) *Differential item functioning on the Scholastic Aptitude Test* (Research Memorandum No. 87–1) (pp. 1–6). Princeton, NJ: Educational Testing Service.

Thissen, D. (1988). *MULTILOG user's guide* (2nd Ed.). Mooresville, IN: Scientific Software.

Thissen, D. (1991). *MULTILOG user's guide (Version 6).* Mooresville, IN: Scientific Software.

Thissen, D., & Mooney, J. (1989). Loglinear item response models, with applications to data from social surveys. *Sociological Methodology, 19,* 299–330.

Thissen, D., & Steinberg, L. (1984). A response model for multiple-choice items. *Psychometrika, 49,* 501–519.

Thissen, D., & Steinberg, L. (1986). A taxonomy of item response models. *Psychometrika, 51,* 567–577.

Thissen, D., Steinberg, L., & Fitzpatrick, A. R. (1989). Multiple choice models: The distractors are also part of the item. *Journal of Educational Measurement, 26,* 161–176.

Thissen, D., Steinberg, L., & Gerrard, M. (1986). Beyond group mean differences: The concept of item bias. *Psychological Bulletin, 99,* 118–128.

Thissen, D., Steinberg, L., & Wainer, H. (1988). Use of item response theory in the study of group differences in trace lines. In H. Wainer & H. Braun (Eds.), *Test validity* (pp. 147–169). Hillsdale, NJ: Lawrence Erlbaum Associates.

Thissen, D., & Wainer, H. (1982). Some standard errors in item response theory. *Psychometrika, 47,* 397–412.

Thissen, D., & Wainer, H. (1983). *Confidence envelopes for monotonic functions: Principles, derivations, and examples* (Technical Rep. No. 82–37). San Antonio, TX: Air Force Human Resources Laboratory.

Thissen, D., & Wainer, H. (1990). Confidence envelopes for item response theory. *Journal of Educational Statistics, 15,* 113–128.

Thorndike, R. L. (1982). Item and score conversion by pooled judgment. In P. W. Holland & D. B. Rubin (Eds.), *Test equating* (pp. 309–317). New York: Academic.

Thurstone, L. L. (1925). A method of scaling educational and psychological tests. *Journal of Educational Psychology, 16,* 263–278.

Tittle, C. K. (1982). Use of judgmental methods in item bias studies. In R. A. Berk (Ed.) *Handbook of methods for detecting test bias* (pp. 31–63). Baltimore: Johns Hopkins University Press.

Tjur, T. (1982). Connection between Rasch's item analysis model and a multiplicative Poisson model. *Scandinavian Journal of Statistics, 9,* 23–30.

Tucker, L. R. (1951). *Academic ability test.* (Research Memorandum No. 51–17). Princeton, NJ: Educational Testing Service.

U.S. Congress. Hearing before the House Committee on Education and Labor. Subcommittee on Elementary, Secondary and Vocational Education. *Truth in Testing Act of 1979.* 96th Congress, 1st session. H.R. 3564 and H.R. 4949.

U.S. Congress. Hearing before the House Committee on Education and Labor. Joint subcommittee on Elementary, Secondary and Vocational Education and Postsecondary Education. *Educational Testing Act of 1981.* 97th Congress 1st session H.R. 1662.

von Mises, R. (1931). *Wahrscheinlichkeit, statisk und wahrheit.* Leipzig: Deuticke.

Wagner, C. H. (1982). Simpson's paradox in real life. *The American Statistician, 36,* 46–48.

Wainer, H. (1986). Minority contributions to the SAT score turnaround: An example of Simpson's paradox. *Journal of Educational Statistics, 11,* 239–244.

Wainer, H., & Kiely, G. L. (1987). Item clusters and computerized adaptive testing: A case for testlets. *Journal of Educational Measurement, 24,* 185–201.

Wainer, H., & Lewis, C. (1990). Towards a psychometrics for testlets. *Journal of Equational Measurement, 27,* 1–14.

Wainer, H., & Mislevy, R. J. (1990). Item response theory, item calibration and proficiency estimation. In H. Wainer, N. J. Dorans, R. Flaugher, B. F. Green, R. J. Mislevy, L. Steinberg, & D. Thissen, *Computerized adaptive testing: A primer* (pp. 65–102). Hillsdale, NJ: Lawrence Erlbaum Associates.

Wald, A. (1943). Tests of statistical hypotheses concerning several parameters when the number of observations is large. *Transactions of the American Mathematical Society, 54,* 426–482.

Wald, A. (1944). On a statistical problem arising in the classification of an individual into one of two groups. *Annals of Mathematical Statistics, 15,* 145–162.

Wendler, C. L., & Carlton, S. T. (1987, April). *An examination of SAT verbal items for differential performance by women and men: An exploratory study.* Paper presented at the annual meeting of the American Educational Research Association, Washington, DC.

Wigdor, A. K., & Garner, W. R. (Eds.). (1982). *Ability testing: Uses, consequences and controversies, Parts 1 and 2.* Report of the National Committee and Documentation Section. Washington, DC: National Academy Press.

Wild, C. L., & McPeek, W. M. (1986, August). *Performance of the Mantel–Haenszel statistic in identifying differentially functioning items.* Paper presented at the annual meeting of the American Psychological Association, Washington, DC.

Wild, C. L., & McPeek, W. M. (In preparation). *Identifying differentially functioning items in the NTE core battery.*

Wild, C. L., McPeek, W. M., & Koffler, S. L. (1988). *Concurrent validity of verbal item types for ethnic and gender subgroups.* GRE Research Rep. 84–10. Princeton, NJ: Educational Testing Service.

Wilson, D. T., Wood, R., & Gibbons, R. (1987). *TESTFACT: Test scoring, item statistics, and item factor analysis.* Mooresville, IN: Scientific Software.

Wise, L. L. (1985). Project TALENT: Mathematics course participation in the 1960s and its career consequences. In S. F. Chipman, L. R. Brush & D. M. Watson (Eds.), *Women and mathematics: Balancing the equation* (pp. 25–68). Hillsdale, NJ: Lawrence Erlbaum Associates.

Wood, R. L., Wingersky, M. S., & Lord, F. M. (1976). *LOGIST: A computer program for estimating examinee ability and item characteristic curve parameters* (Research Memorandum No. 76–6). Princeton, NJ: Educational Testing Service.

Wright, B. D., & Panchapakesan, N. (1969). A procedure for sample-free items analysis. *Educational and Psychological Measurement, 29,* 23–48.

Wright, B. D., Mead, R. J., & Draba, R. E. (1976). *Detecting and correcting test item bias with a logistic response model* (Research Memorandum No. 22). University of Chicago, Department of Education.

Wright, D. J. (1987a). Assessment of unexpected differential item difficulty for Asian-American examinees on the Scholastic Aptitude Test. In A. P. Schmitt & N. J. Dorans (Eds.), *Differential item functioning on the Scholastic Aptitude Test* (Research Memorandum No. 87–1) (pp. 1–27), Princeton, NJ: Educational Testing Service.

Wright, D. J. (1987b). An empirical comparison of the Mantel–Haenszel and standardization methods of detecting differential item performance. In A. P. Schmitt & N. J. Dorans (Eds.), *Differential item functioning on the Scholastic Aptitude Test* (Research Memorandum No. 87–1) (pp. 1–26). Princeton, NJ: Educational Testing Service.

Yen, W. M. (1984). Effects of local item dependence on the fit and equating performance of the three-parameter logistic model. *Applied Psychological Measurement, 8,* 125–145.

Yule, G. U. (1903). Notes on the theory of association of attributes in statistics. *Biometrics, 2,* 121–134. (Reprinted in *Statistical papers of George Udny Yule,* selected by A. Stuart & M. G. Kendall. New York: Hafner, 1971).

Zieky, M. J. (1987). *Summary of the development and implementation of the index of differential item difficulty.* Internal paper dated May 5, Educational Testing Service, Princeton, NJ.

Zimowski, M.F., & Bock, R. D. (1987). *Full-information item factor analysis of test forms from the ASVAB CAT pool* (Research Report 87–1 [revised]). Chicago, IL: National Opinion Research Center, Methodology Research Center.

Zwick, R. (1990). When do item response function and Mantel–Haenszel definitions of differential item functioning coincide? *Journal of Educational Statistics, 15,* 185–197.

Author Index

Subject Index